TABLE OF CONTENTS

Foreword
Analysis of opening narrative
Season 1: 1967

- *Beachhead*
- *The Experiment*
- *The Mutation*
- *The Leeches*
- *Genesis*
- *Vikor*
- *Nightmare*
- *Doomsday Minus One*
- *Quantity Unknown*
- *The Innocent*
- *The Ivy Curtain*
- *The Betrayed*
- *Storm*
- *Panic*
- *Moon Shot*
- *Wall of Crystal*
- *The Condemned*
- *Counter Attack*

Season 2: 1967-1968

- *Condition Red*
- *The Saucer*
- *The Watchers*
- *The Vise**
- *Valley of the Shadow*

- *The Enemy*
- *The Trial*
- *The Spores*
- *Dark Outpost*
- *Summit Meeting (Part I)*
- *Summit Meeting (Part II)*
- *The Prophet*
- *Labyrinth*
- *The Captive*
- *The Believers*
- *The Ransom*
- *Task Force*
- *The Possessed*
- *Counter-Attack*
- *The Pit*
- *The Organization*
- *The Peace Maker*
- *The Miracle*
- *The Life Seekers*
- *The Pursued*
- *Inquisition (Final Episode)*

- **Episode 22, Season Two: "The Vise" - Fade to 'Blacks'?*

David Vincent: The personification of 'white privilege'

- *Money is no object*
- *The Lincoln Continental: Re-habbed or Contractual?*
- *Purchase of buildings, warehouses, real estate, etc.*
- *Immediate contacts and access*

ANALYSIS: SPACE INVADERS VS. ANGLO INVADERS

- ***"The Invaders": The Issue of Gender Bias***

Conclusion
References

FOREWARD

White supremacy is what it is – the umbrella ideology for the white race wherever it is at in the world -- but it has a plethora of supporting mechanisms aimed at control and domination of those they oppress. One of those mechanisms is the media in general and television and movies, in particular. Like money, television is a tool that can project images that serve as the ultimate confounding of things: these images can make the small appear large, the weak appear strong, the ugly appear beautiful, the wrong appear right, the impotent appear virile, the cowardly appear courageous and so on.

The 1967 television show, "The Invaders," in my view, was one such mechanism - a powerful and well-done television show. The haunting theme, done by Dominic Frontiere opened the show up and enticed viewers to watch as this one man stumbles across the landing of an alien space ship. According to Wikipedia (2017), The series was a Quinn Martin Production (Season One was produced in association with the ABC Television Network, or as it was listed in the end credits, "The American Broadcasting Company Television Networks").

Furthermore it appeared by watching every episode that time and care were exercised with putting together the different locations, settings and overall ambience of every show, as well as the wardrobe and the way that each room was set up. By today's standards the technology was someone antiquated, but nevertheless I was captivated by the overall theme of the show: one man has to convince the world of something that they are not ready to accept.

At the time of its airing I was only 13 years old, but I was labeled a "gifted and talented" student and so I observed, talked and wrote about things that bored the shit out of my friends and associates. But there is no doubt that I was at home in the evening when "The Invaders" came on, because I wanted to see what would happen when this white man was treated like a pariah, much the same way that black people have been over the years.

Even at that pubescent age I wondered as I watched, "what is his motivation"? He is standing against the world to save the world from these beings who look just like his race looks! Remember that Martin Luther King, Jr., was marching and the South was being exposed and racism was being confronted, but that was largely black on white. David Vincent's mission was a little more difficult in many respects: he was a white man trying to convince other white men that the aliens that were trying to take over the world looked just like they did! In reality, this would be a cause for unifying and joining the aliens to "go get the niggers!" But alas, this is TV and they want to make white men appear to be progressive freedom fighters, of which David Vincent was but one.

As a youngster watching episodes of "The Invaders" I nevertheless wondered, why are all of the aliens white? And when it comes to humans, why is everybody that David Vincent encounters also white? Sure, there were a few episodes that featured a Mexican venue and some Latino brothers and sisters, but for the most part the aliens, the humans and the context was usually lily-white. That was then, and I would grow to become a scholar at some of the finest schools in this country. And I learned how to engage in critical thinking and how to research whatever subject area peaked my interests.

In May of 1974, *Black Scholar* magazines printed an article titled, "The Cress Theory of Color Confrontation and Racism." In that article the author, Dr. Frances Cress Welsing, explained in her theory of "color confrontation."

> … the initial psychological defense maneuver was the "repression" of the initially felt thought or sense of inadequacy – being without color and, of secondary importance, being in deficient numbers, both of which were apparently painful awarenesses. This primary ego defense of repression, was then reinforced by a host of other defensive mechanisms. One of the most important was a "reaction formation" response whose aim it was to convert (at the psychological level) something that was desired and envied (skin color) into something that is discredited and despised … (Welsing, p. 35).

This theory answered most of the questions I had regarding why white people were, as a collective, generally fucked up. Even the ones who are not dominative racists still as yet sit back and watch their hate-filled brethren wail away on black people. So I hold the quiet ones sitting in their suburban living rooms as being just as guilty and responsible as those club-carrying, "we-hate-niggers"-spouting assholes.

Welsing further explains:

> The whites desiring to have skin color but being unable to achieve
> this end on their own, said in effect, consciously or unconsciously,
> that skin color was disgusting to them and began attributing negative
> qualities to color and especially to the most skin color – blackness
> (Welsing, pp. 35-36).

Though heavily Freudian in its interpretation and analysis, Welsing's thesis is one excellent starting point to figure out just why these white people act the way they do. They seem always willing to play the victim in matters of race and are rarely willing to admit to anything even remotely racist, so what other explanation could there be? And it also explains the images and the movies and television programs that they produce. As Mao taught long ago, "He who controls images controls minds, and he who controls minds has little, if anything, to worry about, from bodies."

The question that has to be asked as you see these "invasion" movies and television programs is why would the aliens invade the most powerful nation on the planet earth, and the one that has a history of hating any creature who is "different." Furthermore, why masquerade as white men and women when this is the race of the human species that is perhaps the most despised on the planet and the one with the most heinous history?

Each show was divided into parts: "Act I," "Act II," "Act III","Act IV" and then "Epilogue." Well-timed, each segment was well directed and each actor, even the guest stars who were introduced at the beginning of each show, seemed to take their roles quite seriously. The narrator's voice was unique with plenty of baritone, and the titles of each show further enticed viewers.

At any rate, we come to 1967-68 and the ABC show, "The Invaders." The thrust of the show, created by Quinn Martin (who was also responsible for "The Fugitive") can best be summed up in the opening narrative, which I will analyze in the following section.

Although it was claimed that these aliens wanted to either destroy or enslave the inhabitants of Earth, these aliens got the benefit of the doubt. For instance, these aliens continued to be referred to as "people" and on-going statements that, "they look just like us." As I stated earlier, it wasn't until season 2, episode 22 that the show decided to feature some Black people in starring roles – which is why I devote an entire section to that particular episode under the sub-heading, "Fade to Black."

As a narration from the episode called, "The Peacemaker" stated, "For two years, David Vincent has been waging war on two fronts. One against the aliens, the second an attempt to enlist allies in high places – while there is still time." And even as the last episode ended, David was still fighting, and the group that he was able to form over the years – the "Believers" – were right there with him, getting more and more attention from the powers that be, convincing them that these aliens were already here and were not bullshitting around. Not a single black person among them.

The sub-heading of this book is, "A Chronological TV Review and Case Study in Intergalactic White Privilege. White privilege is functionally defined by Peggy McIntosh as, "societal privileges that benefit people identified as white in some countries, beyond what is commonly experienced by non-white people under the same social, political, or economic circumstances." According to McIntosh, whites in Western societies enjoy advantages that non-whites do not experience, as "an invisible package of unearned assets". (McIntosh, 1990)

Furthermore,

> White privilege denotes both obvious and less obvious passive advantages that white people may not recognize they have, which distinguishes it from overt bias or prejudice. These include cultural affirmations of one's own worth; presumed greater social status; and freedom to move, buy, work, play, and speak freely. The effects can be seen in professional, educational, and personal contexts. The concept of white privilege also implies the right to assume the universality of one's own experiences, marking others as different or exceptional while perceiving oneself as normal.(see McIntosh, 1990).

What you just read describes white folks on this planet. What I have done is taken what was presented on "The Invaders" and the aesthetic and racial choices that were made in terms of alien embodiment and clearly show that the writers, producers, actors and all associated with this show felt it would be totally believable to believe that beings from "a dying world" would come to Earth and impersonate a minority species with pink skin – white folks. They had to do so knowing that "white privilege" would enable them to get away with whatever it was they needed. And as my analyses will show, these white aliens would be able to purchase land, acquire closed down mining camps, rise to the rank of captain and major in the military and assume power that no black man would ever have. In light of this "white privilege" is not just and Earth-bound manifestation; because of the reputation of the white race, such privilege now extends far beyond the outer reaches of the galaxy.

The fact is the episode titled "The Condemned" proves that the alien invasion was about imitating "whites only." In one scene Vincent is told by a Communications Director named Tate that the aliens are trying to retrieve a file that "contains a list of eleven key aliens here on Earth and their positions of power in this country and England, France, Germany, Russia. My lab has become the hub, the nerve center for transmission of messages from the Mother planet to these leaders. Dunn can't risk having the names on that list exposed." See? All lily-white countries and the aliens have leadership in all of them. How did they do it? White skin gave them an entry pass and their research on the respective countries did the rest.

I admired David Vincent's tenacity, courage, perseverance and eloquence. He believed in something and acted on what he believed in. There are a lot of people today who don't believe in anything. From what I was able to observe he paid for his own gas, plane tickets and registration fees to various "conferences" that the aliens were sponsoring in their quest to bamboozle witless earthlings. And of course, he had the advantage of "white privilege" which time and time again enabled him to get into military bases, hotels, government offices and the like, *sans* credentials, simply because of his whiteness.

For these reasons, I was interested in this show and now, some 48 years later, I devote this book by way of my Africentric views and keen analytic abilities to you, the reader, regarding this TV program, it's characters and its "us versus them" thematic patterns. Don't get it twisted: in addition to serious analysis, I also literally transcribed every word of many of the scripts as that dialogue related to setting up the show. I spared no expense in time and energy making this a book that would make a valuable contribution to the show itself, the genius of Quinn Martin, and the role that "race" played throughout the two year run of "The Invaders."

And let me reiterate: I literally transcribed nearly every key scene of every episode because of the depth of the dialogue, the deep-seated profundity of scientific conversations and the interest generated by the combination of both. There is not another book like this one.

Therefore, let the critique and commentary begin.

ANALYSIS OF OPENING NARRATIVE

Remember the opening narrative of the 1967 TV show, "The Invaders"? First came the roll of the tympani (sometimes known as a kettle drum) that set the stage for the macabre narration. The deep monotone voice added additional eeriness to the description, and the opening narration beings with the deep throated announcement of the title: "The Invaders."

Then came the introductory narration, and it is therefore most worthy of analysis:

> INVADERS: alien beings from a dying planet. Their destination: the Earth. Their purpose: to make it *their* world. David Vincent has seen them. For him it began one lost night on a lonely country road, looking for a short cut that he never found. It began with a closed deserted diner, and a man too long without sleep to continue his journey. It began with the landing of a craft from another galaxy. Now, David Vincent knows that the Invaders are here, that they have taken human form. Somehow he must convince a disbelieving world that the nightmare has already begun …..(emphasis original)

This could describe what white folks in this country did to unsuspecting African people during the beginning and during the slave trade. Let's do an ideological juxtaposition of the previous narration and compare and contrast the coming of the aliens and the incursion of white folks into Africa and then later, into the ghettoes of America.

"Invaders: aliens from a dying planet." So what we have are people with a technology that is superior and nevertheless they couldn't keep themselves from dying off. It is never stated why the planet was destined for doom, but we can figure that something was done that worked against their best interests. Since these aliens seem to have so many human qualities, we can assume that their demise had something to do with greed. It is a quality that they have displayed throughout the two years of the episodes.

Now look at the aliens from this planet. Their nation was brand new and as a collective, they didn't know their asses from a hole in the ground. Sure, they had some foundations like "Manifest Destiny," and "White Man's Burden," but their economy was a local and regional one that wasn't going anywhere until a Catholic priest recommended that instead of using the Indians (who knew the terrain, got sick when they came into contact with white people and were considered "humans" on some level), go to Africa and kidnap some enslaved "sub-humans." And that's what they did and at one time the southern U.S. economy was number one in the world because of black labor and cotton. The "dying" planet called the United States was thereby saved.

The narration continues: *"Their destination: the Earth."* Why? According to scientists, there are a number of parallel universes out there, many of them with environments that should approximate the one that existed on that alien world. Why would you scan this planet, see how fucked up the people are – especially the white ones that you choose to imitate – and nevertheless want to come here? In my book this is a mis-calculation that shows yet another human-like quality (in addition to greed): stupidity.

In the historical example the destination was "Africa." These white boys went over there fronting as missionaries, coming in as mercenaries and then rounding things up with a kind of military approach. More than 60 million Africans died during the Middle Passage – the trip from Africa to the Caribbean and then onward to the United States. Stuffed into the bottoms of ships, dying in droves and forced to eat by using a maniacal funnel-type instrument known as the speculum oris. And this is just the tip of the iceberg, which is why whites folks try to clean up their dirt by acting as if Africans sold one another into slavery or worse, that we *wanted* to come over here because the African unemployment rate had reached double-digits!

"Their purpose: to make it their world." There are several different outlines regarding what these aliens plan to do. During some episodes they want to poison the human race with radiation. On other ones they want to use major storms to wipe out the humans. Vincent claims at other times that their purpose is to "enslave billions." Here's my point: if these aliens want to land on a planet rife with xenophobia, racism, hatred, polluted waterways and smog-filled skies, then once again, I have to say that with all their technology, these are nevertheless some stupid beings.

The purpose was to make Africa theirs, and they had been doing it for centuries prior to the American intervention. The Dutch moved in on South Africa for the diamonds and took over that section. And the Portuguese, the Spanish, French and other Europeans in general had a field day raping the continent of its natural resources. Today, China is involved and some of the ass-backwards African leadership, just like some of the treacherous Earthlings on the television show, are aiding and abetting today's "aliens" in the pillaging of the Motherland.

The narration further claims that, *"David Vincent has seen them. For him it began one lost night on a lonely country road, looking for a short cut that he never found."* A short cut? To where? For what? This guy has no kids, no wife, no girlfriend and he's riding in a new car, chillin,' on his way back from who knows where. What's his fuckin' hurry?

In the case of some historical comparison, Father Bartolome Las Casas had seen "the black people" in Africa. He told his white pals that they were strong, they had farming experience and they would make excellent "servants." This is what paved the way for the enslavement of millions of Africa people. Vincent was in the wrong place at the wrong time, witnessing something he perhaps should not have seen, and African people were in the wrong place at the wrong time, trusting white people (just like the Native Americans did), allowing them to visit their lands, selling the ones captured during war to these strangers, having no idea of the devilish nightmare that was going to be imposed on them. "The invaders" walked away with black human capital and build an empire because of the "theft."

Moving on: *"It began with a closed deserted diner, and a man too long without sleep to continue his journey."* See? Too long without sleep. All he had to do was pull over on the side of the interstate and take a nap. All he had to do was turn on the radio and find an "oldies" station. Surely, with black people burning down the country in the real world, the writers could have found something for him to do. But noooooo! He decides to take a short cut into a wooded area, pull over, take a nap in an area he's never been in before.

Just as David Vincent was dizzy and blinded with sleepiness, the white man was likewise blinded by power, and the belief that he could take the Jewish-built ships and haul a gang load of Africans first, to the Caribbean to be "seasoned" and then on to America to be force to work from "can't see in the morning until can't see at night." If Vincent thought he was tired, imagine how the African brothers and sisters were after working, getting their asses kicked, being forced into sex with white men and getting lynched or gunned down if they said nary a word.

And we all know what happens after that: *"It began with the landing of a craft from another galaxy."* No, that's not where it began. It began with what I described: a planet of people led by idiots who focused on the one planet that has enough firepower to wipe their asses out. It began with another idiot who decides to risk his life by taking a nap in an area that he didn't recognize and has never been in before. It seems to me to be a relationship made in heaven.

And in like manner, it began with the first coming of ships from Africa and the white man spotting naked black people who he immediately became jealous of. He had a choice: befriend them and learn or trick them and steal their natural resources. He chose the latter and informed his white brethren in other parts of the world about these "savages" that they staggered across and that the land was rich with diamonds, gold, bauxite and other natural resources. The aliens landed that night on the initial episode of "The Invaders," and they landed in like manner to disturb, disrupt and destroy the lives, villages and culture of African people.

And as a result of all this, *"Now, David Vincent knows that the Invaders are here, that they have taken human form. Somehow he must convince a disbelieving world that the nightmare has already begun."*

At least in the case of David Vincent, he got a warning sign and was therefore working to warn his brothers and sisters. In our case, there was no warning because the kidnaps took place in the name of "progress" and the Christian Bible, in the hands of these white "invaders," provided the justification for the kidnaps. After all, we were the sons of Ham and were therefore "cursed" with black skin. And that myth carried the slave system before and during the institution was up and running in the southern sector of the United States.

Throughout the series "taking human form" meant looking like white folks. That is what made David Vincent's job so difficult: he had to expose other white people and as we know, the white race more often than not give their own people the benefit of the doubt; usually they can just blame it on Blacks or Hispanics and be done with it.

Quinn Martin, the descendant of an "Invader" of sorts (he's white, ain't he?) offered a great tale, but one that Black people are not unfamiliar with. From ships arriving on the west coast of Africa and through the horn of Africa to intergalactic flying sources, the mentality is the same.

Therefore, with that having been said, I now bring you view views of the 1967-68 television show, "The Invaders."

Season 1 (1967)

.1. Beachhead

The opening episode, from which the narration just shared serves as the intro to every show thereafter.

David has seen the saucer landing on that night but up this point he hasn't seen any "aliens." But the plot continues anyway, so the next day he tells his business partner and even the police lieutenant. They accompany him back out to the site and they meet two young people who claimed to be honeymooners who were "out there last night", camped out in their RV, and didn't see anything. David returns yet a third time, alone and confronts the couple and he and the guy get in a fight. This is the first time we see one of the aliens glowing red. This is what happens when they die: therefore there is never any leftover evidence or residue that this alien ever existed. At any rate, David is knocked out and taken to the hospital.

As would be the case time after time, we have to wonder how he's paying all these hospital bills. What kind of insurance does he have? He's a highly regarded architect, but you never see him going to the bank to make a withdrawal or writing a check. When he goes to dinner or out to have a drink (which is quite frequently), he's always reaching in his pocket and pulling out cash. He's also a chain smoker and as alluded to, rarely turns down a drink. How he can do all this international travelling, get into fist fights with these aliens, survive on-going torture is beyond me. But remember: this is a presentation of how the white man wants others to see him, not as he actually is in the real world.

At any rate, he's alright and he suspects the sheriff of being an alien. Up to this point he had no reason to believe that there was any on-going shape shifting taking place, but he just seems to "know." He finally convinces Landers to come back to an alien site he has stumbled across, the "home town" of the honeymooners.

So many questions are posed but not really answered. Thus far David could well have been a raving lunatic or a paranoid schizophrenic. But wait: that's right – he's a white man and therefore, as the entire show clearly demonstrates episode after episode, he has the benefit of "white privilege." White people in 1967, as now in 2017 – a half a century later -- can travel anywhere in the country they want to, from the ghetto and barrio to the richest neighborhoods. Black people have to take care where they can gas up at, what towns they travel through and in fact, there were and continue to be places called "sundown towns," so named because black people weren't allowed on the street after sundown. And I ain't just talkin' about the Deep South: there are places in California, where I grew up playing interscholastic basketball, where these sundown towns like Antioch, Lodi, Orinda, Lafayette and Piedmont, to name but a few.

I mention this because Vincent was truly a "free man" and that was important in his quest to "spread the word." He got the benefit of the doubt because he was a white man and even though many looked at him skeptically, he was not the target or immediate hate stars akin to those described by John Howard Griffin in his book *Black Like Me*.

For those of you who don't study or read, the title of this episode, "Beachhead," was well named. A beachhead is a place that is set up to give someone or a group a foothold on an area. It is defined as, "an area on a hostile shore occupied to secure further landing of troops and supplies." In other words, this initial episode lets us know that the aliens have not only "arrived," but that they have established themselves, not only in the small town that Vincent was in, but in major ports throughout the country as we will find out from week to week.

.2. Title: The Experiment

The story opens with an old man on a plane, Professor Curtis Lindstrom, a man who has documented proof that there are aliens on earth. But before he is seated, he looks out one of the windows of the plane and notices that one of the traffic controllers is an alien. We find out in this episode that the extended pinkie finger is the way you can tell the aliens apart from "regular" humans, and by "humans" I mean white folks. Almost every single alien through the 43 episodes is white .

There are some exceptions, but remember, this is 1967, the country is aflame and white folks are trying to pacify the community, not address issues of race. By making this an aliens vs. humans scenario, people can come together and pray that Vincent (the lone white man) can save the world (a declaration that he makes innumerable times throughout the series) and therefore, ameliorate the real life black-white racial tensions that are taking place outside of their suburban homes.

At any rate, Dr. Curtis Lindstrom, a professor, has boarded a plane and for the previous three months he has been writing articles and giving speeches about the landing of aliens on the planet. He is now headed to a conference in New York. One of the recurring identifying traits of the aliens (since they are all white) is that their baby finger is extended. The professor is seated near the window and peers out of it and sees one of the air traffic controllers, clad in rainproof gear, peering back at him from the ground. The professor therefore knows that he has not only been identified, *but also targeted*. Their hands and the deformed finger let him know that they are aliens.

Professor Lindstrom tries to make a run for it and his son Lloyd and his doctor, Paul, attempt to stop him. The professor feverishly tries to explain that, "This plane could be a death trap for me," but Lloyd a grown man himself, stops him, but they eventually both de-pane. He and his son watch as the plane takes off and then explodes in mid-air. (Shades of "Final Destination" movies that would be made some 50 years later).

The newspaper the next day carries the headline that forty people died in the crash. Vincent is reading the article as he is riding an interstate bus. Lindstrom is described as a "noted astro physicist. In less than a week, "at a meeting of his colleagues," Lindstrom is supposed to announce his "findings": that aliens have landed on Earth, to the rest of the world. The narrator says, "Then, perhaps, David Vincent could put down his burden. It all seemed so simple."

Yeah, right. A scientist who won't be believed and a crackpot architect as his backup? Give me a break. But this is the plot and I'm just here to share it with you and offer up critique and commentary.

An interstate bus stops at the Pennsylvania Bus Lines in Covington, and David gets off. He tells the driver, after handsomely tipping him, to "see to it that these bags get to the Covington Hotel." This is yet another theme of the on-going series: David stays in high end hotels and can always afford long-term stays. I realize that he's an architect, but unless he's a millionaire (which is never mentioned) where is all this money coming from? And if he has so much money in this, the second episode, why is he riding the bus?

A priest meets Vincent at the bus stop and says that he's been sent there by the Professor to escort him to the professor. While that is going on Professor Lindstrom is debating his doctor, Paul Mailer and his son Lloyd, who are trying to convince him to check into the hospital so that he can get some much needed rest. The professor tells them, "the invaders are real, they are here amongst us. And they intended to wipe us out like bugs!" he says.

What evidence did he know about being "wiped out like bugs"? Even the photo evidence that David view would later view would find had no proof of a genocidal campaign. There were no recorded conversations that would lead anyone to think that mass murder was a motive of the aliens. I liken this unsubstantiated conclusion made by professor Lindstrom to the made up and embellished lies that white men spread about the "Indians are out to massacre us" or "the niggers are going to burn the nation down," all done to justify their own racist attacks on both groups. Was this the case with Lindstrom? Who knows.

At any rate, Lindstrom makes is clear to both Lloyd and Dr. Mailer that he is afraid for his life, but finally agrees to allow them to take him to a hospital., but he intends "to go to that meeting on Tuesday" and "will not be silenced."

Meanwhile in the back of the cab with the priest David notices its taking too long to get to the professor. This is when we find out that the cab driver and the priest are both aliens and are kidnapping David. Vincent kicks open the cab door while it is moving and jumps from the car and takes off, boarding another bus that is headed in the opposite direction and just happens to be pulled to a stop across the street. He is able to escape the two aliens for the time being.

In the meantime there are two other aliens are at the hospital rigging Lindstrom's room. A few minutes later, Davie walks into the professor's room and introduces himself. He has talked to the professor on the phone, and Lindstrom remembers his call. David tells the professor that he agrees with him. "They're afraid you're going to share your knowledge with me. We've got to get out of here right now." David warns. David asks him to go into hiding where no one can find him before the upcoming conference.

One or the hospital orderlies walks in and is surprised to find David there with the professor. David lies and claims to have identification and asks the orderly to go check. The orderly turns around and says, "That's just what I'm going to do," as he turns around and leaves closing the door behind him. The professor then asks

David, "What do they (the aliens) look like?" David replies, "I have a better question: how did they know I was coming here to see you?" That is not a better question – in fact, it is a fucked up question. Because if David answers the doctor and says, "They look like you and me," then the professor would have a better idea about who it could be who snitched on them!

Somehow, we can agree that the aliens knew that David was coming to see Lindstrom. The orderly re-enters the room with Lloyd and Dr. Mailer. Lloyd, Mailer and the orderly tell Vincent to get out and he agrees to do so. Before leaving David implores the professor: "Please Dr. Lindstrom, do what I ask you to do before it's too late. I know them better than you."

What is Vincent talking about? Lindstrom is an astrophysicist and he's been studying these aliens for at least three months and we have no idea how long David's been on the scene. But we do know that David hasn't been involved in any research or study, he hasn't cracked a book and he has no real intimate evidence to back up his rants. So how can David had the gall to claim he knows the aliens better than Lindstrom when he (David) couldn't even tell that the priest and the cab driver who had just abducted him were damn aliens?

David goes to see a detective who calls the hospital and is told over the phone in front of David that Dr. Lindstrom's son checked him out of the hospital earlier that day. Here is another important point that should be made here and that will be raised throughout the two years of this show: Vincent has no kind of federal or local law enforcement identification. He is not even a private detective. He's just a peckerwood using the benefit of nice suits and white privilege to come and go as he pleases. For instance, how did he find this detective in the police department? Why would a detective take Vincent's word that the professor was in trouble? Why wasn't David held under suspicion for having such information which turned out to be unsubstantiated?

The professor is in his room at a place called the Pine Cone Inn. The female caretaker is leaving after asking him if he needed anything. He tells her that he doesn't need anything so she leaves. Lindstrom then locks the door right behind her. Two men (aliens) sit in a car outside and when the woman drives off, they get out and enter. There is no security whatsoever. Lindstrom is scared as hell, exits his room and goes out into the hallway to place a call on the pay phone. Lindstrom is attempting to make a call to the Covington Hotel where Vincent is staying, but the two men interrupt his call after there is no answer in Vincent's room. He leaves a message stating that he "has proof" but has to hang up because the two men, claiming to be government agents, walk in. They show some ID and tell him that his son is worried about him. Lindstrom nervously leaves with them.

The doctor goes along with the men and one gets his suitcase. They ask him if he has the proof. Lindstrom wonders how the men knew about "the proof" when he was the only person who knew of the existence of the evidence. Now he knows he's up shit creek. Lindstrom attempts to make a run for it but gets his elderly ass kicked, is quickly subdued, and taken away by the two aliens. .

The next scene a car is found at the bottom of a gully, burned. The police and fire people are there. The son is distraught because his father was in the car. Dr. Mailer says that professor Lindstrom was mentally ill and was very sick. Later at the funeral parlor, Lloyd looks over the casket where is father is laying. David walks in. "Perhaps if I'd been with him or if I had gained his confidence sooner." How did David find out about the car accident? How did he know that Lindstrom had died and the funeral home where Lindstrom was at? He was not a family member – how could he access such information?

The son thinks Vincent is disturbed, "even more than my father was." Vincent walks over to him and tries to explain to the young man: "A plane blew up. His car went over a cliff less than three days later …" The son remains in denial.

No one knew where his father was but the son remembers that the only people he told were "two government agents" because "they showed me their credentials." This is more than Vincent has done in any episode: he shows nothing more than a driver's license and cannot prove that he represents anything or anyone other than himself. He has no juice, no clout but seems to come and go in government, civic, political and military circles any time he chooses.

Davie explains to Lloyd that the elder Lindstrom had phoned him and left a message that he "had proof," -- actual photos -- that aliens exist. David informs Lloyd that someone had also ransacked his room as well. The son agrees to help David later, but for the time being he wants to be alone with the body of his father. He promises David that they he will help him the following day.

The priest comes from out back after David departs. "You did every well," he tells Lloyd. The son's head is hurting and he is in excruciating pain. "It will all be over soon my son," the priest says.

Meanwhile David and Dr. Mailer are at Lindstrom's office listening to tapes of Lindstrom regarding aliens. The doctor says that the tape is an interview from the hospital, and it is all that they can find. They have already searched Lindstom's house, which is in another city. David tells Dr. Mailer that he's going to head over to the Inn where professor Lindstrom "spent his last hours." Meanwhile, Lloyd continues to digest pills in an attempt to make the headaches go away. Dr. Mailer sees him and asks him where he got the pills. Lloyd continues taking them and this raises Mailer's curiosity. Lloyd says he got the pills from a doctor in New York before he came to town. Mailer palms one of the pills to take for analysis.

Back at the Inn, the cleaning woman comes into the room as Vincent is searching. . She finds a post office receipt showing that a registered package was delivered to a New York address – where Lloyd lived. The woman reluctantly gives David the receipt telling him that she never could "resist a handsome face." David leaves with the receipt and the minute he does the woman gets on the pay phone and calls Lloyd at his father's office informing him of what just took place. Lloyd has another headache and it is clear that he is under some type of mind control.

David goes to New York to Lloyd's apartment where the package was delivered. The landlord lets him in although he knows better. David gives him a generous tip and he man side steps protocol and the law. The landlord comes into the room with David and informs him that he placed the package on the bureau. David opens the package and finds a silver box. In it are photos of the flying saucer landing and a sworn statement from the doctor as well as others. There are other pictures of some type of chamber with giant tubes in it (the type that the aliens use to change into human form). There is also a photograph of an alien saucer landing.

The phone rings and it's Lloyd. The woman tells him about David having the address of his pad and in the next scene we see that David is already there in New York. Lloyd calls his place and David is there to pick up the phone. Lloyd doesn't raise any concerns about David being in his apartment, but asks him if he found anything. David tells him, "I've got enough here to blow the lid right off, thanks to your father's hard work." (Earlier he said he knew more about the aliens than Lindstrom did, remember?). David tells Lloyd he's not taking the info to the conference, but instead, he's going to Washington on the midnight train. He spills his gut to Lloyd and informs him that he has an old army buddy with the CIA, Jack Ryan. "By noon tomorrow, everybody in the world will know," David promises.

Lloyd gets off the phone and immediately makes a call to someone and tells them that David found the material and is going to Washington, taking it to Jack Ryan and will meet Jack at his apartment. "I'm glad you're pleased," Lloyd tells whoever it is on the other end of the phone and then hangs up. Dr. Mailer then comes in with the pill and tells Lloyd that he has had the pill analyzed and it is nothing that anyone has ever seen before. It is at this point that Dr. Mailer realizes that Lloyd has been brainwashed. Lloyd tells Dr. Mailer, "My father was an enemy. What happened to him was necessary.' The doctor turns and makes a run for it.

Dr. Mailer heads for a pay phone and gets on the phone to report an emergency. He's calling David's room, but David is headed to the elevator. Dr.

Mailer is still in the phone booth as someone is walking up to him. The doctor tries to run and get into his car, but even as he does, someone is in the back seat. The person grabs Mailer from behind and this is the first time we see the round glowing orb (metallic disc) that the aliens use to place on the neck of earth people killing them and simulating a cerebral hemorrhage.

David arrives at Ryan's but unbeknownst to him, the apartment is a fake one (across the hall from Ryan and his real apartment) and the man seated there is not Ryan. Lloyd is already there it's the wrong apartment. The priest enters and David gets knocked out. An alien grabs the case. "We'll take him to Maryland?" Lloyd asks. "Yes, to Maryland," the priest nods in agreement.

David wakes up in a room and the door is locked. He's in there with Lloyd. Lloyd is continuing to repeat the statement about his father being an enemy. He then turns to David and asks, "What are you afraid of? They're not going to execute you. They're going to change your brain patterns, that's all." Lloyd adds matter-of-factly, "Their goal is to convince people that there never was any proof, just an old man's nightmare."

An alien comes in. Lloyd has another headache and takes yet another pill. David is escorted out of the room by an alien who takes David into a lower level chamber where David is placed into a machine, akin to an MRI/x-ray machine. The priest is helping to run the machine which is obviously seeking to change David's brain pattern as the aliens watch. David is taken off the machine and immediately tries to fight the aliens, but he gets overpowered. "You are a very foolish man, Mr. Vincent. Can't you understand that there is no escape?" one asks him as he grips David by the throat.

David is taken back to the room where Lloyd is still being held, wakes up in a bed in a room with Lloyd staring at him. "You've been sleeping all day," Lloyd says. "It's not going to do any good to fight it," Lloyd says. Lloyd begins repeating the "my father was an enemy" rant. Vincent grabs Lloyd and takes the pills from him. They wrestle and Lloyd passes out. Two aliens come in to escort Vincent back to the chamber. Prior to their entry, David manages to hide Lloyd on the floor behind the bed. David is placed back on the machine for his second dose of radiation.

Meanwhile, Lloyd wakes up. He walks out of the room (which was not locked) and goes to the downstairs area where David is being programmed. He sneaks up behind the man at the master controls and throws a chair into the computer electrocuting the man and blowing up the system. David shakes free from the machine, and the aliens are dying. David and Lloyd are fighting the aliens. Lloyd is getting his ass kicked but David saves him. The place is on fire as

David helps Lloyd and they manage to escape, burning down the evidence of course. The priest burns in a fire ball of sin.

David and Lloyd make a run for it out of the mine and he is trying to save Lloyd but he's too tranced out. His last words implore David to never give up. And then Lloyd dies in David's arms.

Then comes the on-going epilogue and "moral" of the show: "For David Vincent, another beachhead destroyed. For the invaders, evidence that the human race can never be enslaved …"

The fact that "another beachhead" implies that there is more than one, and the fact that these aliens can infiltrate hotels, doctor's offices, construct beachheads in mountainsides, abandoned army bases and the like all over the country and do just about everything they need to do – courtesy of white privilege – *shows that indeed, the human race CAN be enslaved.* After all, this is the same skin color of the group that enslaved millions of African people, remember? This episode was called "the experiment," was it not? And wasn't the abduction of black people by this country's decision makers deemed an "experiment" of sorts?

.3. The Mutation

The aliens might not be from this planet but they sure know how to design some fine ass bitches. In this case it's Susanne Pleshette, a Hollywood darling from the '60s and '70s. In this one she is an alien, posing as a stripper, who helps Vincent and in doing so, she falls for him. After all, we learn, she's not like the rest of the aliens: she's a "mutation" and as such, she can experience "love". Ain't that a bitch? There were and are people on THIS planet who don't know what "love" is, but here is this alien being who claims she's got what Bruce Lee would call "emotional content." We'll see.

It's been three weeks since the report of a crash and the reports have brought reporters and a host of people, including David Vincent, to the town of Rosario.

Vincent is riding in a jeep with two Mexicans. He tells them to stop and tells them that they are going around in circles. He asks how far it is. The Mexicans tell him what they have seen, bright lights and strange noises. Vincent suspects it's a scam. After looking around the threesome heads back to the jeep and that's when the Mexicans make their move. They knock the shit out of Vincent and rob him. They jump in the jeep and take off leaving him in the desert under the steaming hot sun. The narrator will later refer to this as Vincent being "betrayed by his own kind and left to die under a blazing sun …" His own kind? The aliens look more like white people than these Mexicans did! But that's a story for another time.

The setting is Rosario, Mexico and Vincent has fallen for yet another ambush (there were scores of them throughout the series and he always came out unscathed) but gets away). In this one he comes across miscellaneous rumors of a crippled spaceship, and an air force fellow comes to Rosario County to check on rumors of a fallen aircraft. After getting jacked, Vincent begins walking and is parched and very tired. He falls to the ground but manages to continue. He looks up and through a dizzying haze, sees a flying saucer in the distance. It has landed and there are beings going in and out. Is it a mirage?

Vincent makes it into town and visits the clinic. He now has a new set of sun glasses, the reporters that were in town have gone, but David Vincent remains "to begin the search again." One concerned person, who we later learn is named Fellows who was sent by the government, tells him that they've used planes and helicopters looking for "this thing" and asks him, "Do you know what we found?" David says, "Nothing. Up the creek. I've been there before." And he continues walking down the street of the town without even giving the lone reporter a glance.

He tells the government man, "Mr. Fellows" that he's sure he saw something out there – a disabled space vehicle. Outside of the court house David finds his jeep and asks a deputy, "what about the men who rolled me?" They could not be found but the jeep is in good shape. The officer watches Vincent sign paperwork and asks him to "take your nightmares out of here." David replies, "When I'm finished" and walks across the street. Two teenagers in a hot rod crank up their car and nearly run Vincent down. An older man who knows who Vincent is pushes him out of the way in time.

David goes into the bar after thanking the man. The man, whose name is Evans, follows him and says his name is Evans, claiming to be a freelance reporter. "It came to me that if David Vincent were right," it would be quite a story. Evans says he found somebody who "is telling the same story that you are. They know exactly where this space ship is right now." He won't tell David until he agrees to give him (Evans) the exclusive.

Off they go to meet the source, who is an exotic dancer on stage dick teasing a lounge full of people. Vincent and Evans enter and are seated. She now has on a robe and walks over to Evans. He introduces her to Vincent and asks her to tell Vincent what she knows. They are seated and she claims she was coming back from Mexico sightseeing and it was getting dark. She made a wrong turn, but didn't know it. She started to get scared and pulled over to the side of the road. Being a cockhound, Vincent falls for a story from a stripper says she saw a saucer.

Evans, the reporter, is the one who introduced her to Vincent. Her name is Vikki, and she ultimately agrees to accept a $200 payment to show Vincent where the saucer is (originally Evans offered $100, but she hesitated and Vincent added the extra hundred). She says she will take them out to the site where she saw the ship. She will meet them in front of the hotel in the morning. David asks her if he can buy her a drink, but she tells him she'd better get back to work. But it is clear that there is some chemistry between them.

Fellows is watching both Evans and David. Evans goes back to Vikki's room and walks in. He hands her something. He uses a disk to contact other aliens and tells them "we will be ready tomorrow." So now we know that both Vikki and Evans are aliens.

The next morning Fellows is still tagging behind at a distance. Meanwhile, Vikki, Evans and Vincent meet. "You got the money?" she asks Evans and he gives it to her. David and Vikki have serious eye contact. David and Vikki get into the jeep while Evans stays behind. Off they go with David behind the wheel. She tells him it's a couple of hours away. "Let's just get this out of the way and cut the small talk, huh?" she says to him as he speeds toward their destination.

Meanwhile, the curious government agent Fellows is at the bar asking a lot of questions. The bartender doesn't know where Vincent and Vikki went, but they hired Vikki and when the boss called the place that she was sent by, they said they never heard of her. This raises even more suspicions and Fellows goes to Evans' room with questions. He walks in and an alien communications device is on the desk, but Evans is able to block it from the view of Fellows. Evans offers nothing so Fellows leaves and immediately Evans gets on the communications device and tells his fellow aliens, "they're on their way. Departure time nine plus seven." Whatever in the hell that means.

David fires up a cigarette and spots a ring on Vikki's finger as she's lighting his cigarette. David asks her if she wants to stop and get something to eat. She nods in the affirmative so they pull off onto a side rode and pull up in front of a small cantina/diner. David goes inside after offering to help her out of the Jeep. She rejects his help, he says "suit yourself." Vikki enters on her own. As they sit at the bar waiting for their meal, a fire breaks out in the kitchen and the flames land on a young boy whose shirt is on fire. David goes into the kitchen and puts the fire out, although the fire also burns his shirt. He is wounded but the little boy's mother thanks him and he goes to the porch area to take off his shirt and put cold water on the burns.

Before going to the porch, David notices that throughout the ruckus, Vikki showed no emotion or concern whatsoever. She comes to the porch and asks if he needs help. As he puts water on his wound he asks her, "What's wrong with you? You sat there watching like it was a floor show or something." David grabs her and she says, "You're hurting me." David replies, "I didn't think that was possible." David lets her go and continues to tend to his wound. Vikki wants to help and she offers to apply cold cream because "it's good for the burns." They stare at each other. Could it be love? "Do it yourself," she says putting the cream down and walking off.

The duo gets back on the road. We notice that the space ship is still being repaired by the aliens as they are waiting for Vikki to arrive with Vincent. They arrive at a spot and Vikki tells him to stop because the ship is "over there, over that ridge." David instructs Vikki to wait in the jeep but she comes along anyway. As they are walking to the ridge to locate the ship, Vikki then claims she made a mistake, trying to save him from getting killed, but it's too late – David has spotted the ship and the aliens. But they've also spotted Vikki trying to assist David and they aim and fire a laser beam that destroys the jeep. David and Vikki make a run for it through the mountainous terrain. The aliens are in hot pursuit. She says they'll kill her because "they think I warned you." Without hesitation David takes her hand and together they begin to run for their lives through the mountains.

David must be in great shape, because Vikki is getting tired but he continues to run with her in tow. She tells him that the ship was in trouble she says. "You were getting too close," she says. She tells David that she doesn't know why she wanted to help him. Meanwhile Fellows, who is supposed to be headed back to Washington, is on the phone saying he'll take the next plane out.

The aliens are still searching for Vincent and Vikki, and they continue to run. David doesn't trust her. He wants to know more but she says that he wouldn't understand. Almost right away he tells her that he could TRY to understand." This is known as communication, the same type that white people in real life during that time period simply would not extend to black people. That is what the civil rights movement, the black power movement and all those riots were about. Black people were demanding to be HEARD and listened to – we wanted to get some understanding. But this alien female is white, Vincent is white and as a result, though she is from a galaxy thousands of miles away, there is an almost immediate meeting of the minds.

Vikki tells him that as a youth she "had this thing in me, this difference." She says that her "father" had the difference too. He stood up against the others and they killed him. She tells David, "I can't be like the others. Life means something," she says. Now let's take a look at this for a moment.

The title of the episode is "The Mutant." In other words, Vikki is some kind of mixed race half-breed who, unlike the other aliens who have no feelings, has the capacity for care, concern, and appreciation. The human qualities she has are those that involved emotion and feeling – two elements that the white man has NEVER shown to or displayed toward black folks. Remember the year of the airing of this show is 1967 and white people are running to the suburbs and calling it "white flight." That's how much compassion they had for us in the real world. But on this TV show, these aliens- who adopt the appearance of white people – are cold blooded and lacking in emotion, but this one has good qualities because she is the most like a human. This is straight up bullshit.

Not only that but Vincent shows his racism. He tells her that he cannot be with her because they are not alike, that she came in a different form and that she lives far away. This is what white people tell black people when they are explaining why they (the blacks) cannot live next door or in the same neighborhoods! "You're different." "You're of a different color." "You're of a different race." More on this later.

In the meantime, the aliens are closing in so off they go once again.

An alien walks up on them and he and David begin fighting. David disarms him and is getting his ass kicked. Vikki just stands there as David is being thrown all over the place. The alien swings, David ducks and the alien falls off a cliff. This is where you see the dead alien body turn red and then disappear. "That's what happens to us when we die here on earth," she explains to David.

Fellows is in a tax and goes into a lounge. He's asking for Vikki and the b bartender doesn't tell him anything. The cab driver comes in and tells him to hurry up if you are going to catch that plane. Fellows takes his bags out of the car and decides to stick around.

Meanwhile David and Vikki come upon a ranch house. In this episode some Mexicans actually play a major role, and it is the first time any people of color appear in these early episodes of "The Invaders". Their shack is where Vincent and Vikki hole up to hide from the aliens. The two of them just walk in and state that they are being chased and the Mexicans immediately offer them security and solace. Miguel, the husband, talks with David while his wife comforts Vikki, "You're one of them, I can't trust you." She replies, I'm different." He tells her, "You came millions of miles in a different form, from a different place.

David asks Miguel if the truck outside is operable. After informing them that they "have troubles of our own," Miguel nevertheless says that David can use the truck but that "something in it is broke." David tells Miguel that he can fix the truck and Miguel informs him that there is a station nearby called Dos Lobos. Miguel then gives David his rifle. "You may need this." David heads out, walks past the chickens and the corral to the white truck. He raises the hood and appears to know what he's doing.

The question is how? This peckerwood is an architect. When did he find time to learn how to be a mechanic? The truck is one of those old ones, so how does he know he can fix it? Again, white supremacy means that the white man is all-knowing in all capacities and gullible audiences take it for granted.

Vikki runs outside and says she wants to go with him. He tells her she'll be safer at the ranch house. David asks for gasoline and Miguel tells him it's in the corral. David fetches the gas can and puts it in the back of the truck. It is very important to note that has David opens the corral door to fetch the gas can, Miguel shouts that he make sure that the he close the gate behind him because it should always be closed. At any rate, David tells Vikki he'll make her go to the authorities with him. She says she can't do it. "Take me with you David," she asks. Then, check out this spurt of emotionalism: she tells David that for the first time she cares and feels. "Before I met you, I was ashamed of caring because there was no one to care for. But now there is and I want to stay with you," she says.

This is a teaching moment.

Take the case of interracial relationships. The boy and the girl, from different racial or ethnic backgrounds, meet and fall for each other but they know that their love can never be. So what is the first thing the white girl says to the black boy who is hated by her father and mother? It's the first time she's "cared" for someone. And that "care" may or may not be sex-related, but one thing is for sure: the brutha is getting paid so in a motherly type of way, she is "caring" for him! This scene from "The Invaders" shows an alien falling in love with a man of another race and risking being ostracized (and killed) by her own race members. See the similarity?

The fact is, as fine as Vikki was, there is no way that a single white boy would reject her advances. He could have at least screwed her! But not the gallant and noble David Vincent. He again has to remind her that she came from a different place and in a different form. This is evidence of racism once again. He has not seen her other form; all he knows is that if she's an alien, she has to somehow rejuvenate in order to keep that form. So why not do what the typical white boy would do: fuck her in her current form and then bust a cap?

At any rate, David takes off in the truck headed for the Dos Lobos cantina to find a phone and as soon as he pulls away, Vikki contacts her people and tells them where he is headed and tells them he is meeting a man named Fellows. How would she know about Fellows? But she's learning earth lessons well, isn't she? What do they say? "Heaven has no rage, like love to hatred turned, Nor hell a fury, like a woman scorned."

David arrives at Dos Lobos and tries to call Fellows but Fellows is on the phone in his room. Fellows is informed that it will be two hours before a plane is gassed and ready. Fellows puts down the phone and it rings right away and it's David. Vincent tells him, "The ship – I know where the space ship is," he says. He tells Fellows that Evans is an alien but unbeknownst to Fellows, Evans is downstairs on another phone listening in.

Meanwhile, the aliens find the shack and go inside. Vikki knows she's a goner. The aliens are holding Miguel, his wife and young son at gunpoint. Vincent returns to the shack, where Vikki is trying to stall the aliens. David pulls up and sees the corral door open, something that Miguel would never do. He gets out of the truck with rifle in hand. He calls out for Vikki. She is pleading a case for David's life. "How can he hurt us? When the space ship is gone no one will believe a word he says. It's better not to kill him. With him dead people will ask questions. They'll wonder. It's better not to kill him." The aliens space her off.

She runs out the door to warn David but one of the aliens shoots her down with the gun. She glows and disappears the way they tend to do when they die. In other words, she sacrificed herself for this earth man against her own people. After that comes the shootout, with David using the gun he borrowed from the Mexican. David shots down three of the ambushing aliens. As would be the case in episode after episode there were no witnesses. He looks around and watches as the space ship takes off in the distance.

David is back in town in the ranch house with Miguel and his family, and Fellows walks in. The space ship's gone. The girl is gone, too," he tells Fellows. Fellows doesn't believe him. David says he "killed" Vikki. Why isn't this asshole arrested? The Mexican man and woman testify that horrible strange men broke into their house and that "he (David) helped us." Fellows says a couple of days ago he would have had a quick answer. But now, he's not so sure. David asks when will you be sure – *when it's too late?!*

The moral: "For a moment, in the desert south of Rosario, a man and woman came together across a void of space and time. Two people, star-crossed, from alien worlds. In the months to come, David Vincent would remember that moment" The fact that these were "alien worlds" is what makes the fact that everybody involved has pale white skin even more unbelievable! The white man is attempting to pawn himself off as a universal majority when he's but a shriveling minority on THIS planet!

This is the first episode to show how the aliens glow bright red and burn up before they die.

.4. The Leeches

Thus far we have established the fact that the aliens have established a number of "beachheads" around the world, that they have the machinery and technology here to convert themselves from alien to human form, that the human form that they chose is that of the Caucasian-American, and that from time to time their space ships tend to break down.

In this episode, "The Leeches" we begin to see just how far reaching the alien grasp is on its takeover. Not only do they have key geopolitical outreach, but they have been able to infiltrate, imitate and control the lives of powerful white people who in turn, control hundreds of lives of earth people who are apparently unaware of what is going on.

In "The Leeches" we find David in Maricopa County, which his in Arizona. According to the Arizona website and other sources, Maricopa County is located in the south-central part of the U.S. state of Arizona. As of the 2017 census, its population was 3,817,117 making it the state's most populous county, and the fourth-most populous in the United States. It is more populous than 23 states. The county seat is Phoenix, the state capital and fifth-most populous city in the country.

Remember that "The Invaders" was televised in 1967, and may have been ahead of its time. The fact is that Maricopa County today, some fifty years later, is setting population records for days. According to a website called AZCentral.com,

> The Census Bureau says Arizona's Maricopa County has replaced Texas' Harris County as the county with the nation's highest annual population growth. Maricopa County includes Phoenix and most of its suburbs, and its estimated population now tops 4.2 million. Maricopa County gained more than 81,000 people between July 1, 2015, and July 1, 2016, an average daily increase of 222 people. Harris County had an increase of nearly 57,000, or about 155 per day on average.

But we hail back to the days of the airing of "The Invaders." The previous stats were simply shared to make it clear that those who did the selection of the various and diverse locations of this TV show did not scrimp or take any shortcuts. So from Mexico we find the frequent traveler David Vincent now in a county whose largest city is Phoenix.

As the episode begins, we see that the hi-tech machinery that the aliens exhibited in the segment called "The Experiment" is now more complex and again they have secured some kind of underground lair where there is technology at work all over the place. In fact, it is an abandoned mining facility and how they find it we never know. Did they purchase the land legally or were they just interlopers? The condition of the outside of the camp made it appear abandoned so one would think that they had just camped out in it and modified it figuring they would never be noticed. Maybe they were just alien "squatters," who really knows?

A man, who we later know as professor Markham is being dragged down the stairs and placed in a chair, with one alien promising that "we've extracted almost all the information." Markham tries to fight back and makes a run for it, gets past the stairs and into the tunnel, turns a corner with aliens in pursuit. They get outside of the mine shaft and the old man is getting away. Three aliens, laser guns in hand continue to look for him but he manages to squeeze down in between some rocks and is able to elude them.

We know this because in the next scene we cut to a psychiatrist's couch and Markham is waking up shouting "Don't let them find me!" The doctor tells him to take it easy and lie back down. An aide gives Markham gets a shot and this settles the professor who dozes off muttering, "No more, no more …"

David Vincent is getting off yet another plane, this one at the Maricopa Airport. A man is there waiting to pick him up as the narrator tells us, "Two men with their eyes on the heavens, coming together in a small southwestern city." Warren Doneghan, the president of JAE – Jet Age Electronics – is there at the hotel waiting for David. He is there with another man named Tom Wiley, who introduces himself to David, who is dressed like a pimp, complete with custom-fitted suit and dark shades.

Warren, who is the driver, escorts Vincent over to meet Donegan. They get into the car and Donegan asks Vincent to sit in the front seat while Wiley drives. The reason is because Donegan suspects that a gray sedan is following them. Wiley tells Vincent that Donegan always thinks someone is following them, hinting that the doctor of paranoid. The black Lincoln continental, which we see in a number of episodes, speeds away toward Donegan's factory.

Donegan introduces Wiley as his best friend and body guard who won't believe alien beings are here. "That's why I sent for you," Donegan says and adds "you will be paid for your time." David says something like "that would be a welcome change," implying that he is risking his life and doing all this travel on his own dime. The question is why? All this risk to save humanity and he has not children, no wife, no real home life. In fact, he was on his way home from a conference when he initially spotted the alien space craft. This is a lonely ass dude who is on a mission for who knows what. But we are supposed to believe he's like the Blues Brothers: on a mission from God!

According to Donegan five men – all scientists of some type – have disappeared without a trace in recent months, each an expert in his own field. Most recently Dr. Markham "showed up" and was diagnosed as insane. Donegan fears that his own "disappearance is being planned." He says those after him are an enemy but he specifically believes they are aliens.

He continues his explanation and tells David to look at the fields of the men who have disappeared. Markham was an oceanographer, Wanamaker a mathematician, Millington an expert in psychology, Roddeman was in military science "and just last month Bill Hastings from Cal Tech." Donegan, still in the back seat talking continues: "Add it up Mr. Vincent and tell me what you get." David says, "A pattern." The driver says, "Congratulations Warren, you finally made a sale." David says, "Mr. Donegan if they have a list it figures that you'd be on it. You're the best in your field."

They pull into the plant and the gated security signs them in. Inside an office in the factory they are developing a plan. David suggests that Donegan allow the aliens to kidnap him and he and Wiley will be following him. They plan to place a monitor of some kind on Donegan and use it to trace his whereabouts. Wiley is skeptical and suggests that "we know this off right now and give this gentleman a ride back into town." But Donegan likes the idea, Wiley is his friend and eventually there is agreement. Donegan has to fetch something from his office and asks Wiley to accompany David to the commissary.

In the office Donegan is searching for papers and a blonde woman is there. It's his wife, Eva. As he continues his search he talks to her without even looking up, informing her that he might have to leave town "all of a sudden." She asks for how long and he tells her that he is not sure. It is clear that they have problems in their marriage and they stem from his obsession with his job and as a result, he is not paying her much attention. She is concerned but he tells her that, "You're making a whole lot out of nothing" and then walks out to go "take a shower." Wiley is standing near the bar as Donegan leaves the room but then asks Wiley if he will escort Eve to a party that night because he (Donegan) doesn't have the time. Before heading upstairs to take his shower he tells his wife to "trust" him.

When he leaves she begins spilling her guts to Wiley, who is more than happy to listen. She thinks her husband is seeing another woman, but Wiley tells her that's not the case. She tells him that even if he was, Wiley wouldn't tell her, but he walks over to her and reassures her that indeed, he would. She tells Wiley that she is finished with her husband. He turns to go home and change clothes so that he can escort her to the party that night.

`Donegan and David are in his study viewing film that he's taken over the years. The film is of the route he takes home from work each day. Friday is Tom's day off and that is the day they believe they can set it up for the aliens to kidnap Donegan. "Tom's day off is when they'll probably hit," Donegan says. "This is the shortcut." David tells him, we have the problem of time and place," but Donegan pulls out a bugging device that he claims has the most powerful transmitter ever made, one that he owns the patent to. It has a forty mile range so Tom and David should be able to trail them when the kidnap occurs.

Pay close attention to the confidence that these men have on alien activity. They have confidence that the aliens are highly organized. At about that time David asks Donegan why he's sticking his neck out. "You made four national magazines last month." Donegan has no answer but asks David the same question, and he too, has no response.

Now hold on one god damn minute. Here we have two men who are obviously well-to-do and don't care a real care in the world. The professor has a large home and a giant plant that he is in charge of. Neither man has any bills, or so it seems. But this is why I call this "The Bruce Wayne Mental Disorder." Why? Because Bruce Wayne is Batman's secret identity and he's a billionaire. But he risks his life, for no pay, puts on a damn outfit and goes to battle with the most sinister villains in the history of crime. Now we have David Vincent and Donegan doing the same thing: risking their lives, but when you ask them why, neither has an answer. What kind of bullshit is this? Are we to believe that, like Batman, they do what they do for the sake of humanity and justice? Name a white man in the real world who does this kind of thing for free. You can't.

David and Warren wait in a car on a side road overlooking the road that Donegan will be taking. They have the monitor and its working just fine. Donegan's sports car is a yellow convertible and off he goes. A huge semi-truck comes down the highway and pulls to a stop blocking the road which is only one lane. Here comes Donegan. "He won't be able to get past that van," Tom says. "I know," says David. Two men get out of the truck. One walks over to Donegan's car and tells him he's having truck problems. A second alien comes up from behind and knocks Donegan in the head. He then gets in the car as several others roll out ramps into the back of the semi-truck and drive Donegan's car up into it. Tom and David are watching intently.

The men close up the back of the semi and take off. Tom cranks the car and something happens and the hood blows open. The engine disappears in red glow like aliens do when they die. It's been rigged. The car has obviously been sabotaged and they lose track of Donegan.

David and Tom prepare to leave in a helicopter – just like that. Neither of them has any juice but somehow they've got a helicopter. So off they get ready to go in what is more likely than not a company copter. As they walk toward the copter, Eve is shouting for Tom as David waits. She slaps the shit out of him. And like a typical white boy, he does nothing about it. She acts worried and consoles him with a hug as David watches from a distance. Tom promises Eve they will get Donegan back. "Are you sure that you want to?" she asks. He reassures her that he's more certain than she is. Again, she apologizes and asks forgiveness. He says nothing The copter takes off with Tom at the controls.

Tom is flying with David on the passenger side. David tells him that the hospital where they are keeping Dr. Markham is right outside of Tucson. "He's our last lead." In the meantime, the semi-truck pulls up and three aliens escort Donegan out of the back of the truck. "There's no point in hoping, Mr. Donahue," one says. "Your friends are not coming, not now – not ever." Two aliens then escort a struggling Donegan into the back of a white panel van and it takes off. These guys have resources and are organized to the max.

At the hospital David and Tom visit Dr. Markham. He's in a small cell in a coma like state. Again, we find David exercising the kind of clout that exists only in the minds of the white man. He and Tom go into a hospital without a single medical credential or ID, and in the next scene not only do the invade the professor's privacy by peering into his cell, but then they get to listen to the tapes the professor made before he snapped. As they play the tape with the hospital officials attending they hear the professor say, "They're not people like us … not human. O god what they did to us. Terrible pain … leeches. They're leeches. I gotta get out, understand that. They're buried in hell. What kinds of beings are you? Don't do it anymore. Noooo. Noooo!!"

These words could have been uttered b any African that was captured and then enslaved by the white man. The same sentiments regarding the fact that the treatment was brutal and that these white people are "not like us." And was enslavement not a major example of the white man "leeching" off of the skills, strength and energy of those he had enslaved?

David remembers the words, "buried in hell." What could they mean? Markham was found some forty miles north of Silver City. Tom and David get back into the copter and continue their search for Donegan. The monitor begins to buzz loudly as David barks out instructions (orders?) to Tom to turn here and turn there. Meanwhile, the white panel truck pulls into an abandoned mine area and escort Donegan into one of the mining shacks which has, of course, been renovated. The aliens take him downstairs to the same area where we earlier saw Markham being tortured. The aliens find the bugging decide on Donegan and snatch it off. One alien crushes it beneath his boot heel.

The copter is flying low and is running out of fuel. Tom wants to turn around and head back to the laboratory but David begs for ten more minutes in the air. In the meantime there is a room where all the kidnapped scientists are lying on cots. Donegan is thrown in with them and he comes across a colleague, Hastings, from Cal Tech. It seemed that they had worked together the past year on the coast and Hastings vaguely remembers. He tells Donegan, "The aliens put you in a chair and attach a metal helmet to your head. It hurts. It hurts from deep inside. Then the machines probe the brain and take from it whatever knowledge they want. A lifetime of learning and experiments and they take it from you."

Several things can be gleaned from Hastings' brief explanation. The extraction process with the helmet sounds an awful lot like the electric chair that the white man uses under the guise of "capital punishment." As far as extracting knowledge, also known today as intellectual property theft, no one has a longer history of doing that that the European, be he Greek, Portuguese, English, British or American. Much of what they have today was stolen from African and the Aztecs. Today they call it "cultural appropriation."

The aliens enter the room and grab Donegan. A third one comes in and points a probe of some kind at him. Cut to the helicopter which is now out of gas and has landed as David checks a map. He raises the issue of having seen Tom and Eva at the airport and how "close" they seemed. Tom says that he has every right to say what he wants. After all, he explains, he's been in love with Eva for over a year. David looks at him: "This is none of my business. Leave me out of it," he says. Tom keeps babbling. He and Donegan were in Korea together. "He lives and breathes and sleeps for that factory," Tom said. He says he wished so many times that Eve could be rid of him. He says he can't be committed to something that he can't believe in and doesn't believe that they are ever going to find Donegan.

Tom has had it. He says he's going to quit and blames David for losing Donegan in the first place. He starts walking off toward the highway, which is three miles away, and tells David to "get back on your own." Meanwhile in the mine, Donegan is being strapped to the chair. The machine is turned on as Donegan writhes in pain.

David is continuing his search, on foot, across a mountainous hot desert area, akin to the terrain we saw in the episode, "The Mutation." David looks up and sees a man staggering toward him and immediately pulls out a revolver. Where did David get it? This is the first time in the series that we see that Vincent has a gun, and if he had one before, why didn't he use it?

At any rate the man's name is Millington, and he is one of the kidnapped scientists who has managed to get away. He's dehydrated so he faints in David's arms. Before he faints David tells him, "I'll help you but first you have to show me where they kept you." Before passing out Millington tells David "there are too many of them and they are too strong." He gives David directions – just over the ridge (just as the space ship was in "The Mutation," remember), and then he passes out.

But alas – it's a trick! When David walks to the top of the ridge and has his back to the man, the man gets up (he was faking it) and points a laser gun at David.

But just in time Tom has returned and shoots the alien, who glows red and disappears. "What was that thing down there?" Tom asks David. "He called himself Millington, he's an alien and that's how they die here on Earth," David explains.

Tom explains to David that he changed his mind and came back after he saw a jeep come out of nowhere and drop that man off and then take off. Tom saw where the Jeep came from and he and David go to the hill just above the spot. David says, "It's a mining camp, or what's left of one. Looks like it's been deserted for years." The words "buried in hell" come back to David's mind, the words used by Markham to describe where he was held when he was being tortured.

David tells Tom that he's glad he came back. Now both of them are armed with their r evolvers. Don't ask me how. In the alien laboratory they can see that their fellow alien has not returned. Meanwhile, David and Tom creep into the camp. David and Tom get past a guard and into the mining entrance where the machinery is being used. David sneaks up on the alien and karate kicks him knocking him out. And this brings us to another teaching moment that has to be addressed before moving on.

The fact that Vincent can just go about the world chasing aliens without an apparent care in the world, booking rooms in any hotel or motel he wants, never missing a meal, spending much of his time in custom-made suits is one thing. But this shit about being a crack shot and being able to fight beings who are stronger is going too far. Where did Vincent learn how to fight? How did he become so fearless? The answer is simple: in the white supremacist universe the white man must be seen as being the best in all things. And when it comes to competing against alien beings, this myth becomes all the more important. After all, Vincent is an "exception" and is not like the other humans.

Back to the mine where a second alien security guard is walking up the way. Tom sneaks up behind min, and easily knocks him out. David goes up one tunnel and Tom another, both with guns at the ready. David finds an entrance. Tom comes across a wooden panel and can hear machines on the other side. He pulls out his pocket knife and begins trying to pry off the paneling. Meanwhile, David is watching as two aliens are serving nourishment to imprisoned scientists. David follows the aliens carrying the food trays into the cell where the scientists are served. David sneaks up and knocks one out. Donegan tackles the other and they begin fighting David, seeing that Donegan is getting his ass kicked, comes over the knocks him out with his gun butt.

David and Tom want to rescue the other scientists and get them out of that room. Tom gets the panel door open and sees the brainwashing machine and an alien operating it. He enters the room, another alien comes in and Tom shoots him. He then shoots the alien at the controls and both glow red before their bodies disappear. Tom is out of bullets and a fight begins and Tom is getting his ass kicked.. Another alien is walking in as the fight continues. An alien who was floored reaches to a panel and pulls down a lever which leads to the mine beginning to cave-in. The cave-in gets worse as David and Donegan rescue two scientists and get to the outside. Tom is trapped and shouts out for David but when David tries to run back into the mine he is blown off his feet by the explosion that destroys any proof that aliens were ever there. Tom therefore dies

Back at the hospital everyone is being treated. Donegan comes in and its been three days since they escaped the aliens. He shakes David's hand and it is then confirmed that Tom didn't make it, nor did one of the other scientists. It is reported that nothing is left of the mine, just debris. While David was being treated, Donegan went to Washington to tell them what happened, but got no help. "They listened and were polite and even sent down an investigator," Donegan tells David, "But nothing was found." Washington is willing to admit that there was some kind of a plot, but they spaced him off nonetheless.

The scientists they rescued "are worse than Markham," Donegan says. "Their minds are gone." Donegan asks David, who is lying in a hospital bed, "Was it worth it what we did?" "Yes," David answers. "We destroyed what they were doing and we destroyed them". Before he leaves Donegan says, "Get well, David. And don't quit."

My questions are, first of all, who's going to pay for that hospital stay? Where are all these funds coming from to enable these men to globetrot and chase aliens? Donegan says he's not going to quit and David shakes his hand and tells him he'll be counting on him. David asks him how is his wife, and Donegan claims that Eve is doing alright and that he loves her. And he's going to do his best to convince her of that.

The narrator leaves us with a moral: "Two men with their eyes on the heavens will now share a common knowledge together. Together they have faced the invader. Together they have learned the grave threat that he represents to the human race. And now as they again pursue their separate destinies, they remain more than ever men with their eyes on the heavens."

.5. "Genesis"

It starts off with a motorcycle cop pulling over s a station wagon. As the two cops prepare the paperwork a car filled with teenagers speeds by prompting one of the officers, Officer Hal Corman, to decide to give chase leaving his partner to deal with the station wagon. The cop pulls over the wagon that the kids were in, and they ask why. He says it was due to the broken headlight. The cop hears something and the two large teens say it's nothing, but the cop, flashlight in hand, goes to the back of the wagon anyway.

The cop orders the back tail end door opened and one of the teens says that inside is a girl who is a little "oiled up." The cop insists. Whatever was inside was glowing and the cop asks, "What is it?" but not before one of the teens takes out the metallic orb that can kill and make it appear as if the victim had a heart attack, and places it on the cops neck. He falls dead. They then speed off in the wagon.

David pulls up in a cab in front of Newport General Hospital to visit a police officer who is in a state of shock, "He has been driven to the state of hysteria, a sight that has him on the fringes of madness," as the narrator tells us. "His incoherent words describing a creature not of this world and a strange metallic disk." So here's David, dressed again to the nines, leaving the cab driver a tip and going into a hospital located in a Rhode Island city that he's never been in.

A woman is there arguing with a psychiatrist insisting on staying with the officer. It's the officer's wife, Joan. The explanation is that his mind has shut down. The psychiatrist, Dr. Grayson, has papers for her to sign so that the officer "can be taken to a place where he can get the help he needs." Joan doesn't want Hal taken away but another man, Lieutenant Greg Lacaster tells her that she HAS to do it.

David goes to the front desk and introduces himself as a "friend of Hal Corman. The lieutenant, who just happens to be getting some water from a nearby fountain, overhears Vincent. He walks over to him, shows him ID and asks to speak with him. He asks David for ID and asks him where he was last night. David shows him the airplane ticket. The cop wants to find the man driving that station wagon. He's going to hang on to David's plane ticket and David tells him which hotel he is staying in, then gets on the elevator and leaves.

Hal lost his rank and his future, according to his wife. He should have been at a desk at the precinct instead of out on the street. She blames Lacaster. David is ringing the doorbell at the house when Joan walks up. David wants to talk with her because her husband had an 'experience that I may know something about." What kind of experience? She asks. She lets him into the apartment.

Lacaster and the cops find out that David was, indeed, on Flight 402, about the background information on him describes him as "a kook who believes that aliens have landed." This is interesting because it appears that white privilege trumps background checks. Vincent has gone into five different cities thus far, walked into laboratories and government offices, shows some ID (probably nothing more than a driver's license) and has a jacket that refers to him as a nut? Only a white man could get away with this kind of dual lifestyle and at the same time keep a pocket full of money – and a loaded revolver.

At any rate the phone rings at the cop shop and someone is calling to tell Lacaster that Joan has brought David back up to the hospital with her. He tells Lacaster to get back down to the hospital right away. If he doesn't let her see her husband she will have him taken out of his care. "Can she do that?" Lacaster asks. "Of course she can do that!" Grayson informs him. Before hanging up Grayson tells Lacaster, "If nobody stops her I won't be responsible for what happens."

Lacaster is warned before leaving the office that the captain has kept him on despite the fact that he acts like a lone wolf. Lacaster's not listening and leaves out the door.

Joan, Lacaster, David and Grayson are meeting in Grayson's office. David tells Lacaster, "I don't care what the report say about me, the facts behind it are true." What? How can the facts be true and he doesn't care about them? The facts are that he is acting like a damn paranoid schizophrenic going around the country with no proof claiming that aliens have landed. Only a white man could get away with this kind of bullshit without being locked up – like 64-year old Stephen Paddoci did in Las Vegans in September of 2017 when he was able to secure 37 rifles and gun down hundreds of people from a hotel room despite the fact that his father had been on the FBI's Most Wanted list. But he, like David Vincent, had the benefit of white privilege.

So with no guarantees, no medical credentials and knowledge provided by Grayson that one word out of place could send Corman into an even deeper coma, Joan allows David into the room anyway! With Joan, Lacaster and Grayson standing near, David leans over the bed to talk with Corman He says, "We may have something in common. We may have been through the same experience. Hal, try to remember the metal disk, the metal disk you talked about that night. A metal unknown to us, warm very warm. When it touched you it began vibrating. Someone held the disk in the palm of his hand and it began vibrating. Is that what happened?" Hal's coming out of it but then faints back into deep sleep.

Vincent and Lacaster walk out. "I got through to him," David says. He tells him to put a guard on the door. "He's seen them. They can't afford to have him talk." All they need is one minute alone with him and it'll look like a cerebral hemorrhage," Vincent explains.

David is in his hotel room going over paperwork when there is a knock on the door. It's one of the cops, the one who was talking to Lacaster about being a lone wolf. He shows ID and then says that Corman is dead, and that he died from a cerebral hemorrhage. David is distraught and the man asks him to come with him, which he does. They enter an underground parking garage and he tells David the car is straight ahead. He's got a metallic orb and tires to place it on David neck but David is too quick. They begin fighting. David is kicking his ass as the man now has a gun. David disarms him and goes to grab the disk, but the man knocks him out. Lacaster pulls up and the man begins shooting. Lacaster shoots the man in the back and he glows red and dies.

When hotel management and the cops arrive, Lacaster lies and says that they heard no shots, just a backfire. He orders everyone out of the parking garage until he "checks the damage."

They found the wagon that the kids were joy riding in. Lacaster questions Vincent and David says, "You know what you saw. What you choose to believe is up to you." He tells Lacaster that the sedan station wagon was the car that the alien was in the night they were stopped by Corman. "Who was that man I shot?" "It wasn't a man, it was an alien from another planet. You saw my file. I've been tracking them. You just saw one die," David explains to Lacaster.

David hands Lacaster something, a ticket stub, that he "found in the front seat." What? This asshole has been tampering with a crime scene! He's not a cop. He should have been arrested right there! How does Lacaster know that it's really something he found or was something he planted – the way they do when they set up black people?

The station wagon is traced to the Newport Sea Lab, and when David asks questions we learn that the wagon belongs to Selee Lowell, David thanks the lieutenant for following him and reminds him how he (David) said that he was glad to be tailed because he might be needing help. Lacaster said he came to the hotel to pick David up after Hal died. "He didn't just die – he was murdered," David says.

David and Lacaster both arrive at the Sea Lab and find Ms. Lowell. But she tells Vincent and Lacaster that "everybody uses that car. The keys are always in the ignition." They Sea Lab exists because they got a grant for the secret experiments taking place at the lab that they are conducting. The fact is, the aliens are creating life, experimenting with primordial conditions. "Mind if I wander around a little bit?" Vincent asks Selee, who is the coordinator of the project. . Of course, they allow it.

Once again he presents no identification. Lacaster is a cop but he has no warrant and there is no probable cause for him to actually enter the facility. He can search the car – which he had already done back at the station – but if the Sea Lab is doing top secret work, this seems to be out of his jurisdiction. And it is certainly out of David's. But once again, white privilege reigns supreme and both men head into the facility. Lacaster reminds David on the way in, "Remember: this is police business. I'll ask the questions." David says nothing as they head in.

They get directions to Lowell's office and in the meantime she's outside arguing with a man named Ken, about the grant. He's telling her to keep quiet about a man disappearing because he doesn't want the grant to be jeopardized. He asks her to give him just a minute to check. He and Lowell walk up ion her and the man. This is when she informs them about the station wagon. She asks to know about what happened to Dr. Lanier – he's the head to the sea lab. He went home because he as sick. Lanier went home and since they live in the same building she checked and there was no answer.

She tells them about the new wing being built and that it has to be finished by next week because of some kind of meeting that is scheduled to take place. When Dr. Lanier took over the lab everything changed and they no longer want a lot of publicity. "Ken and I are the only ones left from the old staff," she says and then offers to show them something.

She takes them into the new wing and shows them something floating in an aquarium. "It's life," she says. They've been sending electricity through a mixture of sea water, amino acids and other compounds we know in the sea lab. She's spilling her guts about what is supposed to be top secret to two people who she presumes to be cops? This doesn't make any damn sense and sounds like a fireable offense to me!" This is only on a very small scale – now I'll show you something else."

She unlocks yet another door and shows them the new wing, already staffed and you can hear a typewriter (say what?) going in the background. Now get this: David asks, "Mind if I wander around?" This bitch says, "I guess it's alright" as she and Lacaster are going over to talk to Ken. David is walking around, sees two large doors marked "Generator Room" and bypasses it. He then proceeds to walk up some stairs, un-escorted, as if he owns the place. A man is working on huge cables and David observes, "That looks like enough electricity to power an entire city." The man says he doesn't work there he's just doing some installation.

David walks back down the stairs and into the area where Lacaster, Dr. Lowell and Ken are interacting. She tells Ken that she's going back down to headquarters and he tells her she need not come back that evening, to take the rest of the day off. The threesome then head for the car and pull away. As they do, Dr. Harrison, the head man, is glaring at them.

Harrison and Ken are talking and then Harrison displays some kind of hand-held "hypnotic orb" that is changing colors and places Ken in a trance. If they lose Lanier, who is a veritable "scientific genius," the alien timetable will be set back for months. Harrison wants Ken to "bring him back," referring to Lanier – to "give him human form once again." The loss of Lanier would set back alien progress for months – maybe even years.

When they walk into the station Lacaster has a call, and it's from Joan. She says that although her husband has passed away, he told her some important things. He told her that about a warehouse and where it is located. David is suspicious: "A man who has been in a deep sleep comes to with just enough information to tell his wife – a woman who considers you responsible for her husband's death - to give to you? It's a trap." Lacasther insists "That was Joan Corman's voice!" David says for him to check it out because someone could be imitating her voice.

Lacaster storms out of the office and when he does David goes over to a phone desk and makes a call. That's right: in a police station and nobody knows him from Adam's house cat, but because of white privilege he can treat a phone in a cop shop like it's his own personal line! David calls a number on a piece of paper to speak to Mrs. Corman. He finds out that she left town an hour ago to visit relatives. David asks Lowell if she knows what the warehouse is. She knows.

Vincent is asking for help with Lacaster. "He's in danger." The detective tells Vincent that the station wagon is outside and the keys are in it. Now isn't that convenient. The utility man that David spoke with earlier is giving Ken instructions about the power generators. Harrison orders to utility man to add more power. David and Lowell are in the station wagon and she asks for an explanation.

David tells her, "We're being invaded by beings from another world. I believe they've already taken over the Sea Lab. Meanwhile a formless scuba suit is being elevated and placed on a slab. Ken opens up the front mask of the suit and peers in: "We're ready, Dr. Lanier."

The aliens are in the new wing, ascending the very stairs that Vincent had scaled earlier and two of them are toting a sheet that contains a limp. Lifelike substance to be placed into a giant glass vat. They dump it into the boiling water below. Meanwhile, David and Dr. Lowell pull up. She says they should be going to the police but David convinces her to give him "just five minutes. He checks some doors and goes around to the back. A man walks out with a revolver and says, "You, come with me." David raises his hands and goes inside with the stranger. Lacaster is already inside having also been captured. "For what it's worth, I apologize," he tells Vincent. "Now you know," David says.

David describes what Lacaster is seeing. "This is a regeneration station, to keep themselves in human form. They can get rid of us without leaving a mark or a trace, they can induce a simple heart attack. The two men simultaneously go into fight mode and begin doing battle with the two aliens. The aliens re-gain control of their guns and place Vincent and Lacaster in separate regeneration tubes. The glass being to lower around them, but in another part of the building where the transformation is taking place, the generators are using all the power. Right then the power goes off and Vincent and Lacaster are freed. A fight resumes in the dark.

Vincent and Lacaster get away and lack the door. David jumps out of the window with Lacaster right behind. They get in the car with Lowell behind the wheel. "The Sea Lab, quick!" David says. "looks like every light in the city is out." The aliens have their own generators. What the cop saw in the back of the station wagon was an alien form that had not been fully transformed and it drove him mad. "And it's been at the Sea Lab all day," David says as they speed toward the lab.

The "thing" is being transformed and all the power is being aimed at the aquarium he is in. The upcoming meeting is very important. Harrison continues with the hypnotic orb and Ken is under its spell as Ken tells them they heed "nothing but time." Lanier is b beginning to take form. The threesome pull up outside. She tells them there is a door in the control room. Lacaster asks what do we do when we get inside? Vincent says they make a phone call and he becomes a hero. "If not do you know where a fifty year old cop can get a job?" he asks.

Lowell goes through the front door and meets a colleague and engages him in conversation. David and Lacaster sneak into the side door. They make it downstairs through the control room and right into the area where the experiment is taking place. They see the lifeless form being transformed. David tells him to make his call and he walks over to a pay phone. What? They are increasing the power. He gets caught by a scientist who also has Lowell and David. They walk into the lab. A fight ensures. "No guns." Vincent tells Lacaster to cut the generators. Now he's fighting an alien, and busting up test tubes all over the place. Lacaster cuts the generators. Ken has a gun and takes aim, but he can't fire it. He looks at Harrison and shoots him. Harrison glows and dies Lanier's form is becoming distorted. Lowell sees it as blood is coming out. She's gone mad!!!!! Lacaster rushes her out as David rescues Ken. Everything then burns, as expected.

At the hospital David and Lacaster meet and he gets plane ticket. David tells him he's not going to the FBI. Ken is back to normal and Lowell is out of it. She had a breakdown. "Will you ever tell 'em what happened?" he asks. David has another ally and everything else is conjecture. They agree to go have some coffee.

The narrator offers a conclusion: "One cup of coffee. A few stolen minutes. A last small gesture of defiance for a crusader who fought, and won a crusade and knows he can never claim the victory."

As David and Lacaster leave, a man in a doctor's uniform is watching, pinkie finger extended. He's an alien.

And so it appears that they are everywhere and that they've done their homework. They are prospering, building, constructing, filing the necessary paperwork and generally succeeding in a country that is majority white and that benefits from white privilege. If you are white the human decision makers look the other way and that is all the aliens needed – and all that they took advantage of. David has got his work cut out for him but luckily he, too, has the benefit of white privilege.

.6. "Vikor"

A telephone installer, minding his own business atop an extension boom ladder the kind that are controlled from a remote panel and is steered and guided from the box that the installer is in. As the box rises, the installer peers through an upper level window in the security building of Vikor Enterprises, and sees a figure glowing in a transparent tube. The figure is in human form but from time to time you can see the skeleton. He's spotted by a man in a suit, lowers his boom and takes off running at full speed. He gets into the truck and a security guard attempts to stop him. He seems to have had a heart attack meaning the security guard placed the metallic disk on his neck while they tussled.

His co-worker pushes the guard aside and they take off, busting through the security gates as the truck speeds off. He runs off and spills his guts and the newspapers print the story, which David Vincent gets ahold of . David read the story about how before the installer died, he had seen a glowing man. According to the narrator, the story was investigated by the police "and then promptly forgotten."

Again, we have the issue of white privilege. A man tells the cops he sees a glowing man in a tube. But despite the far-fetched content of such a story, the white man who reports it nevertheless gets the benefit of the doubt and the police use their manpower to "investigate." They find nothing and then forget about it. Do you know how many "cold cases" there are of missing black people who these white detectives and cops intentionally ignore without even bothering to look at the essential evidence? Again, "different strokes for different folks." '

David is actually walking up the long driveway leading to the security gate of Vikor Industries and stops at a check in booth. The place is in Fort Stock, Florida and David has come to look into the matter. (Where is this peckerwood getting all these plane tickets?)

In an executive office the company leader, George Vikor (Jack Lord) is chewing out Nexus, the man we earlier saw overseeing the alien transformation tubes. Vikor is telling him about how he doesn't mind killing (he's a veteran) but he cannot tolerate stupidity. Vikor is in on it with the aliens. Nexus tells him that if his conscience is bothering him, "just remember your stake in it." He's made some kind of bargain with the aliens, use of the facility in exchange for "power, all the power you can use," as Nexus puts it.

An army hero, Sgt. George Vikor is running Vikor Enterprises. He has all of his memorabilia on the wall in his office as a reminder of his past patriotism - a former hero who conquered Hill 312, and in doing so, killed over 13 "enemies." But now it's a new day as he knowingly leasing out part of his place to – the Invaders. He wants power and money. Commander Nexor is an alien and promises Vikor "all the power you could possibly use." DAVID immediately lands a job as a security job under the name David **Baxter** (keep this name in mind –it would be used again in an episode about a black man).

At any rate the phone rings and it's the police informing Vikor that there's something up with his wife. He hangs up and tells Nexus he has to go see about it and then vacates the office. (Have you noticed that on these TV shows, people of high rank leave their offices and leave people standing or sitting inside of them, never apparently worried about theft? What's up with that?)

As David stands at the security gate checking in, that black continental passes by, presumably being driven by Vikor. David tells the security guard that he's looking for work. He is told that they're not taking any applications right now but that he could leave his name and address. The security guard writes it down and for some reason David tells him that he's staying at the downtown YMCA. He tells the guard that he's not particular or "fussy" -- "even if it's unskilled" -- about the type of work it is.

Here comes white privilege. The guard asks him, "Do you drive, Mr. Baxter"? David answers "sure" and is then told as the guard looks through some papers that, "we may have something for you later on." Damn! Is that all it takes? Black people are so accustomed to being told "we'll put your name in a file and will call if anything comes up" so many times that we can see it coming before it gets there! This white man, out of the blue, literally walks up to a security gate, talks to a guard and lands a job!

Vikor gets to the police station and the man behind the desk tells him that she was driving ninety miles an hour when they stopped her, and that this was the second time. He adds that she's been drinking, too. "Are you going to file charges?" Vikor asks. Then adds, "See what you can do." HE is allowed into the interrogation room where his wife his and at first glance you can see that the bitch is crazy as a loon. Vikor asks what happened. "Was it another long afternoon and you were lonely?" A trend is being set in these first few episodes: white bitches being ignored by their husbands so they seek affection elsewhere and in most cases end up in the arms of some extraterrestrial!

She's still drunk and is making an ass out of herself. "I left a top level meeting to come here," he says. "I have hundreds of people working for me and soon will have hundreds more." He tells her, "One of these days I'll hand you the world." She says she would settle for just some company. The desk sergeant walks in without even knocking. The paperwork has been completed and she's free to go. "My wife won't be doing any driving for a while." Hey- driving. Wasn't David just hired as a "driver"? More white privilege.

David is brought to the Vikor's house. He's been hired as the new chauffeur for Ms. Vikor. She's getting a message and comes out wrapped in a towel. David was hired an hour ago. She gets on the phone and calls her husband, but he's not in. Vikor gave David the keys and "I'm not to give them to you under any circumstances." "Really? Then please bring the car around," she says. It's a convertible Thunderbird. She tells David to wait outside and she'll be out. He once again asks if he can look around and she says that it's alright "but don't go into the security building, they're sensitive to strangers.

The place is huge and outside there is a lot of activity, people walking around in suits. They can't all be aliens, but how are we to know since the aliens are also peckerwoods?

David umps up on a dock and ascends several levels of stairs – like he's running the place. He finds his way to the skywalk and runs across it and descends down more stairs as if he knows what he's looking for. A security guard intercepts him. His pinkie is extended. He's an alien. Two more grab Vincent and beat the shit out of him. They grab him and take him back to the main building.

Meanwhile Vikor walks back into his office and his wife is sitting behind his desk in his chair. "You know Sherry, I love you very, very much. I don't like the idea of scraping you off the highway," he tells her. The phone rings and its Nexus. He tells her "it's one of the investors. He's only here for a few days and I can't keep him waiting." He escorts Sherry to the door.

She wants to know why her husband is so concerned about "these people." He says that they can make him the most powerful man in the …and she interrupts and adds "cemetery." "Who are these people? When they buzz, you jump?" What are they doing to you?" He tells her, I told you they are foreign businessmen." In walks Nexus with a guard holding David. "He entered the plant at 11:47 with Mrs. Vikor. At 11:57 he was found in the security section," Nexus snitches. David says he was looking for Vikor's office. Vikor says "you were here this morning. You know my office isn't in the security building." David replies, "Yes, but I got lost, these buildings all look alike. I was on my way to tell your wife that I was on my way to the gas station because the car is almost out of gas. Then your storm troopers jumped me."

Vikor asks Sherry to leave the room and she tells him she's canceling lunch. She wants David to drive her home. "We won't keep him long," Vikor promises. But he allows David to go ahead and he leaves with Sherry and closes the door, leaving Nexus and Vikor in the office. He tells Nexus that he questioned David thoroughly and that if he was from Air Force intelligence or the FBI he would not have been caught that easily. He tells Nexus that if he doesn't trust his judgement, "Why don't you check him out yourself." Nexus apparently likes that idea.

David and Sherry get to the house. "If there's nothing else, I'll put the car away," he says. She asks him if he wants a drink and he says no. She pours one for herself and then turns to him and asks him why he lied about there being very little gas in the car. "I filled that tank myself last night," she says. She is putting it all together. "I think he's manufacturing more than industrial machinery in that plant," she says. "And I think you know what it is, and that's why you're here."

David walks into the living area, coolly pulls out a cigarette without asking for permission to smoke, and fires it up. Of course this was long before America came to its senses about smoking, but the point being made here is that this guy seems to have very little respect for other people's turf, territory or space. In other words, he gets too familiar too fast – the way a lot of white people tend to do when they are in the presence of black people.

David tells her that her husband is working with a "foreign power" and that there may be some kind of invasion. She asks, "What foreign power?" and David replies that he can't tell her that. "What do you mean you can't tell me that – you've just accused my husband of treason!" David looks at her: "They're alien beings, creatures from another planet who are here right now trying to take over. Your husband is helping them. Is that specific enough?"

She doesn't want to believe him. David tells her, "I've seen their space ships. I've seen them, too. I'm not alone – others have seen them." "You've seen them too," David continues to explain. "At the plant – some of them have mutated hands with a crooked fourth finger." "This is a joke. A stupid tasteless joke. I don't enjoy your sense of humor, Mr. Baxter," she says, still clutching the glass of alcohol. She tells him to leave, he turns and then she stops him: "Tell me what we can do to help him," she says.

Vikor is in his office listening to an old record of his fame as a military officer and soldier. He lost an entire platoon but continued to fight on to the top of some huge hill, "personally killing over thirty of the enemy and then, badly wounded himself, radioed Italian headquarters until Hill 317 was ours." He replays the applause that is heard on the record and turns it up. He obviously misses those days as a hero because now it is clear that he is selling out the planet in exchange for power.

Meanwhile Sherry pulls up at the plant and exits the car with a brown brief case. A security guard walks out and she says that her husband may have forgotten it and asks the guard to take it to him. The guard does so and when he leaves she gets back in the car and David, who has been hiding, gets out and runs for the security building as she drives off.

David manages to slide under a storage door that was not all the way closed and gets into the building. He attacks a security guard from behind (again, the assumption that he must be the baddest muthafucka on the planet), and they tussle before David pushes him down some stairs. David walks past a bunch of crates and slides open a large door. He sees the pods where transformations take place. He walks across the room as if he owns the place. Meanwhile, a van speedily pulls up, parks and unloads some glowing people, obviously aliens who are slowly losing their human form.

Men usher them into the building. There are numerous tubes David discovers and he hides as they drag the aliens into the area and place them in tot tubes. Glass tubing encircles them as their transformation beings. David watches intently. Meanwhile Nexus and Vikor walk over to the building. The aliens who manned the machine walk out and slide the door behind them. They have left the machine on a kind of self running mode. He again hides as Nexus and Vikor walks in and observes the work. Vikor's job is to fill the new production quotas, according to Nexus.

The phone rings and Vikor is told that a teletype has come in. He and Nexus leave to go check it out. The tubes raise up and David makes a run for it. The men who were in the tube come out as aliens discover their knocked out buddy. One sounds an alarm. David is running his ass off and hides in some bushes. He jumps a cyclone fence and is off

Back in the office, the teletype has information on David. Nexus explains to Vikor: "Without these (regeneration) tubes, my people cannot maintain human form." Vikor snitches, 'His real name is David Vincent – he's a mental case." Then how come he got the job? Vikor has turned on humanity all the way. At one point he says, "Our precious human race – cowards, liars … Their promises are as phony as they are."

David has hitched a ride with a man in a white pickup truck, and is dropped off in the front of the plant. David stops a police car and asks an officer for help. The officer says "sure thing" and asks him to get in. He knows who he is. David subdues him and then runs off to a bar and gets on the pay phone to Sherry. He tells her that some of the local police are aliens and that they have to go to the FBI office in Miami. He wants to use her car so he can get out of the area. She doesn't know her phone is bugged and she is being eavesdropped on by an alien who looks like he's Hispanic or black.

Sherry comes to Wilson's Tavern where David was at and she gives him a gun "Let's go, I'm driving." A cop car pulls up with the eavesdropper and the officer he subdued earlier. She knows they bugged her home. Vikor walks up and grabs his wife. The cop says that Nexus told him to bring her but Vikor overrules him. They walk into the tavern - Vikor, Sherry and David and are seated. He asks Sherry why she's helping Vincent and she blurts out, "I know all about your foreign investors, why they are here and how you've been helping them." Vikor turns and looks at David. "What kind of poison have you been feeding her?" he asks.

"She knows what's going on at the plant – the regeneration chamber, the tubes you're manufacturing," David said. "So that's what you told her, huh?" Vikor replies, obviously pissed off. "Your source of information is a psycho, Sherry. His real name is David Vincent. He's a mental case. He's been treated for delusions and fantasies, tells wild stories about things that simply don't exist," Vikor tells his wife. David tells him to show her the third floor of the security building and "show her how crazy I am."

Sherry believes what David is saying and tells Vikor she wants to see it. As I write in my book, Transformers: Sex and Role Changes in America, the white woman is the new white man as he has adopted the status of demi-god or meta-human. She calls the shots verbally and physically whereas in past centuries she did it on a more subtle and seductive tip.

And in bitch-like fashion, Vikor walks into the next room of the bar and stands in front of the fireplace. Sherry follows him while David goes to the front of the bar and notices that the police car is still there. Sherry asks her husband, "Why are you doing this awful thing?" He rubs her cheek and says, "For you." He tells her that they'll be running this planet and we'll be right on top with them!" David walks in and says something about his venture coming at the expense of the human race. Vikor accepted the deal because, once he got back from the war in Korea, he found that even as a "hero," he couldn't get a job.

He has a plate in his head and a wooden leg – so he sells out the human race in exchange for power. David tells Vikor that the aliens will kill Sherry because she knows too much. "You wanted the world, now you've got it. What are you going to do – give it to them?" David asks Vikor. Vikor says they might destroy him and David explains, "They're going to do that anyway. You've got every vital piece of information we need to destroy them." Vikor says he never realized that Sherry would be in danger. He agrees to help but they have to let him do it his way and it might take some time. David wants just enough time to get in touch with the FBI.

Outside he tells the officer to "take Mr. Vincent to the plant." The officer says, "But Mr. Nexus …" Vikor is firm: "Take Mr. Vincent to the plant and make sure nothing happens to him. Keep him under guard in my office until you hear from me or Mr. Nexus." Vikor offers to take Sherry home. "We'll send for your car later." They get to the house and he tells her that he'll call Nexus and get things settled. They hug and she goes upstairs to bed.

Vikor gets on the phone but there's a knock at the door. It's Nexus and he's already in the house. He tells him he's got David Vincent "under guard at the plant." Nexus asks, "And your wife?" There's two other men there and they prepare to head upstairs for Sherry. Vikor blocks them: "You've got Vincent, what do you want with my wife"? Sherry comes downstairs and enters the room right in the middle of what's taking place. The aliens grab her. "We must all make sacifices," Nexus tells Vikor. "There'll be no pain – it'll be a simple suicide," Nexus says. "An unhappy woman who drank too much and drove too fast and finally turned on the gas." "Dear God George, help me" she begs as two of the aliens hold her back.

George paces away from them and with his back to them all says, "I can't let you do it." Nexus walks over to him and says, "Must I remind you of the rewards that lie ahead for you? Wealth and power beyond your wildest dreams?" Nexus guarantee Vikor: "A slave population of billions. But you won't be a slave, you'll be a master. You're a very sensible man, Mr. Vikor. How could you possibly give up so much for so little?" George is confused and walks out the patio door as Sherry screams for him.

Nexus gets on the phone and calls the security main office. They've been ordered to kill David, who is sitting right there. The Hispanic alien with an metallic disk approaches him. David pulls out his gun and shoots them both. They glow and burn. David runs out and heads to a police car, gets in and takes off. Sherry is asleep on the couch when David rushes into her house. The aliens have turned on the gas so it appears she suffocated. David finds a bug that was on the phone on the ground and breaks out a window so she can get fresh air. Vikor gave David the gun.

It's a lie. He's speaking into the bug that is on the phone knowing the aliens will hear. The aliens play it back for Viktor and believe he gave David a gun. They believe he is a key man. "He's lying, he's framing me. Can't you understand that?" Vikor screams. Two aliens grab him and place the metallic disc on his neck. He's dead. In other words, David set this all up and it led to the death of a man. And thanks to white privilege, he STILL got away with it.

The next day he tells Sherry, "They've destroyed every shred of evidence in the security building. " The police said he died of a cerebral hemorrhage. She's looking at his medals. David tells her, "I have to go." "Where?" she asks. "Wherever they go," he says. He says he's going to go on like this 'for as long as it takes.' Only a white man in America with no job could make such a damn claim. This is the first episode where the regeneration tubes were shown in full functioning action.

Conclusion? "As the invaders move, so does David Vincent. They must be exposed, they must be stopped, and if David Vincent doesn't do it, who will?" This is that "Lone Wolf McQuade"-type mentality that the white man wants to convince the world that he possesses. The white man's tendencies, at least in America, have been those of a mob leader, a gangster, and a group oriented thug. He never goes one-on-one with men of color. He attacks in mobs. David Vincent's lone quest is a part of that "pioneer spirit" that white folks simply crave. And that is why the show was so interesting. But remember: just because they feel good about what they see and are told about that "lone wolf" approach doesn't mean that they practice in real life. In real life, their tactics are more akin to what scholar Oliver C. Cox referred to as "the manhunt tradition." Like wolves – they hunt in packs, even when the prey is alone.

.7. "Nightmare"

A car drives up to the entry to an old ranch style farm and a woman, Ellen Woods, gets out of her car. We later find out that her name is Ellen.

She walks and then spots a barn. She is carrying a purse and a binder and slowly advances after hearing a buzzing sound. She peers through the door and then walks inside. A man approaches her. He has a blank look in his eye. She has brought his school books to him. Two other men stand nearby and all the men appear in a trance. The young mean picks up a stick and chases her out of the bar. He is summoned back in by the two elder gentlemen and the woman gets away.

They go back to the computer as she flees down the road, forgetting her car. She stumbles in an old corn field as the men manipulate a computer dial. As she runs a cloud of locusts can be seen descending on the area. She ducks into another old bar and secures it from the locusts. She panics, but it is clear that the machine in the barn is what is controlling the swarm.

Back in town is Grady, Kansas. The narrator provides context as he announces: "Thirty miles from the geographic center of America, at its very heart, is the town of Grady; population 5,312, principle industry, and farming. Grady,

Kansas, the American gothic: rigid, proud of its tradition, protective of its own, resentful of any threat from the world outside." While the narration is taking place, some local hicks watch as the over-dressed David Vincent, newspaper in hand, walks down the sidewalk toward one of the houses.

`Oh, and one more thing: that description that was just given is the same way most of these towns and cities are when it comes to working in unison to keep black people out.

The headline in the newspaper is "Third Locust Attack on Grady." He walks into an apartment building and knocks on a door. The people across the hall peer out and tell him, "She's moved" and they make it clear they don't know where. The man who has been watching him blocks the hall as he prepares to leave. "Lookin' for Ellen?", a man named Ed asks. And then asks, "What about?" The man says that questions would just upset her, but David is not convinced. The hick tells him, "Just forget it fella. Just catch a bus and get out of town." David says he'll think about it and walks past Ed and back up the street. The nosey neighbors peer out and complain about the insects in the air.

David walks up the walkway to a house and knocks. "It's me," he says. An old man named Oliver comes to the door with his lunch and says he's one of those newspaper fellas from the city. Oliver is the principal at the school where Ellen teaches. He says he doesn't know where Ellen is. "I've talked to five people in this town and it seems like everybody is trying to keep me from talking to her," David tells him. The old man tells him why that is the case. According to Oliver, Ellen was always a nervous and sensitive "girl." A year ago, just before she was to be married, both of her parents were killed.

According to Oliver Ames, Ellen refused to believe that her parents were dead. She was in the sanitarium in the city for a few months and since she's been back she's been doing fine, "except for this business about locusts." Oliver says a bunch of questions might upset her again as Ellen descends from the upstairs and says that indeed, she would not be upset. The man tries to get her to go back upstairs for rest but she pushes past him and walks over to David and asks, "What would you like to know?"

David introduces himself and his first question is about the newspaper article. "You say you saw a metallic box and the box brought the locusts." She says "The box I imagined I saw." She goes on to explain that when the newspaper men found her she was still hysterical from the locust attack. She now says "There was not box … It was all in my mind." David nevertheless wants to know what it looks like, but Oliver interrupts: "Mr. Vincent, she just told you she imagined it." David ignores him and re-directs back to Ellen. The Danielson's the men in the barn when she walked in, now deny ever having been in the barn that afternoon. David asks "what frightened you so much that you ran over to the next barn?" She's getting upset and he's getting aggressive.

David's grilling gets rougher: "You said it did once. Why are you lying??" She runs back upstairs. Oliver asks David, "Will you please go!" He leaves.

David is talking down the street and walks into a café called The Lunch Counter. Newspaper in pocket he sits at the counter and orders coffee. He asks the woman for the people who own the farm, the Morgans. They moved just yesterday. A man maned Danielson bought the farm. The guy, Ed, comes in and grabs David. Along with two other men they gang up on David and beat the shit out of him and leave him lying on the floor. "You get the message? Stay away from her!" Ed shouts as the three leave. The sheriff and deputy come in. The sheriff says that he had it coming and the carry David off.

David wakes up behind bars. A sheriff lets him out. "We're giving you a break, Vincent. We're driving you over to the next town, Myers Point, to catch the bus," he says. They escort Vincent out to the car. Meanwhile Ed comes to visit Ellen. "That guy's not going to bother you anymore," he says as they hug. She tells Ed that David believes her." How can he believe and I don't?" she asks. Now she's having doubts. "Nothing you do or say will ever change the way I feel about you," Ed promises. "As God is my witness Ed, I saw Danielson in that barn and his son and Constable Gabbard. It was a metallic box with dials and things. It made a loud, whining noise." She says she believes what Mr. Vincent says – that it brought the locusts.

They hug once again and she says she's sorry and he consoles her, telling he that he's love her "ever since we were kids." He says he's going to stay with her until she forgets about these locusts and all these things, that he won't leave her.

The sheriff's car heads down the road, one in the back one driving. He tells the driver to pull over. David jams down on the accelerator and they begin to fight over the wheel. The car goes into a corn field. David jumps out of the car and runs off with a sheriff shooting. He gets David in the arm and now is looking for him. David is crawling through the cornfield. The cop says "put me through to Danielson." David is wounded and passes out in a cornfield.

Back at Oliver's house, there are locusts hanging in the sky. Ellen runs downstairs and says, "The locusts have comeback." She wants to get to the Danielsons and the barn and see the locusts. He restrains her but she snatches away. He says he can't let her go. He tells her to go to her room but she gets away. She jumps into her convertible and takes off.

Locusts are approaching. David gets up to make a run for it even as Ellen is speeding down the highway. Naturally, she sees him and pulls over. White privilege on television and in movies always equates with perfect timing. At any rate, she gets out of the car and runs to where he is. Both are headed for the huge barn and silo where the machinery is located. They meet in the field and continue to flee. He's wounded but manages to grab her hand and they continue their flight. David forces the steel door open with force (yeah, right) and they are out of harm's way for the meantime. Up the stairs they head and they enter a room filled with hi-tech equipment. A map on the wall has "Grady" encircled as David scams the room, which appears to be a laboratory of some kind. There are glass terrariums filled with locusts.

A chunk of raw meat is found and David dips it in a flour substance and puts it in one of the cages with the locusts. They converged on it and begin devouring it – down to the bone!

A short time later David and Ellen vacate the structure where the alien machinery is located. The locusts have disappeared. They look around and all the short grass and greenery that was there just a few minutes ago is gone – nothing but dirt remains. They head back to Ellen's car (with David driving) with the sheriff and another man watching with guns in hand. David has taken over. He tells her what to do as he drives her car, he knows that the aliens are going to do and acts as if he's an expert in predicting their behavior. He's going to make a call "from that lunch room there." Always a lunchroom, a café, a bar or a lounge somewhere conveniently nearby, places that a black man could NEVER enter without being given the once over.

David enters as Ellen takes off and once again, he finds a public phone and once again, he has exact change. He is calling in an emergency. He's talking to the sheriff who is not a part of the alien conspiracy. When the deputy, Jim Walton gets off the phone he calls someone and that person is an alien in Grady and tells him that Vincent called in an emergency and he called from a café. The alien tells his assistant as he leaves that, "I'll go over and pick him up."

Meanwhile David is changing his blood stained shirt (what is he going to change into?) in a back room at the café. Ellen goes back to her house which is filled with townspeople. She goes to the pone as people stare at her. There is no answer. She tried to call Ed to stay with her until the police get there. Oliver asks her what happened out there, what did you see. She now knows that he's one of them. She's hesitant and says she can't remember anything. She says she wants Ed to take her back to the sanitarium. The townspeople walk about and tell her everything is going to be alright. She doesn't want to be alone with Oliver.

David exits the back room and has a seat at the counter. He orders a coffee and describes the double silo. The man says that it used to belong to a fella named Kirby, who sold it to Ned, the sheriff. Some people from out of town came in and took over the property, according to the cook behind the counter. The cops pull p and David spots them. He ducks out the back door as the sheriff comes in, gun drawn. It's Ned. David has gotten away, so Ned leaves.

When Ed gets to the house Oliver refuses to let him see Ellen, claiming that doctors claim that it would not be good for her. Oliver suggests that she be admitted to the Forsyth Clinic, and the townspeople who are watching agree with him. Oliver said he is driving her to the city because the doctor's insist on her getting there was son as possible. Upstairs Ellen tells one of the old ladies that she wants Ed to take her to the city, no one else. The old woman is part of it and tells her that everything will be alright.

David is walking down an alley and right into the back door of Ed's house – as if he has some authority to do so. He calls for Ed but Ed's not present. Meanwhile Ned comes to Oliver's house and they talk outside. Ellen is downstairs and Oliver is forcing her to go outside. Other townspeople grab her and she says "He is trying to kill me." The old woman call her a "poor twisted child" and then one of them put her to sleep with chloroform on a towel.

Back at Ed's house David is waiting and then Ed walks in. He asks, "What are you doing here?" He walks off to the side while telling him to get out. Here is Vincent trespassing and that's all this guy, who had beaten David's ass earlier, acting like nothing was wrong? David immediately begins the grilling: "Answer me this: "Did you talk to Ellen?" Ed says, "Ames wouldn't let me." David tells him – twice – that "Ellen's going to be killed. Now we've got to stop it!" David tells him to call the hospital because the aliens don't want the publicity. Ed, phone in hand, does exactly that. He's calling the Clinic in Wichita.

Ned is walking up the street and over to Ned's house. David ducks behind a pantry door. Ned just walks right in and asks if he seen "that Vincent fella." Ed got the answer that David wanted him to get and then hangs up and lies to Ed about not having seen David. Ned leaves and David comes out of the pantry. "There's no such hospital," Ed says. He and David immediately head out even as Ellen is being placed in a station wagon by Oliver. A man is chauffeuring them and the man tells him that Danielson is read

Ned comes into the house with David and they ask where Ellen is. The nosey old townspeople tell them that Ellen just left. Ed is on the phone. He orders some guy named Carl to stop the car that Ames is driving because Ellen is in it. Off they go to give chase. Ellen is waking up. As Ed and David are driving, Ed says he isn't saying that he does or does not believe David but asks, "Why Grady?"" David says he has a guess and that guess is that Grady is three miles from the middle of America. David says he thinks that the aliens are going to try to send signal vibrations from the silo, "vibrations to reach every part of America simultaneously." He continues: "Insects will attack from every sector of America, all over there must be millions of insects." He tells Ed that in that silo "I saw butterflies eat flesh." They got the owners of the surrounding farms to sell out, Danielson and Gabbert bought them. Now those silos are surrounded by private property owned by them."

A constable who is not an alien, the one that Ed called, blocks the road and tells David and Ed that the car with Ellen in it never passed hm. David and Ed backtrack and head back to Danielson's place. Meanwhile, the station wagon pulls up and Ned is there waiting. Ellen tries to make a run for it but Ned grabs her. Here come David and Ed. Oliver runs into the barn. An alien with a shotgun walks out and shoots at the car. They run over him and he turns red, glows and dies.

Ned runs out of the barn as David and Ed hide. Ellen jumps Ned and is thrown to the ground. David karate kicks the gun out of Ed's hand and they begin to right. They go into the bar and one of the bug terrariums falls over and Ned is killed, glows and dies. Oliver and his associate run to the computer room. Oliver hits a self-destruct dial to get rid of the evidence, no doubt. Ed has Ellen and the silo – and the evidence therein -- blows up.

Ed walks back into his house while David and Ellen (now wearing her hair down) are in the kitchen). All the alien sympathizers have left town, Ed says. "We can't prove anything, can we?" she asks. David says he wants them both to talk to the FBI. She says that all she wants to do is be left in peace with Ed. I can't live through another nightmare (title of the episode) – people looking at me as if I'm crazy." She asks David if he understands and he says he doesn't, "not after all we've been through." Ed agrees with Ellen and says "we're not going to talk – ever."

"Alright. Good luck to the both of you," David says as he leaves the house. The narrator tells us, "Grady, Kansas – proud of its tradition. Protective of its own, Resentful of any threat from the world outside. David Vincent has faced the invader here, and for a little while, that threat has been pushed aside.

Interesting how a place like that can be protective of its own and proud of its traditions and resentful of any threat from the outside world. What was just described is the tradition, rationale and ideology of much of white America, urban and rural, when they stole the land, hunkered down and then heard three fearful words: "the niggas is comin'!"

.8. "Doomsday Minus One"

For some reason, some leaders at a U.S Army Base Proving Grounds in Utah summons Vincent after discovering that as general the base commander is in cahoots with the invaders. The plan for the aliens is to detonate an anti-matter bomb at the same time and place as a scheduled nuclear test detonation and cause millions of deaths.

As the show begins, we find that at the U.S. Army Proving Grounds, there is a large crater, the product of a small meteor. Major Graves is concerned about security and asks his superior, Ted if he can get more. Ted excuses him and tells him he'll let him know. Graves gets on the phone and Spence is asking for Vincent: "He was supposed to be here yesterday." Spence is worried. Now he's trapped in a pay phone booth and the door will not open. People are sitting around, presumably aliens. The bartender walks from behind the bar, pts money in the music box and lets him out. Spence tried to make a run for it, but the metallic orb is placed on his neck and he is killed.

The narrator tells us, "David Vincent had received an urgent call from a man he never met, to come to a hotel he'd never heard of, in a desert he'd never seen. But he came, because the message spoke of alien invaders. A man he'd never met had disappeared. The hotel he'd never heard of seemed menacing, but the desert he'd never seen promised him an answer."

A car is following David on the highway. There is a huge semi truck in front of him and he passes it. David talks a side road and hides behind some trees. The car continues on the highway. He pulls back onto the highway and continues is travel.

David gets hired once again, this time as a civilian employee.

He meets a man, Major Graves, who appears to be a general. He says he was tailed from the motel. They are standing outside Graylock Crater. Spence said the crater was caused by a space ship and he said it because he saw a space ship just last week. Major Rick Graves is working with Vincent. David asks Graves if he believed Spence and Graves says "I'm in charge of security – I HAVE to believe him." Not only hat, but Spence was one of his closest friends.

Graves wants proof. He wants Vincent to get a job on the base. Graves tells him that everything has been arranged because he (Vincent) is "supposed to be an authority on these people." Oh, "people,"eh? Let's take time for a little teaching lesson about white privilege and their concept of "race" for a moment.

"Race" is a term invented by the European so that the division of humanity would be easier. We were all "people" but that would put us all on the same level of another one of his inventions, "the hierarchy of being." So he had to "rank" the races with Black people being at the bottom. Knowing this, take note of how throughout the entire two-year duration of "The Invaders," there are on-going references to these alien beings as "people" and in fact, the term "alien" and "people" are used interchangeably. And do you know why that is? It's because the choice of skin color of the aliens was the same color as that of the Earth bound white human! All whites are therefore "people" no matter where they hail from; it is the person of color who ranks somewhere else on "the chain of being."

At any rate, Graves has set it up for Vincent to be hired and he'll have to use his own name because he's "already used it at the hotel, it's too late to change now," Graves says. Graves tells him that if he gets "jammed up," he (Graves) knows nothing about it. He tells David that he has men out looking for Spence. David looks at him: "Eight to five you never find him," and then walks back to his car.

David pulls into his motel and ironically, there is a man buffing a silver Lincoln continental. David asks a room service attendant whose car it is. "It's Mr. Thompkins' car," he says. Remember that a Lincoln Continental has continued to appear in show after show. David watches the chauffeur buffing the car and notices the extended fourth finger, a sign of the aliens.

Later, the Continental driven by the Chauffeur and Thompkins pull up at a remote mine. Turpin walks in and meets with General Beaumont. Beaumont asks him, "Whatever happened to Charlie Spence?" "General, don't you think it's rather childish to worry about the death of one man when you've agreed to the death of a million?'" Thompkins asks. The general has agreed to work with the aliens but right now will refresh Thompkins' memory. Thompkins warns him that if he decided to change his mind, "What chance would you have to save your precious world"? Thompkins tells Graves that "Spence is dead" and also tells him that if a man named "David Vincent" shows up, to let him (Beaumont) know.

Wouldn't you know it? From a hilltop a few hundred years away is David, peering through binoculars at the interaction between Graves and Thompkins. He watches as Thompkins pulls away.

In yet another café (Taylor's Café), David is meeting with Graves who reminds him that he is supposed to be on his own. "This morning a man named Thompkins left the Desert Winds motel and drove to the desert." Graves claims he's not interested. David tells him he should be because he's an alien, the same one who followed me to the crater yesterday. Graves said that the man described by Vincent was General Beaumont, the commanding officer of the post, "one of the finest men I've ever known," he says.

Graves says he'll handle the aliens. He tells David to go after Carl Wyatt. Widafe is some kind of engineer/architect. The next day Graves and Vincent go through the hiring motions with a guard present and he tells Vincent that he is not to go onto any restricted areas on the post. And the office of Wyatt is in a restricted area, 'in building C, Room 109." They shake hands and as they do, Graves slips David a pass card of some kind. When David leaves he passes by General

Beaumont. After David is gone he tells Graves that he thought he had met "that man before."

Graves had submitted a request for additional security personnel and Beaumont tells him that he submitted it "through channels." Graves knows how time consuming the process is. Beaumont looks at his watch and says he is late for a meeting, but as he turns to leave Graves tells him, "Ted: I want you to postpone the tests." "Why?" "Because I asked you to," Graves says. When asked for a reason all Graves says is that "I have nothing concrete sir, but something stinks on this post."

Beaumont knows that Graves knows something. "My boy died in Korea," he says. From that point on he "couldn't think, couldn't feel. I was empty. I thought for me it was the end." But Graves and his wife Ethel and the kids "came along and filled the void." He adds, "Try to trust me Rick. Try to forget whatever it is you think you know," and then he walks out.

Somehow David presents a pass to one of the guards. He's asking to see Mr. Wyeth. "He's in the machine shop," he's told. David is again walking around a building with no escort or security. He knocks on one of the doors that has a colonel's name clearly marked on it. He's going through a desk that is loaded with blueprints, sits down and fins a locked desk. He pulls a pen knife out of his pocket and unjams it. He comes across more blueprints and unfolds them. He hears someone coming and stands up in time. In walk Wyeth and two guards.

"Mr. Vincent was supposed to come to the machine shop but instead he came here," Wyeth says. "Funny you know my name," David says. The MP wants to take David over to Graves but Wyeth insists that he be taken over to Beaumont.

When they get to Beaumont's office he says that Vincent has violated the rules and the breach will cost him. With Graves standing right there he orders the MPs to take David to lockup where people from the Justice Department will then pick him up and take him in. Cut to the front desk and two men come in to pick up David. The desk sergeant asks to see ID and the men evidently present it. One man signs a form and Vincent is brought out. They handcuff David (in the front) and walk out with him.

In the meantime, Beaumont has sent for Graves. He gives him leave orders. "Are you ordering me to leave, Td?" he asks He says there is something to tell you. He says two agents picked him up and this makes Graves leave the office in an attempt to help David. In the car David is I the front seat with an alien sitting in back and one driving. They pull off on a dirt road. A bright sun is shining but it doesn't affect the driver a bit or the guy in the back. David knows they are aliens.

The glare is blinding as they pull up to a vacated spot. David is let out of the car. "Another disappearance?" David asks. "You're not going to disappear Mr.

Vincent. You're going to have an accident;." Still cuffed David tackles one and begins running. They are after him in the car. David is dodging them and heading for land. The car goes off the edge and two figures are glowing meaning they're dead. Still cuffed David begins walking.

David and Graves somehow hook up in a small bar. They were aliens, David tells him. This is where Vincent tells Graves that the aliens "have a mutated fourth finger." "If you didn't suspect something like this why did you have Spence call me in the first place?" David asks. David has questions: "And where is Spence? How did Wyeth know who I was even before he met me? And why did the Justice Department send out agents so quickly to pick me up?" When Graves says he has no answers David suggests that he call the Justice Department and ask them if they sent any agents.

Beaumont is in the back seat of a

car with head alien Wyeth, who is concerned that "two of my men were killed" and that Vincent is running around and that "he is a man who knows too much." So the aliens are considered men" in the same line as Vincent, eh? Wyeth wants the nuclear test to be re-scheduled, to be moved up and to take place within 24 hours. A committee has been invited to observe the test next week, Beaumont explains. "They'll have to be disappointed," Wyeth says. "Of course, by next week they'll have other things to be worried about, won't they?" A special truck bringing the device from the saucer is now en route, Wyeth tells him. The special truck is refrigerated because the elements are "highly unstable." One the device arrives all they have to do is take it over to the test site and set the timing mechanism. Wyeth tells him, "Believe me general, this is the one chance that your kind has to survive." "Tomorrow at noon," Beaumont assures him.

David and Graves are in an office and Graves comes in and informs him that the nuclear test has been "moved up to noon today." "Beaumont is the key to this whole thing and we don't have much time. We've got to face him with the truth," David tells Graves as if he (David) is the boss man. Off they go.

The truck is unloading the device as aliens and Wyeth watch. It is 11: 20 giving them 40 minutes. "Remember, don't set the timer until you reach the detonation site," Wyeth tells Thompkins, another lead alien.

Meanwhile Graves and David pull up in a jeep on the side of a building, Graves gets out and walks into the building down some stairs and finds Beaumont. He tells him he has something to tell him but that he believes that he (Beaumont) already knows what it is. He asks why the test time was moved up and Beaumont claims it was for "technical reasons." Graves tells him that there's a man outside that he wants him to see. "You have to see this man, and if you won't, I'll have to go over your head." Graves admits that the man that he wants Beaumont to see "is a man I smuggled back onto the post last night – David Vincent."

"How did you find him," Beaumont asks. "He found me," Graves says, "And how did you know he wasn't still in jail?" Beaumont knows that Graves knows so Graves goes out to fetch Vincent as the device is on its way to the site. In the meantime David is spilling his guts to Beaumont and tells him he saw him talking with Thompkins. He tells him that the Justice Department never received a request and" as a matter of fact, they never talked to you." He tells Beaumont about the aliens. Beaumont says, "You know what a busy morning this is, General. I'm sorry you chose to expose me to the imaginings of obviously a diseased mind."

David goes into lecture mode: "General, if you continue this collaboration you'll be serving the cause of beings dedicated to one thing – the destruction of mankind, the takeover of this planet. Now I can't believe you'd knowingly do something like this, not a man with your record …" The general tells Vincent he knows nothing of his record that his record adds up to 100,000 men dead because of his orders. My own son dead because he believes me because I said his would be the last war." David asks, "Whose words are those, your alien friends?"

Graves says he's going to call the Pentagon, but Beaumont tells him that outside of that room there is no one who would ever believe anything he says. "Time is running out," Beaumont says. "As it did for Spence, General?" Graves asks. Beaumont explains that Spence had to die because he was getting in the way of what he and the others were planning to do. "Whose plan?" David asks twice – theirs or yours? And here comes the explanation:

Beaumont says they made it up among themselves. As he explicates:

> " … a world gone totally radioactive, stripped of all life, is of no more value to them than it is to us. Mr. Thompkins assured me that of great sacrifice to his people they were able to land an anti-matter bomb on the earth. Six of their craft were destroyed as well as their crew, blown to oblivion – just to get that one bomb on the earth. Their matter is the opposite of "ours" and when it gets together it fuses and detonates. If it is detonated underground it would blow the earth off its axis by several degrees. Beaumont thinks that earthquakes, tidal waves and floods would kill millions but there would be no nuclear bombs and finally there would be peace. "Billions die –doomsday comes today at noon!"

David exclaims. "Then what do the invaders do?" he asks.

Beaumont says he doesn't care about being killed by the aliens, claiming that there is enough evidence in his safe to expose the aliens. David tells him to call the Pentagon to find out if his evidence is still in the safe. Beaumont says he trusts Macintyre who he's known all his life. Graves seconds David: "Call him!" Beaumont gets on the phone and asks for the Pentagon. Meanwhile the aliens are bringing the device to the restricted area site. We find out that Beaumont is told that McIntyre died this morning. "What about the evidence?" David asks. Beaumont asks the person on the phone to check his safe and gives the person the combination. He wants an immediate report and will hold on.

The aliens are preparing to plant the bomb as they uncover a tunnel. Beaumont is informed that the safe was empty except for his birth certificate. Graves tries to stop the aliens but is told an army truck went through the site five minutes ago. The aliens didn't inform him where the detonation area would be. But David had found the map earlier. Its three miles from where they are now. Beaumont is still in shock. Graves orders a squad of men sent into the test area. Beaumont is told to cancel the detonation and does so over a loudspeaker.

Vincent and Graves get Beaumont to join them when they show him that the aliens have been one step ahead of him. The threesome head out to the site as the device is being unloaded and primed for detonation. A shootout between the army and the aliens. They burn turn red and glow. The shoot Thompkins who glows and dies. Beaumont is wounded. They jump into the truck with Graves following in a jeep.

Beaumont sacrifices himself by driving the bomb out into the desert where the alien are blown to bits. "I'm going to deliver their bomb right back to them," he says. It's almost noon. He tells David to bail out. He orders David out of the truck and then pushes him out as he drives the truck. Graves pulls up in the jeep, picks him up and they follow the truck that Beaumont is in. The lead alien and several others and the truck are there. He blows up everything.

The episode ends with Graves having testified at length (3 hours) to an Army board of what took place, but failing to convince it that anyone other than 'persons unknown' had breached military security." The verdict was "attempted sabotage by enemies unknown."

"The earth turns on its axis, unaware of the disaster that never happened. And David Vincent goes forward again, very much aware that a far greater disaster that lie ahead. The final disaster brought by – the invader."

.9. "Quantity Unknown"

This is one of the key episodes where David's taking advantage of outright white privilege enables him to access information and devise strategies that no other human being could have ever had the gall to come forward with.

A small plane crashes on a mountainside, but there are no bodies. A ten man search crew is on the scene and they note that there are no bodies anywhere. One man shows his supervisor a box and inside of it is a silver metal cylinder. He tells his boss that he found it in the cockpit and it is observed that, "It's practically weightless." How can something be without weight? He is ordered to take it to the lab. On the way the delivery truck is stopped by two security guards and the guard is killed with the metal orb to the neck. They go into the back of the transport van and open it up. A real security guards shows up and there's a shootout. An alien is killed, glows and dies. The human security guard is shocked his colleague is down. The remaining alien shoots him and then makes a run for it, leaving the van open.

More security guards arrive. They're human. He tells them one of them flowed and burned up. All this is b being observed by the alien who got away and flees into the hillside.

A small plane crashes, leaving no trace of its victims. Two security guards killed, a killer disappears in a burst of flame with the killer fleeing into the hills. According to the narrator these are news items too incredible to be taken seriously except by one man: David Vincent. Why is that the case? Why couldn't some other people read the articles, take them seriously but just not have time to deal with the bullshit? Why is the white man always the "lone wolf" who just so happens to be in the right place at the right time? More on this later in the book

David goes to the funeral, figuring some aliens might be there. David is spotted standing nearby by several people. "Isn't that the fellow that was at the hospital, one asks? I wonder who he is?" The other guy, Harry Swain, one of the security guards who drove up late, tells him "I don't know.

David walks up to the security gate at Sperrick Laboratories and introduces himself to security. He asks for Mr. A.J. Richards and they ask if he has an appointment. Time for white privilege to enter the scene: he tells him he has no appointment. No here is a major facility with tens of thousands of gate fencing around it, security guards and the like, and Vincent walks up asking to see the head man – with no appointment! It has already been established at the funeral in the discussion between the security guard and another man that Vincent is not a family member.

And yet the plot continues.

He tells once of the guards, "Tell him that I have information about the attack on the mail truck." This gets the attention of both guards. One gets on the phone as Vincent waits outside of the fence. Harry Swain, the lead guard, open it up. One of the men is the one who arrived late on the scene.

Inside the office he same guy at the funeral takes yet another pill. They enter an office and the female scientist, Diane Oberly, is excused. David is offered a seat but rejects it. The man asks, "Just what is your interest in this?" Vincent then says, "Does it matter if I think I can help?" What? This white boy truly has a God complex. Does it matter?

Vincent explains that the people at the newspaper office told him that there was a cylinder on that truck, "a strange weightless cylinder." After admitting that he can't prove it, but he BELIEVES that the cylinder is what they were after, even after the man in charge tells him that there were a number of valuable items on that truck. David wants to see the cylinder and almost demands to do so. He is led to a woman, Diane Oberly, who is asked to show Vincent the cylinder. Just like that.

Diane comes out with it and David immediately grabs it and looks it over. HE asks questions about it and she says that have been busy working in some government projects. David believes that the man and the woman that the people who want that cylinder will stop at nothing to get it. "They will blow up this plant or do whatever they have to do," David says. Now he's making terroristic threats – sounding as if he is a part of it. If he weren't a white man he would have been arrested or detained on the spot.

But the shit gets deeper. This man who is charge asks DAVID what they should do. Vincent immediately suggests that they "set a trap." What?? The man asks the woman "How long will it take you to duplicate this?" She picks it up and says "a couple of hours." "Okay: go ahead with it."

Just like that the man calls the cop "to go along with this" and an article titled "Strange Cylinder To Be Transferred Today" already appears on the front page of the local newspaper. The stage has been set and a "courier" arrives. ____ is the driver and the head man has the box with the cylinder in it. David is following in his car. There is that continental again, the one driven by the man, this time a light blue in color. They pull up at the airport and place the fake package on the loading bin outside with other suitcases. Why?

David and one of the detectives watches. People are coming to pick up their bags from the cart. A man goes to the pay phone. He shakes his head at one of the other guys who was about to pick up the box and everyone scatters. The people are warned off.

David is back at the lab and the woman who conducted the experiments is there. She and David go into Richards' office. "That phony cylinder is in Cleveland safe and sound," they tell him. ____ has run a check on David and found him to be a "full time dedicated crackpot. He specializes in false alarms." The head man turns his back. David walks out, dejected. The woman, Diane, watches him. As he waits for the elevator the woman comes to him. She apologizes. He asks her to run more tests on the cylinder as the security guard watches. Diane says she doesn't want to get involved. Here comes the old due and stares David down. He boards the elevator with him and pulls his gun. He thinks David is one of the aliens and has a gun pointed at the back of his head.

They get off the elevator and walk down the loading dock. He checks David's hands to see if he's an alien. He thinks David came to the hospital to make sure that his friend was dead "and now you're here, looking for the cylinder." David makes a run for it and gets the goods on the old dude. He says he knows about the aliens. He shows David a picture of his family. His daughter told him they saw space ships. His wife went with her and he heard them scream. He got there just in time to see them die, he says. He's distraught.

Now he knows David knows as well. Harry Swain knows that "they're all around us." David says he's there to help. David tells him he's at the Crescent Hotel, Harry gets off duty and will come see him. David gives him back his gun. They get back on the elevator.

That evening David s in his room and there's a knock. It's Diane from the lab. He allows her in. She tells him she's frightened and she needs some help. She says she conducted more analysis of the cylinder and tells him "the metals resemble nothing on this earth. "She's a scientist and says that it's not just the cylinder but she also has the feeling that she's being watched all the time. Every time she begins to work on the cylinder she gets this feeling.

She is curious. "What could they want from us?" she asks. Then she asks for just one piece of evidence from him that she's "Not just imagining things and that these people exist." Again, though alien they are referred to as people. Keep this in mind.

The phone rings. It's Harry Swain and he thinks they're on to him. He's cornered in an alley. They came at him with disks and he fought them off. He's at a little bar. He says he'll be in one of the booths. He tells her he has to go. "Is Harry Swain a friend of yours?" she asks. She tells him she has some kind of interest in the cylinder. She says that all of a sudden he's become her best friend. David tells her she doesn't have to worry: "I understand Harry Swain." They leave the hotel room.

David walks into the bar and finds Harry. He sits down in the booth. Harry is scared shitless. He tells David that whatever they're planning, it's going to be soon. David convinces Harry that they need to get that cylinder. Harry says that there's a man in New Orleans who is in military intelligence. He could make the cylinder the number one project at the Pentagon. David asks if Harry can get them through the gate. He says he can but that the cylinder is in a vault. David tells him that "the girl" has access to the vault. David tells Harry that he wants to "get the girl" out of there because the aliens have already killed and they would also do the same to her. Harry stares at him: "They're getting ready to destroy the human race and you're worried about one girl?"

Off they go. As they leave one of the aliens is at the bar. He turns and watches David and Harry depart.

At the lab Diane is on the phone talking with someone – she's an alien!

Outside the lab David and Harry are near the fence. He tells David about how the guards make the rounds. He gives David the address of the man in New Orleans in case they get separated. Harry unlocks the gate and in they go. They enter the lab. Harry walks ahead and gives David the coast is clear sign. He waves David in who scurries through a side door. Harry walks into the main office. He tells the man he let his wallet, he pulls his gun and knocks the man out after he opens the internal door. He waves David in. He hands David the guard's gun and carries the body behind the desk. David walks into a lab where lights are flashing. He spots the cylinder box. Loud piercing sound scan be heard. He walks up behind Diane and she's working on something, using a laser on the cylinder

She spots David and he tells her he came for the cylinder. She says she's been trying to cut into it with a laser beam but to no avail. She says Mr. Richards is on his way over to look at it. David snatches it from her and walks off. Harry has tied up the guard and Richards can see that the outside fence has been messed with. Here comes Richards into the office area. He walks up on Harry and informs him, "Main gate is open, Harry". He tells Harry to take care of it. He's on his way up to the lab. Harry tries to talk him away but it won't work. Richards doesn't fall for it. He's on the elevator.

David has the cylinder. Diane is trying to talk him out of it. Harry shot Richards and has his gun pulled. David wants to call a doctor but Harry says no. Diane goes to call a doctor. Harry bogarts her and pushes her to the floor. He grabs the cylinder and tells David to come with him. They both abandon her. A security guard arrives. Harry tells David to go. Harry shoots the security guard in cold blood. Another one arrives. Harry ducks back into the lab with Diane. Two more guards arrive. A shootout takes place and the machinery goes up in fire. Diane is grabbed and the two security guards run out. Harry appears trapped.

David arrives at the office of Frank Griffith (one of the aliens, the one who saw them in the bar). Harry was killed in the fire. The papers said there was no trace of the body. Griffith asks for the cylinder and reaches for it. Harry walks in. He's the alien. They knew who David was all along. "You made it easy for us

David," Harry says. Griffith says, "We rather enjoyed using you, of all people, to help us."

But when Griffith opens the box, it is empty – no cylinder. David pulls his gun. He shoots Griffith who glows and dies. David runs out of the building. He looks for the cylinder that he hid. He finds it. Harry is right behind him. Harry is chasing David upstairs and downstairs outside of the huge building. David is trapped. Harry has a disk in his hand. They both fall into the water below. The cylinder rolls away as they fight near a waterfall. David throws Harry off the waterfall. He's not dead. Harry reaches for the cylinder but he begins to flow rd. He's dying He touches the cylinder and it disappears along with him.

David phones Diane from a distance. Richards is going to be alright and thanks Diane for not snitching. Harry Swain was an alien. She asks him if she will see David again. He says he hopes so and then hangs up.

Moral: "For David Vincent, every friend is a potential enemy. His enemies understand this; Someday perhaps, his friends will, too."

This is the kind of shit that leads to paranoia. How in the FUCK are your friends a potential enemy? If that is the case, that is on you because a "friend" is more than an acquaintance and friendship is earned through trials and tribulations. Maybe that is the way with white folks; surrounded by all that white privilege and having been led to believe that they actually "earned" what they have, maybe they can be free and loose with who, among their fellow race members, they deem to be "friends and enemies." As black people, we have no such luxury.

.10. "The Innocent"

Nat Greely
Mitchell Ross
Sgt. Walter Ruddell
Who was the innocent, you might ask? In my view it was an alcoholic who, like Vincent, just happened to be at the wrong place at the wrong time, got recognized by some aliens and then went on the lam to keep them from finding him. At the same time his wife and child were innocent bystanders and it was his love for them that ended up bringing to an end what might have been a major breakthrough in exposing the aliens.

U.S. Government property, Clement Air Force Base. A man, General Mitchell Ross, is looking for a "Sightings report" and it's not in the file. He asks Sergeant Walter Ruddell about it, "Last week the Ambrose report was missing and now this." They need the report for the committee meeting tomorrow. Someone enters as sergeant Ruddell leaves. It's an MP and he asks for "Captain Ross and says that Captain Gardner wants to see him." The man walks toward him and pulls his gun. "You'll come now – sir." He tells him not to argue. The captain makes a move for his brief case and grabs a gun. He shoots and the MP glows and burns. He was an alien. The sergeant comes back in and he and the general see nothing but the burn marks.

Important reports are missing, and they are vital to a committee meeting. "In a decaying lobster port in Maine, David Vincent searches for a man who has seen the invaders. A fisherman named Nat Greeley who has taken one of their weapons, a strange metallic disk. For a day and a half, Vincent has combed the tiny waterfront town. But Nat Greeley has disappeared."

A military officer with a subpoena recognized Vincent and presents him with a subpoena, as he's been summoned to Washington by a Captain Ross. "We know what you're looking for," the man tells him and hands David the paperwork. He says that David can follow them to the airport in his car. Two men from inside the boat watch as David drives off after the officers. Both men are aliens (extended pinkie fingers).

In Washington, in an office, David is getting grilled. He has filled Ross in on what he knows and the man doubts him. David knows he's seen them die which is why he raises the doubt. He's also yelling at a man who is obviously a high ranking military officer as if he (Vincent) were calling the shots. He finally admits, "I've seen it. So what? Have you ever heard of the Peterson Committee?" Peterson is in the Office of Defense and they've asked him to form a committee to look into his findings. David had never heard of it. Ross wants David there with him to testify on Monday. David lights up a cigarette. David tells him he's been through it all before. "If I get up there and testify before them, under oath, what makes you think they'll believe me?" "Don't you understand? There are two of us this time. Two of us who have actually seen them," Ross exclaims.

"IT's a lot of words, a lot of talk. What we need is proof!" David yells back. Now the man I'm looking for is in Maine. He can give us that proof." Ross tells him, "Nat Greeley is the town bum, the town drunk, his testimony wouldn't be worth two cents. That's why we dropped the whole thing with him," Ross explains. "We need you here to testify. Now if you think he's that important we'll send a couple of men up there to find him." "Do that and he'll never come out of hiding," David warns. He says "I know how frightened a man like this can get."

David implores, "Now let me do it my way – please!"

Meanwhile two suited men with attaché cases walk the dock and approach a boat where a young boy is working up on a mast. He calls for his mother, Miss Greeley. They ask for Mr. Greeley. The main claims that they practice law in

Augusta. He says her husband isn't there. They claim that her husband is the last living descendant of someone who left him $83000. She says that she thought Nat's mother was an alcoholic and only had one great uncle, Sam Burkett. The man says they have no time to waste, all that money stands to go to the sailor's fund. "Where CAN we find your husband. She says when he come back she'll tell him about it. She hands them back the papers and they walk away.

She watches them as they leave. She then immediately looks up a contact number. The kids says "Ma, they said we'd be rich." She tells the boy, "We'll be rich when it rains ten dollar gold pieces." She speeds through a directory of some kind, and it's the family Bible. "Your uncle Sam died when he was fourteen," she says. She tells the boy that the men were just playing some kind of trick. She tells the kid she has to go ashore. Then up walks David. He introduced himself. She tells her husband is in danger. "If you want to save your husband you better persuade him to see me." He hands her a card. "Call this man – he'll tell you who I am. It's an air force number." David leaves.

She runs off to a pay phone. David ducks into a Belle Harbor store unit that has been abandoned. He walks around and finds Ned. "That disc you found is one of their weapons. That's what they're after, that's why they're trying to kill you," David explains. "You saw them get off a space ship." "They're men like me," he says but David corrects him. "They LOOK LIKE men." And here is another teaching lesson about race.

What does a "man" look like to people like these? They are male in gender and white in skin coloration. That's all you need and the aliens knew that when they were researching the human race. They knew white people were racist and were the easiest to convince of their superiority. By lulling them to sleep, the aliens were able to buy property, rent huge warehouses, purchase abandoned military bases and mines, invest in corporate America, infiltrate the government at all levels, and establish a foundation for an eventual takeover. All this is based on the mutual belief, by the white Earthling and the alien, that "white" is the only race of merit and therefore the only one that counts.

Back to our story.

Now Ned, where's the disk?" He says he doesn't have it. "When they tried to kill me I hid it," he says.
David tells him to show him but Ned refuses. "I ain't leavin' here until they're gone," he nervously tells Vincent.

"Ned, we need that disc to convince the government that they're here, NOW," David says. "If these invaders aren't stopped, not only is your life in danger, but everybody's." He gives in. "There's a wharf at the foot of Grover

Street," he says. "You meet me there at six o'clock, after its dark. He then tells David to get out and David turns and leaves.

Later on the two men who came to the ship earlier have returned. The little boy sees them and again goes to warn his mother. The boy tries to run but the men grab him and bring him back down to the boat. "Mrs. Greeley, I'm sorry to intrude again," one of them says, "But there are a few things that we are going to have to settle. This concerns you, too, young fella." They then escort the kid up the stairs into the boat with his mother.

Later on, Ned's finds his father's hiding place, claiming she wasn't followed. She tells him that two men told her that they wanted a disk "and they said they wanted Mr. Vincent, too." You've got to do it. She is insistent and he keeps telling her no and she swears she cares about nothing more than the two of them and their son. "If you don't give them Mr. Vincent they're going to kill us all!"

As David waits feverishly for Ned, he sees him and his wife standing down the way, walks up and is immediately grabbed and then knocked out with a chloroform-filled rag. As they take off with Vincent, Ned takes a swig of alcohol.

Vincent is brought to a building and met by Magnus, the head alien (played by the incomparable Michael Rennie from the 1959 movie classic "The Day the Earth Stood Still"). There are four or five men, along with Greeley, on the porch of the building as Magnus greets them all. Greely is not one of them but according to Magnus, "He's been useful in returning our property and bringing you." They order Greeley inside and Magnus asks Vincent to come with him. "I want to show you something." There it is: a saucer. They approach it.

David walks up the plank and enters with the aliens. They then enter a chamber and Magnus asks, "Do you care to inspect our space ship, Mr. Vincent?" They tell Vincent to take off his overcoat because he won't be needing it. He tells David to sit down and he'll "explain" to him and that "there is nothing to be afraid of."

"I know how you feel about us, Mr. Vincent. I don't blame you. We've committed blunders too – we've used terror, violence, we've even killed. The history of your people is filled with those same blunders. What happens when one civilization finds another one less advanced? We've learned, Mr. Vincent, at great cost to you and us. Now we've got our orders: it's got to stop. Now we've taken our first step … We're here to help to contribute our knowledge to your lives," and convinces Vincent to follow him. Magnus shows him the inside of one of the space ships where he uses a mind-control device to try to brainwash David into believing they have decided on a peaceful approach. David is strapped into his chair and lights come on. The ship appears to have left Earth.

Vincent lost consciousness during the "short flight" and when he comes to he is in a place that he always wanted to be. A place that was once a valley until a drought came and destroyed it – many years ago. The window of the ship opens and there it is in front of him. Vincent sees a place where everything he always wanted. "Shall we go, Mr. Vincent?" Magnus escorts him outside into this incredible world, the valley that was once dying, but is no bountiful. They leave the ship and walk toward the huge structure, an architectural firm that Vincent always dreamed up.

IT's so real, even his car is there as he and Magnus pull up. The car is the silver version of the Lincoln Continental that appears in episodes from time to time. David is very satisfied and asks them how he did it. The dam that he once wanted to build in the canyon has now been constructed and a larger one is under construction. Santa Margaretta is what the area is called. His old friend Billy is there, Billy Stearns. He says he's working for the aliens. He said he fought them until Magnus made him understand: "David, the knowledge."

Stearns has to make a call and will meet David on the other side of the building to show him the dam. As he walks off David notices that he's not limping. Magnus tells him, "Injury, disability – those are human concepts, Mr. Vincent." "You mean you can work miracles like that?" David asks. "We can do whatever you want," Magnus says.

As they walk to the other side of the building woman's voice is shouting: "David! David!" Her name is Helen and David runs out to meet and holde her. They hug. He tells her he never forgot her. She rushes him to her car, a convertible and David gets in. He is so happy to see her.

She explains to him that it's a different world, where what we want most can be accomplished. "David, they can teach us how to get what we want, how not to let human emotions get in the way of what we want." She says she has a house at the lake and asks him to stay with her. Vincent is having doubts. HE says that the town the whole valley, the damn none of it was in the newspaper. She tells him other things were in the past. He said he was there a month ago and none of this was there. "There's something wrong," he shouts. It's all wrong." She begins shouting for Magnus and they end up pulling up in front of the architecture building. David jumps out of the car and looks back: the car and Helen have disappeared. He looks around; the building has disappeared.

He is now in the middle of a field with people saying "Stay with us, Mr. Vincent." He's back on the ship in the chair surrounded by aliens as he moans, "it's wrong. It's wrong. Magnus is saying "Stay with us." He wakes up –"It was all in my mind." Magnus says that they will try again, only this time it will be done a little differently.

Back at the headquarters Magnus sits with Vincent and tells him that his reports inform him that neither he (Vincent) nor Greeley bothered to show up. Somehow the mind-fuck doesn't work on Vincent for long (wouldn't you know it), and when Vincent realizes they are lying, Magnus forces him to telephone Ross and claim that his story was just a hoax, to tell Captain Ross that "you know nothing of us or of our activities. That we exist only in your imagination." "Is that why you tried to brainwash me – so I'd believe that you were here for the benefit of mankind?" Vincent asks.

But wait a minute: a well-placed bullet to Vincent's brain would remedy all that. After all, he's by himself, no one really gives a shit about him or his quest, the aliens have the advantage and they could therefore just bust a cap in his ass the way the white man did John F. Kennedy, Martin Luther King, Robert Kennedy and all the other people who were becoming a pain in their collective pale asses. But noooo! Instead, some kind of hi-tech brainwashing designed to "win over" Vincent, which in many ways is a sign of defeat, don't you think?

David tells Magnus from the other side of the desk in the office, "You're afraid of the Peterson Committee … You're afraid of my testimony." Now doesn't it sound like Vincent is the one holding all the cards? He's surrounded by alien beings who could easily put one of those metallic disks on his neck and simulate a cerebral hemorrhage the way they have done so many times in the past. Instead, we are witnessing some kind of high powered "negotiation" between a superior race and one lone human being who is considered by most of his own people to be a complete and total asshole. What gives?

David refuses to make the call, but they bring out the drunk, Greeley. "They're going to kill my wife and boy unless we do something they want," Greeley tells David. Greeley wants David to make the call but David says "if I do the investigation goes to pieces, and they can continue safely with their plan." Greeley kneels and literally begs David to make the call – he even begins crying.

They call Captain Ross. David lies and tells him that he found Greeley but they didn't find out anything. "Scratch us off your list. You'll have to appear before the committee without our testimony. There are no aliens and there never have been." Ross tells Vincent he wants him in his office but David hangs up the phone. "Thank you Mr. Vincent," Magnus says. Greeley is now free and walks out. But first he tells Vincent "I wouldn't have done this except to save my wife and kid. I've never done much for them," he says. He says the aliens promised him and then walks out.

David begins to fight them, turning down a drink. They pour alcohol down his throat. Greeley says he can find the highway but the aliens say they've provided a car for him. He is ushered inside, but they knock him out and then pour alcohol over him. Inside David is being plied with alcohol that puts him in a daze. Magnus hands him some car keys and David passes out on the floor.

He is lured outside, still in daze and placed in the back seat of the car with two aliens. They drive off. Now its day time all of a sudden. David is dragged from the alien car into another car and places in the passenger seat with Greeley on the other side behind the wheel, knocked out. Magnus puts the car in neutral and send it down a narrow highway toward a cliff. David comes to just time, of course. David tries to grab the wheel as the car careens back and forth. The brakes don't work and the car is at high speed. David maneuvers the sharp curves even though he's in a daze. They enter a construction area and the car turns upside down but of course, David survives. Greeley crawls out first and then drags David out as the car lies on its roof.

The two of them watch as the car blows up. Back at Calment Air Force Base, David meets with officials. Ross doesn't belief him anymore. He reminded David that he too had seen the aliens but now he (David) has been discredited. "Tell them about your little trip to Venus or wherever it was," Ross quips. Ross sent men up to the mansion where Magnus was doing business "and they found nothing. So why don't you and your drinking buddy go and find yourselves another bar?" he asks.

As they begin to wind up their meeting there's a knock on the door and an officer comes in to advise Ross that they're going to go clean up the rest of the area. David recognizes the man right away. After he leaves David tells Ross, "It's Sergeant Rudell," he was one of the men that Vincent saw when he was being brainwashed on the ship. Ross stands up and tells both Vincent and Greeley to "get out of here." They leave.

Ross gets on the phone and calls security. He orders a check on Rudell. "I want to know everything about him." David and Greeley walk off as the narrator concludes: "A trip to a nightmare world. A committee disbanded, another defeat. Another hope lost for David Vincent. Maybe. Or maybe it's a hope begun."

.11. "The Ivy Curtain"

In most of the episodes of "The Invaders," the women were the ones who were fucked up. They might have had bad spouses as well, but the women were the betrayers and weaklings. Sometimes they converted and ended up doing heroic things – before they died. In this episode we find a combination of all of the above.

Barney Cahill is a pilot who is flying to transport aliens – for the money, of course. Stacey, his wife, works as a dispatcher at the same small airline at

Midlands Academy. As what might be deemed a precursor to the 911 attacks where pilots were trained at American schools and used their skills to destroy the twin towers, this was a theme that this episode of "The Invaders" revolved around.

In this segment, the "academy" is a training center. How did Barney get into this situation? During one of his flights Barney was forced to make an emergency landing in a storm, one of his passengers is injured. Barney warns one of them to lie on the floor and use a coat as a pillow and prepare for the landing. All of the passengers in the transport plane do as they are told as Barney warns from the cockpit, "It's gonna be rough!" There is a strange instrument on board that is encased in a wooden box. Barney lands the plane and all seems to be well. He goes back to check on the passengers. They lift the box (it takes three of them) and Barney checks one of the men.. To Cahill's puzzlement, the "man" is not in pain or bleeding because he is an alien! "No blood. No pain. He's not even bleeding," Barney observes. The men, all aliens in white shirts and ties, stare Barney down as he continues to ask, "What do you want? What do you want?"

Once again David rides a bus into a town. Don't ask me why. Mr. William Burns is an educator and business educator. Here on the planet earth for less than a year. In other words, he's an alien. David is following him. He first spotted him at an alien installation in Miami and then later, in Omaha. Now he's followed him to Karen, New Mexico, a town with peaceful streets. Burns gets into a station wagon that has Midlands Academy on the side of it, a place that David is sure "shrouds the presence of the invaders."

David, who once again is right next to a pay phone and also just so happens to have correct change, makes a call, He glances through the directory and looks up the number for Midlands Academy. Now he's got a car and heads for the Academy. The sign points to where it is although it can't be found on the map. David spots the station wagon that Burns was transported in. he parks his car and walks over to it, looks in. "Road signs can be very misleading and this one seems to have taken you to a dead end," a man in a suit says as he creeps up behind Vincent. Another man appears from behind the station wagon.

It's Burns, and he wants to know why Vincent has been following him. David attempts to lay out a lie by claiming "I don't know why you think I've been following you," but before he can get it out the second alien attacks him from behind, and knocks him out. They have his ID, a California driver's license. They hide his car.

Meanwhile, Barney comes to in the office of the Academy administrator, Dr. Reynard. Barney wants to know why he's there. Their initial plan was to kill him, but then they decided on "a more practical alternative." "Like what?" He admits he's scared. "You are a pilot, Mr. Cahill, and we need a pilot," Reynard says. He tells him that their students come from distant regions and we transport them to various training centers that have been established throughout the country. Although Barney says he's not going to get caught up "in any smuggling operation," an assistant brings Reynard a box; he opens it and pulls out a handful of cash. "You will be paid one thousand dollars a head, cash on delivery." He then hands Cahill the thick stack of bills he is currently holding and tucks it into the pocket of his leather jacket.

In the meantime the station wagon pulls up outside. Burns gets out and goes to the back tailgate to unload Vincent who was faking it. When the tailgate is opened, David subdues Burns and then scampers into the foyer of a building. He looks around and seeks the Office of the Dean and a large waiting area. He ducks into a room that is flowing red and hears a woman screaming. He looks up and there's a woman in pain being shown on some kind of television cube. It's a training room and there are men around a table being shown the image and told that "this is a human emotion known as fear. Before you leave this Academy, you will be programmed to simulate fearing varying degrees of intensity. You will learn the language of emotion just as you have learned the language with which you are now communicating." David ducks back outside the door

The voice continues: "You will learn to use fear as a weapon. To twist anxiety into hate, suspicion into violence, cowardice into surrender. The mastery of this technique will make the destruction of the human race inevitable." David quietly closes the door and exits back into the hallway.

He avoids two alien janitor types and goes into another room. There are bodies lying on beds and are being programmed by computer. The people sit up like robots as David closes the door. He ducks out a side door and sticking out like a sore thumb he hides behind a corner and watches people scattering around the campus. He gets into the back of a van and closes the door. It is the van that Cahill is being escorted to. Cahill gets into the passenger side as the van drives off.

Reynard is shown Vincent's ID and he recognizes it. He has a file on him. "Take this to the programming room," he says to the aide who brought the information to him. He gets on the phone. Meanwhile, the van is headed down the highway. David opens the back door of the van and creeps out on the rear bumper. When the van stops at a stop sign he jumps off.

Cut back to the programming room. The people are still laying on their respective beds and being programmed. Bush comes in, pushes some new buttons and now the programming is about David Vincent. Vincent is described and told "he is an enemy to our cause" and "Must be destroyed."

David is still walking around the town has if he was born there. He comes across the airport where Barney Cahill is working. His wife Stacey is behind the desk and tells David that Barney is out on a flight and David wants to see him. She asks if he was another reporter. He says he's covering a story for wire services and will be out of a job without seeing Barney. She's going to close up. For some reason David feels dazed. Two aliens wait outside of a bar and then enter. David and Stacey are already inside at the bar talking.

She leaves to powder her nose and one of the men walks in. David spots him. He grabs some change off the bar and heads to pay phone (there seems to be one readily available everywhere Vincent goes). He looks outside and sees the other man standing outside near the car. He pretends to be going or a smoke. The man has a metallic disk and attacks David. They begin fighting outside of the pay phone. David fucks him up and then makes a run for it. The second man comes outside to render aid to his knocked out pal. When Stacey comes out of the ladies room David is gone. Vincent left a big tip, from which Stacey orders a double.

Stacey comes home and Barney is waiting. She tells him, "If there's one thing I can't stand, it's a reformed drunk." They are obviously having problems as she changes for the shower. She says he's her husband who is old enough to be her father. Meanwhile in the emergency room David is being looked at. Two cops come in and show ID and claim someone was trying to kill him. What? David tells them about Midlands Academy. He says it's a front for people who want to take over the government. The two "cops" are suspicious. One cop says he smells liquor on David's breath and the doctor wants to keep him overnight.

Meanwhile Stacey steps out of the shower. She walks up on a stack of bills. He says it's the beginning of a new world, $3,000 dollars. HE makes a toast to her "To bigger and better things." He asks Stacey if she wants a new dress or new car, anything you want. She wants to know where he got the money. Now all of a sudden they get romantic, kiss and he's going to get some pussy. Typical and perennially successful female sex education maneuver.

Meanwhile, at a simulated nightclub in one of the rooms of the Academy, Reynard is walking around checking out the actions and language of the simulated young people. Young people are talking politics. He's training young people to act like humans. "If we are going to poison their minds, we must be sincere and convincing," Reynard tells a young blonde. "Will you please put it into practice?" She nods obediently. An aide summons Reynard who goes into the hallway. He looks outside and a police car is pulling up with Vincent in the back seat.

The two cops don't buy the story about enemy agents. Burns is running interference saying that he won't' interrupt the students. The lead man comes out. They have a search warrant and present it to Dr. Rayon. David leads the way but Burns continues to interrupt him. He room that David saw is now changed over to look like a regular study hall. David takes them to the next room but it's locked.

The cop demands the key. David goes across the hall and the other room is a recreation area with ping pong, rock music and kids dancing called "the recreation room." They go back across the hall to the room that was locked and David opens it. It's a lecture hall, apparently a science class of some kind and there is nothing out of the ordinary about it.

David says they've changed everything around. The lieutenant says they've seen enough. Burns hands Vincent his wallet back: "You must have dropped it somewhere." David takes it and leaves. There's that continental again, this time it's white with black interior. Inside are Barney and Stacey and its brand new. She suspects he's into something illegal. He says he made a legitimate deal but just can't talk about it. She appears to be worried. Where did all this "care" come from?

As Barney gets out of the car Vincent walks up on him. He says he's giving David three minutes. David asks him if he knows who those people are. He says he doesn't care. "Maybe you haven't seen those training academies. Well I have. They're being taught to act like us, to infiltrate our society and to eventually take over," David explains. Barney asks who are "they"? David says he needs proof. Barney thinks it's a loyalty test and isn't going to help. Stacey walks in and spots Vincent. You know my wife?" She says "Yes, we met in the office yesterday."

David asks him not to take the people he picks up to the academy but bring them to the airport and he'll have the cops waiting. Barney says he has it all worked out. "Barney I know them – it won't work" David says. Barney agrees after Stacey bats her eyes and tells Davis to tell the police to be there in two hours.

Off Barney goes to pick up a fresh batch of students. Stacey phones the Academy. Barney is at the pickup point and is waiting with his plane. The flying saucer is seen taking off and behind him are four "students." "Did that thing bring you here?" he walks. He grabs one but gets the stares down. They board the lane. Barney can't believe his own eyes. David phones the cops and says more agents will be arriving. The cops promise they'll be there. A police car with two men pulls into the midlands driveway and they get out. The driveway is partially blocked. Two aliens wait with metallic orbs. Meanwhile Barney is flying in with men in the back. He radios ahead to get landing instructions.

David sees aliens pulling up at the airport. He knows they're going in to talk to Stacey. The man on the ground has been killed and an alien has been taken over by Burns. David bursts into the airport dispatcher room. He locks her into the fenced in office. David kicks the door in and begins fighting with Burns. David kills Burns and he glows red and dies as all aliens do. Vincent is now on the radio and talks to Barney. He tells him to get back up into the air: "Don't land, the people from the Academy are here, they've been tipped off. Don't land."

Barney takes back off after nearly landing. David says he'll call the police in Albuquerque. Barney doesn't have enough fuel to get to Albuquerque. Barney knows who blew the whistle – it was Stacey. "Tell Stacey I said, "Thanks a lot," and then he signs off.

Reynard, the head man is concerned. He runs outside and looks to the sky and sees the plane flying in, way too close. Headed straight for the Academy. Barney says he's 'over the school, right smack on target. The aliens are running into the building and Barney crashes into it.

Stacey goes to the bar dressed in black. She sees David at the bar. Birney's funeral must be over. It's the bus stop bar and the bus is leaving. She tried to reach him at the hotel but she was told he checked out. David is pissed. He picks up his suitcase. "All I wanted was some money," she said. "I've got to catch a bus," he says and walks out.

I am not sure what the title,"The Ivy Curtain" actually meant. As a college professor myself I am familiar with the concept of the "ivory tower" as it relates to the somewhat elite posturing of university administrations and also of "the Ivy League," those schools on the east coast that are supposed to be the best of the best (e.g., Brown University, Columbia,.Cornell, Dartmouth College, Harvard, Princeton, University of Pennsylvania.and Yale). But since the Academy in this movie was a front for something much more sinister, it was actually a "curtain" aimed at hiding the real motives of the invaders.

"An indoctrination center destroyed where new arrivals to the planet Earth could learn the finer points of human behavior. A day later, David Vincent leaves the little town in New Mexico, grimly aware that sometimes human behavior can seem as alien as creatures from another world."

And well it should. Hasn't this series shown that white people from Earth and white people from "way out there in the galaxy" are pretty much one and the same? Both sets of people have pale skin by choice; both sets are colonizers; both sets are heartless warmongers when it comes to relating to people who are different. Of course "human behavior" can seem alien if the humans are the white ones. They are the moral freaks of civilized society!

12. "The Betrayed"

"Three months ago, David Vincent had come to the Carver Oil Fields in Houston. There had been reports of unexplained lights, and that same night two watchmen had been found dead. The verdict in both cases: cerebral hemorrhage. Now, suddenly, after endless nights of photography, David has found proof that the invaders are here.

It seems that three months earlier, David Vincent came to the Carver oil fields, located in Houston, Texas. The narrator tells us that "David found proof that the invaders are here. And that's not all he's found. Simon Carver owns the Simon Oil Company and of course he has landed a job with the company (as he's been called in to "design a plan)." Carver's black butler is "Henry," and it seems that David has been dating (read: fucking) Carver's daughter, Susan, and they are quite familiar with one another. Evelyn is Carver's secretary and she lives in the mansion with Carver and his daughter.

One night David has a long lens camera with him as a saucer is taking off. A truck pulls up and stops as David watches and takes pictures of numerous aliens unloading the truck and placing something inside of an abandoned railroad car. The saucer takes off. DAVID climbs atop the railroad car and then enters a railroad car , scaling down a ladder. What he finds is that inside of the railroad car is a hi-tech chamber, which we later learn is a regeneration chamber for the aliens. Walking around as if he owns the place, David is taking pictures aplenty. He turns something on by accident alerting several aliens outside. One is climbing the ladder on the outside of the car to check it out. David managers to grab a tape. As an armed alien comes inside they begin fighting although the alien has a ray gun. David kills him he glows red and dies. David scales the ladder and gets outside of the rail car. Off he goes.

Say what?

Continuing, the next day David arrives at the mansion where he is residing. It's the home of Simon Carter, the president of the oil company. So he can just drive up and knock on the door. According to the narrator, "Now finally, three months of waiting and watching are about to pay off."

Carter comes to the balcony outside and asks who it is and tells him it's five o'clock in the morning. Carter calls for Henry, a black butler who says, "Mr. Vincent" but David walks past him like he's a non-entity. Carter descends the large stair case in his robe and again asks David what's going on. He tells Carter to get the security guards out to field one right away, adding that he doesn't have the time to explain fully. "Make time," Carter says. David shows Carter the computer tape that he "found inside an abandoned tank car." He tells David that there's nothing in that tank car but rust and it's been siting there for a long time.

He escorts David into his huge office area through double doors and pours coffee. David tells him that field one is where two men were killed. Carter explains that those men weren't killed but David tells him that they were two men, both killed by cerebral hemorrhage, and were therefore killed "because of this tape."

Carter's daughter, Susan, head full of extensions (or a wig) comes down and asks what is going on. Carter tells David that he hired him to design a plant, "not to give me some cock and bull about some guards. Carter hastily swallows some pills and summons Harry. The brutha comes in and he orders "get me some clothes." Carter believes this bullshit and gets on the phone and tells someone to meet him at Field One. David tells him his car is outside and the old man snaps, "Mind if I put my pants on"?

Why would a man this powerful be so accessible, and feel obligated to personally go and check on a supposedly broken down train car? When the old man leaves to change Susan tells David that she loves his charming manner and when he takes her out. He tells her he will explain everything to her when he gets back just as the Oldman comes in screaming that it's time to go. As they head to the door Evelyn comes down the stairs. She is the secretary for Carter but lives on the premises.

The security guards arrive and one scales up the car but David and Carter are already there. David tells him that it's not the same car. Carter is pissed and orders David to come to his office later. He then, with the assistance of one of the guards, gets down from atop the train car and heads off.

David arrives at the location of Taft School of Electronics. David walks into the building looking for the director, Neal Taft. He walks up on Taft who is soldering a computer and Taft asks, "Who is it? FBI? FCC? Licensing Commission?" David walks over and introduces himself. He says he has a special job for him. "A computer tape?" he asks as David hands something to him. "You tell me," Vincent replies. David went to NASA and then to the university and was given his name. "My former bosses," Taft says. "You're a specialist in cryptography," Vincent says. Taft had been canned by both NASA and the university "for non-conforming," he says, which David says was "breaking the rules – but never inefficiency."

He needs the tapes decoded but Taft says that when he tells him his price he might change his mind. David reaches in his suit pocket and pulls out an envelope. Taft opens it and sees the cash and is satisfied. Taft asks what side of the law he's on and D avid tells him he doesn't have to worry about the law, but adds, "IF anybody finds out aabout this tape, your life won't be worth a cent." Taft tells him to forget it because "it's the kind of trouble I don't need." David tells him to keep it because "you're safe as long as I don't know where you are." HE tells him to take the tape and disappear: "I'm the one they're looking for," he says.

Taft tells David he will meet him tonight at ten o clock, and for him to start walking south and "if there's nobody following you, I'll pick you up." David agrees. David pulls up in front of the Alamo Hotel (of course he finds parking right in the front) and goes into his room where he is attacked by two aliens. One charges him with having stolen something that belongs to them. They've already searched the room. As one holds him down on the couch, the other pulls out a hypnotic advice and gets David to spill his guts about who has the tape: "Neal Taft." David tries to fight back but they kick his ass and leave him there – ALIVE. What?

The time spent with all this hypnosis and negotiating with Vincent could have just as easily been spent putting a bullet in a chamber of a .38 special and blowing his fuckin' brains out. Could it not?

At any rate, David manages to make the appointment and tells him that he was roughed up. They go over to Neal's car and take a ride. Meanwhile, the old man goes into his office and his daughter is waiting for him. She's worried and asks him who Arnold Mayer is. He was the old man's former business partner and he (her father) stole Mayer's technique. He didn't admit it, the girl figured it out. She asks him why he did it. "Don't you want to know WHO I did it for?" he asks. She hugs him and says "I know who you did it for."

In the car Max says there is a list of equations. There are coordinates that represent longitude and latitude coordinates, one of them right here close to Houston, he explains. His brother Joe is looking into the information. Susan, huge tits and all is by the pool. Evelyn is by the pool waiting for her. Evelyn wants the address of Neal Taft and what they've done with a certain computer tape. She says she'll tell the old man's secret if Susan doesn't get her the tape. Susan agrees.

Susan meets David that night to convince him to get rid of the tape. He tells her he doesn't have it and can't tell her where it is. There is a phone call for Vincent even though they're in a bar. Someone wants to meet him in fifteen minutes. David excuses himself and Susan gets on the phone. She tells someone that David is meeting someone in fifteen minutes. She's telling Evelyn. "Don't thank me Evelyn. Don't thank me."

Neal's brother Joe arrives at the meet and is met by two aliens. They eat the shit out of him and leave him there and take off in the car. They hit him with the car and speed off just as David walks up. "Joey Taft?" he asks. Joey tells him that Neal is at the university in his lab. Meanwhile Susan walks into see her father. He wants to talk to her. He repeats that he stole the formula from Mayer and as a result Mayer killed himself. He sent Mayer's wife money all the time but "Nothing could ever wipe out the stink of what I did."

She thinks she solved the problem and that they can go back to living the way they always lived. Meanwhile, Neal and David are at the hospital waiting to see what happened to Joey who got run down. David tries to explain his theory to Neal: "If you could destroy our fuel supply, planes couldn't fly, ships couldn't sail, we would be disabled. We could be attacked." "attacked from where?" Neal asks. "Outer space. You know it's possible, I'm saying it's true." The tank car was a homing device that they bring down in order for one of their saucers to land.

The doctor comes out of the back and it is clear that Joey didn't make it. "Vincent: my brother just died," Neal says.

Vincent goes to the house to meet Susan. Susan comes downstairs. Her father has a plane to catch. She told her father she didn't' want to see him anymore. David knows that she knew about Taft and had a hand in setting him up "I never told you his name," David says. They got the wrong Taft.

It's the next day at the oil fields. David and Neal pull up with a map. Taft and David have a map and figure that the oil fields are an alien landing site. Meanwhile, Taft uses his old NASA contacts to get them to come to the flying saucer landing site. "If your story is right, this could be a landing field," Neal says. David tells him to take the information and try to convince them. "I was canned for non-conformity, remember?" Neal asks. "How many chances do you think we're going to get before they wipe out the human race?" David asks.

Meanwhile, Evelyn and Susan are in the old man's office (he's taken off on a plane trip to New Orleans) office when two men in suits, summoned by Evelyn, enter the old man's office and close the doors. She introduces them to Susan as "Friends." Evelyn tells Susan that "they" have a schedule and if they don't meet it by 9pm it could stall the alien strategy for a full year, maybe two. We can't afford that. I've been made aware that I've failed and if I fail again, I die; and if I die you die and your father dies." Evelyn convinced Susan to go see David and try one more time to get that tape.

Susan arrives at David's hotel room. Susan spills her guts about what he has found out. David tells her to tell Evelyn that the tape could not be decoded. "Is that the truth?" she asks. "No, but they have to go through with their plans," David says. "Tell her that the tape is in a safe in Taft's office. I'll make sure it's there, its sure to convince them, but promise me you won't go back to the house. Take a plane. Disappear for a couple of days … Go to the airport to make that phone call.

She agrees and adds, "There was one thing I wasn't lying about – I do love you." He grabs her and gives her a deep kiss and she leaves. As soon as she leaves Taft walks in. David says, "Better call your friend at NASA. It's happening tonight."

Susan is at airport trying to call her father to warn him. She gets through to him at his meeting in New Orleans and tells him that he's got to meet her at the Mirador Airport because his life is in danger. He evidently agrees, she hangs up and as she is walking out, Evelyn and two suited aliens grab her and take her to the railroad car headquarters.

But David and Taft are already there spying. They see the aliens taking Susan into the train car. Two men come out and are looking around. Susan is being interrogated. The ship is on the way. The aliens use the hypno orb on Susan and she spills her guts and tells them that she was lying. They order the lead alien to turn the ship back and then they execute Evelyn, who has become expendable.

With Evelyn dead, the aliens call and order the space ship to turn back, because they have been found out by David and Taft. Aliens evacuate and take off. The contraption begins to glow meaning its on self-destruct. David comes to rescue Susan and pulls her out. They get away from the rail car and it immediately glows and disappears right in front of the three of them. Susan is dying in his arms.

Aliens evacuate and destroy rail car, and as usual, NASA and the FBI arrive too late. The old man is bent over his desk grieving as David explains David says, "She was special. What she did was special." And walks toward the door. "Vincent, she DID love you," the old man says.

David gets in the car with Taft. Taft says that if there is anything he can do and David thanks him. How about taking me to the airport?

Closing message: "A girl's life. For David Vincent, a very personal reason why the war must go on … Why the world must be alerted, why the invader must be destroyed."

.13. "Storm"

This one centers around a cast of Hispanic characters, from the priest (Father Joe) to his daughter Luis and an alien Hispanic named Luis.

Two men watching a news clip. A hurricane has just hit Miami and 26 people are dead. One of the men viewing the film is Dr. Gantley, and he observes something the other two men do not: a boat floating in the water that avoids a hurricane. Not only that, but an entire town avoids a hurricane and the boat just happens to be from that town. The doctor gets on the phone when the film is turned off and asks "you tell me how a hurricane of this kind appears in February?" He calls Father Joe and asks if the Father is going back to St. Matthews beach that evening. He wants to ride along with him and will meet him down at the emergency station.

One of the men in the room is silent and has that look, so you know he's an alien. Cut to the emergency station where ambulances are busy. Father Joe is waiting. As fate would have it a huge palm tree hits some electrical wires and almost hits Gantley. Father Joe rushes over to make sure he's alright. The strange man, with extended pinkie, has followed the Dr. to the meet. Now you know that the aliens know what they know.

David arrives in a cab as the narrator tells us, "In the nightmare world in which David Vincent moves, there is seldom reason or logic. So when a hurricane that appears out of season blankets a 600 mile area, yet spares a single town, such a storm becomes a part of that nightmare world and prompts a phone call to a meteorologist named Gantley and brings Vincent to a fishing town near the Florida keys."

David checks into the hotel. Gantley has a room but he's not in. A Latino sailor, Luis, said that Gantley went out on one of his boats on the water but he'll be at Father Joe's at lunch time. The sailor wants for David to heat to his room but he as a pinkie issue so he's an alien. Gantley is in a row boat and pull up to the Ship. He boards and looks around. A sailor comes up behind him as Gantley finds a mysterious machine, but too late. The alien uses the metallic object and kills Gantley.

Out for a walk, David strolls past a church, attached to a fine big house. He's waiting for Gantley as two teens work on a hot rod outside. Inside, Father Joe and his daughter Lisa appear to be also waiting. Lisa has been on edge for a couple of weeks. The doorbell rings and its David who is looking for Gantley who is having lunch there. Father Joe says he was expecting him a half an hour ago. "I'm father (Joe) Carelli." The phone rings and Carelli is told by Luis something. He hangs up and we come to find that Gantley is dead. David asks how it happened "Was it an accident?" "Cerebral hemorrhage," he says. David knows what it was. Father Joe leaves Vincent in the house with Lisa. He asks for papers or any reports but she knows nothing. "You might check his room at the inn," she says.

She says he was a very strange man. David walks into the church area of the complex and someone e is playing the organ. The quiet suited alien walks in and closed the door behind him. The organ player looks equally ominous. The suited man reaches in his pocket and they encircle David who tries to make a run for it. A fight ensures. David is jumped from behind by the organist. David kicks his ass. The suited alien has the metallic disk and they fight. David reverses it, places it on the aggressor's neck, and the alien glows red and dies.

The other man gets up and he and David continue fighting. The hot rodders are outside while the fight takes place. David judo flips the organist and ends up getting knocked out. The organist picks up the metallic orb and the teens are at the door. He leaves and the teens get in as the organ is playing because David has fallen on it. They go over to revive Vincent.

As cops pull away from the church Father Joe walks outside with a doctor, who has to go deliver a baby, tells him to keep things quiet. The doctor apologizes for not being able to do anything for Dr. Gantley "I know you were very close," he says as he drives off in his station wagon. Father Joe walks back inside the church. The organist has a computer system set up inside the church, very complex, he opens it up and begins operating it.

Dr. McLeuen calls out to Luis hoping there's not going to be another storm, and then both move on. Louis heads out on a small boat. Back in the house Lisa tells Father Joe that David had been saying crazy things, like he was out of his mind. David us upstairs resting. Lisa drugs the tea kettle that she is about to give to David. David is in best and Father Joe sits down to talk with him. Lisa overhears their conversation. Luis Perez owns the boat. Joe has been there three months and Luis has been there much longer. Lisa walks in intentionally to interrupt their conversation. The Father insists that Vincent drink the tea, not knowing it is drugged. She stares as he consumes it. Come on Lisa, let's leave Mr. Vincent alone." They leave the room.

David wants to tell him that Gantlet was murdered. "They tried to kill me when I tried to enter your church." When Father Joe asks who he's talking about, David says, "Beings from another planet." He says that the hurricane could have hit every big city from here to Washington and now there's another one coming. "These beings – what do they look like?" Joe asks. "Like us – just like us," David says. "Except some of them have a deformity of the hands." The drug is taking effect and David has to lie back down. David takes another sip of tea and passes out.

Father Joe is headed back to the Inn leaving Lisa alone downstairs. Back on Luis' ship. They are uncovering the machine and setting it. The organist at the church is at the helm inside the church and the machine on Luis boat is set. It begins to glow red as Luis gets back on his small boat and heads back to the mainland. Rays begin to penetrate the air and a hurricane being to materialize from the machine on the ship. Lightning and dark clouds take place.

David wakes up and its 4pm. (Why didn't' they kill this asshole when they had the chance?) He has a splitting headache as he realizes he's been drugged by the tea. He falls down and is in a daze. David staggers to the door, sweaty armpits and all, still dazed. He sees Lisa downstairs with the organist that he fought earlier. David tries to make it down the stairs but falls much of the way. He sees a phone but he's moving in slow motion. He reaches it but falls to the floor. Lisa rushes in and finds him unconscious. She snatches the phone from the wall as she looks down at a passed out David Vincent.

The winds are becoming increasingly fierce and Father Joe sees Luis in a hotel lobby and they are both concerned that this storm will be worse than the one that hit Tampa. Father Joe shares what Vincent told him with the doctor who is far too busy in the crowded area to deal with it. The phones are out and Luis volunteers to take Father Joe down to the area hospital. Off they go as back at the house Lisa continues to prepare drugged tea for a knocked out David. Why not just poison this asshole?What is the delay? Why do aliens get chance after chance to rid the earth of this single-minded butthole but sit around playing those "Joker versus Batman rig-the-special-death" type bullshit? Bust a cap in his ass and get on with the invasion, dammit!

Lisa pours the tea and tells him he's had a bad fall. He tells her he saw her talking to a man. She says there was no man. David tells her to call the cops because the man was one of the ones who attacked him in the church. She tells him he was imagining things. She hands him the drugged water and David rejects it. "Sooner or later you're going to have to eat or drink something. I can wait," she says. David looks at her. "They put you here, didn't they? I'm not going to drink. I could be driven insane." She tells him, "Only the first effects are like insanity," she says. "After another glass or two it will become like a dream," she calmly explains.

"And what happens to New York, Washington, Boston?" he asks. "This is just the beginning, isn't it? There will be other cities. Pretty soon the whole world," David babbles. "And what happens to Father Joe?" She says, "We wouldn't hurt him. He's been very good camouflage for us ever since he came to help us rebuild our church," she says. "Your church?" he asks. She tells him that four months ago it was empty, which is why she took the assignment. Now she's mad. She walks over to David and tries to force the water on him. He knocks the glass out of her hand.

They begin to tussle and as David throws her on the couch, Father Joe, Luis Perez and another man walk in. Lisa, tells the entering group of men that David assaulted her. Joe sees her torn blouse and knocks the shit out of David, and then feels guilty for doing it and apologizes. "You're a sick man," he tells David. David wants to say something but Luis is behind Father Joe showing the metallic orb, implying he will use it if David says a word. David backs off.

David is escorted out as Father Joe remains behind to console Lisa. "I should have never left you here alone with him," he says. Now check this out. As Luis watches them leave, four men get into the car with Vincent in tow. One man in the front seat and one man on each side of David, who is riding bitch in the back seat. What kind of shit is this? Luis then heads into the church. He joins the quiet alien who David had fought with in front of the control panel. The simulated map shows the hurricane is headed for Miami.

The car with David in it runs into a police road block because of the storm. The men tell the cop with the flash light that they're taking David to the hospital. David tells him "They're going to kill me." The men say that David is sick and needs help. The cop says, "Mr. Vincent, I know each of these men. They wouldn't wanna hurt you or nobody." David's fast talking works: "IF I am sick, YOU take me to the hospital," he says. The cop goes for it. David then gets into the front seat with the cop as the others look on. What??? And check it out: the cop leaves with the sirens blaring!

Joe sends Lisa over to the inn, but first he has to stop at the church. He wants to say a prayer for Mr. Vincent. He feels badly that he treated David so badly. He is a true believer. She offers to come with him to the church and he agrees. The cop and Vincent pull up and the cop gets out of the car to tell the sheriff. When he does, David steals the police car. Father Joe and Lisa walk in and see Luis and the other man operating the alien machine. Father Joe is shocked but Lisa is not. "What's going on here?" he asks. Luis pulls a gun.

"Vincent was right. He was telling the truth the whole time. Why me? Why my church? Why did you seek me out/" Luis explains that Lisa was put in Father Joe's house to watch him, and if he got out of line, to kill him. Father Joe tries to stop the computer operator but Luis knocks him out with a blow to the head with the butt of his gun. Father Joe gets on his knees and prays. Meanwhile Jesus …. I mean David… pulls up outside of the church in the police car. He can't get in the front door so he goes around to the side. He climbs through a window (which happens to be unlocked) and sneaks upon the group. "When will I die?" he asks Lisa. "When Luis says so," she answers.

The hurricane is at full throttle. Father Joe says that he was praying for Lisa. As they talk David crawls in on his stomach. David jumps Luis and the gun hits the floor. Father Joe now has it. Meanwhile, Luis the alien takes suicide pill and jumps atop the computer machine, destroying it as well. Joe has Lisa and the alien at gunpoint and threatens to shoot. "Whatever lives is a child of God, isn't that what your religion preaches, rather?" Lisa asks. "Priest or hypocrite? Which are you?" I think I know which. Priest." Joe lowers the gun. David grabs is and limps behind the escaping duo but loses them.

Let me interject something regarding that "priest or hypocrite" issue. I view them as overlapping realities. In order to be a priest you have to accept some of the most misogynistic and racist tenets ever developed. You have to swear to things that you don't practice. And in far too many cases, you like to screw young boys in the butt. So to be a priest is to be a hypocrite but not to the religious tenets of racist Christianity: *you are a hypocrite to natural laws and the laws of humanity.*

Moving on, the next day David's taxi has arrived at Father Joe's house. "Any news about Luis' fishing boat?" David asks. Father Joe says that it will probably wash up on a beach but David says he doubts it. "They always disappear," David says to Father Joe. David surmises that they would allow the hurricane to hit them this time because if they allowed it to once again bypass Matthews Beach it might arouse further curiosity. Father Joe says, "I'm sorry your search had to end like this. I couldn't let you kill last night – not as a priest." David says "I understand." "I'll pray for your success David," he says. "Pray for us all," David replies as he heads out the door

"Two men, two searches. One searching heaven and earth. The other searching in the corridors of the human conscience. The search continues." More philosophical bullshit in an attempt to elevate Vincent's mission to the level of sacred observance. How are you going to "search the heavens" when the "enemy" that you are sworn to kill – beings from another planet – are from those "heavens." Give me a break.

.14. "Panic"

A young man flags down a truck and tells the driver that his mother is dying and that he needs a ride. "It's my mother. She's had an accident back at the house. I've got to get to town to get a doctor," the boy yells. "Look pal, that's against company rules," one of them says. The boy continues to plead and the two uniformed men in the truck fall for it. (By the way, before the boy gets into the truck and just so happens to sit on the passenger side, the reason is because these two men were seated with one of them behind the wheel and the other sitting directly behind him in the back seat. What kind of bullshit is this?

He gets in and as they head down the road, he sees two men parked on the side of the road in a car, panics, and asks to be let out. The drivers stop and the boy gets out and runs down the gully on the side of the road, but the men in the car spot him. As the truck heads on, the two men speed to where the boy got out of the truck, stop their car and go after him.

The men in the truck have their own problems. For some reason they are still seated the same way. The one in the back seat notices the driver swerving and asks if he's alright. The driver says that his arm is hurting in the same spot where "the kid grabbed me." A farmer in a white pickup pulls over to help and opens the passenger door. He and the man in the back seat look on as the driver is now bent over the wheel, apparently frozen to death. "He's frozen like a block of ice. It's summer," says the second driver.

The narrator tells us, "A truck driver's bizarre death only added to the growing panic in a remote corner of West Virginia. Nine had died in a 48 hour period – all frozen. Six hours ago it became the responsibility of Dr. George Grunday of the United States Public Health Service, to bring this epidemic to an end – to find an answer to deaths to which medical authorities had found no answer. " (Can you find an answer to an "epidemic"?)

The narrator continues: "One man suspects the nature of this true and terrifying blight. That its sources lie somewhere out in the vast reaches of space. That man: David Vincent."

A cop actually introduces Vincent to the doctor in the hospital ward. "I think you should hear what he has to say," the cop says. "Alright Vincent, you've got a minute. I've heard you have a theory that is going to solve all my problems," Grunday says. "Not theories – facts," Vincent chastises him. It seems that David has already talked to the dead truck driver's partner, a man named Bagley. "Bagley said they picked up a hitch hiker, shortly before Larsen died, he touched him. Now you find that hitch hiker, you'll find the cause of all these deaths," David explains. "Is that a fact?" the doctor replies. "A man about 24 or 25 years old wearing a red plaid jacket."

The doctor's patience is wearing thin. "You listen to me Vincent. I interviewed this Joe Bagley less than an hour after his partner died. He didn't mention any hitch hiker." David says that he was afraid of losing his job (violation against picking up hitch hikers). Vincent has been doing his homework and has even taken a map and marked it up. "Now this is where the truck crashed; right here is where Bagley said the hitch hiker left the truck. Now two victims were found down here before the crash, an hour afterwards a linesman's body was found up here a mile into the hills. The trail leads right down the hill to Morgan's Corner."

David continues: "Now assuming the man is still on foot, that's who your men should be looking for – between Morgan's Corner and Top Pines Crossing." The doctor says, "That's all very interesting. As soon as some men become available, we'll check on it." No, they should have locked Vincent's ass up right then and there. He's too interested, has too much information and he's not even qualified to be "working a case," has shown no identification at all. For all these hick cops know he could be the one responsible!

Then, more gall as Vincent says, "Well give me a car and I'll check it myself." What? Give you a car, muthafucka? A police car? At taxpayers expense?

With no identification or nothing even remotely resembling a law enforcement credential? Lock this muthafucka up right now for having such supreme audacity!

One cop says he'll see what he can do while another one, in the background, has been eavesdropping and staring Vincent down – obviously an alien. (You seen one white man you seen 'em all). The alien cop contacts the two aliens who were looking for the kid. He is assigned to keep his eyes on David while the other two continue their search.

The aliens pull up in front of some kind of knick-knack shop and the kid is seeking directions. The old woman is trying but the kid is hyper. He lies and claims that he just wants to be with his girl but the father is looking for him. He then comes over the counter and ducks behind it, continuing to plead his false case. The two suited aliens enter the woman lies to protect the kid as he crouches down. They know she's lying. "He may be back this way. We'd appreciate it if you'd keep your eyes open. And be careful – he may be dangerous," one of the aliens tells her. They leave the premises and she gets on the phone. She knows the kid is lying. He tells her to put down the phone. He takes the phone from her and hen touches her hands. He smiles, pats her hands and leaves.

A cop car with David and the friendly cop speed toward Willow Creek. The alien cop is in the back seat. The top at the curio shop and go in. Other cops are there and the woman is found dead, frozen to death. He and the cop are going to split up and meet at Prince Crossing. The kid is on the run. David sops at a gas station and the attendant tells him others asked about the guy in the red jacket. One detective is still in the wash room. David goes back and the deputy is dead. His gun is gone. The aliens got him. The other deputy took off after the kid. "That truck out front – is that yours?" "Yeah" And David, promising to bring it back later, just gets in the station's truck and takes off. What kind of shit is this?

David catches up to the cop, passes him up and turns onto a dirt road. He sees the kid. "Need a ride – climb in," he says. The cops sees David pick the kid up. The kid jumps in. David speeds to the closed down motel. The cop car pulls up. The cop pulls his gun and starts looking for David. David bushwhacks him and takes his gun, knocking him out. The kid runs for it but David stops him. David tells the kid – "you drive." He still has the gun on him.

As David the kid drive off the cop wakes up. The kid's name is Nick – Nick Baxter ((Keep in mind this surname of "Baxter" because it is used in several episodes). He's behind the wheel and David is on the passenger side holding a gun on him, and yet tells him his name. "Keep your hands on the wheel. I know who you are and what you are," David says. David puts on some gloves and says "you know what the gloves are for." David tells him he's taking him to the sheriff. I didn't mean for them to die. I couldn't help myself. I can't help being sick," Nick says. "We're not all animals, believe me Mr. Vincent. We're not all bad – just like human beings aren't all good. You've had your Capones, Neros, Hitlers. So have we. The rest of us have to take orders whether we like it or not. Mr. Vincent, believe me – a lot of us don't like what we have to do."

Time for a white privilege teaching moment. This "great man" approach to identifying who the "bad guys" in history are is another white dupe.

David stares at him: "That's what the Nazis said after they'd taken Europe." The kid hits the brakes and David tells him to keep driving. "You'll have to hear me out or shoot me," Nick says. "I'll do just that. I'll blow your head off before I let you contaminate another human being," David says. Nick says he'll make a deal with him. "This sickness – it's a kind of virus, its communicated by touch, slow death for me, freezing horrible death for your kind. Only my own people can help me. You get me to them and - I'll give you evidence of our invasion plans. Better evidence than me. We've just built a new landing site near here, a saucer is coming in tomorrow morning, just after dawn. When it takes off again, I want to be on board." "Where does that leave me," David asks.

"We'll be at the landing soon," Nick says. He tells David he can have the authorities waiting when they land. David continues to point the gun. "Drive."

The alien cop calls the other two suited ones from his police car and describes the direction that Vincent, Nick and the truck are headed. He then also takes off to follow. The suited cops form a blockade on the dirt road and here comes the truck. Nick comes to a stop. He recognizes them. David tells him to turn off over there, which Nick does. The aliens are now in pursuit down the long dirt road. David keeps Nick from running over a couple that are bicycling and off the road they go into a small marsh. "I suppose you never intended to kill those kids out there, huh?" David asks. They must now abandon the truck. "Move out." (What about the station you borrowed the truck from, asshole?)

The bikers come around the corner and look at the wreck and David shouts for them to get out. They vacate immediately. At the same time the suited aliens in the car appear, guns in hand. They check the truck and begin their search on foot.

David and Nick are walking around and getting deeper and deeper into shrubbery and forestry. Nick tells him that a dozen of "his people" are looking for them right now. "You can still save yourself." Nick says. "By letting you go? Forget it," David replies. "Tell me something: just who you trying to save? Your precious mankind? Are they really worth it?" Then there is a sound in the nearby brush. "Face it, Mr. Vincent: they're savages." David looks at him and asks, "And what are you?"

David tells Nick to get on his feet but they begin to tussle. David, still gloved, has the gun as the two tumble in the deep grass. David tosses Nick off and retrieves the gun. The sound in the trees gets David's attention and he orders whoever it is to come on out. It's a young woman, about Nick's age. David asks her if she lives near there and she says yes. Her eyes and those of Nick's continue to lock on each other. David gets to his feet and asks her if she has a phone. Nick prepares to speak but David tells him to shut up. She says she doesn't have a phone and Nick says, "Go on, get out of here!" Again, David tells her to shut up. "Don't let him frighten you. He's trying to scare you away so I can't get help," David tells the girl. "I have to get in touch with the sheriff. He'll tell you if I'm dangerous or not." (What?)

David asks her where her house is and she slowly leads the way, with Nick behind her and David, with gun, bringing up the rear. As the three walk up an old man sops chopping wood as the dog barks. Her name is Madeline. David tells the older man he's working with the sheriff. "The nearest phone is down at the Bugler Café, about three miles walkin'," the old man says. The old man tells David he looks rather peeked and says he could make the call for him for a price. David asks how much. The man says ten bucks. David says how about just being a good a citizen? He asks David and David says he has no money and extends his hand. David cocks the gun. The man turns back to David "Five bucks up front." The old man takes off: "I'll be back in a couple of hours." He's carrying a shotgun with him.

Madeline, David and Nick enter the house. David locks the door. He gives the gloves to Nick. "You wear these from now on," he says. David gives the small house the once over and then asks her if they have any rope. She tells him yes and he just so happens to walk over to the table and get some. He orders Nick to stand up against the support pole in the middle of the room and ties him to it. He germane shepherd just sits there and since their arrival, has not barked a single time.

Madeline asks, "You gotta tie him up like that?" David ignores her. "Want me to watch him for a while?" she asks. "When do you think your father will be back?" David asks. (The old man had told him "a couple of hours"). "Some time after dark" she says. She and Nick cannot stop staring at one another.

The two aliens and the alien cop meet with the owner outside of the Bugler. An innocent, she tells them she hasn't seen a man in a red plaid jacket being accompanied by another guy. The cop leaves to go check out a possible siting and the two suited aliens go into the small café to have some coffee. Back at the cabin Nick continues to work on David as the girl is standing over the oven preparing Nick some eggs. "You really should get some sleep, Mr. Vincent. It's a cinch I'm not going anywhere," he says. Then he turns his attentions to Madeline.

"I guess living way out here you don't get to town very often, do ya," Nick asks. She says she likes it there and Nick says, "You're kind of lucky – it's nice out here, clean air, nobody buggin' ya." As she heats something up on the grill she says sarcastically, "Sure, it's great. Every girl's dream." HE tells her, "At least it's out of the rat race. Not like …." "Not like where?" she asks, continuing to focus on the food she's preparing. He says "forget it" and that he doesn't want to talk about it.

So David cockblocks. "He wants you to help him get away," Vincent says. She brings a plate of food over and stoops next to Nick. "He was right," Nick says. "That's what I was angling for. Wouldn't you be doing the same thing if you were me?" As he stares deeply into her eyes he asks, "Do you know what it's like to be a prisoner? To have the whole world fall in on ya?" There's no way out. How would you know? How in the heck would you know? She's falling for it and looks over her shoulder to David: "What do you want me to do with these eggs? He can't eat with his hands tied."

"His hands stay tied," David says. The girl is exasperated. "Oh yeah, he's dangerous. You've got the gun, but he's dangerous." She stands up: "Why don't you let him make a break for it? Then you can have the fun of killing him?" She walks off into a back room and David decides to follow her back there – to "explain."

But she cuts him off: "Alright, I promise I won't try to help him," she says. David says, "If you do decide to try to help this handsome, clean-cut all-American boy, you could very well become victim number eleven." (Pay close attention to the white nationalist description that Vincent gives of Nick – an alien who only LOOKS human, but still white is white, right?)

Madeline retorts, "Look mister, why don't you stop treating me like I just got off the Christmas tree, huh?" (What?) She tells him, "I been to the big city. I been married and I been ditched. And it takes a lot of man to fool me." David tells her, "He's a good salesman. Ten people are dead because they listened to him. She walks out of the room and Nick starts in on her once again. "Madeline, I never killed anyone." She turns some music on. "I'd like to think you believe me," he says. "I was miles away when it happened. I can prove that." She sips on coffee. "Do you have witnesses?" He tells her he was on his way to catch up with them but "Vincent caught up with me."

He tells her the witnesses don't live far away. As he talks to her David is drowsy and fighting to stay awake. He then falls to the floor, with the gun remaining on the table. Madeline walks over to Nick: "Look you tell me who they are and maybe I can go see them for you." He tells her he has to go himself. "Help me Madeline – I've got to go see those witnesses." She's standing right next to him as his hands remain tied behind the post. He tells her to "take a chance on me" and that once he talks to the witnesses, he'll give himself up. She cuts the music off.

By the time David comes to they are both gone, and so is the gun. A car pulls up as the old man returned. He has two aliens with him. David grabs the rifle and shoots one who glows and dies. The old man watches as a second one is killed. He can't believe it "What was that?" what happened?" Where's Madeline he shouts shaking the hell out of Vincent.

Meanwhile Nick and Madeline are walking with the dog. She says that she doesn't remember seeing any houses where they're headed. The dog is barking and Nick says "all that racket could give us away," he says. He then reaches down, bare handed, and touches the dog, knowing he is killing it. Back at the cabin Gus and David study a map. Gus says they should drive to the sheriff's office. David tells him there's no time. "If people die as soon as he touches 'em, what'll happen to Madeline," he asks. "As long as he needs her he won't' harm her," David assures him. "After he gets there, then what?" Gus asks. "We just have to get there first," David says.

Sill perusing the map, Gus says, "Wait a minute. There is a little meadow. How big is one of those things?" The meadow is called Idlewild Flat, and that is where Gus and David head for in the dark of the night. Madeline is calling for Charlie the dog but no answer. Nick says he went home on his own and she wants to look for him. Nick pulls the gun on her. "I haven't come this far just to get lost. Now move," he tells her at gunpoint.

Gus and Vincent come upon Charlie who is as frozen stiff as a board. They are still less than a mile from Idlewild Flats. "It's going to be light soon, let's go<" David says. Morning comes and they've arrived at the Flats. There they see the saucer and a loading truck. "Dear God" Gus exclaims. "Up until now I didn't care if the whole world dropped dead. But when you realize it suddenly can happen ..." Gus says.

Madeline and Nick come walking up the meadow. Gus wants to take the ladder up the tower. Vincent tells him to wait as he heads down toward the couple. Nick is becoming increasingly ill. David drop kicks him from behind and snatches Madeline and off they run. Nick staggers and follows. The saucer continues loading and Madeline has seen it. Now Nick sees it. David tells Madeline to stay behind. Nick heads for the saucer. Gus fears that they'll all get away. Nick is climbing the tower to communicate. Nick sees him and aims the gun. He shoots at Gus. Nick shoots him but not before Nick can sound the alarm. Nick continues shooting and Gus falls to his death.

Nick turns and heads toward the saucer. The saucer is hovering and glowing as he walsk under it. The ship fires a single beam and destroy Nick and off they go. Madeline rushes to her father's body.

David is driving and Madeline is headed toward the city. He offers to drive her but she says she wants to be alone. She asks why her father did it. " guess he thought the rest of the human race was worth saving, too." "Did we really see that saucer?" she asks "Yes we did."

David drops her at the bus depot. Thank you, Mr. Vincent. Goodbye."

Freezing deaths apparently ended, and an alien landing site exposed. Grudging victories for David Vincent. But the invader still walks unheeded on the planet Earth. Somehow, some way – he must be stopped."

Strange. That's the same thing that the First Nation people said about the white man when he first staggered onto American shores. Interesting that the aliens in "The Invaders" are hated by people who are "aliens" themselves.

.15. "Moonshot"

Again, we find ourselves in the "Florida Keys (recall the episode, "Storm") and it's eight days before the first United States moonshot is scheduled. Two astronauts on vacation, Marlin fishing.

Major Banks and his pal appear stranded as something is wrong with the boat they are on. A copter hovers above a boat, two aliens at the helm. First a dark red gas covers the boat the then flies off. A man on the shore sees it. It looks like a fog but when the window is opened below deck, a gas enters and the men appear to fall dead. One crawls to the radio and gives a call for help. "Something happened. It's not fog. Red – I can't breathe," and then he dies.

According to the narrator, "The nation had been stunned. The newspapers screamed of a fishing accident and a strange, inexplicable red fog. Two men slated to walk on the face of the moon … had perished. For David Vincent there was an answer, terrifying in its implications. And so he came to the Florida Keys to find the radio operator who had received the last words of the dying astronauts.

Bear in mind that the first man to walk on the moon was Neil Armstrong but that didn't take place until July 16, 1969, meaning that this particular episode was ahead of its time. Apollo 11 also included astronauts Edwin "Buzz" Aldrin and Michael Collins, but Armstrong was the one who stepped onto the moon.

Back to the story.

David pulls up in the parking lot and walks up on a crowd of reporters. There's a press conference going on inside the building. David has no credentials and is trying to walk in with the press crowd but the security guard stops him and asks for a pass. David, a pathological liar it seems, tells him he left his pass at the studio and that the press conference was put together so fast he must have left it behind. As a former newspaper editor and journalist, you do not leave a press pass behind when you're going to a press conference because you KNOW you are going to have to present it.

The guard insists, so David shows him is driver's license. As soon as the guard sees it he says, "David Vincent." He seems to recognizes the name. David says he has to get inside and the guard says that he has to go check the name with the "security office." He tells David to wait there as another guard is standing behind him.

An eyewitness, Charlie Coogan saw it, and he is being questioned inside an office. They want to know if anyone else saws what he saw and he tells them no. But he's homeless and lives on the beach "I saw fog out there, red fog. I haven't had a drink in six days," he says. A man hands the interrogator Vincent's ID. "So he did come," he says. "Send him in, Gavin Lewis, head of security says. He tells one of the guards to take Mr. Coogan home. The phone rings. It's Angela, his wife. She has to tell him something about Hardy. She says she'll wait for his call as Gavin stares at Vincent's license. In walks David. "I'm Gavin Lewis, security," he says. Vincent comes straight out with it: "I want to talk to that radio operator." "What do you want with him, Mr. Vincent," Lewis asks.

"Information about what he heard," David says. Who does this asshole think he is, walking in off the street, no press credentials, demanding information about it obviously a very delicate matter? "You can get that out of the newspapers tonight, can't you?" Lewis asks. "I said COMPLETE information," David replies. "I had a check run on you, Mr. Vincent. I know who you are and what this obsession of yours is," Lewis says. "Men from another planet, aliens. Alright, that happens to be your particular hang-up. What does that have to do with us?"

Stop right there for a minute: there you have it again – "Men" from another planet. Men? Don't you mean "beings" or "creatures." The use of terms like "people" and "men" interchangeably with aliens make the so-called invaders sound like some Mexican immigrants! But the subtle racism behind the point is that since the aliens have chosen to adopt the white man's physical form, they get the benefit of the doubt even over "non-white" human beings. After all, to be "non-white" means to be "less than" white or "without" whiteness which automatically assigns you to a category of inferiority.

Back to the episode. Vincent tells Lewis, "I know how those astronauts died, and what that red fog is. I wanna know why they died."

Right there folks: *arrest this muthafucka*. How could he know what it is unless he had something to do with it? Detain this sonofabitch until we find out exactly how he is involved. But no, he's white and he benefits from white privilege. So we must continue with the illogical dialogue.

"Well, they weren't killed by men from Mars I can promise you that," Lewis says. "It happens that it was a form of carbon monoxide." David won't be fooled. "Oh yes, RED carbon monoxide, carbon monoxide you can see" "What is it with people like you? One weird story and every screwball in the country thinks he can get into the act? Even that old man down on the beach says that he saw a red fog." HE talks too much as David's eyes light up. Then a man bursts in to tell him that he can't stall the media any longer.

"Where is this old man? I'd like to talk to him," David says. "Oh no, not until I've had a chance to check on his story, nobody gets near Mr. Googan's place, nobody." Now Vincent has a name. Now check this out: he then tells David, "Now you wait here until I'm done." Wait in his office? With the door closed? David Vincent who you earlier admitted was a fuckin' nut? "Are you holding me?" David asks. "You know I have no authority to do that, Mr. Vincent. You're also smart enough to be here when I get back," Lewis says as he leaves the office. As soon as he closes the door, David sneaks out the sliding glass door window on the other side of the office. Duhhhhhh.

On the beach is the homeless Coogan who is being hypnotized with an orb of some kind by the security guard who is telling him he never saw anything. "I saw nothing. I made it all up," he says. He's been brainwashed. "You made it all up just to get your name in the papers." Vincent drives up and the cop stands there while David talks to Coogan who has clearly been hypnotized. The security guard tells David "That's enough." David knows he's an alien. He pulls a gun and tells David he has five seconds to get the hell out of Dodge. David, not surprisingly, gets a step on the cop and Judo flips him and knocks him out. He finds the orb. The fight is on again. David is getting his as kicked and gets KOd. The man grabs the orb out of the sand and runs off.

The guard's name is Correll and he is taking off as Lewis and his aide, Riley run up and see the cop car speeding off. David charges Lewis with a set up and says Correll ted t kill him. "was Correll part of the setup or was killing me his idea? David accusingly asks Lewis. He tells him to talk to Mr. Coogan after telling Lewis that Correll "is one of them – he's an alien!" He adds, "He's wiped everything out of his mind." Now Coogan says he made it all up. Lewis says "Mr. Coogan you told me…" David now has evidence. You'll never find Corral. He's done his job." "Okay Vincent, we better talk." David picks up Correll's gun and they head back

Correll has arrived back at Lewis office telling the security guard that he has a briefcase to put into Mr. Lewis' car. The guard approves it. Correll does so.

Meanwhile, David and Lewis are in Lewis' office going through paperwork. The paperwork shows that there's nothing wrong with Charlie Coogan. "Did you think that it would?" David asks. David, acting as if he is somehow in charge, stands up as Lewis paces the floor and tells him. "You know, I think it's about time you levelled with me. You give me just enough information to keep me curious, you practically SENT me to Charlie Coogan's place, Why?"

Lewis then spills his guts about his past. It seems that before he took the chief of security job, he was an astronaut who was selected for the moon mission, has his own ideas. . Lewis himself was once selected for the Moon mission, the same one scheduled to go up this week, but something happened one night. As he tells it: "A couple of months ago I was driving home from the Space Center, top physical shape, nothing wrong with me. I was listening to the car radio, and all of a sudden the radio went dead. After that, I don't remember anything. I don't remember going home, going to bed – nothing, until my call service woke me up in the morning. I didn't feel well, and when they checked me out, they found that my blood pressure had gone crazy. Consequently, they washed me out of the space program. But I knew – I KNEW nothing was wrong with my blood pressure. And when I tried to tell 'em, when I tried to make them see, they looked at me like I was some kind of section 8 case. I lost a night out of my life, David. I want to find out where that night went – and why. Maybe you have the answer.

David tells him that they are not going to find the answer in his office. "Whatever it is, it must be at the launch site," David says. Off they go. The valet goes to fetch Lewis' car as he and David wait on the curb. He claims to be in top shape but both he and David chain smoke throughout the episode. "What are we going to do when we find one of these aliens? Are they going to walk up and introduce themselves?" Lewis asks. David smiles. "You said yourself that they look like one of us." Ah-hah!

"There are ways of recognizing them," David says. "First of all, they have to regenerate themselves, and they have an oddness about the hands, a mutated fourth finger. And in f act they have no heartbeat. As David is explaining, Lewis' car glows red and disappears. The suitcase was sabotaged and the poor valet bit the dust. Lewis is standing there with Vincent and witnesses the glowing disappearance of the car. "What was that?! What in the name of Heaven?" Lewis exclaims.

The next day Lewis walks into the office as Riley is doing paperwork. Lewis has been replaced in the astronaut pool by a man named Hardy Smith. Vincent is crashing at Lewis' apartment and Lewis wants to make sure that he (Vincent) gets a security clearance and arrives at the launch site on time. He orders Riley to get ahold of McNally and send over any paperwork or information that he might have

on the backup crew. Commander Smith's wife is waiting in the office for Lewis –
Riley let her in.

Lewis orders Riley that if anyone asks where Vincent is staying to say that
"you don't know." Then he enters his office. Angela is glad to see him, they touch
hands. "Gavin, Hardy will be going up, there is no question," she says. She adds
that she doesn't think he ought to go. She says she believes that there is something
wrong with him. Lewis tells her that now that they've set the date for the launch he
believes she's just nervous. She told Hardy that she had been seeing Lewis and "he
wasn't even jealous." "How can I make you understand? What can it mean that he
has complete lapses of memory? He can't remember the simplest things: the places
that we've gone, or the friends that we knew or even how I like my martinis.

Lewis explains to her that Hardy went through a great deal in Vietnam. "But
if there were anything wrong with him physically or emotionally, the doctors
would have found it out months ago." Then there is a knock on the door. It's Riley
notifying Lewis that it's time to leave for the airport. She says she also has to be at
the airport when Hardy lands. – they want photographs "of the brave astronauts
wife." "Can you come to the house tonight to see Hardy? Please Gavin?" she begs.
He tells her he'll try and she leaves the office.

The airplane lands and David walks in and meets Lewis who asks if anyone
followed him. David says, "no." hardy enters the lobby to a waiting throng of news
men and his wife while Lewis and David watch. David notices a suited man
standing nearby with an mutated fourth finger – an alien. Lewis greets Hardy and
shakes his hand. "I don't think I've envied anybody so much in my whole life," he
says, as Angela stands next to Hardy. "The way you pushed me, the things you
taught me. I wouldn't be doing this if weren't for you," Hardy says. He promises to
look in on him later as Hardy and Angela leave.

David walks over to Lewis. "Who is that man?" "That's Owens," Lewis
says. "Check him." David says. "He's been with the program ever since it started,"
Lewis says. "Gavin – check him," David demands. Lewis shakes his hand in
compliance.

Back at the apartment Hardy is resting on the couch. Angela is sitting on a
chair nearby drinking tea as the doorbell rings. She rushes to the door as he tells
her, "I'm the one who's supposed to get the jitters." He tells her, "It'll all be over
in a couple of days. Let 'em in." Then he goes into a back room and closes the
door. It's the doctor to give Hardy his physical. He asks that she and Peggy go to a
movie tonight. He almost orders her to do so. Angela knocks on the door and tells
him the doctor is in. He's in the bathroom and reaches for what appears to be an
electric razor. But it's something else. He plugs it in. He's energizing himself –
he's an alien!

Lewis and Vincent are in the office at the launch site as Lewis threads a movie projector. He tells Vincent that he checked out Owens who is a medical technician from Detroit and he's checked out ever since he became a part of the program . "I checked his file myself," he says. "Why waste time looking at this film? If you think one of these astronauts is an alien – or all three of them – then forget it," Lewis says. "They've been checked and re=checked, we know who they are, where they were born, when they blow their noses and when they scratch their backs."

David says, "The aliens want this moonshot to go up, and they want this special crew to be on it. Why?" He continues: "Why would they go through so much trouble, just to stop two men from walking on the moon?" Lewis tells David to shut the blinds as David demands to know "the real reason for this moonshot." "If this were simply a walk on the moon your people would have postponed the flight and given the backup people more time," David insists. He tells David that he's told him everything that is unclassified. "I'm a security officer, remember? Vincent closes the blinds as Lewis starts the film.

According to the film three men were chose but only two will actually step on the moon. The man in the capsule will be Dr. Martin Daniels, the youngest man to have flown 31 combat missions in the Korean War. The second member is Colonel Tony LaCava, one of the two men who will walk on the face of the moon. The only surviving member of the original moonshot crew, Macaba was born in Sioux Falls, South Dakota. Now captain of the team, he can be considered the grand old man of the crew. The most recent member of the crew, Navy Commander Hardy Smith, born in New York City in 1935. He volunteered for special duty in Vietnam where he won the Presidential Medal of Valor and the Purple Heart.

While still in Vietnam he was chosen for the astronaut program. Commander Smith underwent medical treatment before reporting to the space agency. In the film he's bandaged up and Vincent says he wasn't hardy Smith. On his way home from Saigon, according to Lewis, his hotel caught a terrorist bomb. The way that you see him now – well the plastic surgeons did a pretty good job. David tells Lewis, "There is an alien on the crew. It's Hardy Smith." Lewis says, "I know Hardy Smith, I'm a close friend of his family. Oh no, you've really gone off the deep end."

Vincent is insistent. "Who was the first man who got assigned to the moonshot program? Tony LaCava, Lewis says. "Well scratch him. If they wanted to get rid of him they would have done it right away. Now, who ranked next – who came after LaCava? Lewis says that he came next and David points out that that is when he started having that trouble with his blood pressure. "Then Banks and

Howell, right?" They're both dead. "Now the crew if LaCava, Daniels and Smith – that can't be Hardy Smith. They didn't change his face with plastic surgery. They got rid of him and substituted a man you CALL Hardy Smith with an alien."

Lewis says that he knew Hardy Smith then thinks back to what Angela told him. "Maybe that's what she meant, maybe that's why she thinks he's changed, maybe that's why she doesn't understand him." "It's not the same man, is it?" David asks. "Why send an alien up?" Lewis asks. David surmises that there is probably something that they saw on those reconnaissance photos from the moon. David starts barking orders and demands that Smith be investigated; he tells Lewis to check his files. "Now we have twelve hours before liftoff, you've got to find something!"

Vincent has literally taken over: he has secured security clearance, he is now bossing around the chief of security, he has convinced that man that aliens are going to sabotage the moon landing and he literally gives orders to both Riley and Lewis. He has even played film critic and social analyst and concluded that the real Hardy Smith was switched by the aliens. No evidence. No photographs and not a lick of proof. White privilege once again reigns supreme.

All Lewis can say in response to Vincent's non-stop edicts is, "God help us if we're wrong." Lewis goes to a man named Stan who can research Hardy's background. Supposedly, hardy Smith had issues with Lewis even before he left for Vietnam. Lewis claims that such a belief is based on issues from the past, but the other guy isn't so sure. Lewis continues to tell Stan, "That is not Hardy Smith!" A medical technician with Hardy Smith's records is summoned.

In the reconnaissance photos that came from a previous flight, some "objects" were spotted on the moon. Lewis has been convinced that the other two astronauts will not be around as witnesses and that the only person's word they'll have will be that of Hardy Smith. The medical technician arrives. It's Owens, the alien who gave Smith the checkup a day earlier. He tells Stan and Lewis that there are no abnormalities. Lewis says, "He's lying. He's one of them. He's an alien. Look at his hand.' Owens has a mutated fourth finger but Stan ignores it. He is going to recommend Lewis' early retirement as Owens leaves the room.

David is still in Lewis' office smoking yet another cigarette, re-watching the footage on the moon crew and Hardy Smith, in particular. Lewis walks in. "I did everything I could. I even saw Owens in there. He had that hand you told me about, but Stan wasn't buying any of it. In one hour that crew reports to the takeoff area and at dawn the shot goes up.

Now get this. Despite what he is just told David gets up and when Lewis asks him where he is going David pompously replies, "To the one person who can prove that Smith is an alien – his wife." And unceremoniously leaves.

A moment for interjection here regarding what Vincent just said and did and the concept of white privilege. The question is who in the HELL does he think he is? He goes to the homes of people without calling ahead, he drops in on high-ranking officials as if he is one himself, and he's always wrapped around somebody's wife or grabbing some woman by the arm as if to shake her back to her senses. This is known as sexual assault. This is known as stalking. This is known as a crime that is punishable by jail time – that is, if David Vincent were a Black or Brown man. But he's white and as you know, America is a majority white nation and those in that majority get the benefit of, you guessed it: white privilege.

Moving on: Vincent arrives at the house and knocks. Angela answers the door. "I'm David Vincent – a friend of Gavin Lewis," he says. He has an idea that what is going on is more than just Hardy and Gavin being "good pals." He says, "I have some information about your husband, can I come in?" Before she can answer and while in mid-excuse for him NOT to enter her home, David slides right past her. He notices right away that she has suit cases packed. "You going away?" he nosily asks. "Yes. I'm going back to Houston. What business of it is yours?"

First of all, if it wasn't any of his business and since you just met him, why in the FUCK are you telling him where you're headed? "On the morning of your husband being shot to the moon, you're not even going to watch the lift off?" he asks. She says she doesn't want to watch it and the nosey Vincent then has the gall to say, "You're running away. Why?" Then he answers his own question: "You know, don't you? You know that's not your husband – that's not Hardy Smith. Liftoff is less than three hours away – you're the only one who can stop it," he tells her.

Cut to lift off. Lewis is present when the white van pulls up and all three astronauts, already suited down, get out and head for the launch pad. "This is what it's all about, isn't it?" he asks Lewis. One of the astronauts shouts back. "Hey Hardy – you gonna join us?" He turns to Lewis: "Gavin, more than anybody else in the world, you're the one I owe all this to." Then after offering him to ride up with him and being turned down because "My job is down here," Hardy tells Lewis: "Look ol' buddy, if something happens to me up there, you take care of Angela." Then he turns and walks away.

Stan is there to shake their hands as they prepare to strap in for the trip. Back at the house David continues to grill Angela. "Would Hardy do to you the things you say he has done?" he asks. She says that he has changed in so many ways, his tastes, how he changes the subject when she wants to talk about the past. David tells her that this is not the same man and that people will die if she doesn't act. David tells her that Gavin Lewis knows as well and suggests that she try to get through to Hardy because there must be some kind of test she can put him through.

David grabs her: "Call him – please call him!! And then turns, picks up the phone and HE dials the number himself! While they are waiting to head to the space craft, a call is piped through to "Commander Smith." It's Hardy's wife. David is standing there listening to her. She says she just called to say good luck and he says thanks, and that's it. She gets off the phone and tells David that she wished him luck: "Hardy's superstitious and always had been. He's like a child about that one thing. Nobody wishes him good luck." Now she knows for sure. "It's not Hardy."

David gets on the phone and calls the block house. She hands the phone to her and Lewis gets on the phone. She tells him she has proof it's not Hardy. Lewis calls Stan over and she relays the message: She says that man is an impostor who is a part of some terrible plot. That man is not Hardy Smith. I'm his wife – I know." Smith is summoned to report to control immediately. He hears the command but he and the other astronauts are already being locked in. HE pushes his way into the rocket after running across the gang plank. He turns everything on by himself and the rockets are ready. Technicians are ordered to leave immediately. The countdown has been sopped but the rocket is attempting to take off.

Up it goes. The space vehicle has lifted off and is about three miles over the ocean. It blows up.

Later that day Lewis and David meet in his office. Like Tony LaCava says, "You can't win 'em all," Lewis says. "Who says we lost?" David asks. What was seen in the reconnaissance photos is still up there and David surmises that it took the aliens a year to get a man that close and they can't risk it again. "Now they'll probably have to destroy that installation or whatever it is," David says. "If they do, we've won."

Owens has disappeared and the "official statement" is given to Lewis. They claim Hardy went berserk and there will be a major investigation. "We just have to wait and see," David says. "And I'll keep trying," Lewis says. Hardy's wife is waiting for Lewis downstairs.

"In the far reaches of outer space, the invader reorganizes his plan for the conquest of the Earth. He's been delayed but he hasn't been beaten." David looks out of the window from Lewis' office and sees Lewis and Angela walking arm and arm to the car awaiting them in the parking lot.

So despite the fact that the Earth is crawling with human impostors and is on the precipice of being "invaded" by them some security and solace can be found in the fact that a white man and a white woman can still feel "safe" enough to go home, have a martini and have unbridled sex. Talk about a fairy tale!

.16. "Wall of Crystal"

A couple sees a truck run off the road. They go to help as a man staggers out from the passenger, glows bright red, then burns up. The female sees it and her man says his leg is broken and since he's behind the wheel, she gets out and walks over to check on the other person who is in the truck. She has to cross the highway to get there but before she can she appears to have passed out. The groom manages to make it over to his new bride who is dead. He notices that the truck has turned over and several large canisters have spilled out, some type chemical rock that the truck was carrying.

He covers one of the rocks with dirt but begins to strangle and apparently dies. "An accident on a deserted highway. A honeymoon couple that dies by suffocation in the open air. A chemical truck traced to a company that doesn't exist. Strange circumstances for which David Vincent can find but one answer: somehow, some way, alien beings from another world must be involved."

David drives out to the site. He pulls over, walks over to the site as a man in binoculars, Taugus, is watching from a distance. David takes a dirt sample and pts it in a plastic bag. A rock still at the site makes him cough, but he collects it. Cut to a television station where Theodore Booth is a big time TV personality and newspaper reporter who wants to deal with Vincent's crusade. They go off the air and his boss walks up to him and tells him that he got a call from David Vincent. "Do you remember him?" Booth says, "Yeah, chicken little – claiming that the sky is falling in." "Don't underestimate him, Ted. A few months ago he almost had you convinced." "That man is a psycho. I warned him about bothering us." The man tells Booth that Vincent says he had proof and that it's worth investigating.

Vincent is waiting outside of Manufacturer's Bank as a cab pulls up and Booth steps out. David has placed the rock in a safe deposit box inside the bank and wants to show Booth. David says he's tried to call the police, the FBI and the CIA but the earliest he can get someone is tomorrow and he fears the proof may be gone by then. The alien Taugus is sitting in a car with a driver watching Vincent and Booth as they head into the bank.

David shows him the sample. "Whatever it is it does something to the air," David says. "The foliage around it was withered and dead and it (the rock) seems to shrink when exposed to the air. "David sets the rock out and then walks away but Booth says, "It looks like a piece of costume jewelry" and then begins to wheeze and lose his breath. Booth asks if he's had it analyzed. He tells David he's on his way to the press club and he'll have it analyzed. David tells him that having that rock could put his life in danger. Booth said he would warn the lab technicians to wear oxygen masks when analyzing it.. "The men (meaning "aliens," but since they're white, the terms can be used interchangeably it seems) know we have this crystal," Vincent says. The rock shrinks when exposed to air. Booth said if it checks out he will use his columns and his television show as a soap box."

As he prepares to leave he asks David how he would recognize these "creatures of yours". David says, "They look just like us. Some of them have awkwardness on their hand, a mutated fourth finger." David again warns him that if they know that he (Booth) is carrying the crystal, "There's no telling what they might do." He pats David on the shoulder and says, "Your paranoia is showing again, son," and he walks out of the bank vault. As David walks Booth out Booth tells him, "Call me tonight about seven. I should have a lab report by then."

David asks him if that is the same cab driver who brought him. Booth says it is, but when he prepares to get in the back seat an alien with the metallic disk lunges toward him. David snatches him out and they make a break for it. The cab takes off. "That was an alien weapon he had," David tells Booth. "Look, you've got to call McMullen right away and tell him you're about to write a series of articles about the existence of alien beings here on Earth." Booth is still skeptical but David assures him, "once you announce your plans they won't touch you. You'll draw too much attention to this story. Booth scurries inside to make the phone call.

David is walking to his car when Taurus walks up to him and says, "Mr. Vincent. I hope you've changed your mind about your little project." David gets into his car. As David prepares to drive off the alien says, "My regards to your brother – and his charming wife."

We then see the home of Dr. and Mrs. Robert Vincent – Robert is David's brother and they don't get along well. His wife, Grace, is an artist and is pregnant with what we find out later is going to be their first child. The doorbell rings and its David. Robert opens the door and he and David exchange a distant hand shake. David and Grace hug and Robert asks him what he's drinking. David says "nothing, I don't have much time …" Robert walks down into the living room and asks, "Mind if I make myself one?" As he mixes his drink he turns back to David: "Well, you're in a hurry: what's on your mind?"

He tells David, "I'll bet it's about those bogey men (he meant "boogey men") from outer space, isn't it? "Then David lowers the boom. "You're in trouble, you and Grace." Robert turns away and David follows. "I know what you think of me. You think I'm a crackpot, a sensationalist out to make a quick buck." David tells him that a couple of hours ago he (Robert) became a target for them."

Because of David's reputation as an alien hunting "nut case," his brother's reputation suffered and he (Robert) found it difficult to keep a job. He had stood behind David once before and feels that he never got anything out of it. In fact, he lost his practice because of it.

He asks Robert to call Theodore Booth at the San Francisco Courier. Then he says "After you call him, arrange for police protection, but don't wait. Bob, if you've ever believed in your life that I ever cared for you, please don't wait." David turns and leaves out the front door. After he's gone Grace says, "He's ill Bob. He needs help." "Yeah, I wish I could help him, I really do," and then the phone rings. It's a woman named Miss Endicott and she is seeking help. He gets the address and says he'll be there right away. In the meantime Grace is looking and before he leaves he says she's had a heart attack.

Robert pulls up at the Endicott house address but there is a for rent sin in the front yard. A woman comes out and meets him and they enter the house. Outside a white van pulls up. Two men come out carrying Robert's body and places it in a van. Back at Vincent's room two aliens wait. Taugus tell him that they have his brother and that he will be released if he (David) follows their demands.

"First, Theodore Booth is not to broadcast or print any information regarding our presence here. Secondly, Mr. Booth is to publish a column completely discrediting you that will contain your confession that you have lied about your experiences with us, and the day that that column first appears in print your brother will be returned to you." Taugus tells David that it would serve no purpose for them to kill him. "Unless I see that he's alright, unless I talk to him – no deal," David says. "I expected you to ask that," says the smiling alien. "He'll call tomorrow about this time. "I'll be waiting at his place," David says. "Oh, and if you value your brother's life, don't call the police" Taugus says as he coolly walks out the door.

David is back at Bob's house as a strange woman walks down the sidewalk. Inside the house David has shared the kidnap with Grace, who wants to know why. "We have no money," she says. "We can't pay a ransom." David kneels down and talks to her eye to eye as she's seated in a chair. "Haven't you listened to me from earlier today? He's my brother. As long as they have him they can keep me from talking to Booth. Now honey I didn't imagine this. They came to my hotel room and told me they had taken Bob."

She stands and is upset and asks why he hasn't called the cops. "Honey you don't know who you're dealing with ….he's their bargaining power. Without Bob they have nothing to hold over my head. Now let me do it my way – you've got to trust me!" "I do? Why? Because you're his brother? Because you say so? How can I trust someone who …." He cuts her off "…might be psycho. Do you really believe I am?" he asks. "Honey, they're going to let Bob call tomorrow at dinner time. Now at least let me talk to Booth before you ruin our once chance to get Bob out alive. Please Grace, please."

After saying she doesn't know anything anymore including who she is, she agrees to listen to David. "Your way. Do whatever you want. God help us if your way turns out to be wrong." Meanwhile a scientist is looking over one of the crocks. As he glances into the microscope with the door wide open, in creeps an alien in a suit. There's two of them. One turns on a gas tank and takes some papers. They leave before the scientist an turn around. When he does he tries to leave but the door is locked. A deadly invisible gas forming because of the rock, which is gradually disappearing. The doctor dies. In walks Booth. The door is locked and Booth enters and can smell the fumes. He molds his breath and finds Harry dead. He begins to wheeze but there's no more rock left – it has evaporated. He vacates the room and closes the door.

Booth picks up the phone and calls the police and reports the accident at Laboratory Analysts Incorporated. He wipes his fingerprints off the phone and leaves. Meanwhile Robert is being held and an alien comes into serve him food. Robet attacks him and knocks him out. He tries to leave where he is being held and notices some kind of lab right across the way. The rocks are being stored. Robert tries to make a run for it but ducks into the booth area. Now he's surrounded and trapped in a room where the rock fumes are getting to him. He comes out and remains surrounded. What an asshole.

Taugus comes out. "may I advise you to save your breath, doctor?" he asks. He tells him that he has agreed to allow him to make a telephone call. Robert refuses to make the phone call but changes his mind when the alien mentions his wife being subjected to "needless anxiety." Taugus says he can convince Robert to make the phone call. Meanwhile, David is in his hotel room trying to get through to Booth.

Back at the alien stronghold Taugus tells Robert that as a scientist he might find the glassed in lab interesting. "Those crystal clusters that you see in there are produced by combining a substance known as Micah, a catalytic agent found only on our planet…" "What does this have to do with me," Robert asks. "When exposed to Earth's atmosphere, those crystals displace the oxygen that is in the air." At that time Grace is pushed into the room by a female alien dressed as some kind of nurse's aide. Grace is in the Booth where the rocks are. Robert is frantic. "Get her out of there, she'll suffocate!" he screams.

Grace is beginning to choke as Taugus explains that breathing oxygen makes it difficult for them, which is why they have to regenerate ourselves. Grace is beginning to fall to her knees as she peers out of the glass prison. Grace has passed out as Robert agrees to make the phone call. "She'll be alright doctor. You just relax for a few hours. We have a phone call to make this evening."

David is now back at Robert and Grace's home banging on the door. A cab pulls up with Grace in it. They both go inside after the taxi leaves. "I think I saw him, David," she says. She said that a woman and two men came and blindfolded her and drove me to a factory of some kind. They took the blindfold off and pushed me into a room. All of a sudden I couldn't breathe – it was like I was drowning." David asks her if she saw Bob. "I think I did" she says but she's hysterical.

David tells her he wants her to pack her bags and get out of town. Just then the telephone rings. "That should be Bob," he says as he answers the phone. David tells him that Grace is alright and Bob tells him that he's "in deep water again, David." Taugus snatches the phone and asks, "Mr. Vincent: have you made the proper arrangements with Mr. Booth?" David says he's tried everything including leaving messages at the station. The alien tells him to "try harder" and that he has "until noon tomorrow.'

Robert's statement about "still in deep water" was some kind of clue for David. He tells her to go pack her things. She asks if Booth knows about Bob. David tells her not yet and she is concerned that Booth might print something before he reaches Booth. "What then?"

Cut to Booth in his dressing room who says they can't print anything. Booth's publisher is calling it "the biggest story of our time" and thinks David has run off. The publisher tells Booth to go to Santa Carla and find Vincent in time for tomorrow's edition. Booth tells him that the messages from Vincent say that they cannot release that information until he hears from Vincent. He says he's seen the information. He really believes they are here.

David is at the Santa Carla airport with Grace. David wired Grace's folks and she gives the key to the house to David. David keeps repeating "deep water again" to himself. He remembers a creek that he and Robert used to go when they were kids. . The old winery is thee – it has been deserted for years. Her plane leaves in five minutes. David is going there but first stops at his hotel room. David is on the phone trying to reach Booth once again and there is a knock on the door. It's Booth. He says he has a private plane he can use. "Is the project on or off?"

David says they can't go through with it. "They've kidnapped my brother." Booth pours himself a drink. After Booth prints Vincent's confession about lying about the aliens and the rest, that is when they will let Bob go. Booth gives it to David straight: "Your brother's life is one. Do you think that his life is more important than the entire human race?" David answers in a way that not only shows white nationalism but also how selfish Vincent really is: "At the moment, the only one I care about is my brother." "Do you know how ironic this is? You are forcing me to use your own arguments against yourself," Booth says. "Now I have until noon tomorrow and I cannot let him die!" Vincent replies. "But if I help you, I will be helping the enemy," Booth says. "I must go ahead with these articles and I must go ahead with these broadcasts, with or without your help."

David says he can't do it because he doesn't have enough information. Booth says he'll do it with the information that he's got. Booth says his publishers will back him and he's going to do it and "I'm going to fight these creatures every way that I know how. I'm going to fight them the way you fought them once – if you can remember," Booth says as he walks out the door.

Somehow in the next scene David has gone back to Robert's house and Grace is there. He asks her why she didn't catch the plane. David says he just came by to return the key, "I won't be needing it." She accepts it and then asks where he's going. "Archer Creek," he says. David tells her that they won't kill Bob because he's about to make them a better offer. He turns and leaves. David wants to trade himself for his brother, whose wife is pregnant.

Booth arrives at the house after David leaves. He introduces himself and says he's looking for David. He wants to have a word with her because she's doctor Vincent's wife. He tells her that his publisher needs David. "If there is no Vincent, there are no articles." He says he's flying back and a solution can be found. She tells him that David is trading his life for Bob's. She tells him that David went to Archer Creek, an old winery. Booth tells her to call the police and have them meet him at the winery. Booth takes off.

David pulls up at the huge winery in a car (where'd he get it?). David is spotted and a voice, sounding like Taugus asks why he is there. David says, "To re-negotiate our arrangement." "Our terms were final," the voice s says to David, who is standing outside in the middle of a quad-like area. "I think you'll prefer my new terms. Look, I'm alone and I have no weapons," David shouts. "Come out where I can see you. Bring my brother with you so I can make sure he's still alive," David says. What gall.

"Very well, Mr. Vincent. Your way," the voice says. Meanwhile, outside of the winery Booth pulls up, but an alien immediately gets the drop on him. "Would you like to join us?" Meanwhile Taugus, another alien and Bob come out into the open. "State your terms, Mr. Vincent," Taugus says. "Simple: my life for my brothers," David says. Taugus turns it down saying "your death would only dramatize Mr. Booth's articles and bring more attention. You know that." David has it all figured out. He says that his brother is a doctor and that he will declare that David is insane and should be committed to an institution." Robert says, "Not a chance, David." "He will later announce that I died in that institution," David continues, ignoring Bob's bravado.

"That's the only way I can meet your demands. I'll be discredited, Booth will lose the source of his materials, my brother will be at home with his wife and child." Taugus says he would accept the terms, "But your brother doesn't seem willing to cooperate." In comes Booth behind the wheel being escorted by an alien. Booth is driving slowly but then takes off. Bob pops an alien and Taugus shoots and the car and Booth both disappear. David and Bob make a run for it. Two aliens hit the destruct button and the entire winery glows red and disappears. Bob and David both watch.

Just then two cop cars pull up. "What's going on here. Some woman called and said there was a kidnap." "The two men that kidnapped my brother were in that building." But there was no building. The cops are smiling. "Sure there was a building." No ticket. No arrest. The lieutenant who was leading the cops turns out to be an alien as they drive off.

Back at Robert's house Grace is drawing a picture of Booth as David prepares to leave. She painted it from memory. "You take good care of my nephew," he says. Bob wants him to stay for a day or two but David says they both have work to do. Robert says that he's seen them and David says he may need him some day. Off he goes.

The narrator concludes, "One man fighting a secret war against a hidden enemy. Someday, when that enemy is defeated, David Vincent will no longer be alone. Someday."

And there you have it – the "lone wolf" scenario that fiction writers love to use in depicting white men as pioneers and fearless crusaders. They did it alone, they acted alone. But tell me: when have you ever known a white man to act alone when there was an issue of race involved? Other than sniping and sneak attacks, American history is replete with examples of outright mobocracy, out of control contagion attacks and again, what Oliver C. Cox referred to as "the manhunt tradition." Even when he hunted lone black escaped "slaves" he had his pals (sometimes the entire town) and hound dogs with him. But the lone wolf is easier on the psyche when you're dealing with "an alien invasion", right?

.17. "The Condemned"

Mr. Tate is going through a safe looking for papers. "Got it," he says. He puts the folder in his suit coat and now is seeking to escape with the help of another man. He walks out of the room and head for the exit. He turns and heads upstairs as people see him. One man hits the alarm system. Tate hides the folder in a compartment. Two men cut them off, they turn and another cuts them off. A fight ensues. Tate hits two of them with his flashlight and the two men run, locking a door behind them. Off they go.

Tate and Ed are in a pickup heading up the highway. They are being pursued by three aliens I a car. The car overtakes them and the truck goes off the road and into a gully. Ed is knocked out. A young girl sees Tate exit the tuck and make a run for it, hiding behind some hill.. The three aliens get out with their lasers and shoot at the truck. It glows red and disappears. Tate sees all this as the little girl screams for her mother. "Mommy, mommy!"

Morgan Tate unknowingly leases his communications laboratory to Invader Lewis Dunhill. But when he finds out that Dunhill is an alien, he steals some very valuable information and they hide it under some stairs. They try to get away, but end up crashing the truck. A little girl is watching what takes place and sees one man killed with a ray gun, vaporize the truck, while another man has run off.

A little girl's story about a truck that melted and then disappeared made it into the newspapers, and this is what brings David Vincent to town, Sands Point, Oregon. The girl saw a man running from the scene, a man that she recognized as Morgan Tate, head of the nearby communications laboratory Peninsula Telecommunications Laboratories.

As men are shown delivering a message in different languages down in a lab (planning steps for an invasion), Vincent waits in the lobby for Louis Dunhill. Louis Dunhill is leaving most of the plant he owns to Morgan Tate. When David asks to see Tate, Dunhill tells him that Tate is out of town for a few days and offers to help. David tells Dunhill he doesn't know where he'll be staying but will call back. David checks out with the security statin and walks past the gate. He looks up to see two men welding some type of pipe. Vincent is attacked by a guard. They get into a fight. David throws him off of a cliff. The body glows and disappears.

David makes a run for it and the kids stop him. The kids saw the man fall but when one goes to the spot where he should have landed, there is no body. He comes back and reports to the other teens, "Joey, there's nobody there." A scuba diver is later brought in and searches the area. He comes back and Dunhill tells him to "look further out." David is arrested.

With the cops at the scene, David convinced them that they need to take a look around the plant. One man, Mr. John Finney, says that he's not authorized to let them into the plant, but the policeman says he thinks it will be alright. Finney explains that they've been "working on some government contracts.' The detective recommends that they talk to Morgan Tate about it. A second man from the lab says that it can't be done "because unfortunately, Morgan Tate is dead." The man says that Finney witnessed the entire fight, and Finney says that he's "almost sure that the man David killed was Mr. Tate.

David's been appointed a public defender and they are in the attorney's office. The lawyer tells him he's got to "level with me" or else they have no case. So David does just that: "I'll begin with telling you that Morgan Tate is alive." Then standing up he says, "What if I told you that Lewis Dunhill was a creature from another planet. He's not working on government contracts, he's working to conquer our government." Lewis Dunhill believes Tate is dead," David continues as the lawyer is laughing at him. "But he knows I didn't do it. He thinks Tate died in a truck that was disintegrated by a spaceman-like contraption. By framing me for a murder that never happened he thinks he's killing two birds with one stone. Now can you take that into court?"

The lawyer replies, "Mr. Vincent, if you're trying to build an insanity plea, forget it. I doubt whether there'll be a death sentence without a corpse. You know, you'd be better off praying that Morgan Tate's body isn't found." In walks the head detective and a cop, and they pass a paper to the attorney. "It seems that a fisherman working near the lab has radioed the coast guard. He's bringing in a corpse that he found in his net." "Tate?" David asks. "Sure looks that way says the detective. The lawyer looks back at David and says, "Vincent – maybe you ought to work on that insanity plea after all."

David, the Detective Carter and a police officer, along with a medical examiner, walk into the coroner's office. He says that identification of the body would not be easy. "There wasn't much I could with the face hitting the rocks like that," the medical examiner says, "Plus two days at sea." The detective walks over to David. "Vincent, I'll make a deal with you. You save the state the cost of a trial and I guarantee that the district attorney will be very grateful. Whaddya say?" David says, "I'm innocent." The detective directs a man who just walked in, "Okay, bring her in" and then tells David to stand to the side.

A woman comes in. It's Tate's daughter. She looks at David and asks if he's the one. They state the affirmative and then explain that the body has to be identified by a blood relative. She wants to hurry up and get it over with. They walk her over to the drawer where the body is, she looks and they ask her if she can identify the body as her father. She says that it's been over nine years and that she's not sure. "You'd know your own father, wouldn't you?" the detective asks. She says she never knew her father. The detective says that "some of the men at the plant have sworn this is Morgan Tate."

He asks her to look once more, she glances at it hurriedly and then asks, "Yes, that's my father. Can I go now?" "Now wait a minute, don't let him talk you into this," David exclaims. "If you're not sure say so, you have good reason not to be sure that's not your father!" The man who allowed her in says, "Shut up Vincent." David tells her it's not her father and tells her to go to 310 Seashell Road and "there's a little girl there. Talk to her, she'll tell you she saw your father alive. When the daughter says she doesn't understand the detective said that they checked the girl out and "it seems that she has a pretty active imagination. She claims she saw a truck melt and disappear. That's right. Melt – like a glob of butter on a frying pan."

David says, "Your father wasn't in that truck. He was seen running from it. She says she'll be at her hotel if they need her and walks out. David tries to talk further but the detective orders that the police officer "get him out of here.' The detective offers to call her a taxi but one of the main men says that he has a company car waiting for her. He then walks over to her: "You don't have to worry about the funeral arrangements. I'll see to it that everything is taken care of." She turns and stares back into the room. "That man, Vincent, said my father is alive." He said some little girl aw him. "A man like that is liable to say anything, isn't he," the man in the suit asks her as he escorts her out of the building.

David overpowers the man who is escorting him outside of the morgue and makes a run for it. David jumps into a car and takes off as the man recovers from the long fall down the stairs. The man is seen talking with the little girl. he is in the car with another suited alien. From the phone he calls Miss Tate. It's Dunhill. He said there are important papers at the pant that need her signature. Someone is at her door and he presses her. She says she'll be there as soon as she can.

It's Vincent at the door. She tries to slam it in his face but he forces it open. He tells her that her father is alive and it won't only save his neck but there's a lot more at stake. David asks if he has a summer cabin where he could hide out. She again says she and her father haven't been on speaking terms. She leaves her room with Vincent with him and heads toward the elevator. Her father would have to see a druggist because he's a diabetic. She gets on the elevator and now she's at Dunhill's office. It's her father's office. She wants to sign the papers and get on her way. Dunhill tells her there are no papers. They asked her to help them get back a very important file that was stolen. The other man closes the door.

Dunhill says that he's discovered that her father is alive and has stolen a very valuable file. "But he owns the company. Why would he steal from himself?" she asks. Dunhill claims that he has been leasing the company from her father, and he only maintained a small building for himself out back. If the file isn't returned, he tells her, they stand to lose everything they've invested. "We'll be wiped out." He insists that she stay with them for a while. "We hope that when your father realizes you're in town, he'll contact you."

He apologizes for the imposition. "But keeping you here with us is our only way to force your father's hand," Dunhill says. "My father is alive, and a thief to boot," she says. "You need not make it sound so sinister. I'll be delighted to help you. In fact I can't think of anything that would suit me better." "I think we're going to get along very well, Miss Tate. Now, how about that drink?" she says, "Make it a stiff one, I need it."

At the Dumetz Pharmacy the newspaper is out with a picture of a handcuffed Vincent being arrested by police. The headline is "Vincent Accused in Tate Slaying." Somehow Vincent is out and he asks a paperboy about the man who runs the place, the Pharmacy, that is. Vincent unabashedly grills the young boy who is running the store while the boss is out on a two hour lunch break. He asks about a man who has diabetes. "Do you remember delivering insulin to anybody"? Who said anything about insulin? Even back in those days there were other medications, were there?

He asks the boy if he can look through the prescription files. The boy rejects the idea at first. Then Vincent flashes a whole one dollar bill and the boy sees it and accepts the bribe. David goes behind the counter and starts his manual search through paperwork. He comes across the name at the Longwood Hotel. He asks the kid where the hotel is and gets directions. Off he goes. After he leaves the kid gets on the phone and calls the cops.

At the Longwood Hotel David finds the room that Tate is in – just like that. Tate, appearing nervous goes to the door. Tate grabs a bottle of orange juice and then goes back to the door. David tells him "I'm not one of Dunhill's people. I need your help, we can help each other." Tate puts on his jacket and cops pull up with guns drawn. "Moran Tate is in room two, why don't you check on it!" David snitches. Tate climbs out the back window and makes his escape and watches the cops pull away with Vincent in the back seat.

He glances over and sees the newspaper with Vincent's picture on it and the headline where Vincent is accused of slaying Tate, Another article says "Girl Identified Father's Body" and it's a picture of his daughter. He gets on the (always too convenient) pay phone in a phone booth and calls Carol Tate. Her calls are transferred to the Peninsula Plant. He knows the number so he calls it. An alien picks up the phone and hands it to Carol. "Hello father. I hoped to have to never talk to you again. But I've never had much luck, so I'll be brief. "Before he can explain she interrupts and tells him, "I want you to return the file that you stole from Mr. Dunhill, do you understand?"

She won't listen: "How many more lives do you want to ruin? My mother? Now these men? She hands the phone to Dunhill as he continues talking and telling her that those men are not what they say they are. Dunhill tells him they're desperate to get the file back. How much does she know, Dunhill asks. "Your daughter knows nothing of the contents of the file. As long as she remains ignorant of it she will also remain safe. Come back with the file, Morgan. Bring it back in person." Then he hangs up.

Vincent is led into the interrogation room where three men are waiting. Tate is there as well. Tate tells the cops that he and Vincent never had any fight and David confirms it. Tate makes up a lie and says he was out for a stroll and Vincent just happened to be there and grabbed him as he slipped and was about to fall off the cliff. The police detective asks him about the long fall and Tate says he was stunned. He said he came to and read the story in the newspaper and came right over to the police.

Mr. Dunhill and Mr. Finney swear that David killed him. Tate asks what his bail is. Reagan is ordered to take Tate down to the cashier's office. The cops tell David he hopes he's grateful that Tate came through. Later in the car Tate says there's a price for the lie he told. Tate tells the driver to stop at a bar.

He and David are seated. An alien is playing pool adjacent to the booth they sit in. Tate says he needs someone to go to the plant to make an arrangement with Dunhill. He wants to make a trade, me for my daughter. "There's' a file they want, they think I have it," he says. "These people are not really people," Tate says. David interrupts: "They're aliens. Yes, I know all about them." Tate says, "I didn't think there was anyone else." "I've been working on this for some time," David replies.

Tate explains: "A year or so ago they came to me about leasing the plant. I needed money desperately. I didn't know all this time what they were dong there. When I found out last week I decided to do something." After ordering a bourbon and water with no ice (with Tate ordering the same), David asks Tate, "What's in the file?" He tells him that the file "contains a list of eleven key aliens here on Earth and their positions of power in this country and England, France, Germany, Russia. My lab has become the hub, the nerve center for transmission of messages from the Mother planet to these leaders. Dunhill can't risk having the names on that list exposed."

A man in a suit walks in, looks at both of them and then walks away as the waitress brings their drinks. David resumes the inquiry. "Where is the file?" "It's still there," Tate answers. "When the alarm went off there was only time to hide it and run," Tate further explains. He said he planned to come back and get it when things cooled down. "David: will ya help me get my daughter out of there?"

"On one condition," David says. "I get that file." Tate agrees to the terms. "we get it, you can take over. Take it to Washington, turn it over to the authorities. I want to see these – whatever they are – exposed." David warns him: "You know what this means: you may be dead ten minutes after you enter that place." Tate looks at him and says, "We BOTH may be."

That night in a bright yellow cab outside of the plant gates, Tate waits in the car with the taxi driver as David is inside negotiating with Dunhill. David says that Tate is at the front gate and will hand over the file when he sees his daughter come out alone. Dunhill says he gets the impression that Vincent doesn't trust him. "She'll be out in a few minutes" he says. David turns and walks out the door.

David returns to the taxi. The cab drives up to meet David. David tells him to back the cab up and turn it around. When the lady comes out we'll be leaving right away, he says. Tate gets out and joins David. David says he can't find the ladder to the roof. Tate gives him elaborate directions about a ladder on the back part of the building. David tells Tate to stall Dunhill as long as possible. Tate says she thinks that her father killed her mother. Her mother was an alcoholic. Her mother told him to get out and six months later she committed suicide. She left a note blaming him and Carole never forgave him.

Carol comes out escorted by Dunhill. She walks over to the cab. "Goodbye Carol," he says. David gets into the cab with her as Tate is now in the hands of Dunhill. The taxi pulls off and the two go back into the plant. The cab stops up the road. David orders the cab to take the lady to the hotel. He walks back up to the plant. David scales a small hill and with wire cutters, cuts the barbed wire fence. What? A security guard sees nothing as David scales the fence and then runs over to a huge ladder and gets to the top of the building.

Dunhill asks Tate where the file is and Tate pretends that he can't remember. "It all happened so fast," he says. David is sneaking in while Tate stalls. David comes down the stairs as an alien slaps the shit out of Tate. "Let me remind you that just because your daughter is at liberty now, doesn't mean that she will necessarily remain so." Tate walks over and actually opens a lower level drawer and hands them the file. Dunhill looks it over and says, "It all seems to be here." David pounces on both Dunhill and the assistant. The fight begins. Tate is getting his as kicked. Dunhill goes for the gun. He shoots, misses and hits the alien assistant who glows red and dies. Tate hits Dunhill over the head with a stool. David grabs the file and takes off. Dunhill shoots Tate who is killed.

David gets to the ladder and scales down. He just happens to have on black gloves. The assistant hits a switch and calls for abandonment of the mission. "Take the usual steps. We have lost Command Roster 1."

The police chief, in a white continental, is taking David back to the hotel after ordering him to be out of town by midnight. David knocks on the door and Carol is packing. "My father send you to hold my hand all the way to Boston?" she asks. David tells her that there are a lot of things she should know about her father but still hasn't told her that he's dead. Instead he asks if she minds if he rides to the airport with her. She doesn't.

The narrator offers the conclusion: "Carol Tate had lost her father to a nameless enemy. But the enemy had also suffered a grave blow: they had lost Command Roster I. In the days that followed, eleven key aliens either resigned, disappeared or died in a tragic accident – the bodies never to be recovered. The invaders' timetable for conquest had received a major setback."

.18. "Counter-Attack"

This is where we meet the group, The Believers, people who know the aliens have arrived and who work to get the word out.

Two men walk into a building, about to ambush someone. They head up a flight of stairs and set the ambush up. Dr. Elliot Kramer is an astronomer who accompanies Vincent as they are headed outside. As they prepare to exit they are attacked by the two men who are aliens. Vincent kills them both, but Kramer is pushed downstairs. But before he dies, he gives some important material to Vincent. A security guard comes down the stairs and Davis orders him to call the police: "Dr. Kramer's dead!"

So Kramer is dead, but he has bequeathed a powerful program that will enable his seven friends, all members of The Believers, to go from defense to attack. David has the brief case that Kramer had before he fell down the stairs. He gets picked up on a dark dirt road by Edgar Scoville, one of the members of The Believers. Scoville asks where Elliot and David gets into the car and tells him that Kramer is dead. By the way, Scoville is driving a black Lincoln Continental. Scoville is nevertheless optimistic telling David that "once we start jamming their telecommunications systems and they lose a few spacecraft, they'll switch radio bands. Without Elliott Kramer, they'll have a more difficult time. Scoville tells David that he'd known Kramer for over thirty years and that, "he was one of the best friends I ever had. I talked him into helping us. Now it seems he died almost for nothing." "Maybe not," David says. "There might be a way to make his work pay off for something permanent." It seems that Kramer had completed calculations that will allow the Believers to create an automated jamming station that will cause navigational malfunctions aboard incoming saucers.

Back at the site the ambulance, cops and reporters are on the scene. They found .38 caliber bullets at the scene. They know that Kramer had an appointment with Vincent. The security guard said he heard no shooting. He saw David leave with the professor's brief case.

At Scoville's house as he serves David and others a drink, he reiterates that what Kramer shared with them gives them the means to go from defense to attack.

"The means to jam the navigational signals the aliens use to get from their planet to Earth. He was more than a scientist – he was a man you were proud to know,"Scoville adds. One of the Believers, Jim Bryce, asks if the computations are complete and Scoville assures him that they are. The doorbell rings. Some blonde , Joan Seratt, who is Scoville's niece, is seated next to David giving him the eye. Colonel Archie Harmon comes into the room and Scoville makes the introductions. Harmon is an aide to the Secretary of the Air Force. Jim Bryce, the man that Scoville handed the file to, is the chief engineer. Joan acts as the confidential secretary to the group.

The Colonel is not with the group. He tells the group, "Mr. Bryce, I don't buy what you people are selling. But when Edgar told me your plans I decided to see for myself. Jamming radio waves is something I understand, and Dr. Kramer is someone I respect. I thought you said he was going to be here, Edgar." Scoville explains that Kramer was killed and promises Harmon that he'll fill him in later.

Scoville sends Bryce off to get to work on those transmitters because he wants action immediately. Bryce leaves the house to begin his work. David wants to leave with Bryce but Scoville calls him back, telling him that he's been through a great ordeal and "what you need now is a good night's sleep." David says, "What I need now is to get to work." As he turns to head out, Scoville signals Bryce with a shaking of his head not to let David go. Bryce turns to Vincent and says that his car is loaded with equipment and there is no room for him and "besides, it's all pretty technical from here on in."

"Go home David. Try to rest," Scoville says. "Why so much interest in how much rest I get?" David asks. "You've been under a strain! Why don't you recognize it? I would be too under the circumstances." David asks him, "Are you blaming me for Kramer?" Scoville comes clean: "Alright, how did they get to him? If it wasn't through you then who?" David said that Kramer used the university computer and he "must have been monitored." Scoville says that he can't believe that Kramer would commit such a blatant abuse of security. "You're calling me a liar," David concludes. Scoville doesn't answer. Joan interrupts. "Edgar you're upset because your friend is upset and (looking back at David) you're feeling guilty. There is no reason to be at each other's throats. Now both of you – please." Scoville immediately says, "Sorry David." David says nothing except, "Joan, can you give me a lift back to my car?"

"Of course," she says but adds, "You two need each other." David and Joan leave. When they leave Harmon asks Scoville, "You still keep that twelve-year old sour mash?" Harmon then asks, "How was Kramer killed?" Scoville says, "If I told you aliens, would you believe me?" Harmon says, "No." Scoville goes over to pour the drink and tells him, "You will – I guarantee that."

The next day Vincent pulls up at a construction site. He is greeted by the police department. One goes into the car and finds a gun. Vincent says it's not his gun and they put him in the back seat of an unmarked car. Aliens are watching as the men drive off. At the police station Vincent is being questioned in the chief's office. The assumption is that David was after whatever was in that attaché case. He then pulled a gun and Kramer fought him for it. You knocked him over the railing and then took off with that attaché case. Well, Mr. Vincent?" David replies, "That's very good but you've screwed up with the facts." "Okay. Maybe a couple of hours in a cell will make you less squeamish." When David asks if he's filing charging the chief says, "We're holding you for further questioning."

Reporters are waiting outside of the chief's door. The chief is telling the reporters that Vincent told him it was aliens who incinerated. Now the world will know. Next day the paper main headline reads. "Architect Held in Kramer Murder." Back at the house, Scoville is pissed, telling Joan that David has lost his grip and that he cannot jeopardize the group just for David. Joan argues that, "Without David there wouldn't be any group." She adds, "Edward – sometimes you frighten me." Harmon is still there. When Joan leaves he asks Scoville, "Is she in love with him"? Scoville shrugs his shoulders.

In the next scene Joan is at the jail visiting David. A wall separates them as they converse. "You must have done something to straighten out this mess," David says. She tells him she thinks he should see a lawyer. "Any lawyer in the country would think I killed Kramer and start to build an insanity plea," David replies. "What's with him – does he still blame me for Kramer's death? Does he see what the papers are doing tome? Does he care?" Joan promises that something will be done. "I promise."

Later David is ushered into the Police Chief's Office. "Want some coffee?" David flatly replies "No." As a tall man stands over in the corner (probably an alien), The Chief tells Vincent "I thought you'd feel more like talking now." David tells him that he's told him what he has to say. The Chief tells David he can go "but stay where we can find you. His attorney has filed a writ of habeas corpus. David says, "I don't have an attorney" to which the chief replies, "Evidently you do."

David leaves the office with the tall man walking behind him. As David heads down the hall the tall man meets briefly with two other aliens and then walks on.

In that black Lincoln Continental, Scoville drives down a dirt road after passing a sign that says "Trepassing Loitering Prohibited." The car comes to a large cyclone fence and the doors swing open. They drive past a lake and down a long road to what appears to be some kind of laboratory with a tall tower. Bryce is inside and busily working and taking notes. Scoville and Harmon exit the car. They observe the large tower and press the buzzer. Bryce lets them enter. "You certainly aren't going second class," Harmon says. "We can't afford to," says Scoville, who explains that the place used to be an FM radio station. "We took it over, Completely revamped it."

David is back at the construction site where he was hired to do consulting. He walks up to the boss and tells him he tried to call. The boss has seen the newspapers and tells David that the board of directors has requested that he be replaced. David argues that he wasn't charged with anything and that "this project is very important to me." It's the first time it seems that David is actually concerned about earning money. At any rate the boss, Mr. Gleebs is told by David that he put a year's work into the project and the board and bank were encouraged. Gleebs says, "David I like your work, but even if you were Michelangelo, I'd still have to replace you. I'm sure you understand that." David says that he does NOT understand.

Gleebs tells him that he will receive a prorated check in the mail. "Change your name. Go away. Forget this delusion." A disappointed Vincent walks away gets into his car and drives off.

Back at the radio station Byrnes is at work under the guidance of Scoville. Harmon is still there, pacing about checking out the environment. Byrnes tells them that the next time the saucers try to land they're in for a big surprise. Harmon, still doubtful, says "we'll see."

David is in a café/restaurant dining with some random blonde. "I hate to see you so unhappy, Mr. …." He tells her his name: "David." "I'm Louise. What's bothering you Mr. David?" He asks her if she's ever been pro-rated – fired. She says she doesn't let things get to her. David says, "They will. They get to all of us. I promise you that." "Mr. David, are you sure you're alright? Would you like to talk? Somewhere else? Because my apartment's right down the street." HE tells her, "You're probably just what I need, but I have to go. You're very nice." He tells her goodbye and gets up to leave. "Mr. David – don't forget your cigarette case," she says handing him his case.

Two men are at the door, offering to buy him a dink. David is drunk and pushes one of them. He knocks David back. Two men grab him and take him out. The blonde has David's real cigarette case and puts it in her purse.

Joan pulls up in her convertible T-Bird. He's outside of the construction site packing his stuff. The lawyer who got him out was named Corwin. David notices that the cigarette case is not his, but says nothing about it. David feels like he's a laughing stock. He wants her to go away with him, anywhere. He knows he's being listened to and that the cigarette case is a bug. He's faking it. "We could live out our lives but then who knows. I only believe in you and me, nothing else matters.

The aliens are listening in. She is trying to convince him to stay the course. "You believe in this," she says. David tells her, "I've done my hitch and I deserve a long vacation. How about it?" He asks her again if she's coming with him. She says "there's no place to hide from them. "He looks at her coolly and says, "Alright – Ciao" and walks off.

The three aliens are in a car nearby. One tells the other two "alright, stand by." David is walking off the construction site and two of the aliens grab him, knock him over the head and toss him in the back seat of the car. Joan witnesses the whole thing and is screaming her ass off.

At the alien's house, a two story white house surrounded by a picket fence (how do these assholes find such housing? Easy: white privilege). David is seated and drinking his ass off (four fingers scotch in a glass). One of them tells him, "You're not a young man, David. Young in the sense that the future is full of options. A murder charge, loneliness, sickness, death – that's your future. ." When David asks them what they want the answer from the lead alien is, "Cooperation." David tells him, "I'm not traitor." The alien tells him, "But you are at a dead end. We know that. David, do you want to die for them? For those people who rejected you? For the society that plans to destroy you? You're an outcast – your only refuge is with us."

David appears to be drunk and says, "You're asking me to betray my own kind. Kill them." "You won't have to kill anyone, David. You won't have to fight any more. We'll take care of you, all of your needs. It could be a good life. (The rationale of the Uncle Tom)

David asks, "Do you read Faust?" And then he quotes claiming it is a story about a man who sold his soul to the devil knowing he would end up in hell (deal with uncle tom conscience or lack thereof).

The alien asks, "Where do you think you are? What do you think this planet is going to be like for everyone but us – and those who work with us? I'm offering you power, David." Vincent says, "I don't want power. I want peace. I want out. Maybe we should talk about money.' "That's easy – a million?"" the alien offers. David says he wants two million, placed in an account in Geneva. He adds that he wants immunity from whatever happens "when you win." "Agreed," the alien says. He looks over at his two alien counterparts and tells them, "You have something to do," and they leave the room.

The alien leans over David from behind: "Do you drink, or do we work?" David hesitates and answers, "I guess we work."

Back at the lab, Byrnes gets up from his desk and tells Harmon and Scoville that "we are now fully operational." The reply from Scoville? "Good boy." He adds, "Their saucers will crash and when they do, we'll hear about it." The phone rings just before they prepare to leave. Scoville answers. It's Joan and he tells her to take it easy and asks if she can get out here. She's on her way. Scoville said that David has let himself be taken by the aliens. "If we do our part, we may be able to cripple the aliens."

David is at the table drawing up something for the aliens, who seek more information. David tells them he was cut out of the loop and they believe him. He says that Alex Kramer was respected by people and that it was Alex's equipment that they were using, as the alien grabs the drawing and looks it over. "You're a very selective traitor, Mr. Vincent. About Alex you know nothing and about the transmitter you are a fund of information.

The alien says, "Well, we'll see. We've taken the liberty of inviting a dear friend of yours in." He opens the door and the two aliens who had previously departed appear with – Joan! David asks them why they brought Joan and the leader says, "Simply because I don't believe you."

In the meantime the tower is emitting its signal under the direction of Byrnes and in the distance we see one of the saucers crashing into the sea. The alien is questioning Joan about where the tower is. She asks him how would I know? He tells her it's an alien transmitter, and he calls it "her group." She pretends she doesn't know what he's talking about and when he asks her who Alex is, and that she mentioned his name at the police station, she says, "Oh yes, Alex Garoto, the lawyer from Chicago." The alien knows she's lying. The second alien calls her "a foolish young woman" and takes out the metallic disk. The lead alien grabs his arm and tells him to wait. "They've all been given a hypnotic cover," the alien says. "It's a pity about David, isn't it? The way he cracked up?"

Just as Joan answers, "David's fine," in he walks accompanied by another alien. He walks over to Joan. "You alright? Did you tell them anything?" he asks. "There was nothing to tell," she says. "They know about the transmitter," David tells her as he looks deeply into her eyes. "And they know that Kramer invented a way to jam the navigational signals. That's right. I told them. And all they want is a confirmation and you can save your life." She looks at him and says, "I don't know what you're talking about.'

David gets insistent: "Tell them the truth. It doesn't matter anymore. Alex double crossed me, didn't he? Well I'm getting two million dollars. You confirm my story and we'll both be safe." She says to David and the three aliens, "He's fantasizing. What have they done to you."? Then the phone rings.

The lead alien takes the phone, says "I see," hangs up and walks back over to the center of the room where Joan and David are. "Evidently he wasn't fantasizing, Miss Seratt. We've just lost one of our ships with a malfunctioned guidance system." The lead alien looks at his colleagues: "Get the equipment ready, we're leaving in thirty minutes." When a second aliens asks if they should leave that night, "We're due in Rockland in three hours." The leader insists, "We will leave in thirty minutes!"

The alien grabs a metallic orb out of his jacket. "What are you doing?" David asks. "We don't need her now," the second alien explains. David says, "If you kill her you'll have to do without me." They try to argue and David repeats himself and adds, "You'll have to kill me, too." Seeing that, the lead alien says, "She's coming with us." "Why?" David asks. "She'll only be in the way." "If anything goes wrong she'll be killed instantly, is that clear?" the lead alien asks. "Nothing will go wrong," Vincent says, then turning to Joan. "David, why?" she asks. "It's for the best," he says. "Better for whom? For what? Wouldn't it be better to die?" David says, "I don't want to die." "Our friends don't either but you're going to kill them. Oh David, in the name of God, you're going to kill them!"

"Let's go," David says. She whines and cries, "David no. Don't," but to no avail.

Five people in a car, three aliens, Joan and David are heading to the tower. David is riding bitch in the front seat. Don't ask me why. They head down the long, winding road. David gives them the code to get through the cyclone fence. They continue the drive around the lake. Scoville is inside, pacing. Harmon and Byrne are also there "We're ready, "Byrne says. A camera is overhead filming the entire room.

Out of the car the quintet exits and heads to the tower. The aliens view the tower. "Reality, monsieur, cold reality." The head alien nods to another one who goes into the trunk for supplies. The two aliens unload equipment, including some kind of laser gun. They then use the gun to blast into the front door of the tower. Joan tries to make a run for it. She fights an alien as David looks on. Another alien goes over to help. The leader tells the other alien to keep working. "Don't do that again," the leader warns Joan.

They burn a hole in the wall, David reaches in and pushes a button. The doors open and he walks into the room. No one is there. The leader picks up an attaché case and enters. Scoville is in a separate room watching along with Harmon and Byrne. It's a setup. They think they are in the real control room! The alien sets up a machine on the control panel and turns a knob. "We're going to have to talk more about this Alex, David," the leader says. "If you let the girl go, I'll tell you what you want to know," David says. "Then you DO know who Alex is." "No - but I can find out," he says.

David breaks for the door and closes it behind him. Outside Joan is still battling with the alien sent to guard her. David takes the laser rifle points it and shoots the alien as if he knows what he's doing. The alien disappears. Jon stares and runs to David. "David you planned this, didn't you? All of it." "I never planned to get you involved," he says. She apologizes and they hug.

The other two aliens are trapped inside the room. Scoville and the others, from a separate room push a button and the room the aliens are in fills with gas. The leader and the other alien begin choking and suffocate. Byrne dons a gas mask and enters the room where the alien bodies are. He looks around and lifts one and carries him to a lab table. "How close to human are they?" "Many light years away, colonel," Byrne says. Yeah, but they're still act and look like peckerwoods, do they not.

Harmon gets on the phone and calls Walter Reed Hospital. The alien's body is glowing red and he is dying. "Regeneration," David explains. "They needed regeneration." The alien says there is no time left. "This time you lose," he says. David points to the camera overhead. "Take a look." The body glows red for the final time and disintegrates. "Fantastic," Harmon says.

They are all gathered back at Scoville's house as Harmon gives a report in the living room. "Naturally, they were all skeptical about the film," he says. "Film can be faked. They know it and they said it." David stands up, "Does that mean we're back where we started?" Harmon says, "Not at all. I went to my boss. If he had any doubts about the film, he had none about me. He's setting up a special study commission. I honestly think you're on your way to enlisting official support. Now David if you need any unofficial support with the police …" David stops him. "No, no. Edgar's taken care of that." Scoville says, "Gentlemen – I have some material in the next room that just came down from Canada."

They leave with Joan and David in the room alone. She admits she wanted to kill him. They walk into the room together implying there's a relationship.

The narrator's conclusion claims, "A new war. A war in which the ability to attack is no longer the sole prerogative of the invader."

Since when, anywhere in the white man's history of brutality, war and pillaging, has his race EVER given the other side the "sole prerogative" of the attack? In fact, the white man has instigated and started more wars than anyone else on the planet. And yet we are expected to believe that before this final episode of Season 1, it was the alien who was doing all the attacking, waging all the violence, and committing all the atrocities while the white man countered with "understanding"? Bullshit! The alien bought himself more time because he was smart enough to disguise himself as another white man! Any "mercy" that was therefore extended was akin to that of "brother-to-brother." In his own words throughout the series, when asked "what do the aliens look like?" Vincent would reply, "they look like us." Of course "us" means white folks.

And let's culminate Season 1 with this addition to the previous "they look like us" statement. Just like the white earthling is the beneficiary of white privilege, the aliens also capitalized on this bias. The white Russian, the American and the Jew, standing side by side, are peckerwoods first and whatever their nationality or ethnicity is, second. And that is how they behave in their personal and professional lives and it is reflected in their policies and procedures. White privilege has never fared so well.

Case closed. On to Season 2.

Season 2 (1967-1968)

The second season was not only a continuation of the on-going benefits of white privilege (by both Vincent, his allies and the aliens), but a ratcheted up version in many respects. The Believers are becoming increasingly organized and are adding new supporters with nearly every turn. There were more than a few unfortunate deaths and we get an up close look at some of the intricacies of the space craft and the regeneration chambers. But for the most part, the second season of the invaders remained a case study of white nationalism and by extension, white privilege.

.19. "Condition Red"

Falling off a horse, Laurie Keller (Antoinette Bower) is pronounced dead by a hunter who happens to be passing by. He walks over to a police phone to report it. It's Dr. Frederick Rogers and he is reporting an accident of a woman thrown from her horse. "No, I'm afraid she's dead," he says. As he turns he sees her being revived by three men, obviously aliens. They grab him and drag him off, walk him past some trees and into a lake where two of the aliens overpower and drown him.

David Vincent, having read in the newspaper that the woman was reported alive by her husband, NORAD Major Dan Keller (Jason Evers), who works as a computer programmer, suspects that she is an Invader: since the aliens have no pulse, an unconscious Invader could have been mistaken for dead. So get this: David has "arranged" to get into NORAD's Combat Operations Center, some 1400 feet below Cheyenne Mountain, a very secret area and as we learn, a perfect target for the invaders. And yet he is allowed in (how?).

Under the name Robert Davis, Vincent is going in as a "free-lance magazine writer." He checks in with the officer in charge and is asked to step over to the side. They have a huge photo of him on the clipboard and the guard calls it in. "You were right about Robert Davis, sir. He's David Vincent," the guard tells the officer on the other end of the phone. "Let him take the tour with the others," the commander tells the guard. The commander hangs up and goes over to his files and looks under Unidentified Flying Objects and under the label in smaller print is the name David Vincent.

The guard says that they want the public and their potential enemies to know about the facility although they won't see anything that's classified. "But I can promise there will be plenty for you to write about," he says as he steers the jeep through a tunnel with David sitting next to him in the front seat.

Meanwhile, inside the command center a General with an attaché case walks into a room full of busy military personnel. He looks around and walks up to a man he known as Major Keller. His wife is the one who had the accident. They converse about installing some "new tapes" by tomorrow. On the tour Vincent and several others are taken to a room that they are told is "the war room." The guide claims they call it "the peace room." "Each object in the sky must be identified and accounted for," the man says. The key to the entire operation is the computer section, which is relied upon for the defense of the North American continent.

David is in deep thought as the tour group is led into another room, filled with computers. They are told, "Naturally, the final decisions are made by men." The group stares at the huge map on the wall. They pass a door with "Top Secret" emblazoned in huge letters and are told that they cannot go in there. Duhhhh!!!

Vincent, in a station wagon, drives up to Major Dan Keller's home. David, claiming to be Davis (a reporter) is invited in and is asked if he wants a drink. "Scotch and soda, no ice please," David says. Donna was his first wife who died six months earlier from a heart attack. Her photo is on the living room table. Why? At any rate, his current wife, Laurie, who he's known for three months, is upstairs. When David wants to know about Laurie, Keller gets defensive. "The PIO (Public Information Officer) said you wanted to know about my home life – to me that means meals, hobbies, schedules."

The fact is, Laurie is the major's second wife. He married her after knowing her only three months. His first wife died of a heart attack. David meets with Stanhope and tells him his theories. Stanhope spent five years in UFO

Investigations. She controls Keller with something in his neck. David tells him the real truth: he's looking into a plot against NORAD. Then this muthafucka has the nerve to look this man in the face and say, "There's a couple of things I'd like to ask you about the second Mrs. Keller." What?? Who does Vincent think he is? He could have been arrested for that and even worse, under what is known as "Castle Law," shot in the ass since he is on that man's turf and appears to be a clear and present threat!

Laurie comes downstairs wearing all white (what gall). She offers to fix them both some lunch, but Keller says, "Mr. Davis was just leaving." Vincent vows, before he leaves, that he'll see Keller again. Keller spills his guts to his wife as to why Vincent was there.

On the road David is behind a camper being towed by a pickup truck. The camper is moving slowly as David leans on the horn. The camper stops and an alien gets out. David sees him right away as another car comes up from behind. David steers the station wagon off the road then makes a run for it. The aliens look for him but he's ditched them. He turns down an abandoned canal as the aliens, with lasers in hand, continue to search. The aliens finally give up and head back to their truck.

Back at NORAD David appears to be acting as if he's running things. "These aliens of yours, why haven't we spotted their aircraft?" the major asks. Someone is buzzing in – it's Keller. The major reveals that Davis is really David Vincent – "you know – the one with the UFO theories" and claims that he knew who he was earlier in the day. "I didn't interfere with him because I wanted to know what he was doing at NORAD."

What? Wanted to know what he was doing at NORAD? He should have been screened and then he should have been placed in limited capacity, not given a damn tour of the facility just because he claimed to be a reporter. Why would NORAD want publicity, anyway? That doesn't make sense. Most of the things they do are on a clandestine and sneaky level. "You don't buy his stuff, do you?" Keller asks. The major admits that "there are plenty of unanswered questions."

Vincent grills this man about his wife and why her fall was handled so mysteriously. "Are you saying that Laurie has no pulse or heartbeat?" the major asks. Before Keller leaves Vincent asks him what his wife was doing alone in the mountains in early morning. Keller answers that she "loves to ride."

I'll bet she does. That's probably why he married her after knowing her only three months!

That night Keller spills his guts and tells Laurie that Vincent thinks she's an alien being. Said in get he says "he thinks you're a heartless alien being." As they hg her ring flows and she gains mind control over her husband. While he's hypnotized she goes to the dresser and takes out a band, which she places around his head. She then turns on a machine and begins draining him for information. He's telling her all the key information about NORAD. The aliens want computers re-programmed so incoming saucers can't be detected. They are using the second wife to control Keller through manipulation with a disk in the back of his neck.

The next morning she goes riding again, but this time David is spying. She stops at a cabin and men help her off the horse. She goes into the house. She gives the aliens more information about NORAD. A man takes information and hands it to an alien at a computer: "Re-program this," he says. Meanwhile Keller is having dreams and wakes up and sees she's gone, once again. He comes downstairs still somewhat dazed and rubbing his neck. The headaches persist. Keller keeps getting post-program headaches and doesn't know why. Laurie goes riding early every morning. She uses that ride to go to a cabin and pick up tapes from the aliens to take back to the base and switch in the computer at NORAD.

The aliens give Laurie some fake tapes to replace the existing tapes at NORAD. She will have her unwitting husband make the exchange. She gets back on the horse as David watches from a distance. Off she goes. David is attacked from behind and fights with an alien. Two men with guns are walking up as David subdues the alien. David makes a run for it. David gets back to the station wagon (how'd he get it back) as the aliens close in. He rolls down a hill as they shoot the laser at the car and destroy it. David is hiding down below as the aliens search the area and are convinced they've killed him.

Back at the house Laurie goes upstairs. She takes Keller's briefcase and grabs a fake tape and puts it in his case. She then sneaks back into bed but he's sitting on a chair nearby waiting for her. He tells her he has a headache and asks where she was. It's four in the morning and she tells him she couldn't sleep. Only a white man would go for this kind of bullshit excuse. "It was so beautiful out there tonight. The air was so clear, the stars were so bright." He said he feels drugged already. He says he had a nightmare, "as if my brain were being scooped out of my head."

He tells her he doesn't want her to go out riding any more in the middle of the night. She tells him she's done it all her life and she asks him if he thinks she's meeting another man. "Do you think I'm sort of creature?" she asks. She talks him down and they head back to bed. But first she heads out of the room for something else but promises, "This time I won't leave you."

The next day David checks back into NORAD after showing ID to the front gate security guards. Keller has his briefcase and takes off the existing tape, hides it in a file cabinet and then replaces it with the tape that Laurie placed in his case the night before. He's hesitating but the headaches occur and he continues.

David is talking with the major when Keller walks in once again. Tapes are being loaded onto other computers by NORAD personnel. The new tapes have been "installed." The phone rings. In walks another General. The shack was empty and dusty, no sign anyone had been near it for years. The aliens cleaned up evidently. Vincent looks like an ass. Keller says he'll bring Laurie in in half an hour. Vincent warns him to take a detail of police with him but Keller disregards the warning.

Back at the house Keller walks up on Laurie. He asks her if she wants to see the inside of the command center. She asks what brought that on and she's concerned. "I didn't think you'd object," he says. She asks him if he feels guilty about marrying her, trapped him with some kind of witch craft. She starts crying and turns on the ring. She places it on the back of his neck and hypnotizes him. He's dazed as she sits him down. "I don't want you to worry – I don't want you to worry at all," she says.

After seating him in his hypnotic state, she makes a phone call and tells someone to "come get me." Keller snaps out of his trance as Laurie is packing her bags. David thinks that Keller has "served his purpose" and the aliens are going to do away with him. Keller staggers to his feet and heads upstairs where Laurie is. One of the guards tells the major about how Keller "checked on" the tapes. Vincent said that Laurie brought something out of the shack in a saddle bag.

Keller asks what happened to him. Laurie says she's going on a little trip they talked about, "don't you remember"? He now sees her for what she is. "It's true. It's true. Why?" he asks. She tells him that they needed a base on the highland and at 10:22 they'll have it. She pulls a gun, they struggle and he shoots her. She disintegrates right in front of him because of her alien composition. Two aliens pull up and head into the house. Laurie had composed a fake "Dear John" letter. As he is reading the letter the driver comes upstairs and shoots Dan twice while he's on the phone with Stanhope trying to warn the military. "Reel 9" are his last words. It is now 10:15.

A detail is ordered to Keller's house. The aliens know that Stanhope was on to them and that Vincent was also a threat. David and Stanhope check the computer reels just in time. The alien who shot Keller takes Laurie's suitcase and leaves the house. NORAD is now under condition red and jets are taking off in attack mode. "Whatever they are, they're not air-breathing engines" one of the programmers says as he looks at the computer screen.

The aliens head to a large silver van. "We have to intercept them," one says. The aim a device at the air and warn the invaders away. The aliens now have their ships retreat. Laurie's "dear John" letter is located.

As Vincent leaves, Major Stanhope tells him that the Keller case will be buried, but that he will continue to investigate. The general's preliminary report on "condition red" explains the UFOs as natural phenomenon. Nothing is said about the change in the computer tape, stating that Keller was concerned about his private life "and simply made a mistake." "Good luck David. Stick with it – for my peace of mind," Stanhope says.

Closing moral: "The Invader has lost a battle. But David Vincent knows that somewhere in space, new strategies already are being devised ... For the war has only begun ..."

How could Vincent possibly "know" about any strategies that were being devised? Does he "know" the aliens? If he did, why does he continue to keep getting duped, kidnapped and nearly killed every time you turn around? The fact of the matter is, David Vincent doesn't know a damn thing and is basically learning on the job! He's "winging it" and pawning himself off as some kind of expert when, in reality, he's a man with a death wish who had nothing going on in his life before he turned onto that country road that night and spotted that saucer. If he had, he would have kept on stepping and minded his own damn business.

How could Vincent possibly "know" about any strategies that were being devised? Does he "know" the aliens? If he did, why does he continue to keep getting duped, kidnapped and nearly killed every time you turn around? The fact of the matter is, David Vincent doesn't know a damn thing and is basically learning on the job! He's "winging it" and pawning himself off as some kind of expert when, in reality, he's a man with a death wish who had nothing going on in his life before he turned onto that country road that night and spotted that saucer. If he had, he would have kept on stepping and minded his own damn business.

.20. "The Saucer"

Cops are searching the hillside after a man called them the previous night because he thought he saw a flying saucer. This time he's got a fuzzy photo. "Okay fellas, you can knock it off," the sheriff tells the deputies. Then he walks up to the man who made the call, John Carter.

It is, after all, John Carter is the man who saw the ship, and it's not the first time he's seen space ships. Every time he calls the cops, the ships are gone by the time law enforcement arrives. "If you had come out last night when I called ..." he tells them. He shows the fuzzy photos to the sheriff and is told, "I think you need a doctor – these things don't make any more sense than you do." But it is clear in the photos that there is some kind of space ship hovering just behind the mountains.

Ironically, a Frisbee comes sailing into the area, blue and white. A man and his young son come and retrieve it. "I told him the wind would carry it," the child's father says to the sheriff. The sheriff asks the man if he's noticed anything strange in the sky the previous night and the man says, "No, not last night or any other night." The cops get in the car with Carter in the back seat. The man and his son are both aliens.

Carter is an unpublished writer who lives alone with four cats and a beat-up motor bike. David shows up to test Carter's claim that he can predict the day and place of the next landing. But if that was the case, why didn't he just have the cops waiting (instead of just responding) so that they could be there? The narrator tells us, "If true, he could bring to an end Vincent's never-ending war against the invader."

At any rate David and Carter meet on a dirt road, Carter on a motorcycle who tells Vincent to follow him in the car. They head up the dirt road, Vincent in a Ford Mustang, and wait and three men in a truck pull up. He saw them the last night of the last quarter of the moon, both times always one hour before dawn. He shows David his photos and he brought a shotgun along as David recommended "It's loaded with double-odd buckshot." The two of them then lie in wait.

The sun is rising. "They should have been here an hour ago," Carter says. "You don't really buy this, do ya?" he asks. "I'm here," David says. "It's a lot farther than anyone else would come," Carter replies. "Since this thing started everybody's got me pegged as some kind of a kook," he tells David. Here comes an old truck as three men exit and climb the mountainous terrain. David and Carter follow and then, through binoculars, Carter spots a saucer landing. David sees it as well.

An eloping couple in a plane is having problems with their engine. They are going to have to crash land in the area. The saucer sets down as David and Carter walk to get closer. The plane makes a safe landing. The three men from the truck approach the saucer and other beings come out and join them. All together there are now five. They all head back to the truck and three get in the back, one in front and another one returns to the saucer.

Carter makes noise and aliens hear and come to see what is up. They have guns. David shots one who dissolves. Carter witnesses it. Another shoots a laser and misses. Carter shoots the second alien dead. A third makes a run for it. David and Carter apparently head down to the ship.

The plane is settled and Ann and Robert get out. There's gasoline all over the place as they walk away from the plane. He says he'll call the plane rental people and tell them where to pick up the people. He apologizes for making a hash of things. They're headed to Mexico and then to the Riviera as he promised. She's much younger than him. He says he'll rent a car and come back for the luggage. "Do you have the blueprints?" she asks. He shows them to her.

David is walking up to the ship, gun drawn. Carter is there as well. "It looks empty," Carter surmises. David begins climbing up the ladder into the ship. Carter follows. Up another ladder to another level within the ship. They both see what is evidently a control room. They begin looking around. "Who's the most important man you know in town?" David asks. He says he knows a state assemblyman and David tells him to go fetch him. "Get Bonning to come out here and you'll be nominated for the hall of fame." He gives Carter a transistor that he's taken off the ship's mantle so he'll have something to show Bonnie. In turn, Carter hands the shotgun and shells over to David.

Carter gets on his motorbike and speed off, but a lone alien sees him leaving. David continues taking pictures of the inside of the control room of the space ship. The eloping couple sees the saucer. He says he saw something big and shiny when they were about to crash. "If they wanted to hurt us they would have done it by now," he tells her as they walk toward the ship. He begins ascending the ladder and David pulls a gun on him. "Back down," he says.

David gets of the ship and hold them at gunpoint. He checks their pulses to make sure that they are not aliens. One of them, Bob, is a scientist, and he and Ann are eloping but they are also carrying $250,000 worth of stolen blueprints that they hope to sell when they reach their destination. Bob is an electrical engineer and he wants to see more of the saucer, leaving Ann and David on the ground below. They are seated. She asks him what happened to the other beings. "Did you mow them all down?" "It's not as bloodthirsty as it sounds," David says. She asks him why and he tells her that they (the aliens) want to take over this planet.

Bob comes back. "Annie! You've never seen anything like this in your life. They're light years ahead of us!"

Carter arrives at the Assemblyman Bonning's home. Carter is supposed to be fetching a state assemblyman to bring back as a witness. Carter gets to Assemblyman Joe Bonning's house at 6am. He rings the doorbell and the maid answers (she's Latina, of course). Goon music plays as she allows him into the house. At a nearby gas station the lone alien walks up to the proprietor and borrows a dime for a phone call. He calls an alien who says, "you know what to do." The alien pulls out a metallic disk to place on the neck of the gas station attendant, leaving no witnesses.

The alien who was just phoned is scanning the area and sees Bob, Ann and David sitting outside of the space ship. He is one of the three men we saw earlier in the truck. They get back into it and take off.

Ann is nervous waiting for David's "friends' to show up. Bob says they should go right up to the top. "I don't think this thing even uses fuel, probably some magnetic principle," he says, most excited about the "discovery." She wants to head to Mexico, but Bob tells David he has a friend who had done a lot of work "on all of the Apollo projects."

Meanwhile, a cop, Sheriff Thorne, pulls up and meets with the Assemblyman Bonning. Carter is with him and he believes him. Carter gives Thorne something that was from the control room of the saucer, the transistor that David had given him earlier. Thorne agrees and climbs in the back seat with the Assemblyman and the eager beaver Carter in the front.

Back at the saucer, David is pacing with the shotgun while Robert and Anne sit around. Ann wants to steal the car and get the hell out of there and catch a plane. David says he's going to go have a look around as she continues to put pressure on Robert: "What's more important: that thing (the saucer) or me?" Robert doesn't want to steal the plans that they now have in their possession. She says she's going with or without him. He says he's going to stay. He hands her the $250,000 worth of blueprints. She snatches them and takes off.

Bonning pulls up and they get out and find a wounded man whose car was taken by the aliens. Thorne and Carter help him into the car and put him in the back seat. The cops sit next to him with Carter and the Assemblyman in the front.

Ann gets into Vincent's Mustang and peels out. David sees her leaving but it's too late. Off she goes in the fastback. He runs back and asks Robert why she took his car. "I need that car, our lives may depend on it," David said. "Will you just shut up! I just lost everything in my world and I could care less about yours," Robert tells him. Then he has something to explain. "My company had some blueprints for a new computer. I don't know whose idea it was to take them, hers or mine, but they would have brought a quarter of a million dollars in Europe, enough for us to live happily ever after on … She took your car because I said I was going to stay here with you and see it through. She didn't want to be here when the police came."

Robert says, "I am a fool and a sloppy sentimentalist, but I am not a thief, Mr. Vincent. She will find out when she sees that the envelope is full of blank paper."

Here comes the car with the four men on board. The man they picked up is really an alien who pulls out a metallic disk. He puts it on Thorne's neck and kills him, unbeknownst to the men in the front seat. As he tries to put it on Carter's neck he is busted and he and Carter begin scuffling over the front seat as Joe wheels the car. The car goes off a cliff as Ann turns the corner. Bonning is alive, the alien dissolves and Carter is also hurt. "It's true," the Bonning says, just before he dies.

Ann flags down a truck, but it's full of aliens, five of them. "You were with the others at the saucer," one says as he pulls out a ray gun and goes down to the car where Carter is. He shoots the car and dissolves it. They grab Ann, place her in the truck, and take off.

David continues waking around, one holstered gun and one shotgun in his possession. Robert explains to Vincent that Annie thought he had money and would give her anything in the world. He said he was going to tell her the truth when his $975 ran out. "I thought she'd love me by then."

The truck pulls to a stop as David and Robert watch. They duck inside the saucer. What??? The aliens scale the hillside as David views them on the monitoring screen from the saucer's control room. The lead alien contacts the ship and tells him to press a switch so he can hear them. "We only want the ship. You can go. We'll take it and leave," he says. David says he wants the ship and Robert says he wants it, too. "We have something of yours, too," he says and then they reveal Annie. "They've got Annie David, they'll kill her."

David tells Robert to figure out a way to disable the ship until he returns. David leaves the ship and meets the alien leader who has ray gun in hand. David is also packing. They will release the girl after Robert is out of the ship. They want David's camera as well. He turns it over to them and the alien destroys the film and tosses it. David goes back into the ship. David takes the shotgun from Robert and goes back down. "Annie, start walking to me," he says. She begins as the alien leader orders one man to go to the ship to make sure everything is kosher.

The alien goes into the saucer and signals that all is well. Robert comes down as well. David tells Annie that she is more important to them than the saucer is. "Without me they have nothing to bargain with," she says as she tries to make a run for it. David tells her to "get down" and a shootout begins. Aliens charge as they destroy the bush Annie was hiding behind. Robert shoots one of them. Annie's arm is on fire as Robert rushes to her aide. Aliens charge. David shoots one. Another climbs into the ship as David kills yet another. The ship takes off.

An ambulance arrives later to tend to Annie's burns. Annie is still out but can be saved. Robert says he's going to tell the man he works for what he saw. David says it won't make much difference but Robert is not deterred. Annie wants Robert by her side and tells him to open her purse. She gives him the envelope back and says they don't need them anymore.

To save the white woman, David gives up a chance to expose the aliens. And it's time for another teaching moment.

You have a chance to expose the aliens that you have been chasing for at least a year. You have risked your life on scores of occasions looking for a way to expose the fact that the aliens are on earth. You have submitted yourself to ridicule and scorn throughout this entire process. And because of one white bitch – ONE – you throw all caution to the wind? This is a derivative of the King Kong Syndrome where a super-creature risks all just to get his paws on a boney white woman. And don't forget the fact that he was tripping over African women all the while!

At any rate, the concluding statement: "Two others have seen what David Vincent has seen. Two others now know that flying saucers do exist. The search for Congressman Bonning and Police Chief Thorn will continue for months. Because of their disappearance, dozens of others will begin to wonder reluctantly what David Vincent knows is true: that alien beings now walk the face of the earth."

Do they – or do they just land and walk the streets of various American cities and towns? And furthermore, are the aliens from another galaxy or are they of the earth-born, Euroamerican variety?

.21. "The Watchers"

A man drives up looking for an incoming Washington flight. Here comes that black Continental (again), filled with aliens as the man warns that the people in it "look just like us" and then makes a run for it. Another man, presumably an alien uses the hypno orb (my name for it) and tells the first guy, "Everything is going to be alright, Mr. Grayson. There's going to be a plane landing in a moment." Two men watch (presumably aliens) watch as Grayson then walks onto the airstrip in front of an incoming plane and gets run down. One employee tries to stop it but it's too late. The manager of the famed resort hotel had been driven to suicide, David Vincent read about the fact that before dying, the man had declared that aliens had taken over his hotel. So once again the self-appointed "white knight" goes to the small Virginia airport where the suicide took place.

Meanwhile the word that is circulated is that a man who was the manager of a resort hotel – Grayson – was driven mad, and moreover, that the hotel has been taken over by aliens.

David Vincent is looking for a job. The aliens, led by the new manager of the lodge, insists that everyone clear out until a special plane comes in. The owner insists on complete privacy and they can't share who is coming in on the plane. David keeps insisting and tells the man that he and the guy who committed suicide "were working on the same project." He hands David the manifest with the information on it and says he has to go inside, providing David what he needs without actually telling him.

The expected guest is an "electronics wizard" named Paul Cook. It is Cook who is the key to the missile defense system. As David Vincent investigates, Cook, an electronics genius with an aversion to people, lands in a small private plane with his blind niece Maggie. Vincent asks for a job and the man says "try the bus company" and "if it helps, use my name. As the plane land the two aliens in charge are also waiting along with David.

Cook is accompanied by two guards and a woman named Maggie, who is blind. He is meeting several generals because he can analyze the nation's defenses and suggest improvements. The Invaders want access to those defenses, and they intend to take advantage of Cook's reclusive nature. They get into the waiting limo (another black Lincoln Continental) and head off as David watches.

In a small house near a large mansion, the aliens have set up and are spying on Cook. Ramsey and Sims are his guards. He asks them what they have done with his brief case. HE orders them to unpack his things: "get on with it." Maggie comes out of the back room. "You know what I'm going to do when you die, Cookie?" she asks. "I'm going to check into a hotel with some people in it." Cook doesn't like people and the hotel they are in has been vacated. She says she's going to find a big, gossipy hotel in someplace like New York. He reminds her, "you used to like this place."

He summons Ramsey to answer the phone. Washington is calling asking if he has changed his mind about security. Cook wants things the way they are. Maggie wonders what kind of deal it is this time and "why you should need this kind of protection?" He tells her this deal is larger than usual." She jokes, "The fate of all mankind? You never share anything with me any more do you know that? Why don't you trade me in for a poodle?" He tells her to be the beautiful girl you've always been. She's headed down to the pool: "Maybe there's a sexy lifeguard."

Ramsey hangs up the phone. Cook feels that someone is looking at him. He summons Sims and tells him to check the room out. "I feel like a bug under a microscope," he says. There is an alien watching Cook and working to monitor his voice patterns. "I think I'm getting it now," he says.

David gets a job in a bus terminal (just like that – more white privilege) and walks through the hotel lobby, outside and up on Maggie who is standing near the pool. When she asks who he is and what he does, David bluntly replies, "I go around the country chasing flying saucers." He tells her to take her hand to avoid falling in the pool but she tells him she can swim like a dolphin. He tells her he drives the mountain bus and says he goes around the country chasing flying saucers. He saw her picture in the papers after reading a story about her and her uncle.

She says his approach was different and they should "cool it right here." She walks away. The aliens continue to monitor Cooks' room. He is eating in the lobby with Maggie, Sims and Ramsey. Maggie gets up and leaves. David is still outside creeping around and spots two aliens. He breaks into a side door and hides as Maggie walks down the hallway. She enters room 22A and he creeps in right behind her. She can sense it. David goes through a brief case on the desk as Maggie approaches. "Somebody's here, they're not saying anything," she says. She finds her way back to the door and closes it.

Cook sends Ramsey to find Maggie and apologize for him. Ramsey comes in and busts David and pulls his gun. "Make a move and I'll kill you," he tells Vincent. Now the gang is all there. Maggie exposes him to Cook, Ramsey and Sims. David tells them that he came to stop Cook from making his deal. He accuses Cook of playing games with the aliens because everybody knows what Paul Cook is to the missile defense system and what would happen if he sold out. Vincent warns, "You think you can do business with them, but you can't. Nobody can. When they get what they want, they'll turn on you. They're here to take over the world. Give them America's defense secrets and they can do it."

Cook tells Ramsey to contact Sims and take Vincent downstairs where he can be locked up and guarded. Before David leaves he asks, "What did they promise you, Cook? A kingdom?"

Vincent is taken away and Maggie is hounding her uncle, who calls David a "crackpot." In the hallway a clumsy waiter gets in the way and David makes a break for it. He hopes on his bus and speeds away. Ramsey hesitates to shoot and Vincent is gone.

He won't tell Maggie what the secrecy is all about and she says "we've really lost something, haven't we?" He says, "Maybe so." He says he's helping the government overhaul defense installations. He says he's going to try to upgrade the system, that's all. She asks why they didn't go right to Washington, which is right down the road? He says it was his hang-up. Sims reports back that he has lost Vincent. Cook is pissed and sends Maggie off to her room.

Meanwhile David is trying to contact a special agent in Washington DC. Maggie is walking up the stairs and offers to help her inside. She is at the bus station and he seats her. He pours her some coffee, which she takes black. He asks her why she came: "friend, foe or Cookie's errand boy?" She tells him, "What a pair we are: you blind to everything that's going on and me just blind."

She tells him he couldn't be more wrong about Cookie, that he's not selling anything to anyone. "He's true: red, white and blue," she claims. Vincent said he read the papers on his desk but she says he "mis-read them completely." She asks him not to go back to the hotel because Cook can be one nasty cookie. "Those people at the lodge: I know what they can do, even by Cookie's standards," David tells her. Sims and Ramsey are searching for Maggie. The power station is nearby and Ramsey runs over to it but the door is locked. He enters a small side hatch and opens a door to see complex computer monitoring that is watching Cook as he is on the phone.

He goes back outside and makes a run for it. David has explained the alien presence and his work to Maggie. Ramsey, using a pay phone, calls the bus terminal and David picks up. He tells David about the power station and says he will bring Maggie. He tells him to take Sims and get to cook right away. But two aliens walk up on them. They are obviously about to die.

Three years ago Cookie was driving and got in a car wreck that also blinded Maggie. They are driving to the power station and come across the car that Ramsey and Sims were in. It's crashed and on fire and they are both dead.

David gets back into the bus and the two continue their trek toward the power station. He tells her to try not to think about the deaths of her uncle's secretary and pilot. They arrive at the power station. What could the plan be? He drops her off and heads to the power station (which is the headquarters for the aliens). This woman is blinds, and he doesn't even bother to walk her to her room. At any rate, Maggie tells Cook that Ramsey and Sims are dead. She adds, "It's no joke, Cookie. You're probably next," she says. "They have taken over the lodge, they are all around us. They've spared us so far because we fit into their plans," she argues. "The people that are running this lodge – they're not people and they mean to take us over one way or another, and you are one of the ways!"

(No, but they're white and have blue eyes so they get the benefit of the doubt, right?) And further, you've been referring to them as "people" and "men" throughout the series. Why stop now?

Meanwhile, David sneaks into the power station and finds the hatch door that Sims had previously entered. He goes to the same door and sees just what Sims saw: surveillance of Cooks room. They see Cook being convinced by Maggie to join her in leaving. Two generals are on the way to hear his views. He says he wills cancer his earlier meeting. But all circuits are out. He begins packing his papers and the aliens know they must make a move. One gets on the phone and says, "It's time."

Three aliens leave the power station while David stays behind and walks into the control center. David and an alien get into a fight. David pulls out his gun but is disarmed. David is getting his ass kicked but manages to knock the alien into a power grid where he electrocutes himself and dies.

David wins and immediately phones Cook. Maggie can't see so she doesn't know that the man she is talking to is a Cook impostor. He promises her a military escort out of the area and tells her to go to her room and rest. Maggie leaves. "Just let me know when you hear from David," she says before departing.

The aliens now have the papers. David has been trying to phone Cook but the line was busy. The aliens have the real cook and are kidnapping him (another Lincoln Continental). She thinks she's talking to Cook in the office but it's the impostor. "They want Washington's defense plans," she says. She tells him that he would be easier to impersonate than W.C. Fields. He tells her to go back to her room and lock the door. "And stop worrying." She tells him he's too fast on his feet lately. "I think you're schizophrenic. Two completely different people. I only like one of you," she says.

Meanwhile, the Generals from Washington, DC have arrived and are picked up by the limousine from the Lodge (Lincoln Continental). Vincent is near the pool and two aliens are walking up, the same ones who killed Ramsey and Sims. David watches the men empty out of the limo. "This way to the Conference room, gentlemen," one of the aliens says. Maggie knows that Cook is a fake because he made a statement about contacting the families of Sims and Ramsey. But how did he know they were dead? She sneaks out of her room

The generals are around the table in the conference room. Maggie knocks down a statue in the hallway. The fake Cook has the brief case and is headed to the conference. Maggie can't find her walking cane and leaves the broken statue on the floor b behind. The fake Cook find the cane and knows Maggie is somewhere around

David sneaks up behind one of the aliens and knocks him out. One of the aliens walks up on Maggie. The fake Cook comes down the stairs who has her cane. Now she's trapped. "Maggie listen to me. We never intended to harm you. We need you. With certain restrictions we can continue with me as your uncle," the fake Cook says. David is running up the hall and pulls his gun. He gets the drop on them and forces them to let Maggie go. One pulls a hyno orb and David is woozy but shoots them both. They turn red, dissolve and die. "I'm glad I didn't see it," Maggie says. There are no witnesses and the entire staff seems to have "disappeared.". The power station is empty.

The generals acknowledge that something was not quite right and promise a full investigation. "We'll make a full report as well as your own," one general promises her. "An investigation will be made."

Closing statement: "David Vincent will seek out the invader again ... Facing a world that cannot believe him. Not so alone now. For he has found another who does believe: a girl of courage and spirit – a girl of vision." Why can't she be a "woman" of vision?

(Episode 22, "The Vise," the only episode that featured African-Americans, will be addressed in a separate section of its own later in this book.

.23. Valley of the Shadow"

A couple in the car cruising down the road talking about their honeymoon. Dr. Larousse and his wife Maria are snuggled up as the car goes down the highway. Another car speeds past them and careens off the road, turning over. They pass the car and immediately spring into action. Dr. Larousse goes over to the man in the car and helps him out of the car. The man doesn't want the woman touching him and resists Dr. LaRousse's attempts to help. The woman, Maria, pulls the hurt man off but is cast aside. The man knocks the LaRousse out. The man from the car stares at Maria, rock in hand, and comes after her. Two cops pull up and tackle the man before he can do harm. The woman runs over to check her husband.

This episode takes place in yet another lily-white town - Carterville, Wyoming, a town of 1,216 just south of Laramie. At one time it was a processing center for local copper mines. Now, it's just a small town barely making its own way.

As stated earlier, Dr. Sam and wife Maria LaRousse (also a doctor) are on the highway and a car speeds past them and crashes. They pull over to assist. The man and the doctor begin to tussle because the man doesn't want to be examined. The man, now out of the car, eventually knocks Sam out with a rock and begins chasing Maria up a small hill, but the cops arrive just in time.).

The alien, a man known as "Joe Manners," is arrested and brought to the town's small jail. As can be expected, David is sitting right there in the lobby, hoping to see "Manners," the "man" who killed the doctor. David Vincent tries to convince the sheriff that the Manners is in fact an alien. When asked why he wants to see the man David tells the sheriff that the picture in the paper wasn't very clear and adds that this is a man who "once tried to kill me." David then shows his identification, the sheriff takes a seat and looks things over.

The sheriff tells him there is no hurry but David warns that "in a few days he'll disappear in smoke. I'm just trying to help you." The sheriff searches Vincent after returning his ID and escorts him to the cell where Manners is being detained. The sheriff asks Vincent why Manders wanted to kill Dr. LaRoos and David explains that he (Manders) "didn't want to be examined." He adds, "That man has no heartbeat or pulse," David explains, "and in one or two days, he's going up in smoke." When asked why he thinks the man doesn't have a heartbeat or pulse, David tells them, "He's different, he's from another planet."

David wants to call Captain Taft at the air base. The interested reporter will allow David to use his phone. Meanwhile, the alien wants to make a call to talk to lawyer. He gets on the phone and gets the sheriff to give him some privacy. He calls other aliens and tells them he needs help. "You gotta get me outta here now, right now. I got an Air Force captain on the way."

When Will, the reporter asks David what planet the man is from and what the man is doing in that part of the country, all David can say is, "I don't know." Vincent makes a direct call to Taft. "This is David Vincent. You told me that if I ever caught one to call. Well I'm calling," David says. David reminds him that Regulation 33-6 of the UFO Manual says that he (Taft) has got to check it out. Taft is on his way.

The reporter is adamant and wants to introduce him to another doctor in town. He says he'll get her to check the heart beat and pulse of the man in the cell.

On the way the Captain and his colonel run into a roadblock. The officer may well be an alien.

Meanwhile, Maria is summoned to come in and check the alien inmate's pulse because there was only two doctors in town since her husband was murdered. The reporter convinces her. Taft is at the police station as Maria walks in. David says when she examines the man he will take her word for it and then leave. They agree that the sooner the examination is done the sooner the incident will be behind them.

Taft is now an alien. He signals all enter the cell. The man is backing up. The sheriff goes to handcuff the man, the general intercedes and provides cover as the man escapes out the front door. The cops shoot in a town full of people as the man is running and ducking. He's hit and then turns red and dissolves in front of scores of witnesses. David looks around at the Captain.

Captain Taft declares martial law to keep the secret. He assigns the deputies to spread the word. All communication is cut off. The Captain is still there and claims he is calling the air base. Instead, he contacts the aliens and tells them that there is an emergency. "This is a red call," he says. "I'm taking measures to keep the news from spreading," he says over the phone as David carefully watches. Aliens are on the way. Will, the reporter, wants the publicity that such a story would bring.

When David walks out people are asking about what is going on. A headline has already been printed regarding a "space creature." David goes to visit Maria to apologize for what she has been put through. She still thinks it's a cheap joke. She says Sam's funeral is in an hour and she wants David to attend it and see how important her husband was to the community.

A huge metallic gray van perches atop a nearby hill. Aliens converge and then turn on a huge machine, and all electricity is shut off. Not only is the electricity off, but cars stop running and the city is brought to a literal standstill. But the funeral somehow goes on.

Not one person other than David and Maria come to her husband's funeral. The preacher delivers, "The Lord is my shepherd..' (hence, title of the episode). As he concludes the eulogy the preacher says he doesn't understand and then recites the Psalms. There is a small earthquake and it is clear that the nearby dam is cracking. David walks outside and looks around. People are scattering. Water begins to come through and there are no phones that work. Sheriff sends out a deputy to go find help, to "fetch the army "or anybody you can."

David confronts Captain Taft who plans to murder the entire town. David knows that there is an alien plan afoot. The deputy that was sent to find help is on foot and he and another deputy come across the van with the mechanism inside. They have rifles and the aliens have lasers. The deputy says he's going up there. They shoot at him and dissolve a huge bolder. The two deputies flee. David is trying to negotiate with the Captain, telling him that destroying an entire town would be too big a risk. The Captain tells Vincent that, "a harmless mist will put them to sleep. It won't affect my people." (They're "people"?). The Captain says his people will escape before the flood hits.

David brokers a deal with aliens. If they leave the town alone, he'll say it was all a publicity stunt designed to get the prisoner alien (Manders) out of jail. David is willing to lie his ass off to save the town and explain away what those people saw with their own eyes. The Captain tells him that his people are on the way and he has an hour.

He has the sheriff on his side now. They go to see Maria once again. The sheriff tells her it was a scam; David even tells Maria it was a hoax. The sheriff needs a way to quiet down the town. She'll print up bulletins on a hand press and distribute them around town. "Please, I want to do this," she says. They get Will to help with the goal of "bringing this town back to sanity again."

The Captain and Vincent meet face to face again. Meanwhile Maria is getting the people to believe her story. Will is there but she counters his eye witness sighting with the claim that it was "an optical illusion." The people know there is a reason for batteries to stop working. The preacher says, "Before God and man, is it possible that you could be wrong?"

The deputies return and talk about how the town is surrounded and that there is a machine that "is sucking up all the electricity." Up the street march men from the army. They are carrying huge brief cases – more likely than not they are also aliens. The General tells Vincent, "You had your chance" and to not cause any more commotion because "the people are serene now. Cooperate – and I'll let you live." Vincent smugly replies, "Sure you will."

The aliens who arrived in army trucks and dressed like army infantry have everything under control. The head army infantryman is actually General's boss and vows he'll have an accounting to make once all this is over. David tells Maria that he wishes there was something he could do to get the people to resist. Maria says it won't work because the people are too passive and there would be a lot of bloodshed. David and Maria say their goodbyes.

David goes in to negotiate, but offers to hypnotize the people into going back one full day. They give Vincent a gas mask as the mist is being sprayed and it covers the town, freezing everybody motionless. They then bring in a machine and set it in the town square. The announcement is made: "Obey this voice. To the town square you will bring every last item artifact since nine o clock this morning. You will tell of an unusual magnetic disturbance. Tomorrow at nine in the morning you will awaken and you will have lost one full day." The people get into position to obey the edict

The aliens alter time and everything goes back one full day. Gas is released, and the entire town is hypnotized to go back to 9am the previous day. This time David denies ever having seen Manders. This time around the funeral takes place and it's packed with people. Again, the Psalms. Maria doesn't remember Manders or for that matter, David either.

So he's saved an entire town – of white folks. Not a single black face on the screen throughout the entire episode. So when the title contains the word "shadow," you know something evil or bad is taking place because a shadow is associated with darkness and in Euroamerican culture all that is evil, dirty, bad and inferior is associated with darkness or blackness. The town, being lily-white, is saved by a "white knight" who represents the savior of the world (Jesus?)

The closing statement: "Carterville, Wyoming. Principle industry – contemplation of the past. Population: twelve hundred sixteen people. All unaware that they have been given back their future."

So this episode, "Valley of the Shadow" addresses an area that the white man has long been obsessed with: time and the control of history. In this episode we saw where time literally was able to "stand still" because of the manipulation of the (white) aliens. And when it stood still, history was able to be revised and altered. Today in 2018, is this not what the white man is still trying to do? Witness all of the retro TV channels that are promoting a time when black people were segregated and nearly invisible on the air; shows like "Happy Days," Laverne and Shirley," "Donna Reed," "Leave it to Beaver," "My Three Sons" and so many more.

Not only that, but the history books around the nation are being "revised" to make sure that issues involving black power are not mentioned and even the piecemeal civil rights movement is given short shrift.

"Valley of the Shadow" made it clear that white people were thinking about control on a number of fronts. These episodes pointed out the control of the oceans, control of the mountains and of space and time. White supremacy is the only functioning racism in the known universe. If this isn't evidence of a "God Complex," then I don't know what is.

.24. "The Enemy"

Gail, a ranch woman, rides up to the gate of her farm and gets out of her Jeep to open it. As she does she hears a noise, looks up in the sky and spots a saucer that crashes on a mountainside in Utah. She gets into a jeep and sets out to locate it, and it is f-u-u-u-c-ked up! The saucer is glowing red as several aliens stagger from the wreckage. As one of them dies, a second one pulls a box from the ship, then pulls out a ray gun and destroys the saucer. He then unpacks several vials from the box, turns and sees Gail. He passes out.

Gail is an ex-nurse and somehow she manages to get the alien, whose name is Blake, back to her ranch, perhaps assuming he is a human. After all, the aliens are white just like the humans who are featured throughout each episode.

The narrator tells us that for two days, planes have crossed and re-crossed the Utah wilderness searching for the fiery object that witnesses swear plunged from the sky. But the planes finding nothing and the investigation is called off. Only one man continues the search. For somewhere in the forbidding mountains may be the remains of an alien spacecraft."

The report of the crash prompt David to "investigate." Once again, no credentials, no badge, no arrest powers, no papers – just "investigating" on his own. Gail believes that Blake (the alien) and his people are peaceful, and she has helped him, fed him and even provided him with clothing. She injects him with a serum that he says is "experimental" which is why he is there in the first place. She continues the objections when he begins to feel pain, telling him that pain is a warning that he needs help. He says he will get help from one of their regeneration stations. He has a rendezvous to make with two friends later that afternoon.

He questions why she didn't let him die. He says "you saw the ship, you've guessed what I am, you don't show the fear emotions humans are supposed to. Why?" She tells him she's just come back after a year in Vietnam and after what she saw there, "nothing's ever going to frighten me again." He tells her he's not like anything she's ever seen but she tells him that he should trust her.

Blake turns to her: "Humans? Oh no. I've heard about you. You fight, you hate, you kill, you betray each other. It's the only way you know. If you do it to each other, you'll do it to me if you get the chance." The phone rings and it's the sheriff, Vern. Sheriff Vern wants to visit, and she declines, telling him that she's working on the ranch. She doesn't even know Blake and yet where she is lying for him already. She says "maybe in a few days" and hangs up.

Then she turns to Blake and says, "See? We don't all betray each other." And yet, didn't she just do it by defending Blake against her own race?

Someone is coming. Blake hides around the corner in the house while Gail covers. She takes an empty shotgun goes outside and gets into her Jeep to go out to the gate to meet the visitor. It's David, of course. He tells her he's trying to get back up into those mountains and she asks what he's looking for. He tells her he's looking for whatever fell out of the sky a couple of nights ago. She tells him there's nothing there and that the search was called off. David tells her that they were looking for a plane – "I'm not." She raises the unloaded shotgun and orders him to "get out" because he was trespassing.

Blake is looking out the window the entire time, but falls to the floor. Meanwhile, the persistent David Vincent, using a map, continues his search. He begins scaling a hill. At the ranch Gail is tending to Blake who is still very suspicious and wants to go back to the clearing. The courier's box is still there and now that the courier is dead, Blake has to finish the mission for him. He tells Gail he needs her help.

David is also searching the clearing, and he finds the box! Blake and Gail walk up on him just as he does. Blake wants to shoot him but Gail asks him not to. Blake orders David to carry the box to the Jeep. David jumps Blake and they begin fighting. Blake has the ray gun and David disarms him. Blake passes out. Gail tells David that Blake is sick and that "he needs me and I'm going to help."

The police are anticipating a storm. Sawyer and Lavin, two men in suits pull up outside (obviously aliens). The one named Sawyer says that his company just brought out the mine and there is enough low grade ore to work, according to their equipment. The sheriff mentions a flying saucer Sawyer is interested. "Just turn your car around and take your car up into the hills," the Sheriff suggests after spilling his guts.

David explains that Blake's body is a shell and that he is not in any pain. Gail says she has medication at the ranch that may help him.

The sheriff sends a deputy Vern out to Gail's ranch to warn her about the storm. Meanwhile, David ties up Blake (hands in front- why?) and tells her, "He's reverting to his old form." Still defending this "man" she just met, she tells Vincent, "We're the killers, Mr. Vincent …How do you know they're not here on a mission of peace? … Anything that's strange or unlike us doesn't have a chance." Two points: (1) then white alien gets the benefit of the doubt and (2) this woman is willing to admit to the crimes of the white race.

She says she only knows one thing: he could have killed me and he didn't. She lectures David on morality and tells him that he's judging Blake by earth standards. She says that, "Anything that doesn't look like us we kill." What? Race is not an exception to the death march of the white man; it is merely a final solution for the whites who don't comply with the overall racial mission!

Gail tells David to untie Blake's hands and he does. She injects Blake and they go into the living room to wait. She asks and so David explains the conversation process to her (as if he's an expert), and still has the ray gun. "Why would they want to take over the world if they can't survive here?" she asks. David tells her that the answer may be in that box. She doesn't want to turn him in. Her father died in one war and her brother died in another one "that they didn't even call a war." She came to the ranch to find some reason, but she can't. Blake is coming to.

The sheriff's car is pulling up, and David goes outside to meet him. He has the ray gun. "Who are you?" the deputy asks. David explains the ray gun and marches the deputy inside, saying that they have a prisoner. Blake pretends to still be unconscious as they walk in. Blake makes a move for it and shoots and murders deputy Vern.

The two aliens who claim to be looking into the mine meet briefly again with the sheriff and then head back out to the farm. Vern is dead. Gail asks why he had to kill Vern and Blake says, "Primitive people whose lives are ruled by emotions." She replies, "Don't you feel anything?" David interrupts and flips the script on her: "You're trying to understand him in our terms. It doesn't work." Gail turns to Blake: "I just want to know one thing: when you're done with us, do we die, too?" He refuses to answer so she turns to David and apologizes. "I should have listened to you," she says.

Blake now has the gun and tells Gail, "It's almost time." She tells him that she is not going to help him again but he insists that he is about to revert. When she tells him no a second time, Blake says that Vincent is his assurance that she WILL help him. "I learned from you how valuable even one life is," Blake tells her. "You won't sacrifice his (referring to David)." David tells her to do as he says. "The longer we stay alive the better chance we have of stopping him."

Gail goes into the other room to fetch her nurse's kit as Blake has a seat. "Why the fancy games?" David asks. Blake tells him that it is no game, that they need those mines on her property to move in their equipment for their "experiments" (in the box). They've come to collect that particular box which will enhance the aliens' ability to live on earth without spending time in the regeneration tubes. Gail re-enters the room with bad news: Blake cannot be regenerated. She shows him the vials of fluid. "They have been smashed. You did it when you killed Vern," she says. "I can't do anything more for you." When he orders her to find another one she tells him there are no others.

Blake says they'll go get one at her village. Vincent asks him about the risk and Blake guarantees him that there is no risk. "You'll see."

In the meantime Vern, who has been killed, is still being looked for by the sheriff. "Maybe he stopped at the Thompson's or the White's (interesting). Gail and Blake drive to town to get more needles as more aliens arrive. There is also a storm on the way. She tells the sheriff she has not seen Vern and that she only came into town to get some supplies.

Sawyer and Lavin look into the sky as the storm breaks. "Survivors," one says.

David, Gail and Blake are now headed to the mine in a heavy storm. David is ordered by Blake to bring the box as his hands begin to deteriorate. Gail decides to destroy the serum as Blake withers. The chemicals in the box changes alien chemistry in certain atmospheres even in their natural form. After that, they'll eliminate the oxygen. They arrive at the mine. He tells David to take the box despite David saying they should keep it in the Jeep. They enter the mining cabin and David places the box on a table. He gets a lantern and lights the room. Gail begins preparing the serum as Blake stands away. Blake tells her to hurry. David is going for wood to start a fire. Gail makes a decision and then intentionally breaks the serum which turns red and disintegrates. The two aliens are trailing them and are headed to the mine to find them.

Blake has a gun trained on them. David asks them what his mission is. They were seeking to change their chemistry to change the atmosphere so that they could live there. They said they would eliminate the oxygen and kill every living thing. "Mr. Vincent, I know now that what I did was worth doing." Vincent tells Blake, "You're like us; you're in pain and you're afraid to die."

David then turns over a table. The box with the chemical is smashed. He and Gail run through the mines Blake, who has a flash light follows after he sees that the box is beginning to glow which means it is self-destructing. Meanwhile David and G ail are trying to find a way out, but there is a cave-in at the entrance. David and Gail go back in as Sawyer and Lavin enter. Blake walks right past them as they run out and shouts for them to wait. Blake staggers out and he's deformed. Blake tells Sawyer and Lavin that he needs help, but they tell him there is no help. They order him to get rid of David and Gail but Blake instead shoots both Sawyer and Lavin who glow red and dissipate.

Blake, however, now near death, vaporizes then begs David to quicken his own slow death, because of the pain in his hands. "Anything to stop the pain," he says. And so Vincent obliges. David picks up the gun and shoots him. Gail says, "I wish we hadn't killed him, David." Still showing remorse for an alien despite all he's told them. And it could only be because he's white.

The next morning Gail tells David she's never seen a storm as bad as that one. "They haven't taken over yet, until they do I'm still a nurse and there's still a lot of people who need me," she says. David tells her, "He wasn't a man." And check out how Gail responds: "To me, he was." She asks him to drop her off in town.

The moral? "David Vincent's war is unrecognized, unheralded. His battle fields can be anywhere, anywhere the invader has carved out a stronghold. David Vincent's war will have no ending until the Invader is driven back to his own world – or until he has made David Vincent's world his own."

How prophetic and relevant. The "lone wolf hero" myth lives on.

.25. "The Spores"

The narrator begins the episode quite hauntingly:

> "Shortly before dawn, a space ship landed near Philipsburg,
> Colorado bringing to Earth a strange and ominous cargo-two dozen
> spores. After exposure to the Earth's atmosphere, each will develop
> and grow into a perfectly formed alien. On the success of this
> experiment rests the possibility of future shipments numbering
> hundreds, perhaps thousands, of alien invaders. And possibly, the
> future of the human race."

How strange. Spores that produce alien life forms, but they come out (as we will see) with the same pink "tone" as the white man's skin here on Earth. Is there no bottom? And recall the analysis of the previous episode ("Valley of the Shadows") where I alleged that the white man was controlling time and space and indeed, had a "God Complex." Well this one is about the literal creation of life itself.

There are two highway cops on the road having formed a barricade, when a van carrying two aliens transporting the spores, appears. The van stops, turns around, and heads away as one cop, the elder, gives chase. Two aliens in back of the van as the van crashes. One falls out of the van and grabs the spores as two men in the back have unconscious. He hides the large case that holds the spores. The old cop comes down the hill to check out the wreck.

The two aliens in back dissolve in front of his very eyes. The third witnesses what the cop saw. The remaining alien Jessup is taken in by the sergeant who witnessed the vaporization of the other two. At the Philipsburg Police Station, the third alien, Jessup, is lying and claiming that he didn't see what the cop saw. They assume that one of the driver's "must have wandered off in the woods." Jessup is, of course, an alien.

They doubt the word of the old cop and take him into a side office. They want to know if he's been "hoisting a couple." He says he hasn't for two years, since he came off suspension. He's got one year and three months until retirement. They doubt his report and they threaten him with suspension with no pay. He won't swear to it under such pressure. The narrator updates us: "Several hours ago, a radio newscast carried a strange report. A deputy sheriff in Philipsburg reported an accident in which the passengers vanished in a burst of flame. A policeman's delusion, or evidence of invaders? David Vincent travels to Philipsburg to discover which."

Here we go again. Since Vincent pulled up at the police station in a car, we have to assume he has an unlimited gas card or major credit card. He can travel hither and yon, wherever he wants to, no kind of law enforcement or government identification – just a white man on a witch hunt. And they allow him inside every single time. It's called "white privilege" and the writers of these scripts had to know about and they surely capitalized on it.

As Jessup is escorted back to the police car he and David pass, not recognizing each other. David is on his way into the police station. David is grilling the head cop. The old cop gives David directions to where the accident took place. Police Chief Mattson is himself an alien convinces the cop that he's just imagining things. "It was an optical illusion," Mattson tells the cop. David leaves.

Later that day, Jessup the alien has searched the scene for the spores and finds the case, opens the case finding the spores still intact. With case in hand, he begins walking down the highway. David sees him walking away down the highway and as you would have it, Vincent pulls up and offers him a ride. Why would Jessup be walking? At any rate, he accepts the offer of a ride from Vincent who is claiming he's going to Milford. They stop at a café so that Jessup can make a phone call. He tells David his car broke down a few miles back. Vincent introduces himself as Dave Harper, a salesman. Jessup tells him he sells seeds and says, "Everything starts off as seeds once."

They pull into the café and both get out. He asks David to lock the car. Some young hot rodders pull up, two guys and a girl. Jessup changes his mind and says he'll take the case in with him after looking over the teens and saying "some people" loud enough for the toughs to hear his comment. All enter the café.

David then sneaks into the outer room of the phone booth and sees the brief case. He overhears Jessup say, "No, they weren't damaged. A few of our people perished … I have to get the spores to the incubation point … I'll get this man to drop me off." David tries to take the briefcase but ends up in a fight with Jessup. The teens hear the commotion and come into the back area and watch these two dudes fighting it out. During the fight one of the teens, Hal, grabs the briefcase and the three teens take off in their roadster.

David gets his ass kicked and is so fucked up that Jessup takes David's car keys out of his pockets and speeds off after the young people. David comes to and orders the waitress to call the police.

Jessup pursues the teens in Vincent's car but they give him the slip, and as they speed down the highway, the girl asks "What do you think is in it?" The tough behind the wheel says, "Well, it's gotta be something we didn't have before." They then pull into a residential garage as the alien, speeding through the area, drives right past the house that the kids are holed up in.

The kids lock the garage that the car is in, take the brief case and look inside of it. One of them is concerned about how "dumb" it was to snatch the case. The leader of the pack, a kid named Hal, tells him, "you heard how he put us down." The girl also opposes the move so the leader tells them if they don't like it they can both leave. Hal then blames the kid who opposed the move for panicking, which caused the man to see him grab the case in the first place. "Now, let's see what we've got."

Hal begins working to open the case. It must be Hal's house because he says he knows where he can go get some tools. He leaves the girl and the guy still seated in the open hot rod as he goes into the house searching for something to use to pry the case open.

In the meantime Jessup calls for more alien reinforcements from a pay phone. "This is Jessup. The spores have been taken. No, they don't know what they have. I can't, I'm driving a stolen car, you'll have to pick me up. Yes, but hurry. If they managed to get it open it could be dangerous."

David is at the police station telling Lieutenant Mattson, "The kids don't matter, but Jessup does and so does that case." Mattson says that the man is just a car thief who took off after some kids who took his case. Realizing he's getting nowhere with the cop David says, "All I know is that I'm responsible for that car." Leaning over the cops desk and raising his voice, David says, "I'm reporting a stolen car to you, it's up to you to follow it through." Mattson asks, "Look, you trying to tell me my duties?" David says, "Looks like somebody has to."

Mattson backs down and turns to the elder Ernie, the one who saw the aliens in the first place. "Ernie, get a description of Mr. Vincent's car and get it out there for routine circulation." David tells Mattson that time is very important but he's pissed off at Vincent's gall and ushers him out of the office, "Take care of him, Ernie."

Ernie and David are in the outer office and Ernie offers to drive David to the spot and adds that something is going on out there and he believes that David knows something about it. "What's in that sample case?" Ernie asks him. "Nothing good," says David.

In the meantime the leader of the guys is using a drill in an attempt to get inside of the sample case. The other two watch. "Whew! This must be the hardest stuff in the world," he says. "Hal, let's take it back," says the other guy. He is the one with the moral compass and on past 'jobs' they could have had, Hal reminds the two of them, it was this young kid who "blew the whistle." He explains, "Yeah, they wanted us to take stolen cars out of the state. You call that a good deal?"

Hal finally agrees that they should take the case back. When the youths fail to open the briefcase they decide to return it, but as Jessup catches up with them, walks up to their hot rod and says, "You took something of mine. I'd like it back." Hal innocently says, "I don't know what you're talking about mister." Jessup snatches the keys from the ignition and orders Hal and the girl out of the car (the younger one has the case and is watching the entire thing from behind another car).

Jessup manhandles Hal and slams him against the hot rod. "Do you want to die, son?" "My brother, he's got it," Hal snitches. Jessup spots the younger one who is making a run for it. Hal and two other aliens get in their car after he tells Hal he'll "keep the key" and take off after the younger kid. They catch up to him and tell him he threw it in the white convertible outside, the one with the black top. But when they get outside, the car has pulled off. He tries to make a run for it but out comes the metallic disk. He's dead meat.

The white convertible's occupants have no idea about the case that has been tossed into their back seat. They have only seven dollars and they just got back from Vegas and losing a bunch of money. So they pull into a motel. "We're tapped out, financially and spiritually and I've had it," the woman says. He spots the case and says, "I told ya something would turn up." He wants a reward for returning it to the owner. "Anybody who locks something up this tight it's either a woman or diamonds and this doesn't look like any woman I've ever seen," the man says. He's going to go look for a chisel to open the case, leaving it on the back trunk of the car.

An ambulance takes the young boys body away as Ernie and David are on the scene. Ernie puts out an all-points bulletin on the convertible. A call has already been put out – Jessup sent it out. How could that be? Hal and the girl are released.

Back at the motel the man tells Sally he's got it open and he sees the spores. They look like large seeds, but the man wants to find the owner. Sally (the woman) is telling him to get rid of them. Sally is leaving and he doesn't appear to be going. Sally grabs her suitcase and heads out – alone.

David tells Ernie about the kid will be found to die of cerebral hemorrhage and was murdered. "Every time things slow down you feed me another zinger, flying saucers, alien invaders." David interrupts: "Wait a minute: you saw two of them die." Now Ernie agrees. They spot Jessup and the lieutenant conversing. "Mattson, how much do you know about him?" Ernie says he's grade A and has cut the mustard around here for a full year.

David tells Ernie that Mattson is one of them. Ernie tells David to get out of his car. Meanwhile cops find the white convertible and have pulled Sally over. They have detained her and Jessup pulls up. He walks over and asks Sally about "a small suitcase." She wants to know how grateful he would be. He offers her two hundred dollars, then makes it five hundred. "For a bunch of funny lookin' seeds? She asks. She'll lead them back to the motel where the case is.

Ernie is in the office with Mattson and decides to check on him as David recommended. He calls to check on Mattson and is told that Mattson died because a kid ran him down last year. Mattons walks back in and closes the door and walks back in, grabs a metallic disk and approaches Ernie. They begin to fight and get into a scuffle. Ernie shoots him, he glows and dies.

Sally comes back into the hotel with Jessup. The man says he threw the box away and now Jessup wants to know where. Some kids have come across it and the three young kids are carrying the case off. "Where are we taking it?" they ask. "We going to plant them?" They plan to take them to the "hot house". They tell a little girl, Liz, that they've got nitro glycerin and are on a mission.

Ernie and David hook back up. He is then even more convinced as to the alien's true nature so he goes with Vincent to find Jessup. David pledges that "if we find that case before Jessup does, they'll believe everything you said." The three kids open the case and the spores are growing larger. They grab one kid and tease him. "Get out here, chicken," the other two say. He leaves. One kid takes one of the spores and buries it in a box of dirt.

David and Ernie catch up to the man and Sally. He tells them about Jessup and says there were a couple of kids up the block when he tossed it. Sally forgives the man claiming "It's the first time I ever knew you to toss in a winning hand."

Jessup and the aliens are going to conduct a house-by-house search for the spores. A kid happens into the police station while the aliens are there and asks for Mattson. He describes a metal case. "We have a car outside, why don't you come with us," Jessup says. Right in front of a BLACK officer who sits there and allows these men to take that boy. He doesn't do shit about it.

The aliens are knocking on doors. At about the same time so are Ernie and David. The little girl doesn't want to talk. But when the cop leaves she tells David her brother has a case full of dynamite and that he's at the hot house. The spores are growing and throbbing. The boys see it and can't get out. A shadow appears and it's Jessup. He orders them to wait outside where other aliens wait along with the boy who snitched. "You kids run!" shouts David as he and Ernie pull up and see Jessup at the door of the hot house.

There's a shootout and David shoots one of the aliens who glows red and dies. David gets a full bottle of whiskey out of Ernie's car and empties it. He then crawls under the car the siphons gas into the whiskey bottle. He makes a Molotov cocktail, lights it and tosses it at the hot house. It's now on fire. Another alien is shot as he tries to escape. You can hear the spores making noises as they burn. The fire consumes Jessup who dies. .

Vincent tells Ernie not to turn in the report because he would not be believed and he doesn't want Goldhaver to sacrifice his pension, which a little more than a year away. "Ernie, chances are they won't believe you any more than they believe me." David adds, "Let's make a deal: in a year from now when you have your pension, if I'm still working on this, we'll get together." Ernie smiles. "You and me. That sounds good. One year and three months."

David leaves and then Ernie tears up the fuckin' report!

Moral: "The destruction of the alien spores becomes a major victory for David Vincent in a continuing relentless war in which victories are few."

If victories are so few and the "war" is still raging on, then how can this burning of a greenhouse with spores be considered even remotely "major"?

.26. "The Trial"

In a place called Jackson City, a man gets cut by glass a foot and a half long, but there's no blood although there was a gash in the man's wrist "two or three inches long" according to the man David is talking to, Gilman. It is Gilman who suspects that the personnel manager (Fred Wilk), the guy who got cut, is an alien but he didn't tell anyone because he knew they'd never believe him.

David asks for and is directed by Gilman to the security office. I ask on what grounds? One again we find this relative stranger walking into a secured area, asking a bunch of questions that don't even involve him, and nevertheless getting clearance and access. While Gilman was spilling his guts to David however, two aliens were up above on a ledge watching them.

Gilman watches and then follows the two suspected aliens down a number of flights of steel stairs into a basement area. But as can be expected, he gets caught. One of the aliens (in a full suit of course) asks him, "Okay Gilman – what do you want?" The alien is armed with a ranch, jumps down from a stairwell and begins attacking Gilman. David and Sergeant Wisnovsky come out of the office and go outside but there is no sign of Gilman. Of course David just happens to duck into the right door and goes down into the bowels of the building where he witnesses the fight between Gilman and the suit-clad man.

The two men fight as David and another man look through the window. One of the men in the fight, an alien, gets his ass kicked and burns himself on a nearby incinerator, killing him. His body incinerates before David and his accomplice get to the stairs. Gilman describes what happened to the man but only David believes it. Wisnovsky places Gilman under arrest for murder.

The narrator informs us: "David Vincent, brought to Jackson City by a reported alien presence must now help a friend account for the absence of that alien. At two o'clock this afternoon, Charles Gilman goes on trial for the murder of Fred Wilk."

Brennan, an investigator hired by David walks up to him and says that he checked out Wilk and he was 'as good as gold.' David reminds the investigator that Wilk had only been on the job for a year and that he needs proof. He found Wilks' transcripts and high school record and reminds David that, "What we need is PROOF." The investigator is getting paid and says he's a "couple of days up" on David's appearance on the scene. David tells him (as in "orders" him) to stick with it and he's going to check out the wife.

David goes to Gilman's house and introduced himself to the wife, Janet, as someone from the insurance company. "Well I've already spoken to the agent," she says. David, a quick liar (as demonstrated in episode-after-episode) replies, "Well this is the industrial accident policy that the company carries." She falls for it and asks s him to sit down.

David digs right in, prefacing his remarks by telling Janet there are a few questions he'd like to ask. Instead of him easing into the questions he really has on his mind, he dives right in with, "How long did you know your husband?" This dumb bitch says that she only knew him a few weeks before they were married. Such an answer is grounds to withhold any insurance payments or at least to question the marriage in some capacity. A few weeks? Come on, man. Anybody can smell setup on somebody's part. But again, this is television and this is the world of white nationalism.

Janet says that they moved to Jackson city about the same time. She says she's from Springdale and has lived there since kindergarten and that her husband is from a small town in southern Indiana. It is only then that she finally uses her brain and tells him, "I don't see why all this is so important." Then the doorbell rings.

A voice is warning her about a man poking around asking questions and he immediately enters the room asking, "What kind of trick is this?" It's a man named Slater and he's the county attorney. He tells Janet that "He's a friend of Gilman's" and orders David out. "The lady let me in," David says. "You lied to her," Slater replies. "That may well be," says David, "And she may have returned the favor." After that insult David excuses himself. Slater warns before David's exit: "You may as well stop your snooping. Gilman killed him and that's all there is to it."

Later, David is in the cell with Gilman and his attorney and even Gilman believes that he killed Wilk. "You destroyed an alien, remember that?" David asks. Gilman tells him that nobody is going to believe it. The attorney says that a self-defense argument won't work because the plain clothes man, Wofnofsky, saw Gilman hit Wilk with a wrench and that Wilk didn't have a weapon. David asks if Wilk said anything, Gilman says no and David says he doesn't believe him. Gilman basically then tells Vincent to fuck off and lays back down on his cot. David reminds him, "Look, I stood by you in Korea and I'm going to stick by you now, so just cool down, okay?"

Vincent then turns to local lawyer Bernard (Russell Johnson, "the professor" from Gilligan's Island) who is hired to defend Gilman, and ask him about the County Attorney Slater and how long he's been in town. Bernard says, "about a year, I guess." David surmises, "Only a year – and this guy was a friend of Wilks." Gilman looks up: Hey, you think he's an alien?" David answers, "They arrived at the same time. He could have arranged to have himself assigned to this case – it's possible." They waived the jury because David believes that they have a better chance of convincing one man than twelve.

Bernard says he took the case only because Bill Cleary was out of town and Howard Mitchell is laid up with arthritis. "I'm not going to stand up in open court and claim that there are flying saucers and that nonsense and I most certainly am not going to include my colleague of being some kind of space monster." David stares Bernard down and says, "You don't have to claim anything. Just ask the questions. Bernard says that when Gilman gets through telling his story, "we may not have any questions to ask."

First on the stand is Sergeant Wisnovsky who testifies about what he saw. When asked if there was any place to dispose of the body, he said only a "large open furnace" and that it was "going like a blast furnace." Sawyer, the lawyer representing the state, then calls David Vincent to the stand. After correcting the attorney about a "murder" and stating it was a "disappearance," Vincent is then asked if he was with Sergeant Wisnofsky at the window, and David has to admit that Wisnofsky's account was correct.

David then admits that he saw Gilman hit Wilk with a wrench but then quickly adds that "Mr. Wilk did not die." Vincent then asks the judge if he can make a statement and, for some reason, it is granted. Despite being told by the attorney that Vincent is not a defendant or a witness, and that such a statement is slightly irregular, the judge allows Vincent to speak. Again, white privilege raises its head in favor of David.

David admits that even Gilman will admit he hit Wilk and that he saw him do it. But then goes into this thing that the definition of murder is the killing of a human being. "Fred Wilk was not a human being." The judge calls an immediate recess, leans over and says, "Mr. Vincent: I'd like to see you in my chambers."

In Chambers, with both Slater and Bernard present with Vincent, the judge begins by making it clear that, "I hope I don't have to remind you that a man's life is at stake here." David says that Gilman saw Wilk "disintegrate," and that this may not indicate that Wilk was a creature from another planet but is surely indicates that he wasn't human. Slater says that the defense is trying to turn the trial "into a three-ring circus." The judge then warns David "against any more grandstanding." David then TELLS the judge that there should be a certain amount of latitude and the judge replies, "Latitude, not license." As if Vincent is qualified to call a judge out.

They then head back out into the courtroom. But Slater holds back to remind the judge that he is being considered for the State Supreme Court, and adds that, "If this trial goes another day, the newspaper will have a picnic, a barbecue. Why can't you just see the governor appointing a man who in effect had announced his belief in little green martians?" The judge tells Slater to get out. What he SHOULD have been doing is holding this asshole in contempt of court and charging him with an attempt to bribe a judge!

Back at Bernard's office Wilk's wife, Janet, walks in and asks David why he's doing what he's doing. David charges her with hiding the truth. After she leaves David tells Bernard that she's probably an alien herself. Bernard has a woman on the stand, Ms. Cole, who saw Wilk was attacked by Gilman. She said he said, "I oughta kill you." During the fight there was no blood. Janet Wilk is next called to the stand. Janet Wilk is married with one child. Before she met Fred Janet was engaged to Gilman. Janet says she also heard Gilman say he should kill Wilk.

She was engaged to Gilman in another city before she moved to Lincoln City. A year later she married Wilk but then Gilman moved there as well. A 15 minute recess uncovers it all. Gilman and __ had a fight and she moved and that is when she met Wilk. Gilman said he killed Wilk because he was an alien and had a couple of drinks. He hit him because it was about Janet. Wilk was an active member of the community and now, says David, "we have to prove that he never existed." David runs into Janet in the hall and he tells her that Gilman still loves her.

Gilman is now on the stand being questioned by Slater. "He married your old girlfriend, didn't he?" "Yes." "And that's why you killed him." Gilman says, "Why doesn't mean anything. He wasn't a human being." Slater comes back with, "Come on, Mr. Gilman. He breathed didn't he? He ate, he cried, he laughed, he walked, he talked – and he wasn't human?" "No," Gilman says. "He was a father, Mr. Gilman – he had a child," Slater says as Janet twists the wedding ring on her finger out of nervousness. " … And yet you claim he wasn't human. How can that be? Can you please explain that to me?"

Slater then calls Janet Wilk to the stand once again. After being reminded that she is still under oath by the judge, Bernard begins the questioning by asking how long she was married to Fred Wilk. When she gets on the stand she admits marrying him after only a few weeks, and that she knew nothing about his past and "as far as I knew he never existed before I met hm." This raises Slater's eyebrows as she continues by adding that her marriage was not good, and "he never touched me, he never wanted to." The judge interjects that, "a wife is a better judge of her husband than a lawyer." She adds, "There was something cold, almost inhuman …" Slater continues to object "to the spectacle of a wife assassinating her husband's memory after he's dead." Not only is Slater overruled but also ruled "out of order."

She told Gilman what she though about her husband. Her son is 4 months, and they were married 11 months. Wilk was not the father of the child. Slater is impeaching his own witness. She says, under oath, that Gilman is the father. She admits being in love with Gilman – and that she still is. She was pregnant when she married Wilk. Brennan, the private investigator that David hired found evidence that Wilke was an impostor. The social security, fingerprints, birth certificate – none of it adds up.

So then that raises an important question: how in the HELL did this white man get that job! How was he able to be on payroll for a full year, with benefits, and rise to the rank of Personnel Manager? No background check? Again, there can be only one answer absent nepotism: white privilege!

As David prepares to re-enter the courtroom he politely allows two elderly people in before him. Unbeknownst to him they are Wilke's parents. More on that later.

A black man is brought in to testify as a fire expert. He's quickly dismissed and his testimony favored Wilk. They have to keep the trial going until seven o'clock until Brennan arrives with the evidence. Prosecutor has a special witness: Fred Wilk Sr. from Omaha, Nebraska! He is there with his wife, both hicks from Omaha, Nebraska. He lies by giving the birth date and claims to be his father. He even has a birth certificate. A woman stands up claiming to be Wilk's mother. Bernard has no questions. Slater thinks he's proven that Wilk was a man.

When the old people leave the courtroom David follows them and questions them. They take the suicide pills, glow and disappear just before Slater comes around the corner and says, "Mr. Vincent: I'd say we have you by the ears. What would you say?"

Evidence is on the way and will be there at 7pm. But private investigator is found in the car outside – dead! Bernard and David discuss how Gilman should plead. Bernard says perhaps second degree murder or temporary insanity. Then David, of all people, has the gall to say, "The whole world is nuts. And everyone in it." If that's the case, then why all the traveling and risking your life? If the whole world is nuts, then the invaders are doing the world a favor by blowing it up!

Janet is allowed to visit Gilman in his cell and they are allowed to kiss and hug. What kind of shit is this? She pledges that no matter how much time he gets, "we're together now," she claims. This is the same bitch who married a man after knowing him for two damn weeks! She has no credibility. As fine as she is do you think she's going to go dickless for two decades waiting for a man that she had previously left and who she didn't even tell he had a kid?

They now believe Bernard, their own attorney, killed Brennan and has the evidence. They found out because Janet saw Bernard walking from the parking lot area into the courthouse holding some papers – papers that David presumed were taken after Bernard killed Brennan.

David walks into a room where the judge and Slater are. The judge now wants to include David as someone who is demented. David breaks a glass by dropping it onto the floor in the judge's chambers and picks up a chard which he uses to cut Bernard's face.

Vincent's gamble pays off when Bernard doesn't bleed and Bernard attempts to run from the courthouse. Sergeant Wisnovsky is just nearby and shoots Bernard when he fails to stop. Bernard then vaporizes in front of Vincent, Slater, the judge and the sergeant. Slater is convinced then of Gilman's innocence and offers no contest in court and moves for dismissal of the charge based on "insufficient evidence". The judge dismisses the case.

Narrator: "Three more witnesses to testify in David Vincent's behalf. When he has his day in court, when he presents his case to the authorities, proving the existence of the alien invaders."

.27. "Dark Outpost"

As was the case with "Valley of the Shadow" with the word "shadow" denoting something dark and ominous (as is the case in Euroamerican culture), it should be clear that an outpost that is described as "dark" is going to an outpost that is a place filled with the macabre, the maniacal and the murky.

Man staggers out of room and collapses on the street. The ambulance arrives. Almost immediately a car pulls up and pulls the ambulance over. Claiming to be the Public Health Services, they claim to be taking the injured man to hospital in San Francisco. They clam the man is suffering from cholera, quickly flash ID, although the car they are in has no identification at all. The "officials" are actually two other aliens who kill the two medics is dead (from cerebral hemorrhage with the metallic disks).and retrieve their comrade who is the injured party. They take the comrade and whisk away in a car.

Elsewhere, David Vincent pulls up in a 1967 Mustang. The narrator tells us: "An ambulance, wrecked on a California highway, its two attendants dead. Cause of death in both cases – cerebral hemorrhage. To the world, a bizarre coincidence. To David Vincent, much more."

David is met by a woman who may be a nurse. She says that the man, Thatcher, who is alleged to have had cholera could not have had it. She says her little girl came down with it just last week and it was "chicken pox – plain old fashioned chicken pox." She says she knows where Thatcher wanted to go before they dragged him into the ambulance. She offers David some coffee inside and he turns it down. Thatcher said a place called Cavanaugh's.

In the next scene a huge truck with the name "Cavanaugh" is backing up to a loading dock. David is already there and decides to take the very steep stairs up the side of the building and goes through a side door. He goes over to "investigation" as usual, sneaks in (as usual), and sees a man placed in a locker. He is able to hide behind a huge number of wooden crates and sees a fence marked "Unauthorized Personnel Keep Out." His favorite words because whenever he sees these kinds of warnings he takes his nosey ass directly into that spot.

The fence is, of course, unlocked and David enters. There are gym lockers all lined up and he opens one and finds it empty. He opens a second one and there is a man in it, appearing to have had chicken pox. He appears to be dead though he's standing upright in the locker. Aliens are busy at work so David decides to duck into one of the lockers. Three of them enter the area and begin hauling out the lockers, including the one that Vincent is in. the lockers are placed on a space ship.

The lockers are then re-aligned in an area on the ship. David slowly opens the door and sneaks out. He peers into another room and walks through several corridors. He ducks into a room and the ship takes off. He falls to the floor from the acceleration of the ship, which has taken off and ends up landing in some nearby mountains. When David wakes up, he is alone (figures) and climbs down from the ship (which has landed, of course) and is on a mountainside. He wonders where he is.

David begins weaving his way through the mountainous terrain (similar to the terrain we saw in the episode, "The Saucer"). He walks upon a girl and some other people excavating rocks. One man says "Welcome to God's country." David asks where he is and is told he's in Bowman County, about 20 miles outside of Griffin. He tells the people (all white of course) that he will show them the space ship. When they get there the saucer is gone! It is a science class and they have a truck, so they all pile in and head off to see David's flying saucer. The group has their doubts but they go along anyway.

They join several other people who were waiting by the truck who introduce themselves as Steve and Nicole. Off they go per David's directions. When they all arrive they climb out of the truck and as can be expected David says "Just over the hill" and when they arrive – no saucer. "It was right down there," he says pointing at what is now a clear space. The group is laughing at him. But in the distance an alien is peering at them through binoculars.

Dr. Devin, the leader of the group is willing to investigate. He tells the group, "He could be a crackpot, but he doesn't sound like one to me. He's an architect with a graduate degree." The girl, Eileen, adds, "with a pair of thirty dollar shoes" (expensive by those standards). They say they were talking about his shoes and it didn't look like he had walked very far. He asks the group to stay off of each other's throats and take the truck back to the campsite. He's going to check things out some more with David.

So Devlin and Vincent strike out. First, they locate the landing pod marks left by the ship. "They unloaded the lockers," Vincent surmises. They then come across some automobile tire tracks. "Hardly extraterrestrial," Devlin says. "They unloaded something that looked like lockers," David says. They continue their walk until they venture across a place that looks like a military base of some kind. A soldier meets them and says "restricted area." They are denied a chance to see the camp commander. David can see he's an alien and they fight. David knocks him out and kills him and he glows red and dies right in front of Devlin.

Without even taking the rifle that the dead alien had stopped them with, Devin and David sneak onto the base and from a hiding place look directly into a control room of some kind. It is a regeneration chamber with a body inside being re-energized. They creep inside and hide behind some large computers.

They watch as the "man" is then released from the tube and is placed into one of the waiting lockers. Next comes the one with the chicken pox who is rolled over and prepared for one of the re-generation tubes. David sneaks up to the control panel and snatches the rotating crystal that powers the machine. The alien masquerading as Colonel Harris returns to the control panel and immediately spots the missing orb and immediately has his men searching the chamber. They give chase and grab Devlin. They place the metallic disk on his neck and he dies instantly as David watches from a safe hiding place. "Search him!" the lead alien shouts. David makes a break for it as they search Devlin's body, runs out the door and hides as an alien runs past him. Of course he easily knocks the alien out and continues to flee across open ground, easily getting away.

Vern and the other guy, Hal, are fighting over the beautiful girl Eileen (played by Dawn Wells, formerly Mary Ann of "Gilligan's Island"). Vern sees David running back. David says they have to get out of there and David tells them he's dead. "They're on their way to get us now. We've got to get into the truck," David says. Here come jeeps filled with aliens, dressed as soldiers. David hides the mechanism he stole in the rim of one of the cars. They tell them, "The camp commander wants to see you," and they are corralled into their car. The mechanism falls out of the jeep and is picked up by the girl who casually puts it into her bag.

The base is actually an alien hospital run by a man named Col. Harris. Vern is the macho one and he warns one of the soldiers not to push him or "we're going to war." They place them all in an abandoned barracks. David tells them the entire story. The girl apologizes to Vern for what took place the night before with Hal. "It's your business – just not in front of me, okay?"

Vern walks over and apologizes to David about the threats from before. "It was nothing personal." David accepts his apology. David tells them that he and Devlin were trying to find proof that the aliens were here. "Find any?" asks one of the group. "Yes," David replies. David tells them he hid the proof which is why "they searched us."

An alien claiming to be "Colonel Harris" comes in in full military gear and introduced himself. "This is a secret military base. And yet you've managed to come in here and steal a vital piece of military equipment." When Vern asks him what is missing he says, "A crystal, a circular-shaped crystal." Harris lies and says that Devlin is alright and is in the infirmary "being treated for a slight injury." David wants to see him and Harris says that he will. Harris says if they return it "we'll forget that you took it."

Hal says, "Give it to them Vincent" as the aliens were leaving. "Which one of you is Vincent?" All the men volunteer that they are Vincent. "Play your games gentlemen – I have as much time as you." Vern was in the army and didn't like being pushed around. Cal says that he's locked up with "two squares, a freak and your ex-boyfriend." Vincent says he knows that they cannot deliver Dr. Devlin, but unbeknownst to the group, the room is bugged and the aliens hear everything.

The device that is bugging the room can also render mass hypnosis, so Harris gives a hypnotic suggestion: "From this moment on you will see what I tell you to see and hear what I tell you to hear. In a few minutes a man will enter your barracks. Listen to me closely, all six of you. The hypnotic light is flashing on and off as they are being programmed without being aware of it.

In walks a man who appears to be Devlin. Hal tries to attack David who easily subdues him. Vern tells him "Give them back that crystal." Devlin says "the colonel knows you have it. You lied about the saucer and you lied about me dying," the fake Devlin says. In walks Harris asking, "Which one's Vincent"? David steps forward and says, "I am." David asks, "Why is it so important. Is it part of your equipment to kill your people?" Harris doesn't answer. "I have it – let them go," David demands. Harris tells them that the base is engaged in a project that could affect everyone in the country.

Harris tells them that if David doesn't hand over the crystal, then all seven of them will be considered enemies of the country and will be taken out and executed. Vern says, "You must be crazy. You don't have authority to do that." Harris orders that the executions, one by one, begin. The first one they take is Hal. HE tries to run for it and David tries to help but gets knocked out. They grab Steve instead.

They actually have a gallows rigged up and from a clear spot in the window it can be seen. One is put on his knees and another is tied to a pole. They are all seeing different things because of the hypnosis. Harris returns to the barracks. "Where is it?" David says "in the air filter of the truck." Nicole says, "Thank god it's over." Harris orders the entire truck be taken apart (they have it on the military grounds). They put the air filter back on. Vern wants Hal to stand with him as they prepare to fight.

Eileen pulls something out of her purse. Vern says he saw Steve hang. David saw him get shot with a pistol shot to the back of the head. Eileen saw a firing squad with six to eight men. "They're making us see what they want us to see," David says. They search the place as the fake Devlin tries to turn them against David. They spot the glowing light on the ceiling. Vern stands on a stool and pulls it down and when he does, the fake Devlin can be seen for who he really is – an alien imposter!

David sees the crystal in Eileen's bag. Steve is brought back in. "No more games, Mr. Vincent. A second one of my people died because we don't have that crystal." Vincent gets everyone released after promising he'll give back the crystal. "Get out of here as fast as you can," David tells them as he is led off. They go to the truck but are cut off by soldiers: "Lieutenant's orders."

They slap David around. In the meantime outside, Vern, Hal and Steve overpower the guards and grab a military rifle. "Get in the truck – get out of here," Vern orders as he heads to save David. He busts into the area where David is being held and fires away as David makes a run for it. Vern blasts four aliens and they glow and die. They pack into the truck and take off.

The real military arrive to investigate but find no evidence, though they do promise all to take things very seriously. "The army report will be thorough and painstaking. But without proof its conclusions will be negative. And David Vincent resumes his war against the high command of another army: the army of alien invaders."

And there are six new witnesses that aliens do, indeed, exist.

.28. "Summit Meeting" (Part 1)

This episode is the first of two parts and represents a major turning point in Vincent's quest to expose the aliens and gain some major support. Not only is a major invasion threat prevented, but he is able to win over an ally from the other side (female, of course) and we get to see how much "juice" this unranked, unlisted, civilian really has when it comes to alien-chasing. The opening narration informs us of the following: "An uncharted island in the Baltics, one hour after dawn. Thor Halverson signals the world's dream for peace, keeps a fateful appointment"

Three men wait for a copter in to an island somewhere in the Baltics, one of them is Halverson. The two men with Halverson are high ranking officials and a man in a suit (an alien) approaches them about "offering a substance to the world" upon the condition that their "presence here is not revealed." Halverson agrees and says that he is prepared to go on with the plan. Halverson says it was a difficult decision to make but that they must do it and therefore he will arrange the invitations to go out today, addressed "to the various heads of state, the usual diplomatic delays will be eliminated."

Halverson and the two chauffeurs turn to leave. The third man, Almquist tells the alien that there will be no witnesses. "One of them is ours," he says. He adds that the other one will be taken care of. The alien turns and walks with his two men back to his helicopter. The first limo with Halverson in it takes off. The second limo, with Almquist, getting into the back seat is not so fortunate. Almquist takes the metallic disk out of his coat pocket and uses it on the chauffer, killing him instantly. He then drags the body out of the car, lays it on the ground and drives off.

We find David finally doing something related to architecture. Evidently working for the Albert Construction Company, he is in a small outside office rolling up some blueprints as the narrator informs us of the following: "A man toils late into the night. A man whose job is only a necessary delay in performing his own self-assigned mission. But that mission, doing battle with the most dangerous enemy in the history of the earth, may be resumed at any moment."

What? How can such a claim be made? The condition of the world, even back in 1967-68 when this TV show was being aired, was in that condition because of the white man. It was the white race that had colonized Africa, ripped off South America and was in the middle of the Vietnam War (which didn't end until 1975), that proved to be the biggest enemy in the history of the world. Today, in 2018, merely ask world leaders about America and its history. Unlike the history classes and "education" approaches that camouflage America's brutality, the rest of the world knows. Who else dropped two atomic bombs on another race of people, and the list goes on. To place that "most dangerous" label on aliens who masquerade as white people is a disservice to history, in my view.

David is padlocking his tiny office when a man in a suit walks up. "Vincent," he shouts. "A friend of yours wants to see you – Michael Tressider." David shouts back, "Why didn't he call first?" The man says, "We'll take you to him" and it is then that David knows it's a trap. He attempts to make a run for it but a second suited man cuts him off. David runs the other way with both men giving chase. David ditches one and when the man comes around the corner, karate chops him and knocks him out. He then goes through his pockets as the second man comes up from behind and gets the drop on him.

The first man wakes up and the two of them escort David to their large sedan to meet Mike Tressider. "That was a dangerous stunt you pulled," David says to the man after getting into the sedan. Tressider says that it wasn't a stunt. "My phones are being tapped and I had to talk to you." David reminds him that "there are public phones" to which Tressider apologizes. "I've been trying to reach you for two weeks, and I had no intention of losing you. Besides I saw no reason to put your life in jeopardy as well as mine by meeting you in a public place." "What jeopardy?" David asks.

Tressider explains: "Three weeks ago I was nearly run down by a laundry truck. I managed to get the license number." David says, "So?" "There was no such laundry nor had any such license like that ever been issued." "You think it's aliens," David deduces. "That's why I picked you up." He says it's a lot more dangerous than it was with that sabotage business a year ago. They drive off.

Still in the car, David tells him, "You look like you've aged ten years.." Tressider tells him, "I haven't been able to concentrate on anything for weeks, particularly since I heard about the radiation." Tressider says that "they've kept it hush-hush, but if the level of radioactivity continues and increases at its present rate, in six months' time the planet will be unfit for human life." David said "it's worldwide?" Tressider says, "Yes, except for one part of Scandinavia where the radiation level has dropped to some degree." David says that according to the papers that's where they've had a rash of UFO sightings. "Exactly," Tressider nods.

The Pentagon is going to make "a little investigative trip over there and I want you to go with me," Tressider says. "What are we supposed to find there?" David asks. "Proof that the aliens are using that little particular corner of the world for their headquarters." "And from their headquarters they're trying to destroy the world with radioactivity," David concludes. "I don't think there's any doubt," Tressider adds. "And in a few months' time, if we don't do something about it …" David interrupts: "We'll all be dead."

Thor and Almquist step out of a first class hotel the next day. "The Americans are last, they have to agree," Almquist says. He adds, "Without the United States, there is no conference." A limo pulls up and they get in. They're headed to the White House.

David and Tressider arrive at the office of General Blaine because Tressider has an appointment. David notices that one of the officers who is leaving is an alien (extended pinkie finger). David decides to follow him. The general calls in Tressider. He tells him that the answer was no. "A couple of weeks ago you told me there would be no problem," Tressider says. "That was a couple of weeks ago," says the general. A couple of people at the state house have since changed their mind – something having to do with "not wanting to rock the diplomatic boat."

Halverson has already met with the President and the general says that he assumes that "Halverson would rather have you not snooping around in his back yard." Halverson has scheduled a news conference for that afternoon. Tressider gets up to talk out. The general says, "Michael – are you sure you don't want to tell me what you're after?" Michael says, "No, I don't want to scare you out of my corner."

The officer that David is following gets out of a cab and enters a club called The Circle. David's cab is right behind and David enters as well. It's a hippie type club and David is looking all around. He even jumps a counter. David runs outside and he's lost the officer who gets into another car and speeds off.

Meanwhile, Tressider is in the back seat of a car being programmed by what I call the hypno orb. He is being told that "David Vincent is your enemy. "We will wait in the lobby. When he comes in, you will take this gun and you will kill him," the lead alien says. "I will take this gun and I will kill him,' Tressider repeats. They then get out of the car and head into the service entry of the hotel. Tressider is left to go in alone while the aliens leave.

David arrives at the front door. After looking around he enters the lobby. Tressider shoots him in the arm and David hardly flinches. Tressider snaps out of it and David talks the security away saying it was an accident. He and Tressider walk to the back to the hotel. "It's a flesh wound in and out," David says in vintage macho fashion. Tressider doesn't remember what happened. "I didn't want to, I didn't mean to."

They check into a motel and as they enter the room Tressider quips, "Not exactly the lap of luxury, is it?" "It'll do," David says. "Unless they followed us here." Although Tressider tells David, "Let's have a look at that shoulder," they don't do it. Instead, they're babbling about Halverson, with Tressider stating, "I just can't believe that Halverson would have anything to do with aliens." David turns on the television and says, "He's an old man. Sometimes old men do strange things. A news report blaring from the TV informs them that the United States has accepted Halverson's invitation to the conference along with acceptances from "the other big five powers."

The newscast then airs Halverson's press conference where he makes the following statement: "It can be no secret that in the past six months atmospheric radiation has been climbing to a dangerous, almost fatal, level …" David notices the man standing behind Halverson is the same man that he saw at the art gallery. He's Peter Almquist, Halverson's chief aide. Halverson continues his presentation: "Two weeks ago, I was presented with the news that they had been successful in developing an anti-radioactivity pollutant. This pollutant, which we call AR-5, successfully eliminates the toxic elements in the radiation-poisoned air. The purpose of our meeting next week is to hold a public demonstration of AR-5, and discuss its distribution to every corner of the Earth. "

And that's the end of Halverson's press conference. The key is that the aliens want to raise the radiation levels on the planet and the only country that is unaffected is that of Premier Thor Halvorsen's country. Some aliens have convinced Halverson that they have the antidote which is called "AR5." Halverson believes them and as a result, calls for a EURAC summit (EURAC stands for European Allied Command) of world leaders where they'll discuss rising levels of radiation that threaten all life on earth. Getting all the world leaders in one place is what the alien plan to do – so they can assassinate them.

Tressider says that Halverson has to know that the AR-5 claim is a complete lie. Why? Because his country is too small and too poor. Tressider believes it's a smokescreen "to keep us from worrying about radioactivity." David is in disagreement and argues, "The aliens don't want to take over a world that is contaminated with radioactivity." Tressider counters: "Maybe they've figured out a way to live with it." David says he thinks they have something else in mind and tells Tressider, "you've got to make sure we're at that summit conference" and tells him to do it "any way you can."

Tressider makes a phone call to a General Blaine. Meanwhile, Halverson is in his office telling a man that "these people have moved in good faith." The other man, Secretary Rosmundson, says he saw steel needles move on electronic equipment but adds that he knows that machines can be made to lie. Halverson asks Secretary Rosmndson , "Have you any reason to believe they lied?" Rosmndson hesitantly answers, "No." Halverson says, "Do not worry about placing your faith in these alien people. Only let your faith in me continue. I would be lost without you, my friend."

Just then Almquist walks into the room. "Am I interrupting something?" he asks. "I'm afraid Secretary Rosmndson has his doubts. Almquist says, "Courage retreats before the onslaught of old age." Rosmndson tells Halverson, "Please think about what I've said," and then gets up from the table and walks out the door. "Do you think he'll take any action?" Almquist asks. Halverson says, "What do you mean? Almquist explains that the secretary objects strongly to the conference and he may try to interfere.

Meanwhile, David and Tressider are meeting with a major outside and trying to convince him that there is a conspiracy afoot. He says that Vincent can show him the bullet hole that shows that attempts have been made on both their lives. He says, "I'm not asking for an investigation, all I'm asking you for is a favor." The

Major is willing to listen. Tressider says, "I want you to get me assigned to the president's conference commission." The major quips, "Is that all? Are you sure you don't want a cabinet post, too?" "Calm down Jake, it isn't that tough," Tressider says, "I've been assigned to these diplomatic missions before. And it should be easy for you to get a temporary clearance for Mr. Vincent, too."

When the Major says he can't do it, Tressider says, "That's alright. I'll just see the President myself." After that threat, the Major says, "Alright: I'll see what I can do" and then gets up and prepares to walk off with the woman who the lieutenant was flirting with earlier. Vincent asks her about it because he witnessed it. "Do you realize how many junior officers are wandering around the pentagon looking for a friendly desk to sit on?" she asks. The Major walks up and asks what the conversation is about. She tells David she resents "the third degree" and the Major tells him that he's out of line, that he's known Miss ___ since she was born, that her late father served under him at Anzio North. He adds, "I trust her with my life."

Now its Tressider's turn to cockblock. "I'm sorry Jake. My friend here does sometimes get carried away. But let me say in his defense that usually it's for good reason." The Major says, "Well not this time" and then escorts the young lady away from the scene. When they leave Tressider tells David, "Better be careful, you're paranoia is beginning to show." David tells him that he saw the young lieutenant in the office, and that Almquist could have gotten the name of the hotel they were staying in from her. Tressider warns David to be careful because "not trusting our friends is not going to get us anywhere." David tells him, "It's kept me alive for the past two years."

In a steam room sits the old Secretary Rosmndson. The steam is coming in heavy and a shadowed figure locks the door and turns up the steam. The old man yells for someone to open the door but no one does. He dies.

In a meeting headed by Almquist and a desk surrounded by big wigs, the word is given to him that, "The last opposition to the conclusion of their assignment has been removed. Secretary Rosmndson has met with a most unfortunate accident." The Major then enters the room and informs Almquist that "there is a small difficulty but it can be dealt with." The meeting resumes.

David is outside sitting in the quad pondering what is going on. He's waiting to meet with Blaine's secretary. David sweet talks Blaine's secretary, Ellie Markham (who is also an alien) in order to secure a pass (diplomatic clearance) for himself and Tressider to get into the Summit. The secretary also has her doubts about the Summit and provides the badges. She tells him that she's concerned and he tells her that there is no danger for her. David asks her to go to dinner and when she asks if he will tell her everything he says "maybe." She tells him her address and they will meet that evening. An alien is watching them who goes to a pay phone and contacts Almquist who then orders the watcher to kill both Vincent and Ellie.

David meets with Tressider who tells David that Rosmndson is dead. He threatens to cancel out of the conference because "it's more than the two of us can handle, that's why." He says he will take the information they have to the CIA and David says, "You know how they'll react. We have nothing we can prove." David says "you're running scared." Tressider then shares with David some background: "I built an empire once, now I didn't manage that by running scared." He adds that, "I spent four years in the war carrying a gun, not a pencil, and I did well enough there, too. But this – this is something else, huh? Two men against – well, you know exactly what we're up against. An enemy we can't even recognize." (Of course not – they're white folks like you!).

David replies, "That's why we've got to keep going. If we give up there are no odds, there is no ball game!" The phone rings and its General Blaine. He's returning Tressider's call. He wants to confirm when the man is coming to pick him up. Meanwhile David is at Ellie's apartment and she is flirting with him and offers him a Scotch and water.

As she fixes his drink and he lights up yet another cigarette, she claims that the last date she had was "back in 1963." "Judging from that the vodka you're drinking, that Scotch must be pretty well aged," David observes. "Ah, you're a detective as well as a spy," she says. "Spy is your word," David replies. She notices he's been checking the room. He notices dust on the books. He is suspicious and when she cuts her finger it doesn't bleed.

Ellie tries to make a run for it, but he beats her to the door. "You're one of them, aren't ya?" David shouts. "Yes I am. But there's something you don't know. David gets on the phone and is calling the police department. She says she will destroy herself if he does. She says she can destroy herself by standing right there, no traces. David puts down the phone and lets her go. "Now maybe we can talk some sense," she says.

"I'm on your side, at least in this," she says. He asks her why he should believe her: "You need this planet. Your people want to take over, don't they?" he asks. "That means eliminating everybody here including me." She says he is correct but then she explains, "The operation my people are planning is extremely hazardous. In my opinion it can only backfire." "Why tell me?" David asks. She says that if she went to them they would destroy her. "Why won't their plan work?" David asks. "Because it would alert your people to our presence here and unite them against us before we've arrived in sufficient numbers to complete our takeover," she explains.

"It's not about the radioactivity is it?" David asks. "Of course not. We need Earth for colonization," she says. When he asks what the aliens are trying to do Ellie tells him that "The summit conference is a fraud. They just want to get everyone together, the delegations from all the countries attending. Heads of state, top assistants, right on down the line, so that they can kill them." "A mass coup d'état," David concludes. She says, "We have men in every country ready to take over as soon as assassinations take place, except that I know it is not going to be as simple as they think. It's the only reason I'm telling you this and perhaps together we can stop it." David asks, "Is Alverson a part of this?" and Ellie says, "no, he's just being used."

David admits that he has no reason to believe what she is telling him. She explains that, "My assignment tonight was to kill you," she says. David says, "You never got the chance." She further asserts, "Your friend Tressider – they're going to kill him tonight." David tells her that Tressider is supposed to meet General Blaine tonight. He asks her "is Blaine one of yours" and she says he is not and when David asks where they are taking Tressider she tells him that she doesn't know. In fact, she "swears" she doesn't know.

Swears? On what and to whom? The Holy Rocks of the Planet Zimzor? The Sand Bats from the Rings of Jupiter? The Four-Eyed Frogs from Uranus? Swear to who? And what credibility would such a vow have coming from a bitch that is not even a human being?

Moving right along, Tressider is leaving his apartment as aliens, under the guise of officials, come to pick up Tressider, but they actually kidnap him. David phones Tressider's room, but is too late, and Ellie tells him that Tressider has been taken to the warehouse. And it appears that the car that he gets into is yet another Lincoln Continental. They are driving and have just crossed over into Virginia. When Tressider tells the lieutenant to stop the car, the Major points a gun at him.

On the phone Ellie tells someone she needs to contact General Blaine. She gets directions to where Blaine is headed. David has a revolver. Where did he get it? Does he have a license to carry and conceal? Who wrote this bullshit?

In any event, Ellie and David head to the secret installation, where Tressider is being tortured and is about to be placed in a regeneration machine. There they are met by General Blaine and when Tressider says, "Well Jake, you're not one of them, so you must be selling out. Blaine says, "Selling out? Just words, Michael. We all sell out." Tressider says, "Not all." Blaine tells him, "You could have been one of the great scientific minds of this century. Instead, you wind up a businessman. Now I can't blame you, of course. The Nobel money is nothing compared to a fat government contract. But I'd still call it a sellout." Tressider is offended and replies, "If I sold out to anyone it was to myself, not my country, not everyone I believed in." Blaine says, "Well, maybe it depends on what you believe in. Me, I believe in what counts these days: strength, power." Tressider reminds him, "You had both!" Blaine says, "With one star, my name on the door and a $600 a month pension? I'm talking REAL power." Tressider shouts, "You're talking treason!" and Blaine slaps the shit out of him.

Tressider claims that he called the president and told him "about your and Almquist. By now the CIA is on the move." "You're bluffing," Blaine says. "Are you sure?" Tressider asks. Blaine says that he will let Almquist decide all that. They are waiting for Almquist prompting Tressider to tell him, "Even in this army all you rate is one star."

Ellie and David are speeding toward the warehouse as Tressider is under interrogation with the hypnotic crystal but resists and knocks the mechanism out of the hands of one of the aliens and it breaks. Almquist witnesses it and decides, "I'm afraid we're forced to become more direct unless you're ready to tell us the truth." They begin a physical beating of Tressider who is sitting in a chair. He still claims that the CIA is "probably on their way here right now."

David suspects a trap. She says she's not going to get out of the car and accompany David because "if something happens to you, someone has to be someone who knows what they're planning, someone who can do something about it." Though warned by Ellie that he'll be walking into "an armed camp," David nevertheless leaves her in the car and approaches the warehouse. Meanwhile Almquist and his crew force Tressider into a room and into an area that Almquist describes as "shock therapy." He adds, "However, if it proves ineffective in your case, we'll simply increase the voltage until it is beyond the tolerance of the human body." He adds that it is a technique used in a number of "your institutions."

Tressider is feeling intense pain as David coolly walks around outside and hears the machine. He opens up an unlocked door, enters the building with no security and walks down the stairs. Gun in hand, he approaches the door to the room where Tressider is being tortured. Tressider refuses to snitch. David kicks open the door, shouts "Hold it!" and then guns down an alien. Spotting two through a window on a door, David kicks it open, falls to the ground and shoots two more, who fall into a machine and are immediately electrocuted.

Now there's a shootout. Blaine and Almquist make a run for it. David fights Blaine and tosses him into a machine as well. But since he was not an alien he doesn't burn. He just dies. David drags Tressider out, and it is clear that Almquist has escaped.

Everything burns up. As Ellie drives them back Tressider is still able to say, "We've got to get to that conference." David tells him, "nothing can stop us" as Ellie drives them to the hospital. She has to go home and pack and prepare to leave for the conference the next day. David asks her, "We still working together on this?" Ellie says she is thus far. David says he's after a lot more than just stopping THIS takeover. I wanna see every one of you off the face of the Earth." Ellie, still driving tells David, who is in the back seat with the unconscious Tressider, "I understand. So if the choice comes down to the survival of your kind or mine, I'll have to destroy you without a second thought"

David informs her that, "We're playing by the same set of rules as he glares at her menacingly.

The narrator sums up: "A summit conference, to be attended by the heads of this world's major nations. But beings from another world will be there, too. And their purpose will jeopardize the security and the future of the planet Earth."

.29. "Summit Meeting" (Part 2)

The theme music blares in the background with bass drums and trumpets sounding. Something incredibly grand is about to take place. And what do we find? The EURAC flag blows in the wind, some 18 miles from the Baltic Sea, the island is host to all of these world leaders, with the President of the United States slated to appear as well. In the reception area is clear while the name of the host agency is EURAC – it's lily white except for a few blacks clad in African garb.

As stated earlier, EURAC is the acronym for European Allied Command. This is more evidence of the globalization of white nationalism. To these white people, they ARE the world – the only people who count. With the exception of a few sellout brown and black dictators, the world is Europe, America, Israel and every other white nation there is. Remember now, white people are but a minority in the world but if you look at films and TV shows, you would think they were 99% of the world's people. In fact, this recent wage of renewed intensified racism by the so-called "Alt-Right" is all about the white man's fear that his race is about to become a minority in the most powerful nation in the world. And he can't stand it.

But let us not get ahead of ourselves. The year here is 1968 but the same fears exist. In light of that, the TV show is white, the aliens are white and so is the hero, the lone wolf David Vincent. And in this episode the world summit is under a flag that makes it clear that "Europe is the key.

While the camera pans the outside and shows helicopters coming and going and shows the flags of many nations being displayed, the human beings from those countries are few in number during this episode. Token African garb, an occasion turban, and a few black and brown faces are flashed and that is about it. More on that later.

A TV reporter is announcing the event: "And so this mountain fortress, home of the European Allied Command, has become the focal point of the entire world. The five heads of state and their staffs have all gathered here, the President of the United States having de-planed just a few moments ago. For it is here, almost directly below where I am speaking, that the conference host, Premier Thor Halverson, will demonstrate at three o'clock this afternoon the anxiously awaited AR-5, anti-radiation pollutant, that Premier Halverson claims will reduce the present dangerously high level of radioactivity by a significant degree. Since last night the famous names and faces have been arriving here, having been carried up by helicopter from the capitol."

Other newsmen are also broadcasting. The show's regular narrator provides us more general context: "A summit conference in a mountain stronghold, 18 miles from the Baltic Sea. There are two who do not share the high optimism of the other arrivals here: David Vincent and his ally and friend, Michael Tressider, who step off a helicopter and into a moment of history. They share the grim knowledge that this conference was initiated, and is being controlled, by alien invaders."

A newsman wants to know if Tressider's company has contracted to produce the AR-5 and he and David walk past the reporters with "no comment" type responses. In a very elaborate setup, the men step onto a giant concrete elevator that slowly descends downward. At the lower level the elevator doors open to reveal a large lobby. It is clearly a signing in area where numerous people are congregating. Ellie is already at the counter.

In the reception area near the octagon, David comes up from behind Ellie. Without turning around she warns, "not now, not here. We can't be seen together. My room, D-12, half and hour." David and Tressider are both being watched. "They've made contact: Vincent, Tressider and Ellie Markham," says one alien over his communications device.

David then boards the elevator with Tressider and they head upstairs. David explains to Tressider, who asks why Ellie is there, that she had herself reassigned to the secretarial pool "so I guess she did." Tressider tells David, "You trust her a lot more than I do." The duo stops at a door down the hall and rings (buzzes) a bell. They are let into an outer office where Tressider leaves his hat and then enter another office where they see Almquist and Halverson. Halverson tells them, "You are both welcome here" and Tressider asks to speak to Halverson alone because Almquist is standing close by. Halverson tells Tressider, "Chancellor Almquist is part of our official family, Mr. Tressider, and if you wish to tell me that Chancellor

Almquist is a representative of an extraterrestrial body, then let me assure you – I'm already aware of the fact."

"You are?" Tressider says with complete surprise. "For some time now," Halverson begins to explain, "And I wish to tell you how aggrieved I was to learn what transpired between you two in Washington." "Transpired?" Tressider says with more shock in his voice. "Did you know that on his orders I was tortured and practically killed?" Halverson says, "Mr. Almquist reported that he interrogated you at length and that minimal force was used only when you became actively uncooperative." David's eyes remain locked on Almquist as the discussion continues and Tressider takes a chair.

Tressider says that what he just heard was "a gross distortion of the facts," backed up by David's saying, "The man's a murderer!" "Rather extreme language, Mr. Vincent, Halverson replies. "Not extreme enough, I'm afraid," David says. Halverson says, "I'm afraid you both are too involved, or perhaps not involved enough – who knows? But what I am trying to do is preserve the very life of this planet, and Mr. Almquist is trying to preserve the life of his. Though it may be possible, although I can scarcely believe it, in his zeal Mr. Almquist could forget the value of a single life, the importance of the fallen sparrow. However, you must remember that there are billions of lives hanging in the balance." Halverson returns to be seated behind his desk. "Billions, Mr. Tressider."

Tressider says, "Is it not possible sir that you are merely being – well…" Halverson interrupts: "Being USED, Mr. Tressider?" "We believe that Almquist and his people are determined to take over this planet." Halverson is hesitant but says, "I'm afraid I cannot believe that." Tressider says, "Then why are their methods so devious? Why don't they simply bring this substance – this AR-5 – to the United Nations?

Now it's Almquist's turn: "You're being naïve, Mr. Tressider. You know as well as I do that should this world of yours discover that it's playing host to uh .. what is the term you use? .. visitors from outer space, the result would be panic, chaos. A proposal of ours would be met by universal suspicion and hostility. We have to find someone to do it for us, someone who is above suspicion. So we came to Premier Halverson." "So, as you can see," Halverson interjects, "I am being used. But for a good cause and with my full consent." Almquist says that Halverson granted them a hearing without prejudging, without fear, and that Halverson has, "A long history to the cause of peace."

David then takes the chair next toTressider and tells Halverson, "Sir we've been informed that this conference has been arranged as a smokescreen, a camouflage." "To conceal what, Mr. Vincent," Halverson asks. "The assassination of every world leader attending this conference," David replies. "That's quite an accusation, Mr. Vincent – rather melodramatic, don't you think?" Halverson counter-queries. "That's the information we have." Halverson says "Thank you Mr. Vincent" and adds that "we will take it under advisement. Now if you excuse me. I must prepare myself for a meeting with your President," Halverson says.

As Tressider and David prepare to leave, Halverson says, "Men, I want you to know that your concern is appreciated." They just look at him and leave the room. After they do Tressider immediately recommends that they get in touch with American security right away. David is still trying to convince Tressider that Ellie is on their side. David convinces Tressider to "at least listen to what she has to say." He agrees to do so.

In the meantime, Ellie is on the phone working to arrange a meeting with Almquist's aide. Almquist walks into his office and the aide informs him about what she wants. Almquist gives the go-ahead. Ellie is still on the phone as she lets Tressider and David into her room. She asks how the meeting with Halverson went and David tells her that "Almquist has him all wrapped up."

Tressider begins grilling her right away, with many of the same questions David has already asked and had answered. At any rate she once again shares the reason she is siding with the humans. She tells the two men, once again, that she believes that the plan will backfire. She believes that f they do, Earth will react "into one unified faction that will destroy us." She tells them one more thing: in reality, the warhead payload does not carry an anti-radiation pollutant, but is instead carrying a deadly gas that will wipe out "every speck of life within a ten mile radius – almost." Whatever its toxic element is, it will not affect the aliens.

There really is AR-5 – but it's only effective at low levels of radioactivity. In the case of a severe attack, it's useless. The current high level of radioactivity is the doing of the aliens, Ellie explains. And they can live with what exists. Ellie wants to get to Halverson to change the time table that will cancel the launch. During her call to his office, Almquist told her it would be in the top drawer in his desk and will leave it for her.

All three of them – David, Tressider and Ellie -- head to Almquist's office down the corridor. David has his gun drawn, as they get to Apartment D-2, which is Almquist's room. The door is, as can be expected, unlocked. David looks into the drawer – nothing. Then two aliens get the drop on them. David shoots one and Tressider hits the other one over the head with a vase, knocking him out. Meanwhile, at the same time Ellie has disappeared, and Tressider is worried. Tressider things Ellie set a trap while David believes that the thugs were waiting there for Ellie. Tressider is going to look for an American security officer. He warns David about going to go look for Ellie. David says, "If we're going to die in an hour, what difference does it make how we go?" he says this as he lights up yet another cigarette.

David goes to Ellie's room and she lets him in. He has his gun drawn and looks around. He holsters it and asks her to explain. She says she's glad he made it. She says she ran because "there had to be one of us left." "There was nothing in that desk," the skeptical David tells her. "Then Almquist has it with him," Ellie explains. She gets on the phone to call Almquist's suite claiming she is from the front desk. He's at the press lounge calling a news conference. David says "we improvise" and the two of them head back out.

Meanwhile, Tressider meets with the security chief but has no success with convincing him as to the aliens' plans. He says he knows how it sounds which is why he didn't bring it to them before. "I'm sorry Mike," he says to Tressider, "There is nothing I can do." Tressider leaves the room but before he does he tells the military man, "Unfortunately, you won't live long enough to realize the mistake you're really making." Now that was a threat, and this military guy, if he doubts the story Tressider told him, has every reason to lock this guy up because he represents, at very minimum, a clear and present danger. But what happens. Tressider is allowed to make his statement and then walk right out the door. More white privilege at work.

Almquist is holding a press conference regarding the antidote 'AR5' during which Vincent grabs a briefcase belong to Almquist. The interesting thing is that while Almquist is at a board pointing to a map, David simply walks over to the table, which is in the front of a room packed with reporters and cameras, and simply takes the brief case, which is wide open, and walks out of the room with Ellie! Almquist sees him as he leaves and realizes he's got the plans! He then excuses himself by telling the throng that he "must attend to final preparations."

Almquist and his aid turn the corner in time to see David and Ellie getting on the elevator. Almquist then puts out the word to all the aliens that Vincent is on his way to share the plans with Halverson. At each turn Ellie and David see aliens guarding key door passages. David tells Ellie to call Tressider.

Meanwhile Halverson is lying down in his office while Almquist feeds him more bullshit and tells the old man that David is a menace. Part of the deal is also that the people of Earth must lay down their weapons and, as Halverson put it, "turn down the right to blow each other to bits." While lying on the couch Halverson adds that, "They'll pay the price for your chemical. They need it. They have no choice." When lied to about Vincent, Halverson accepts the lie and says, "We men with missions are fanatics, aren't we?"

It is at this time from his room that David calls the concierge downstairs and asks to have Tressider paged. I thought he just sent Ellie to do that? But she comes to his room and is trying to seduce him. She almost does as they are very close to one another and she and David debate if emotions are really worth it. She tells him that Almquist doesn't hate him but it is he, David, who hates Almquist. "He's going to win eventually," she says.

"You're so used to emotion you wouldn't know what to do without it. Would you like to learn?" she asks. She further queries, "Wouldn't that be better to have never loved, but to have never hated?" Before she can get an answer the phone rings. It's Tressider calling.

David tells him he has the timetable, every detail and how they're going to polish us off." He informs Tressider that Halverson is under guard and that he's being followed. "We'll meet on "E" level," David says. Tressider knows he's being watched so he has two soldiers run interference for him – Tressider tells them that the man following him is trying to sabotage the summit. That man (an alien) is detained.

Jim is a conference aide to Tressider but is also an alien. He has a metallic disk in his hand. There are 15 minutes to countdown, 25 minutes to launch. The nation's leaders are taking their seats in the observation room.

The three meet in Room E-44 and Tressider apologizes to Ellie for his suspicions –the schedule that David swiped is real. Jim, the aide, gets the drop on them as he enters the room while they are planning. "Please keep your hands down by your sides," he orders. "I understand that you have a document belonging to Mr. Almquist. Please hand it over," Jim says, with the gun pointed at the trio. David tosses the document and it hits the floor. As Jim reaches down to retrieve it, David shouts, "Get down!" and the trio ducks behind some computers and there is a shootout. David slips Ellie the gun and then pretends to be giving up. When Jim stands up, Ellie shoots him. He falls, glows and burns out. "You trust her NOW?" David asks Tressider. "Of course," he says.

"How many of you are here?" David asks. She informs them that there are ten aliens, all told, at the Summit. They have seven more to go through. They try to phone Halverson but his aide, an alien intercepts the call and gives the information to Almquist. Tressider takes the risk to try to get to Halverson, serving as a decoy so David can give him the information. "When that sergeant doesn't report back, they'll be looking for me," Tressider bravely explains. "You'll never make it," David says. "Sure I will. You want until I leave, you wait a few minutes and then you follow," Tressider says. David wants to go but Tressider is out the door. "Who knows? I may fool all of you," he says and then he's gone down the corridor.

An alien intercepts David and Ellie in the hall. "The document please", the alien says but David gets the drop on him and knocks him out. Ellie has the gun. They hear someone groaning. It's Tressider whose been knocked out. Tressider tells David "there's no time. No use." He tells David to get to Halverson, and then he dies. David is pissed, taking his gun and shooting the alien he just knocked out.

David contacts the American Security office in the building. Why is there an American security office in the Baltics? Do all the nations have such offices or just the haughty American contingent? Again, white nationalism combined with its twin cousin, American patriotism. Six of one, half a dozen of the other.

The ten-minute countdown will begin in approximately two minutes, the loudspeaker reminds all in attendance. Meanwhile, an officer comes over and whispers something to Halverson who gets up out of his chair and leaves the room. Halverson and David finally meet. David hands Halverson papers that show that Almquist plans to kill ever human being in the area. Ellie is there as well, and they share the time table. "Please look at this," David says handing him the paperwork. Halverson is amazed – it's right there in black and white, the invasion plans to kill millions. "This paper could be fraudulent," Halverson says. But David reminds him that the plans are in Almquist's own handwriting. (Why would such plans be handwritten?). Halverson says, "It could be a clever forgery manufactured by you and Mr. Tressider," he insists. "Tressider is dead. Almquist had him murdered," David tells him.

Almquist walks in with an aide and denies it all, but an anonymous soldier shows Halverson Tressider's dead body. Halverson orders the launch stopped, but Almquist turns down the request since only he can stop it. Halverson walks over to Almquist: "So it's all been a lie? All of it?" Almquist replies, "I think the word is tactics."

David, Ellie and Halverson run to the jeeps in the hallway, board them and take off down the corridor. David talks the wheel, Ellie is riding shotgun and Halverson gets in the back seat. The jeep speeds off. Now Almquist and an aide give chase in another jeep, shooting all the way. Dodging bullets, David, Halverson and Ellie arrive at the Control Section of the building. David engages in a shootout while Ellie and Halverson enter the booth to try to stop the launch. David shoots Almquist and the aide.

Halverson orders the missile deactivated, but it doesn't work. Only one chance: Halverson presses an emergency launch and in that way, once the missile is launched, he can hit the destruct button. It's a suicide mission.

David and Ellie run like hell. They get back into the jeep and speed away down the corridor. The missile is launched and then destroyed, blowing up the booth and everything burns, including Halverson. David covers Ellie with his body as the explosion rains down. The only complete formula was in the hands of Almquist, and he's dead. Tressider's death is deemed by the media as "a mystery." David and Ellie part ways. Ellie reassures Vincent that the radiation will no longer be a threat as The Invaders can't live in a highly radioactive environment either. "He was a good man," Ellie says about Halverson.

The news media says that the world still faces extinction from radiation poisoning. David is walking to a waiting helicopter with Ellie. "What are your people going to do about the radioactivity?" he asks her. "We stopped manufacturing it already," she explains. "A poisonous world is of no use to us."

"We've been allies for a time, but not friends, unfortunately. So I suggest that you don't count on me next time," Ellie tells David. "I didn't count on you *this* time. If you'd made a wrong move anywhere along the way, I would have killed you," David replies. "Then we understand each other very well," she says smiling. "Goodbye, Mr. Vincent."

MORAL: "It is over. A great man's dream lies buried beneath a mountain. The leaders of nations return to their homes. And David Vincent returns to his continuing war – to rid the world of the Invader. That is HIS dream and he will not see it buried."

.30. "The Prophet"

People all white, are in a choir and their white robes appear akin to those of people who are involved in a cult. David is in the audience and heads backstage without permission (can you say "trespassing"?) Brother Avery, the self-proclaimed "prophet" is telling the throng, "I am the chosen I speak in the name of the Heavenly Host." He later adds, "Prepare for the coming of a million saints!" David bribes a man backstage to go even deeper into the backstage scenario. One of the men is watching him as the man on stage, who claims he is "chosen," begins glowing red and then walks off the stage with the assistance of two fellow aliens.

All of the cult followers are clad in white robes as they lead the man away. David follows walking past two security guards. He exits the back door and sees Brother Avery going into a large trailer. David is escorted outside of a fence and glares up at a sign that reads, "And the truth shall set you free."

The narrator informs us: "David Vincent has seen the prophet. A saintly figure who announces the coming of a heavenly host, whose skin begins to glow at the climax of each service. Evidence that Brother Avery is an alien invader and a reason for Vincent to contact columnist Bill Shea, of NOW magazine.

The phone rings in Shea's room. There's a phone call and as David knocks in the door he is invited in. He is talking to someone about something he saw and then wrote about. He tells the caller that "you don't believe it, nobody believes it, but that's what I saw." He tells the caller where the prophet will be and is headed. He hangs up and turns to David. Vincent introduces himself and reminds Shea that he wrote him a letter a while ago but was never answered. He remembers the letter and tells him, "I think I'm going to like you Mr. Vincent. Now what do you call them – aliens?" David nods in affirmation: "Aliens, anything you want to call them." "And you've seen them?" Shea asks. David says, "It's as you said on the phone, you don't believe it, nobody believes it. But I have seen them."

"What do they look like," Shea queries. "You, or me, or anybody else," is David's response. They uh … well some of them have a mutated fourth finger. They don't bleed when they're cut … When they die, they glow, they glow in an incandescent light …" "This man doesn't die," Shea says, but David explains, "They have regeneration tubes. They're put into these tubes immediately two or three minutes before they do recover." "Recharge the old battery," Shea asks. "You're standing on the edge of the greatest story a writer could want," David tells the reporter.

Shea pours a drink and then is seated on a chair. He wants to know what the "space people" could want in his town. David says, "The preparing for the coming of a million saints," David says. "Are you talking about a mass landing? An invasion"? She asks. "That's what the man's advertising." Shea agrees that it is a great story but adds, "even though there's not a word of truth to it." Shea wants evidence, so David asks him, "What if I get pictures of the inside of that van and the regenerating tubes?" Shea is hyped: "Yes, pictures would be just fine. Then – you've got yourself a deal."

Back at the van Brother John, an alien leader picks up the phone. The alien on the other end says, "You were right. David Vincent." The man on the other end is none other than Shea!

Back at the religious building, a woman, Sister Clara, is lecturing a group of young people, apparently all females. She is telling them that they want more people, youth too. "Now," she says, "You're the captains. We're depending on you" and then sends them off on their way. As the women leave David walks his lying ass up to her and introduced himself. Unbeknownst to him, Brother John is listening from behind one of the stage curtains. David says to Clara, "They told me you are the one to see. My name is Dennis Victor. Last night I saw a revelation. I don't know how to say this …" She cuts him off: "You were spiritually moved." He tells her, "I want to join you." She sits down behind a small desk and says, "If you'll just fill out this card" and hands David a pen and an index card.

She says, "I imagine you want to be a member of the local chapter." David immediately responds that he wants to be a member the organization and that "I want to go along with you as a working member." At first she says no but then explains "we'd be swamped." "Please sister," he says flashing his baby blues on her, "Don't shut me out." He piles it on: "Do you know, have you ever known how desperately someone could need The One? She says asks for a sign and that then he'll know.

Clara is then summoned by Brother John who walks from the stage. "Good morning." Clara says, "Brother John, this is Dennis Victor." David and Brother John shake hands. Clara says, "Mr. Victor believes he's in a spiritual cone." Brother John sits back on the desk and asks, "Can you tell me about it?" Before David begins she adds that, "He had a revelation last night." David says it is as if he were in the same flame as Brother Avery. It's as if he gave me a part of his own vision." "Bless you, bless you," Brother John says.

Clara, who has been smitten by Vincent, adds, "We were talking about him perhaps coming with us – as an apprentice, with your approval of course." Brother John says, "I am sure we are fortunate that Mr. Vincent has been brought to us by his vision. Let us give thanks that he has been led to our embrace." Brother John walks up to David, takes a medallion from around his neck and places it around David's. "Greetings, Brother Dennis."

What a crock of shit! Not only is this white privilege, but the scene shows how weak-minded this white woman, Clara is and also makes David look like some kind of Svengali, some guy who has talked Clara straight up out of her panties. And then, the man who is supposed to be Brother Avery's second in command, comes down from a stage, take her word for it without nary a vetting, and turns over a medallion to this novice. How could this group have been so successful if everybody in a leadership position was so damn stupid?

But remember: this is the way of the white writer. Throughout cinematic and television history, the goal of the script is to make the white man appear infallible and irresistible. He can solve all crimes, defeat all monsters and solve all problems. No woman can resist him. And in the case of the show, "The Invaders," we have seen time and time again that David Vincent, sans identification, legal credentials, experience or inside contacts, can march right into an alien enclave, get a job, gain access and as in this case, talk key leaders out of their positions of power. Although it is clear that Brother John is laying a trap, the point still remains that Vincent is now a "member," not only of the cult, but of the traveling administration. As organizer Saul Alinsky once said, "True revolutionaries do not flaunt their radicalism. They cut their hair, put on suits and infiltrate the system from within."

The next day, early morning, Brother Avery is outside indoctrinating the throng once again. He tells them: "My children, I have come from a sunrise prayer to bless your great valley, to dedicate your broad fields and dry hills …" and as he continues, Brother John walks up behind David and says, "Are you as troubled as I am? Have you foreseen something that has caused you to doubt? David turns and asks him, "Are you testing me, Brother?" Brother Avery, arms lifted, is pouring it on: "Lift me, believe me, sustain me." The throng is spellbound.

Brother John tells David, "I saw it in your face last night, on stage when you thought no one was watching you." The throng then leaves as Brother Avery, arms raised and buoyed by security, says, "Bless you my children. Bless you." He then walks into the back of the van/trailer once again. Brother John turns to David: "You need not say anything now. Only let me show you what I've seen". He then leads David off. They walk between several huge trucks.

We then cut to the two of them on a country road in Brother John's car. They stop and park and both get out of the car. He tells David, "The first time was accidental. I wasn't sure what I had seen." He tells David that the night before last it happened again. "It's just over here" he says as he and David go walking. "This is where you saw the spacecraft?" David asks. "Yes," Brother John replies. "The saints don't come in spacecraft, do they?"

David is walking slightly ahead and doesn't see Brother John reach into his back pocket and grab a pistol. David wheels around just in time, as usual, and the two men begin struggling over the gun. David is getting his ass kicked as Brother John kicks him down a steep hillside. Instead of shooting the defenseless Vincent, fat ass Brother John bolts for the car. Somehow David gets ahold of the pistol that Brother John supposedly dropped and runs back up the hill. Brother John tries to hit David with the car but David dives to safety. John puts it in reverse and tries again. When Brother John tries a third pass, David gets clear and fires two shots through the back windshield. Brother John's body glows red and he dies.

David gets a ride back to town in a pickup truck with Belasco Farms written on the side. It must have been a migrant farm worker because when David exits the vehicle he says, "Thanks amigo." At any rate, two security guards meet David and he flashes the medallion/necklace given to him earlier by Brother John in order to gain access.

David is met by a suited man who says, "Brother Dennis, right this way." The man takes him directly to Brother Avery's office who is having his temples massaged by Sister Clara. David is seated after Clara gives the signal and Brother Avery asks, "Have you been with Brother John?" David answers, "Yes I have." "He instructed you in our discipline?" Avery inquires. David, ever ready with the bold faced lie, says, "Partly. We were to continue when he returned." When Avery asks the male escort if Brother John has returned, he is told, "We haven't seen him, sir."

Brother Avery, still seated asks David, "Did Brother John give you an assignment?" Again David prevaricates: "He suggested that Sister Clara would see to it." Avery then welcomes David.

Later Avery is in his office swallowing some kind of pill and washing in down with a red substance, probably wine. He is preparing to go onstage as the escort is timing him. Brother Avery begins his spiel: "My dear people, I look into your beautiful faces and I know I am doubly blessed." As David watches from backstage, Avery continues: "I am given a sacred mission and I am received into your hearts. I can feel as I can physically experience the stimulus of your love and faith. It flows on from you into my body. And I am humbled before the manifestation of this physical proof in man …" and he continues as David ducks out and Clara sees him. She follows.

Later Vincent tries to get into Brother Avery's caravan quarters by picking a lock and entering a side office. But his breaking and entering is interrupted by Sister Clara who turns on the lights. David finds the hidden control panel in a file cabinet. He tries to talk to her but she tries to make a run for it. He sees that she is bleeding after stumbling over a desk and he knows she is no alien. He claims to be an investigator. "With a divine call?" she quips. David tells her, "I don't believe in Brother Avery, I believe in something else. David tells her he is an alien from a foreign power. Still on the floor, he asks her to help him prove it.

Just then a security guard enters the room. "What is it, Sister?" he asks. "Has Brother John returned?" she asks getting up from the floor with David's assistance. The guard says, "We've started a search for him." David says, "That's one reason why we should discuss this thing thoroughly before we make up our mind," still clutched onto Sister Clara. "I have a great deal to tell you," he says to her. The guard allows them both to walk past him and leave the office. What?? There's a man on the floor seated behind a woman who has obviously taken a bad spill inside of an office that he is supposed to be guarding. They do not account for why they are there together. He takes no report. What kind of bullshit is this?

At any rate, Brother Avery is still on stage pontificating: "I have seen this multitude with my own eyes." As the crowd chants with approval, he continues by claiming, "They have spoken to me" and as soon as he does, he begins glowing red as he proclaims, "I am chosen." A man rides up on Shea who is walking near the trailers (remember, he's an alien) and tells him that the police have found the car of Brother John and that the auto has been towed by the cops. They see the burn marks on the driver's side (where John's body has disintegrated). Shea gets in the car and the two reporters speed off.

Meanwhile, David is still hounding Sister Clara. "Sister, have you ever seen the inside of that recovery van? Why is it so secretive? Why is it kept locked? Why does it have a special high voltage power line?" Clara asks, "How can you think that that's a trick?" David says, "I know it's not a trick, but neither is it holy." He continues: "The glowing – that special incandescence. There's something that happens to an alien being just before he dies or he burns, unless he's put into a regenerating tube immediately, just as they're doing to Brother Avery right now. I want to see those tubes and I want to show them to you as proof." "Alien beings," she says mockingly. "Creatures from another planet – space men," David replies (which in my view means he is hurting his own case).

She calls him "mad" and then turns to walk away. "Sister, think of every question you ever had about that recovery van." She stares at him: "I know what you're doing. You're just like all the rest of them. You have no use for anything divine, anything of the spirit that cannot be proven without space ships or gadgets or tubes." David ain't hearin' it: "Help me to prove it – help me to get inside that van." She walks away from him.

Inside the van Brother Avery is being regenerated in a tube.

David is again walking around back stage as if he's running the place. He walks upon Clara once again. She now says she's glad that David stayed with them, but that she has decided whether or not she is going to tell Brother Avery. She spills her guts and tells David that she hasn't been with Brother Avery for very long. "They've given you a lot of responsibility," he says, typical of a sexist pig who assumes she could have EARNED it. She says she's a good organizer with plenty of experience on her father's political campaign. When David asks who her father is she says, "It doesn't matter."

David walks around and then sits on a desk directly behind her. She has to turn around in her chair to communicate. She says, "I want to tell you something so you understand how wrong you are. I loved my father very much. But then I discovered that he was nothing like the image I had of him. He was – well, let's just say I was disillusioned." David interjects: "Then along came Brother Avery." She says "no, then along came another man who I loved very much, who also turned out to be a disappointment. Well, I wanted out. I wanted as far out as I could get, and I got pretty far. I had money, I could do as I pleased. And found the right set of people to make the trip with. I went pretty much the whole route: LSD, pot – I even started experimenting with something stronger.

Someone outside the office is talking and she snaps, "Do you have to shout like that!?" David offers to get her some coffee and she declines. She continues her sob story: "One night we thought it would be fun, a bunch of us would come down and see the prophet. I don't know how it happened. I was about at the point where I was climbing walls. Sitting there. Seeing doctor Avery. Revelation. I just couldn't take it. When I came out of it in a hospital room, he was there. Since then, he's given me beauty and faith and a reason for living. All that couldn't be a hoax."

David doesn't hear a damn word she says. He immediately asks her, "What if it is? What if it's a hoax? Maybe he's really putting you on, send you back emptier than you were before. You afraid of him? You still haven't kicked any habit – you're still hanging in there, using this whole thing as another trip. She slaps the living shit out of him and then starts crying immediately. He grabs her and says, sounding like a pimp, "There's a lot of dirt in this world, baby. Either you dig deep down and find enough character to face it or you cop out."

What is this – "77 Sunset Strip"? What is all this "cool" language, Vincent talking about drug "trips" and calling this woman "baby" and telling her about a "cop out"? Who is this schizophrenic muthafucka? She's crying away all the time, so his one man intervention may have turned the trick.

At an impound area, Shea and the cop look inside the car and notice how only one side of the seat is scorched.

Meanwhile, Clara meets with Brother Avery and has questions. He finds it strange that this loyal follower would suddenly be so inquisitive. As he is on the phone, Clara hangs up a choir robe and then goes through Brother Avery's desk drawers. She goes outside where David is waiting. She signals him to come inside the van. Despite security, David manages to unscrew a large light bulb from outside the trailer and throw it on the roof to serve as a distraction. He then gets inside the van and takes pictures with the brightest damn flash ever seen. Still never gets caught. But guess who does?

Clara. And it's by Brother Avery. "My child, my child. After all your experience with us, did you really think that I was not blessed with spiritual insight? Come in, sister. Come in, my child. She walks into an adjoining office where Shea is sitting. "Please proceed, my brother, Avery says. "You must forgive me, Mr. Shea. I'm afraid we will have to postpone the interview." "Yes sir. Good night sir," Shea says as he leaves. Avery then turns his attentions to Clara.

"Would you harm us child? After the love we've offered would you connive with the enemies of our faith? Cut to David still skulking around outside the trailers. He jumps a brick wall. In Avery's office he is seated in his chair and she is kneeling on the side of it. There is a knock on the door and it's the security officer. He says, "Gone, sir." Avery says, "Sister Clara, would you please bring Mr. Victor to me so I can re-assure him about these mysterious tubes of his?"

Avery correctly assumes that she has a rendezvous with David and she confirms it. "I'm supposed to meet him in his room at the Gridiron Hotel. The security guard and an aide overhear it. Avery looks over at them: "Bring him here. Use Shea." The guard asks, "And Sister Clara?" "Are the tubes still powered?" he asks. "Yes sir, says the security man. "Then Sister Clara will have a heart attack." Why didn't they just use one of the metallic disks right then and there?

Avery has heart problems which is what the tubes are for. He orders his aides to rig it so that it looks like Sister Clara has had a heart attack. Clara is being held in one of the regeneration tubes. David has the photos and will trade them for her release. Shea comes to David's hotel room. He tells David Sister Clara called him and told him where David was. He asks if David has the film. "Let's go," he says. David says, "It's not here –I stashed it." David pulls a gun on him and asks him where Clara is at. He checks his pulse and then nicks his neck. No pulse and no blood.

He tells David Clara is in the regenerating van. "They're waiting for a call from me. They're waiting for a call from me, to see if I've got the film." "How do I know that she's not dead?" David asks. "It's easy enough to prove," Shea tells him. "You prove it and we'll make a deal," David says. As they exit, two aliens are waiting on either side of the door. They disarm David as Shea picks up David's pistol and simply stares at him.

David has told them that he hid the film in the auditorium, so that is where they head. David demands to see Clara first, and the aliens comply. They go inside and the first thing out of her mouth is, "I can't tell you how sorry I am." David tells her that it's alright and that he has the film and they are going to make a deal. Then, for some reason, they're giving David three minutes, until 11:50 – to go and fetch the film.

David and two aliens walk into the auditorium Shea orders David to tell him where the film is because he believes he's stalling. David reaches in his pocket and pulls it out. He throws it, the aliens begin shooting. "After him," Shea shouts. David is backstage. A security guard comes around the corner and is at the top of the stairs. David disarms him and is able to shoot him. The security guard glows red. Shea is still in the search and both he and Vincent are armed.

Time is up for them to place Clara in one of the tubes. David shoots and kills Shay. "Proceed," says the head security guard. David is on the way. He shoots the power cable which electrocutes on the aliens who dies. David bursts in and shoots another alien right in front of Clara. Avery is in his office alone as he sends out a man to drive off in the van. The van is moving with everything on board. Avery takes a suicide pill. David and Clara bust into his office only to watch him glow and burn.

"There's nothing wrong with me that a good paddling wouldn't cure," she tells David the following day. Sitting across from him with her legs gapped, she again apologizes. "The consensus opinion has it that he was a humbug magician with powers greater than Blackstone, and the electronic bag of tricks got out of hand and burned him up. They say they'll know more about it when they find Shea." "Shea? Didn't you tell them?" she asks. "No," David explains, "That kind of mistake can get me locked up – permanently." Clara offers to tell them. "I'll help you," she says. She repeats the advice he gave her about "copping out." He grabs her hand and says, "Bless you, Sister Clara."

The narrator chimes in: "A man and a woman, two alone in the world to resist a multitude, a mighty host, two who will move on their separate ways. Watching, waiting, fighting the invaders from the sky."

.31. "Labyrinth"

A man is in the doctor's office and the x-ray technician is raising questions about his x-rays – he has no bone structure! Vincent is in the outer office and begins discussing this with the doctor. David says the man was probably hit by a car and David brought him to the closest doctor he could find. His wife summons him into the office and David makes it a point to go into the patient's room. In another room the x-rays show, as the doctor tells Vincent, "your friend seems to have no bone structure."

As Vincent discusses this with the Doctor's wife Mrs. Thorne (the X-ray technician), the alien wakes up uses the alien metallic disk on doctor's neck, kills him and then walks out of the office. David and the woman are looking right at him as she says, "You're not supposed to be out of bed. Where's my husband?" The alien says that he thinks the doctor had a stroke. The alien tries to get past David even as the doctor's wife runs past him to check on her husband, and a scuffle ensues. David tosses the alien against a rack of trays and he grabs a scalpel and charges David, who deftly sidesteps him and tosses him into another rack. The alien stabs himself, falls down and glows red and dies.

David now has the x-rays, and takes them to Drs. Crowell and Harris, who work at an Illinois University (Monroe University) that has been getting funding for UFO research. Now, I don't care if he's a one man anti-alien warrior or not, this asshole STOLE those x-rays. Again, white privilege – the same ideology that allows cops to lie in order to convict a suspect – is the same one that allows Vincent to kill, maim, steal and lie in order to "get the alien" because, even though they are in human form, "they're not really human. (Hmmm. That's the same thing they used to say about black people just before a tar-and-feathering or a lynching.)

As a United Airlines jet lands at an airport, the narrator introduces us: "A small-town doctor has died and his patient has disappeared. But now David Vincent has evidence, x-rays that can prove the presence of alien beings here.

Evidence that he can turn over to a government research project at a prominent Illinois university."

David gets off the plane and is walking through the airport. Two men in suits come up to him. One introduces himself as Dr. Crowell and the other is Professor Harrison. They say they are going to the office at Monroe University and they're glad he brought the x-rays. The three men walk into the science building. "You're sure these are authentic?" Harrison asks. David assures them because he was there when they were taken. Harrison tells Crowell, "Doctor, this is the proof we've been after for two years." Crowell says, "It certainly isn't a human structure." They both have looked over the large x-rays and place them back in the envelope. Harrison says, "Mr. Vincent, I don't know how we can thank you for contacting Dr. Crowell about this." David explains that he read about the government grant to their project concerning UFO research and figured this would be the one place "where my sanity wouldn't be questioned."

No, but I have a question. What in the FUCK is the government doing doling out taxpayer dollars to research some damn unidentified flying objects? This is 1968, and black people are rioting and starving in the nation's ghettos. Important people like John F. Kennedy and Malcolm X have been assassinated and two more – Robert Kennedy and Martin Luther King – are on the verge of it. The nation is in an uproar and these peckerwoods are giving out grants to research some damn aliens? And it took David Vincent's stumbling onto a back road to see the saucer and launch a one-man movement? This is bullshit!

David has a room at the Hammond Hotel and he has to take a 10am flight out the next day "unless you think I should stay." Harrison quickly says, "No, these x-rays speak for themselves. He adds that doctor Crowell will take David back to his hotel "and keep in touch, Mr. Vincent. We may need an affidavit later on." David and Crowell depart from the office. Before they close the door Harrison says, "Rest assured we'll guard these with our lives." David replies that he has a duplicate set of x-rays in his brief case. As David walks out first Harrison and Crowell look at each other.

Harrison immediately gets on the phone and is telling someone, "Vincent has another set of x-rays … He's at the Hammond Hotel." The next morning a cabbie is there as David walks out of the hotel. He gets into the taxi and the driver places his suitcase in the trunk right next to an identical one. The cab pulls into the airport and both men get out. David pays the driver and the driver takes the fake case. David catches the attempted switch just in time, grabs the real case and the cabbie gets in the taxi and jets off.

David gets on the pay phone inside the airport and calls the professors Dr. Samuel Crowell (Ed Begley) and Dr. Harry Mills (James T. Callahan) again, after which he realizes he has been duped by imposters when the real professors claim that they haven't met Vincent yet and are expecting him. They tell him that people sent them a fake wire gram and claimed at David would be a day late. (These aliens are good!). Crowell's daughter, a young blonde says, "Well if you didn't send it, then who did – one of your green men?" David then has the stock explanation: "Mrs. Crowell they are not little and they're not green. In fact they look very much like you – or me." "Good grief," she jokes, "You mean you might be one of them?"

David is introduced to Crowell's daughter Laura, and is immediately suspicious of her when he notices a suspicious-looking scar over her right fifth metacarpal. His suspicions are strengthened when he discovers that Dr. Crowell has only been reunited recently with his daughter. "You really do believe in this stuff, don't you?" she asks. "Your father does, too," David says. Laura tells him that her father "has been taken in by a lot of crackpots."

Dr. Mills, who is from Stanford, is then introduced to David by Dr. Crowell, and they learn that Mills is from Stanford and frequently plays tennis with Laura. Mills cancels his tennis date with Laura so he could meet with David and Crowell. Laura has just recently returned from a long trip to Europe with her mother, and Crowell acknowledges that there's been a "change" in his daughter since she's returned. Crowell has been separated from his wife for fifteen years and Laura has been living with her mother during that time. "As a matter of fact," Mills explains, "She just came back."

Crowell gets off the phone and says, "Professor Harrison is waiting for us – the REAL one." When Crowell offers to call a cab David turns it down and informs the two men that he has a rented car outside. The men then head over to meet with their colleague. When they get there, David opens the case and takes out the envelope containing the x-rays. Harrison says, "They've given us two weeks to show that we've made some progress, or it's all down the drain." He turns to David and tells him that he is very much like the 7th Cavalry.

They take out the x-rays and hold them up to the light. "As you see this is the left shoulder area," David says. Harrison looks at them and is impressed. "These are remarkable Mr. Vincent, as advertised." David tells them he was present as was Dr. Thorn, who is now dead. He adds that Mrs. Thorn was also there and Crowell wants to know if she'd be willing to come in and sign an affidavit. David says, "I'm sure she would. I'll call her and ask her to fly in tomorrow." "We'll also need an affidavit from you," Crowell says looking at David. "The 7th Cavalry will be proud to go anywhere you ask," David quips. "Even before your Congressional Committee."

Crowell says, "We would like you to stay in town until these x-rays are studied." David tells him that staying would be no problem and he is thanked by all. David tells them to please take care of the x-rays and Harrison vows that "they'll be right here in this cabinet, under lock and key." Harrison is the only person with the key. David asks if Dr. Crowell would meet with him the next day for breakfast to discuss a few things. He agrees and David leaves the office.

When David leaves the three men are concerned and hoped that the committee would think that the x-rays are faked. Crowell says that any photographs can be faked, but his main concern is whether the committee will believe David.

The next morning David is at the home of ___ meeting with Dr. Crowell and Dr. Mills. As tea is being poured, Dr. Mills reaffirms to David that "The important thing is we believe you and we're in a position to do something about it. So your worries are over." "Not quite," David says. "How did those two aliens who impersonated you and Professor Harrison know I was coming?" Crowell says he's wondered about it as well. "The three of us and Harrison were the only ones who knew about it," Crowell explains. He said he didn't even tell Laura. Mills says that he told her: "I'm sorry, but I wanted her to realize how important this work was. But no one else, believe me."

The phone rings. Mills is going over to the tennis courts to meet Laura and David asks if he can join. The phone is for him. It's Mrs. Thorn who is at the airport. "I was able to catch an earlier flight. Should I catch a taxi out to the university." David says "no taxis," and says he will come out to get her. Oh, by the way: who paid for her plane ticket? Who made the reservations? Why couldn't these three grown ass men, one of them about to go play tennis, get on a plane and go to this woman's house to get her to sign the affidavit?

At any rate, David and Mills head out to meet Laura at the tennis courts. But then they decide that Mrs. Thorn has to be picked up. So since David wants to talk with Laura, Mills decides while that is taking place, he can go to the airport and pick up Mrs. Thorn. David describes the woman to Mills and Mills and turn pleads with David to be "diplomatic" with Laura. David is dropped off at the tennis courts and Mills is on his way to the airport.

When David crosses the street and walks up the stairs to the tennis courts, he sees Laura talking to one of the fake doctors and chases the alien, who gets away in a dark car that was waiting. David returns to talk to Laura and immediately asks, "Who was that man?" Laura says, "Don't tell me he was one of your aliens." "Who was he?" David repeats. "I think he said he was from Venus," she quips. "That's very funny," David replies in a pissed off tone. "Actually I don't know – I never saw him before in my life," Laura says. "He just asked me how to get to the administration building, then he saw you and he ran." "Did you think that we were exchanging invasion secrets?" "Something like that," David says.

"Oh, I guess I am being sort of hard on you," Laura says as they walk over to take a seat on a bench. "It's just that my father is a research scientist and he's neglecting important work because he's hung up on this UFO mumbo-jumbo. Your being here encouraging him doesn't help him much." "What makes you think it's mumbo-jumbo?" David asks. "Women's intuition. Which also tells me Harry's not coming, right?" "Right," David replies. She tells David, "You should smile more often. You're really very attractive. I think we could be friends if you tried." David ignores her: "What happened to your hand?" She asks him, "Why – what's wrong?" "The scar over your fourth finger – how'd you get it?" David asks. Laura says she got it in a riding accident then adds, "You've got that look again. Is this scar supposed to mean something?"

David says "no, not necessarily and tells her, "One more question and I'll let you go." She jokingly says how do you know I want to? Ignoring her advances David asks, "Your father said you knew I was coming here. Did you tell anyone else?" "Why? Who else would I tell?" David insists: "Answer the question." She says she did not tell anybody and when David asks her if she's sure, she becomes angered: "Don't you trust anyone?" she asks. Then she stands and says, "Alright, I'll come clean. I'm the one, me – I fingered you to the invaders. The guy you saw me talking to – he was my contact. And you know how I got this scar? Falling out of a space ship. Now go play your games with my father and Dr. Harrison and Harry and leave me out of it, please." Then she sashays off.

When Dr. Mills arrives to pick up the woman from the airport, and drives her back to the university, she appears nervous. Mills takes her bag and off they go. Back at the office before Mills and Mrs. Thorn arrive, David is busy "interrogating" Dr. Crowell. He asks how long his daughter has been living with him and asks if during the 15 years they were apart if he had ever seen a photo of her. Crowell catches on to the line of questioning and tells Vincent as much. David apologizes and says, "There are some things that have happened that I can't explain." "How do they involve Laura?" Crowell asks. "I don't know. Maybe they don't," David replies.

Vincent then asks Crowell about the scar on Laura's right hand and Crowell ignores the question. "Well doctor, I thought you had an open mind. Isn't that what this project is all about?" Vincent asks. Crowell caves: "Alright. I haven't seen a photo of Laura since she was eleven. But she's my daughter, Vincent, my daughter. And I will not allow you to carry your ridiculous fears into my home. When you start seeing aliens under every bed, I start questioning your sanity," Crowell tells him.

David looks at his watch as Crowell walks up behind him and says, "When I start questioning my friends, I'm some kind of idiot. Sorry David, I know we're fighting the same war." David almost apologetically says, "Well, I was pushing. I can imagine how it sounded." Crowell says, "the pressures on you must be pretty grim. At least you have allies now, and some real proof." David adds, "And when Mrs. Thorn authenticates those x-rays, when you've gotten to Washington, maybe there'll be an end to this war."

At that time Mrs. Thorn and Mills enter the room with Mills still toting her suitcase. She is introduced to Dr. Crowell and David informs her that "professor Harrison is waiting inside for us." Mills adds, "Good, I'm anxious for Mrs. Thorn to see the x-rays. They knock on the door and then enter. Harrison lets them in and Mrs. Thorn is seated and immediately shown the x-rays. She looks at them as Harrison tells her he is going to have his secretary come in and make a transcription of her statement.

But she surprises them all by telling them, "I'm afraid I have no statement to make," she says. "These are not the same x-rays that I developed in my husband's office." David asks, "What are you talking about?" She says, "I don't know what kind of game Mr. Vincent has been trying to play, but I've never seen these x-rays before." David walks over to her, grabs the x-rays from Harrison and points to them. "Look right here, you pointed this out to me yourself!" She replies, "You are wasting your time, Mr. Vincent. I will not sign an affidavit that I know to be untrue. Now if you excuse me I have to get to the airport."

She stands up to leave and David repeats, "These are the x-rays you made! You know they are!" Then he shouts, "She's lying! I don't know why!" Then he turns back to Mrs. Thorn: "These are the x-rays you made! Tell the truth!" Harrison tells David to let her go, and Crowell adds, "You can't force her to sign an affidavit, Vincent. It would be meaningless." Harrison apologizes for her "having to make this trip" and she leaves. David asks her at the door, "Mrs. Thorn, what happened?" She turns to him and says, "You made a mistake, Mr. Vincent. That's what happened." And then she leaves, closing the door behind her.

David turns and faces the three men. Mills says, "Okay Sam, we're not going to give up. We've still got Mr. Vincent." Harrison asks, "Mr. Vincent, do you still say these are the correct x-rays?" David says, "No question." "Well then," Harrison begins, "We'll have to build our case on your testimony alone."

Mrs. Thorn leaves the building and gets into the back seat of a waiting cab driven by aliens, one driving and one in the back seat. "Is it alright?" the one in the back seat asks. "Yes," she says. "You're sure?" "Yes, I swear, it's alright" she says, obviously upset. The cab takes off.

Mrs. Thorn arrives at the airport, buys a magazine to read, and is then seated. A suspicious looking man is pretending to read a magazine but she knows something is up. She proceeds to the departure gate, places her bag down and is seated. David walks in the door and the man hides behind the magazine rack. He walks over to Mrs. Thorn and again asks her what happened. She asks him twice what happened. "Mrs. Thorn, they murdered your husband," he says. "Help ME," he asks. She says she can't. David asks if it was Dr. Mills who threatened her and she doesn't answer. "I'm not a very brave woman," she says. "Please let me go."

David walks over to a pay phone to place a person-to-person call to a professor Richard Kurawicz. The alien walks out the door but as he does he passes right by Laura. David is asking about Harry Mills and asks the professor to call him back tonight and if he's not in his hotel room, "Try professor Harrison's office at the university." He hangs up the phone, turns around and the first thing he sees is Laura in that bright red dress.

Like the true cockhound he is, David walks up on her and asks, "Looking for someone." She turns around and says, "Shhhhh. You never can tell where one of those invaders might be." She says she let Harry talk her into tracking him down. He asks why and she says, "The usual nonsense. Harry phones and says he's been looking all over for you and asked me if I'd go to the airport and see if you were here." "What did he want? David asks. She playfully goes behind a corner and David asks her to "stop playing games."

She asks him, "Have you ever heard of the Granville Power Company. Ever heard of it?" David says "no." She explains that "It's a deserted power plant about a quarter of a mile out of town on the west road. Harry wants you to meet him there. He says it's important." David asks, "Is this for real?" prompting Laura to answer, "To him it is." David thanks her and walks off.

As can be expected, David is on the road right away and pulls up once he arrives at the spot. Still fully suited including tie, he walks into the abandoned plant through a door that is unlocked. An alien is watching. David goes inside and goes down some stairs where he sees some kind of control room. It is filled with computers and regeneration tubes. He heads back up the stairs, turns off the light and goes back outside. He then phones Crowell and tells him about the regeneration station he's "found." David says, "I tried to reach Mills. He said he was going to meet me out there." Crowell tells David that "Harry is here with me," then asks, "You actually saw this place?" David says "Ten minutes ago."

He asks Crowell how soon he and Harry can make it and the doctor says "We're on our way." David tells him, "If you have a gun, bring it." Crowell looks at Harry as they prepare to leave and says, "Told ya not to sell Vincent short."

It's nightfall and they pull up right behind David's car. They meet with him. David confronts Mills but Crowell referees: "Gentlemen, let's not stand here talking. There's a gold mine in there." The three of them approach the door of the regeneration station.

It's dark and David turns on the light. He tells them "It's right here in this room." When they get there – nothing. "Regeneration tubes, control panels – everything was in this room," David says. Mills says, "Vincent, this place looks like it's been deserted for years." In walks a suited man accompanied by two policemen who Mills introduces as Lieutenant Eaton. David and Crowell are introduced by Mills. The lieutenant looks around and says, "Where's all the stuff?" David says, "They've moved." The cop asks, "And cleaned the place out?"

Crowell apologizes and the cop says that it's alright. "We get all kinds of kooks." David is still looking around. The cop says he's going back to town and Mills says "We'll wait for Mr. Vincent." The cop says, "I don't blame ya. He might try to fly back on a broom stick." The three officers leave.

David comes back to the other two men. "Nothing," he says. Crowell immediately charges David with "putting our entire program in jeopardy." "That's what you want isn't it?" David asks, staring at Mills. Mills says that David is imagining things but David tells Crowell, "He asked me to MEET him out here." Crowell says, "Impossible" and Mills adds, "That's not true." "To make me look like a psycho and those x-rays go out the window," David charges. "Harry didn't call you or anyone else," Crowell vows. "He's been with me every second, from the moment you left Professor Harrison's office until right now."

David then asks where Laura is. He runs out to the car and speeds to the office. He bursts in and there is Laura going through Harrison's desk. "I thought you were out chasing monsters," she says. "I'll bet you did," David says. "Stay away from her," says Mills. David takes the keys to the cabinet where the x-rays are out of Laura's hands. David says, "Dr. Crowell I know how this is going to sound but please bear with me: she is NOT your daughter." Mills says, "Vincent, you are mad." Laura adds, "Or you have a marvelous sense of humor."

David continues. "Tell us about the scar on your hand" which she claims she already explained. "I think it was from an operation to correct a mutated fourth finger." David says, "Doctor, if you don't believe me, check her pulse because she has none. None of them has a pulse or a heartbeat." David approaches her and says "I'll take it myself." Mills tries to stop him and David pushes him into the cabinet. Dr. Crowell pulls his gun and orders David away. "Thank you for suggesting this," he says. He calls David "completely paranoid" as Mills picks up the phone saying he is going to call the police.

The cops are arriving as David continues to try to convince Crowell and Mills that Laura is the key. They won't listen. Mills lets the cops in as Crowell tells David that he is "a troubled man." David tries to tell them that "these are aliens, too. These are not the police!" They lead him out as Crowell observes that the cops are being pretty rough. He says he's going down to the station because they don't like the way they handled him. "He's a troubled man and we encouraged him. Now I think we should help him," Crowell says.

Crowell heads out, which leaves Dr. Mills alone with Laura. The phone rings and Laura answers it. She tells the caller that Dr. Harrison is not end and when they ask for Vincent she says that he's "tied up" at the moment. She says she's more than happy to take a message. It's from Stanford University, returning Vincent's call. They are telling her that Harry Mills is a fake. Mills snatches the phone from her. The caller told Laura that Harry Mills was killed in an automobile accident a year ago. "How said for him," the fake Mills says.

She makes a run for it, goes around a corner down the hall and ducks into an office and locks the door behind her. Mills is at the door trying to get in. He decides to lock her in the office (old-fashioned doors) and takes the key. He walks back to Harrison's office, takes the key off the desk and opens the locker where the x-rays are. Laura is trapped as the windows have bars on them.

The police car pulls up at an isolated building and order Vincent out at gunpoint. When Vincent says that there will be questions when he doesn't show up at the station, the cops say they'll file a report saying that he was put under intensive psychiatric care. "They'll never believe it," David says. One cop, talking too much, says "You forget that we have someone very close to the program. He'll convince them." David says "he?" Now he knows it wasn't Laura. They take David back into the same regeneration station that he and the others were in hours before.

David kicks one down the stairs and is battling with the second. He tries to run for it but David jumps him from the top of the stairs. The battle continues. The first cop is coming to as David is battling. The cop shoots his partner by mistake and then David picks up a gun and shoots the other one. Both glow red and die.

David heads back upstairs.

Meanwhile, Mills quickly burns the X-rays. He goes back to where Laura is trapped and now has a gun, promising not to hurt her. He breaks into the office and has a gun. She, on the other hand, is holding a beaker of nitric acid. He walks slowly toward her. He raises the gun but David arrives just in time to shoot him. He glows red right in front of her and Laura reveals that it was water, not acid, in the beaker. Dr. Mills burns, as aliens do, right in front of her.

Later on, Dr. Crowell says he's still having trouble believing that Mills was one of them. "We have to face it, Ed, Mills was probably diverting most of the valuable information that came to us, "Crowell adds. Harrison says, "Alright, so now we know they're here. But we don't have one tangible bit of proof." David says, "You still have my affidavit," and Crowell adds that Laura can "testify to what she saw." He says, "I'm sure we can keep the program going a few more months" (read: keep the paychecks coming in).

Crowell asks Laura to join their "Crackpot Club." She agrees and Harrison pledges to David that when they're needed, they'll be there. They all apologize and Laura asks him if she can walk him to his car. As they walk to the car, the narrator concludes, thusly: "There are millions who doubt, some who suspect and a handful who know. David Vincent seeks to reveal the dark face of the Invader so that before it is too late, the millions who doubt will know."

One final point: why is the face of the invader a "dark" one? They're peckerwoods just like Vincent and the majority of the cast members throughout the two-year series. We haven't seen a dark face yet (other than a few Latinos here and there)! You know why? Because this is white nationalism and Eurocentric culture and in that culture, "darkness" is synonymous with evil, inferior and dirty, that's why!

.32. "The Captive"

In a building marked Delegation to the United Nations, a man is breaking in. He enters a side door and then turns on a flash light as there appears to be a secret door that slides open revealing a safe, that the man has the combination to, courtesy of a slip of paper that he takes from his jacket pocket. He inadvertently trips a silent alarm, and the security staff catches him in the act after rushing into the room. They shoot him. His identification in his wallet reveals his name: Wesley Sanders and he is from New York.

A female doctor is rushed, the internal doctor is Dr. Katherina Serret (Dana Wynter) who cannot find a pulse and pronounces the intruder dead because she feels no pulse. But the man soon recovers. The man has some kind of mark and after further medical examination Dr. Katherina declares that he is not human, because he had no heartbeat. This comes much to the shock of the delegation leader Deputy Ambassador Borke (Fritz Weaver). Borke says "It's obvious he's a spy," but Serret adds that, "He's not a human being." The alien sits there, staring ahead and saying nothing.

As David appears to be working on some architectural drawings, the narrator tells us: "In a confused and divided world, one thing remains certain: a man must earn his daily bread. And so David Vincent takes advantage of a precious lull in his lonely war." Vincent is going over blueprints in an office as a man walks in and introduces himself as Borke. He gets right to it; "If I were to tell you that we captured an alien, would you be willing to share your knowledge with us?" David asks, "Who's us?" The man takes out identification and at the same time tells him that "one of our medical people read about you in the newspaper and hopes that you will be able to help us."

David glances up from his desk. "Where are you keeping him?" "At U.N. headquarters – we caught him rifling our safe." David glances over at the second man in the room, the one accompanying Borke (the assistant, Josef Dansk) and says, "Yeah, I'd like to take a look."

Meanwhile, Borke and Serret are in a laboratory and Borke tells her that he's sent for a fluoroscope and it should be there in an hour. She continues to look at the skin and questions the man's skin texture, the fact that he has no heart beat or no blood. Borke responds, "If you're suggesting he's from outer space, you really do need help." She tells him that she's sent for an American "who may have experience with these creatures. His name is Vincent. I hope you don't mind." Borke says, "Well then you do have help" and adds, "When the ambassador gets here, I want a full file for him to read." Serret says, "Fine" and asks, "What is it, Peter. Are you afraid to commit yourself?" Borke gets on the phone and says, "Send Sanders to my office."

Vincent and Joseph are chauffeured into some kind of guarded institute where a security checkpoint approves them and the car drives through the gate. Meanwhile Borke is grilling the alien, who goes by the name Sanders: We checked out your social security records, Mr. Sanders. Supposedly you've had four jobs in heavy industry in firms requiring medical examinations for insurance. I must wonder, Mr. Sanders, how your peculiarities have escaped detection. Can you explain that to me?" Sanders is quiet. "Where are you from, Sander?" Borke asks. "How many of you are there?" "Why are you interested in our troop dispositions in east Asia?" Sanders says, "I wasn't. I was hoping there would be some cash." Borke tells him, "There was - in plain sight – yet you managed not to find it."

Borke is getting intense. "Who sent you here, Sanders?" Borke slips the file back into the huge safe and tells him, "If you want to be difficult, I can be difficult, too." He adds, "On the other hand, if you want to be reasonable, I will be reasonable, too." Sanders says, "Don't try to pressure me. We've been briefed on you people. Borke asks, "Who briefed you?" No answer. "Where were you born?" Sanders says, "I was manufactured," and when Borke asks, "Where?" Sanders quips, "somewhere over the rainbow" and someone immediately slaps the shit out him starting a ruckus. They hold Sander up and he shouts, "This is the United States, mister – I've got rights!" Borke stares at him and says, "Alright. We have other ways."

David and Josef arrive at the U.N. building and head inside. As they walk inside Sanders is being escorted by Borke's men.   Josef turns to David and says, "That's him, Mr. Vincent." As Sanders is whisked away, David, Josef and the other man head into Borke's office. As Sanders is escorted downstairs into a back room, a fight breaks out between him and the two men escorting him. Sanders is holding his own until one of the men breaks a bottle over his head and then the two toss him into a fenced area in the room and lock the gate.

David is lecturing Serret, Borke and the others. "based on what you've said, he must be from space," David says. "Now the important thing is to get him out of here as soon as you can. They know you have him and they won't let you keep him." Borke is pondering: "Get him out. Where to?" David answers, "State department security or military intelligence." Borke says, "To YOUR people, of course."

Borke explains that one popular view of flying saucers is that they are made in America. David says, "Yes, I've heard that theory." Borke asks, "Do you believe it?" David says, "You've examined Sanders, do you?" Borke says, "It's arguable" claiming that the nearest galaxy is eighteen trillion miles away but he can stand on the Potomac and throw rocks at a half a dozen biological warfare projects."
"Meaning what?" David asks. Borke says that the fault may not be in our stars, but in our selves. And let's take a break for a teaching moment.

Isn't this the reality behind the creation of "The Invaders" in the first place? White writers and creators –in this case Quinn Martin - decide and believe that a television show about an impending invasion by aliens, tapping into the on-going American fear of a communist scare – would be a hit. And isn't that why the aliens were as white as the "humans" that they came into contact with? Any other difference might tap into the insinuation of a race war, so they make the aliens white and in doing so replicate a kind of "inter-galactic "cold war" that will entice the American public into watching. Yes, "the fault may not be in the stars, but in our selves" is right on point.

Now, returning to the analysis.

Dr. Serret looks on as the men debate the issue. "That we are underlings," she adds. David walks across the room to Borke. "Mr. Borke, is there anyone up higher that you can ask?" He says that he'll do it when he's ready, but until then, he wants to "weigh all possibilities."

David says, "You're weighing impossibilities, you're wasting time! He's proof that they're here, they'll kill to get him back, you must get him out of here!" Borke says, "Mr. Vincent, I've listened and I'm not satisfied." Borke orders Vincent taken downstairs. David says, "You're not taking me anywhere, but when the two other men flash their guns, he has a change of heart. "I don't suppose you care that I'm an American citizen?" David asks. "Until I learn who Sanders is and what he represents, I want you to be my guest," Borke says and then signals for Vincent to be carted off.

When Vincent and the two men escorting him downstairs leave the room, Serret walks over to Borke and tells him that, "You are risking Vincent's life by putting him down there with that …" Borke interrupts and tells her to "keep an open mind." With that he turns on a tape recorder hidden in his desk so that he can hear what Sanders and Vincent may or may not have to say to one another.

Borke tosses him in the same fenced in jail cell as the alien! The alien Sanders has game. As soon as the gate is locked he goes to work asking, "Vincent – how did they get you? They didn't get anything out of me. Did they work you over, too?" David asks, "What are you talking about?" Sanders says, "Come on, you can level with me. David locates the bugging device. The alien Sanders is well aware of Vincent's history and Sanders suspecting that the cell is bugged by Borke, tries to implicate Vincent in a plot by making out that Vincent is a comrade. Vincent finds the bugging device and rips it apart, at which point Sanders tells Vincent that it won't be long before 'his people' come to rescue him.

"I think they heard enough, don't you?" Sanders asks. "They won't believe it, "David says. "Don't bet your life on it," Sanders confidently states. They stand face to face as Sanders tells him, "You'd better pray that I find some way to get out of here. I don't know how long my people will wait before they blow this place up, but they will. And your government will be blamed for it. I think you know what will happen then," Sanders threatens.

Meanwhile, the security guard at the U.N. gate announces the arrival of "two police officers from Point Pleasant. The two men in the car are suited and clearly aliens. But because they are white they get through with the security guard telling them that, "The deputy ambassador will see you." They drive on into the gated compound.

Serret, in the meantime, is continuing her research in the lab as Vincent walks in. The man escorting him goes back outside into the outer office but leaves the door open. "Please, sit down," she says. David doesn't sit down but instead directly asks her, "Did Borke believe what he heard on the bugging device?" She answers, "Yes, perhaps because he wants to." Vincent explains that after he found the device and turned it off, "Sanders told me the truth. Unless he's released soon, his people are going to blow this place sky high." Serret asks David, "Do you believe it?" David answers, "Yes I do. They have to keep their presence here a secret. You must talk Borke into either turning him over or releasing him."

Serret tells him that she cannot talk the deputy ambassador into anything. "I'm a subordinate here. Mr. Borke is a nervous man, a very careful man. He may not know exactly what he has here, but whatever it is is more than what he wants to deal with," she says. "The ultimate weapon: creatures created to do America's bidding? Outer space people here to do God knows what? No, he's just going to sit tight, do nothing, and wait for someone else to make a decision." David is pissed. "That's great. That's just great. What dragged me off my job, what brought me here to say what I had to say, yell in my face, lock me up. What sense does it make?" David argues.

Serret then gives him background on how eleven years ago she was raising chickens on a Connecticut farm. She did well and went to a university and it cost them seven years "and a small fortune to turn her into a scientist." She adds that, "We can try to change the deputy ambassador's mind, Mr. Vincent, and I will try, but failing that, we have no alternative but to follow him." "To the grave?" David sarcastically asks. The escort re-enters the room meaning it is time to go.

Meanwhile, Borke entertains the two visitors. He is having caviar and asks them to sit down for sandwiches. One of them says, "I'm afraid we have no time, Mr. Ambassador." "Do you not drink on duty?" Borke asks the two men who have remained standing as he is seated at his desk wolfing down food. "That is one of the present prerogatives of democracy," he adds. "Our hardest work is done at cocktail parties." The aliens want to get down to business.

"Mr. Borke. The man we are looking for is blond, medium height and about 35 years old. You might call him handsome," one of the men says. "He goes by the name Sanders, he's been seen in this area, we believe he's hiding somewhere in the compound." Borke takes a break from his meal and asks "Gentlemen, would it be rude if I asked to see your credentials?" Both men show Borke their credentials. He then tells them, "As a matter of fact we did have some trouble here last night. Someone tried to break into our safe – right over there. The alarm went off but by the time we got there, the thief had gone. Right out that window."

The two men doubt the story. "Did you see him?" Borke says, "No." They ask him, "Why didn't you call headquarters?" Borke tells them, "Nothing was stolen. Privacy is very important here." One man asks him, "Do you mind if we have a look around?" Borke reminds them that "this is a foreign embassy," but one of the men says, "This is for your own protection, Mr. Borke." Borke agrees, says he appreciates what they are doing and escorts them out. They ask him what's upstairs and he tells them "living quarters – you can check them if you like."

Then they ask him what is in the basement. When Borke begins to make excuses both men pull their pistols. "Downstairs," they insist. On the outside of the store room where David and Sanders are being held, Borke loud talks to warn the two guards inside. They get behind the door as Borke and the two men enter. The aliens are shot and glow red and die, right in front of everyone, including Sanders. Borke is in shock.

Later, upstairs, David is sitting in Borke's office and is asked, "Have you ever seen one die?" David says, "Yes," and then answers a spate of questions regarding how long does it take and "do they leave any residue?" David says, "A speck of ash, or soot. Why?" Borke things the men were a part of American biological projects designed to burn up so as to leave no evidence. Borke apologizes for locking David up. David says, "Then let Sanders go right now," but Borke insists, "I've got to know the truth, I've got to be sure."

Borke tells David that in 1944 he was beginning his intelligence work at this company. It was simply not possible in 1944 for anyone to come up with an atomic bomb to effect the outcome of the war." He talks about the places he went to collect all the evidence and found that it was not possible. He says he was shocked when in August of 1945 he heard the words over the radio, "Hiroshima." Borke called it a marvelous piece of misjudgment on his part, and says "never again." He looks at David: "What you are asking me to believe is simply not possible." David tells him, "I can't blame you for playing this thing safe, but this is not being safe, you can have us all killed!"

Borke tells him that if there is even half a chance that he is right, "Do you know what they will do to me?" There's a knock on the door – it's Borke's aid, Josef. "We're ready sir," he says. Borke then says to David: "Come with us."

The two enter a room where the assistants are describing to Dr. Serret what they saw when the aliens glowed and died, comparing it with magnesium flare. Sanders is then stood behind an x-ray machine. "What do you make of it?" Borke asks Serret. She answers, "He's not of this earth. No chance." Borke then asks Sanders, "Is that right?" Sanders quips, "Go take a flying leap, Jack." Josef plays back the tape where Sanders was setting up David by asking him "How did they get you?" when no such situation occurred. But on tape it sounds as if Sanders and David are in cahoots.

Borke turns off the tape. "Sanders, where were you made?" he asks. Sanders says, "If I tell you, what happens to me?" "You will stay alive! Now where were you made!?" Sanders says he was made in Langley, Virginia and Serret immediately responds, "Nonsense." Sanders says, "Look, I'll tell you anything you want but first we've got to make a deal." Borke tells him, "Any deals you make you'll make back in my country."

They begin to escort Sanders out but he manages to break free. He puts on an oxygen mask and inhales but it is snatched away and he is whisked back off to his cell. David explains that he was trying to kill himself, I think. Another way of keeping their secret." Serret says, "Of course, pure oxygen must be fatal to an organism like that." David turns to Borke: "If they were made here, quite obviously we wouldn't make them vulnerable to oxygen." Borke says to David, "There will be a courier plane tomorrow morning at Kennedy airport. You and Sanders will be on it." Then he leaves the room.

Serret offers David help so that "at least you won't be alone anymore." David tells her he'd like to talk to her alone. David says, "Borke may not be entirely wrong. Alone – please." She asks the aide to stand outside and he hesitatingly does so. David grabs her and puts his hand over her mouth telling her he's sorry for what he's about to do. David has tied Dr. Serret up and slipped out of the office, out a window and climbs down a trellis. Dr. Serret knocks a pan down and the noise alerts the guard who comes in and unties her.

Another guard goes after David who is on the run. Joseph comes in and tells Borke, "Vincent is on the grounds." He gets on the phone and orders the guard to electrify the fence. David gets to the fence and checks it and sure enough, it's electrified. He just so happens to find a wooden plank that he props up and manages to get over the fence. Aliens with laser guns are coming down a hill looking for him. They capture David.

In the next scene, David is in the car with some guy who is an alien and he tells them everything. He says that Borke thinks that Sanders is some kind of super-weapon made in America." The man says, "The animosity that you people feel toward one another is almost beyond belief. Of course we'll have to destroy the compound." David warns him that the tension could cause a nuclear war, a blood bath." The alien tells him, "You have left us no alternative." David's mind is working and he asks, "How soon will Sanders need regeneration?" The alien asks, "Why?" David suggests that they let Sanders incinerate and "when he's gone, so is the evidence."

The alien informs David that Sanders has another nine days, time enough to reveal information to any government. "We cannot take that chance, Mr. Vincent." David says, "I might be able to get him out." "After my men failed," the alien asks. "I know the house and there's a doctor there who might be able to help me," David says. The alien initially says he can't take the chance, but David convinces him to give him until tomorrow morning. The alien says he will give him two hours, "Until five this afternoon. If Sanders is not free by five o'clock a helicopter will be sent to obliterate the compound," the alien promises.

David is dropped off and the aliens take off. Serret is talking with Borke. He asks her what she thinks of Vincent. She says now they can do things his (Borke's) way. David walks into the State Department but he is followed. A man comes in and says that Washington has referred to him "as the man who has been so insistent about alien creatures." Now the official is really skeptical. "Oh, I see. And this prisoner is one of those aliens, I suppose?" David says, "Yes. But if you don't believe that, I was a prisoner there. I'm an American, and that makes it your business, doesn't it?"

The official answers, "Yes and no. Technically, the compound is foreign territory. The only way we can get in there is for them to ask us for help." David is frantic: "So what do you do, just stand by and let this happen?" The official seems to cave: "I guess we could give them a call." He does just that and someone answers the phone who may be an alien. "We have no prisoners, this is a diplomatic mission." Serret is listening and Borke is eavesdropping. The official hangs up the phone and says, "Well, we gave it a shot,Mr. Vincent."

David prepares to leave. The official asks David if he can join him and David is pleased. Off they go. All of a sudden the car starts to sputter. The official says, "That's funny – I just got it back from the shop." He gets out of the car and says he'll fix it, "just give me a second." Another car passes by them and pulls up down the road. Two men get out and begin walking back to where the official is working on the car.

David gets out of the car and sees the official knocked out with the hood up and two men running away. David walks up the compound and knocks out the security guard. He runs up the driveway to the front door. The guard wakes up and phones ahead. "The gate. David Vincent is on the grounds. And he's armed!"

David creeps back to the compound headquarters and scaled the same trellis that he had escaped on earlier. He enters Serret's office and she spots him and tries to make a run for the door, but he stops her and manhandles her. "Don't scream, don't do anything until you've heard me out, please!" he orders. He tells her that the aliens have given them an ultimatum, that Borke has ten minutes to let Sanders go or this entire compound will be bombed at five o'clock! He orders here to tell Borke that "right now." He then asks, "Won't anyone accept responsibility around here?"

She asks for one reason why she should believe him. Again, he snatches her and leads her to the balcony window and opens the door as a helicopter is flying overhead. David orders her to get Sanders up to the office right away. She tells him she was ordered not to move him. David then paternalistically asks her if she has a gun. "If you think Sanders and I are working on the same side, in THIS we are," he tells her. She says she has a gun but she won't commit treason. David grabs her again: "You have about five minutes to save your country!"

She sheepishly gets the gun from her desk as the helicopter prepares the bomb. Joseph and Borke are staring at the helicopter and wondering what it is doing. She lies to them and says she saw Vincent running in the forest. They fall for it, leaving David alone to descend the stairs and go to the cell where Sanders is being kept. Meanwhile, Serret is telling Borke about the potential bombing. Borke doesn't believe her. "Forget about 1944 – commit yourself!" she says. Borke slaps the living shit out of her. She pulls the gun and orders Borke to have Sanders come up "or I'll kill you."

He gets on the phone and orders Sanders to be brought to his office. Sanders is fetched by the guards but David is in the outside room waiting and gets the drop on them. "Alright Sanders, I'm gonna get you out of here," David says with his gun pointed at the two guards and Sanders. The helicopter is about to make its last pass as both Borke and Serret stare out of the window at it. "I'll have you executed for this Kathleen, I swear I will," Borke tells her. "I hope we both live long enough," she replies.

David and Sanders climb the stairs and make a run for it. Outside they both go, as Sanders waves the helicopter down. Borke grabs the gun from Serett and runs for the front lawn where David and Sanders are. Borke chases Sanders and begins shooting. The alien laser mises and burns down a nearby fir tree. The helicopter takes off. Serret comes running outside. "Are you alright," she says. "I know nothing about biochemistry but I know a great deal about weapons and no weapon on earth could have done that," Borke says. He now agrees with David and pledges to "mention the incident in my report." Serret tells Borke "they might laugh at you" to which he replies, "A man does what he has to do, regardless of consequences."

The three of them head back into the compound.

The next day Serett gets out of a cab and enters her office. David is already there. "We'll beat them," she says. She's taking a commercial flight home but David asks her to stay out of sight or take a boat or stay in this country. She feels she has to go back and warn others although she feels "very close" to David. She leaves.

The narrator tells us, "A long and lonely war and yet the invaders, seeking to take advantage of the differences between nations, have provided David Vincent with an ally, half a world away."

.33. The Believers"

Let it be noted here and now that this is the group of people who, over time, have decided to agree with David and in their own individual ways, have accepted and provided evidence that the invaders are truly here on Earth.

A Mr. Charles Rosselli checks in with security for a meeting with Charles Russell and it look urgent. He exits the elevator and steps into a meeting, immediately apologizing for apparently being late. Inside the meeting room at the Singeiser Electronics Computer Building are a group of people, among them David Vincent. All are apparently waiting for an incoming call on this special red telephone. It rings and David picks it up. Vincent says, "Yes, and the four here make ten. We don't think there are that many of them here yet. He says something about having a year at most and that they're not exactly aware of what the "time factor" is.

On the other end of the phone is Edgar Scoville who says that "we may have something to add onto that." He tells David that on page three, paragraph two, they have a "fair fix on their galaxy." Scoville is at the head of a table in a room of about six people. "And when we get that down, we can tell how long it takes them to get here and then – we start to track them. And who knows? We may have a little fun raising Cane with them for a change." Scoville tells him that they need computers for that and that he "can fly out to San Francisco the weekend of the 29th. David is informed by one of the people in the room that the computers will be available.

"Anything else we haven't covered?" Scoville asks. "We'll be sending two reports to you this week, weapons reports and internal communications," David says. "That's a start," Scoville replies. "Anything else?" No one in the room has anything else to offer so David tells him, "Nothing here." No one on Scoville's end, either. Scoville tells David that they've opened bank accounts, one in New York and one in San Francisco. It's going to be a pleasure doing business with you, friend." The phone call is over and David tells his group, "We have a deal."

This is the episode where David will finally get a long time colleague, Edgar Scoville. You may remember them working together in the episodes, "Counter Attack" and "Task Force."

One of the group says that with such organization it could be "the beginning of the end." David adds,"Or the end of the beginning." They group leaves the room by the elevator and head outside. Mr. Singeiser is walking with a woman and the security guard watches as they leave. Outside a bright light encompasses them and shots ring out. David tells them to run. He has his brief case and gets in a car, but a man is inside with a chloroform-laced handkerchief. David is knocked out as the security guard peers through the passenger side window.

Three of the group were killed, including Mr. Singeiser.

David is being pushed down a hallway on a gurney in some type of hospital setting, it appears. The narrator tells us, "Finally this happened. A group of people have banded together – Believers – who see and know what David Vincent knows: that alien beings have found their way here and that they must be destroyed. A group of believers who by their very nature, become the aliens' chief target for extinction."

David is placed in a room, and in a chair and injected with something. An alien stands over him. David comes to and is immediately told that he is in a facility thirty feet below the ground and that "there is no escape." They have information on the other Believers and the show him the files that they found in his briefcase, labeled "hand weapons a,b, and c, nomenclature and ballistics. The alien keeps reading the labels: table of command, regeneration, vulnerability to electronic detection." The alien tells him "There has been a great deal of research."

Apparently being interrogated, the alien says, "Who are the others? I want them all." David says, "There are only four of us: Singeiser, Farnam, Rosselli and myself." The alien asks, "How many of you are weapons experts. Somebody else prepared these reports. David answers no more questions. A hypno orb is used on him and he wants to know about the group. Somehow has found a way to render alien hypnosis useless. He proceeds to resist alien hypnosis, and does not divulge any details about the group of believers. The lead alien tells his flunkies to put David "in Room 8."

He will sleep until the following day and the lead alien pledges, "By then we'll have them all." Some of the information that David gave them was falsified as they have checked. The lead alien comes into the room and is given the information. "The names Vincent gave us were false," he deduces. He adds that "Frederick Bell was killed in Korea in 1952. And there is no record at all of any of them." "He gave us those names under hypnosis," says the aide. "He's found a way to render hypnosis useless, says the lead alien. "They must, each of them, have undergone hypnosis beforehand and had a set of false statements planted in their subconscious mind. They're anticipating us – that makes them dangerous."

At any rate he's in a Tulsa Hospital, formerly run by U.S. Military Intelligence. Now the aliens appear to be in control. David is escorted down a hall by a talkative alien and then led into a room. The alien then pulls a gun and tells David, "You won't feel a thing. It'll just look to the world like you disappeared." He adds, "It's not that I wanna do it …" And then gunshots ring out from another part of the building, diverting his attention but with the gun still trained on David.

Suddenly a pipe bursts and smoke is being emitted. The alien comes over and David jumps at the chance and there is a struggle. David is getting his ass kicked when men in military uniforms and gas masks come in with machine guns and blow away the alien and carry David out (how did they know which one was which?)

When David wakes up he is being tended to by a nurse. He is in suite 405 in a military hospital in Tulsa she informs him, "Which makes you a very important patient," she adds. An officer walks in and says, "I hope you like the accommodations" to which David says, "Yeah, they're fine." The man introduces himself as Colonel Newcomb, United States military intelligence. He says he found him because his men were on the way to the Singeiser plant to make sure it wasn't attacked. "We've been keeping a tag on it for some time," he claims. Newcomb claims his men didn't intervene during the attack: "We did, but we arrived too late."

The Colonel says, "There's no need for thanks. The important thing is the safety of the group" because they have reason to believe that they are all in danger. He says, "We have to collect the others and put all of you under direct protection." The nurse prepares to give him another shot but David says, "Before you do that, I'd like to see the sunlight," as Colonel Newcomb is staring outside of the blinds. "You've been away from the sunlight for three days" and the doctor would prefer the exposure to be gradual. "Is that really why you won't raise the blind?" David asks as he grabs Elyse's arm forcing her to drop the needle.

David tells her, "I can't find a pulse. Why is that?" They've been busted. In walks Newcomb and tells them, "Alright. Get out." He goes over and hits a switch and what appeared to be sunlight was actually a lit up room. He tells David, "There is no way out of here." He then walks out.

David is then put into general circulation in the alien prison and heads to a lunch room where he decides to eat, sitting alongside a room full of aliens and next to a blonde. "You're the new prisoner, aren't you?" she asks. Then she says, "Meet me later in the library." David does just that. She walks over and sits at the table where David is, She slips him a note that says, "Don't go." The alien guard leaves the room. "Have you been here for long?" she asks. "Five or six days – I'm not sure," he says. She tells him she would have come earlier but just found out about his arrival. She adds, "We've got to get out of here."

She tells him her name is Elise Reynolds, a psychologist. She tells him, "They needed me. I was doing work in an area that was of some interest to them. I've been here for nearly three months." David has his doubts: "Can't help ya," he says standing up and walking to the book shelves. She follows, explaining, "You must. You have to. They're planning something and we've got to stop it. Listen to me: They brought me here because I'm a psychologist working in the field of crowd behavior, mass responses to disasters. They plan to attack the cities by starting fires and floods and power breakdowns. They plan to cut the leaders off from contact with the people. They're planning to start it in Los Angeles a week from tomorrow. And if they succeed, they'll have a way to turn every major city into a panic-stricken mob."

Vincent believes that she is also a 'captured' human and she says she knows a way out. She shows him blood on her arm: "They don't bleed – or maybe you don't know that," she says. He feels her pulse. "Satisfied?" she asks. "There's no way out of here," David says. "Yes there is." She then struts out of the library and is stopped by an alien guard. She shows him a pass but he says it's the wrong one. David comes out and walk up behind him and then hits him with a vicious kidney punch that somehow knocks him unconscious.

They head down some stairs under Elyse's direction, David with the keys he took off the alien he just knocked out. Meanwhile Torberg comes down the hall and spots the fallen alien. He sounds the alarm.

There's a window but its high up, so David stacks some crates and uses a convenient pry bar to take down the board blocking the window. He then lifts her to go through first so he won't see her panties (she's got on a short skirt) and off they go through what appears to be a duct. On the other side they go through a room and exit. Now they're on the outside and off they go!

The scene is Hollywood-Burbank airport. David is on the phone talking to Scoville. "We have a company suite at the Station, stay there," Scoville says. He says he will send Bob and Mary out and they can help in Sacramento. "This time, take care of yourself, will you?" Scoville sarcastically asks. David says he'll get back to him the next day. Two aliens walk up, one with a metallic disk in his hands. They make a run for it and get into a taxi headed for Hotel Stanton. The aliens get in their car and follow. Elyse spots the car following them.

David tells the driver to make a left turn and asks the driver to lose the car that is following them. "Let us out on the next corner and then head for a police station. If they see we're not with you they'll let you alone," David tells the taxi driver. The alien car continues after the cab after David and Elyse hide behind a corner. Somehow they arrive at the hotel, a five-star number where they are served by a waiter and violin music is playing. David fires up a cigarette. David tells her they have to split up, when she asks why he says, and I quote: "I have a job to do. That's all that I live for." He says he doesn't want her help: "I can't afford to worry about what happens to you."

She informs him, "I'm not a fragile China doll. She says she's never needed anybody to look after or take care of her. "I have no one to worry about and no place to go." He asks her if she has a family although she had a brother she used to take care of – "in fact, I raised him" – But he died. She doesn't say how or when. Just that "he died." And David accepts this shit because she's blonde, has big eyes and a dress up to the crack of her pussy.

He stands up, walks around and then begrudgingly says, "Tell me about their plan." She informs him that the aliens have compiled a list of 300 key officials to replace on the day of the attack, people whose job it is to keep the city running. "On the day of the attack, they plan to kill as any as they can," she says. "Other units will be sent out to immobilize the communications and power systems. According to the research we've done, the hour after the blackout is most critical. When they have heard nothing from their leaders, people begin to panic. The aliens plan to broadcast a message across all channels, saying that a major earth quake has developed along the fault line, and that people should evacuate whatever way they can." "Mass murder," David says. "Yeah – what can you do about it?" she asks.

He tells her about the group: "There are seven of us working against the aliens," he explains. "They killed three of us the night they captured me. I'll take you to meet them. Better get some sleep."

The next morning Elyse and David arrive by taxi at a large home. A home nurse opens the door and they go into the living room and meet a man in a wheel chair. He is Professor Hellman and he and David know one another. He apologizes that he could not be at the meeting. Hellman says he heard about Singeiser and the rest and adds, "Yes, you were careless – all of you." He then turns to Elyse: "Ms. Reynolds you must remember this: your life does not belong to you now." He asks about the planned assault.

Elyse goes into her attaché case and tells Hellman she made some notes. "There are a few pages missing, I hope they make sense," she says, handing a notebook over to the professor. The attack is slated for Los Angeles in five days. Professor Hellman says he'll have to study the notebook but tells David, "From what you've told me, we should be able to neutralize the assault by protecting our essential communication parts and our key officials – that is, if they will believe us." Hellman says he will contact the mayor's office tomorrow after he's worked out a proposal. David says this is a lot of work for such a small group to which the professor agrees but adds, "We cannot afford to add more of us than is necessary. I believe you better go now and I will call you tomorrow," Hellman says.

When Vincent and Elyse return to the hotel, and get relaxed. "What kind of psychologist were you?" David asks (although she answered the question earlier) "Clinical,' she says. She tells him that she worked in a "veteran's hospital," dealing with combat stress. War cases, you know, adjustment to disability." "What made you choose that line?" he asks. She tells him that there was work to be done. He says, "I would have thought you'd be interested in children," to which she asks, "What would make you think that?" "You said you raised your brother," David replies. "When did he die?" She said her brother died three months ago and adds, "The aliens killed him."

She explains they were out driving in the car. "He was sixteen, just got his driver's license, and there was a turn on the road, and we had to stop because somebody had set up barricades." She said some people came up to them and "there was something strange about them." She says she doesn't know what happened but "next think I know we got hit. Charlie got hit, Charlie got hurt. So they left him there to die." She's been whining and moving her neck as if begging for a massage. David finally walks over to her behind the couch and puts his head on her head as she cries.

Later, Vincent gets a call informing him that Hellman has suffered a 'heart attack'. That means that more likely than not the aliens got to him with one of the metallic disks. David hangs up the phone and tells Elyse, "Looks like we have to start from the beginning."

The next morning Elyse and David catch a cab over to the hotel room of two of the believers and introductions are made. David briefs them about the situation: "mass hysteria, panic – it's supposed to start in L.A." Elyse hands the man the notebook as both men express that they are upset about the loss of Hellman. The man says, "I loved that old goat." David says, "I know. You did your post-graduate work under him." The man says he has a couple of friends in Sacramento, and adds, "From what Scoville told us, I think we go with everything." David says, "Fine."

They give out assignments and then part ways. Two shots ring out when David and Elyse walk out. The man is shot as David and Elyse duck back into the apartment. David calls a doctor and then he and Elyse duck out of the back window and climb a fence. Despite her short dress you never see her panties.

Vincent then calls Scoville and while discussing events drops a fictitious name 'Jansen' which is picked up by Elyse. David is testing her – he wonders why every time they seem to make a step the aliens somehow are there to circumvent their activities. She argues with David about his sending people off on missions where they could get killed. "What kind of monster are you?" she asks. He tells her straight out: "If I have to I'll sacrifice you, too. They all knew that from the start: Singeiser, Hellman and Mary. They all knew it. So does Jansen – and now you know it." She asks him, "If you die, what'll I do?" David tells her, "You'll finish it."

"It's up to you to meet Jansen," David says. "By myself?" she asks. "By yourself," he repeats. "Tell me what to do," she says. "It's almost daylight. Take a cab to Fourth Street and Hopkins Avenue. On the southwest corner there's a phone booth. At 6:00am the phone will ring, you answer it. It'll be Jansen. He'll give you an address where you can meet him. You go there immediately and tell him everything you know." She asks, "Will I ever see you again?" David says, Jansen will tell you then. It's after five, you'd better get going."

Vincent sends Elyse to meet Jansen at a disused warehouse. Just as she looks down at her watch the pay phone rings. Someone on the other end tells her to walk and get there at 6:15. Then she makes a phone call herself.

Two suited men (aliens, no doubt) are at the meeting point looking for Dr. Jansen. Instead of Jansen, David walks out and as they pull guns, he shoots both of them. They burn and die.

Elyse heads to the meeting place, the abandoned bus terminal. David grabs her. She got there at seven clock when she was supposed to be there at 6:15. David knows she's lying because he gave her explicit instructions. He tells her, "There is no Jensen. I made the phone call. You've been working with them right along, haven't you? You sent them here to kill Jensen the same way you set up ____ and his wife. They never intended to immobilize Los Angeles because they're not strong enough for that yet. So they find out about us and destroy us. But they couldn't break me so they sent you."

She tells him that the aliens told her that they weren't going to kill anybody. She says the aliens said they'd kill her kid brother if she didn't do it. David said, "your brother is dead," but she says that was not true – her brother is still alive. She says they said they were going to take him to a base or something where they could treat him. David asks her if she actually saw him and she says she talked to him on the phone. David explains "you didn't see him because he's dead! Your brother's dead because they let him die inside of that wreck!"

Now she knows she's been duped. David tells her "Harry, Dr. Hellman and Mary – died for nothing." A car pulls up with three aliens (all in the front seat) and they get out to search for the duo. They spot Vincent's car and go into the terminal to search. One gets on the car loudspeaker: "Vincent, we know you're in there. You haven't got a chance. You might as well come out now." David tells Elyse, "There here to find out about those other two they sent." He tells her he needs her help.

Torberg, the alien on the loudspeaker issues his last warning and suddenly Elyse comes running out of the terminal. "Don't shoot! Don't shoot!" She runs over to them, tells them Vincent is alone and claims he's on the other side of the terminal, prompting two of them to go to find out. David watches the men walk past and after they do, he guns them both down. The remaining alien, Torberg, the one on the loudspeaker, takes off in his car as David returns to the outside and Elyse. Again, she sheds tears.

Later on the phone rings and it is implied that David fucked her. After the phone call David tells Alyce, "If I have to, I'll sacrifice you, too. They knew that from the start!" Three more aliens arrive and Vincent manages to eliminate two of them when Elyse helps Vincent by creating a diversion. The third alien escapes. Vincent returns to the group and Elyse is being g grilled by the Believers, who charge her for getting two of their members killed. Her defense is that she didn't do it voluntarily. "They blackmailed you once, why couldn't they do it again?" Scoville asks. She says now that her brother is dead, "They have nothing else to use on me."

She says she doesn't want revenge, she "wants to stop them." One of the Believers asks, "What makes you think you're tough enough?" When Scoville asks her if they let her join, what she can do for them she says she's a trained psychologist and a good one, and she knows them. The vote has got to be unanimous. And it is. Elyse is accepted as a member.

Moral: "There are seven of them now – Believers … Aware of the presence of alien beings here. Determined to destroy them. Perhaps for us it is the end of the beginning. Perhaps for the Invaders, the beginning of the end."

Here's the question I have: is the purpose to chase the aliens off the planet or to kill them off, root and branch? The end game seems to differ from one episode to the next. If they are "invaders," then the goal should be to stop the invasion from being successful. But as was stated in the previous concluding narrative, the Believers are "destined to destroy them." Destined? Destined by whom? God? Destined to do what: murder off a race of creatures whose planet was dying and who therefore made the survival-oriented decision to find another place to live? In any case, White privilege and white supremacy are alive and well in America!

.34. "The Ransom"

-The setting is Harper County, Vermont. David Vincent is in a car with a man named BobTorin who says he was raised there. David wants to show him something at the Walden Ski Lodge. He and Vincent arrive in order to investigate and as they get near the aliens' regeneration chambers, some "exotic circuitry" outside, in a disused outbuilding they are fired on by an alien guard. They enter through a cellar and, on getting inside they tussle with two more aliens and kill them, but a third alien leader calls on the guard to stop firing just as Torin gets injured. Vincent and Torin then capture the obviously important alien – the leader -

- with the intention of bringing him to Washington and the alien leader only has seven hours before regeneration is required. The alien guard then alerts his cronies: "They've taken the leader … We've got to get the leader back!"

The leader warns David and Torin, "You'll never make it to Washington." The head for the Lexington Motel, where David goes to the phone booth to call Scoville. It seems that the aliens murdered Torin's wife. The alien continues talking: "Unless I am released, there will be a terrible retribution." The leader has to regenerate in seven hours or he w9ll die.

Scoville tells Vincent to take the alien leader to Belding Army Base and to ask for Colonel Gentry (John Graham). Scoville sets out to meet Vincent at the army base. However, the aliens, desperate to rescue their leader, are following Vincent and Torin along the road and finally catch up with them at the motel. When the police also turn up at the motel, the aliens trick the police into leaving by labeling it a prank summons, but in the meantime Vincent and Torin and their alien captive get away on foot from the motel.

The alien tells them, "We will withdraw. Our war will be over, Mr. Vincent, and you will have won – all for my release." He tells them he is that important.

As the police take off, David, Torin and the alien escape through a window and are now on foot headed to a farmhouse. Torin heads for a car or go to the airport and meet another ally. Woman lets David and alien leader in. In the farmhouse are Farmer Cyrus Stone and his daughter Claudia and when Cyrus produces a shotgun. Meanwhile, the aliens have the farmhouse surrounded and cut the phone lines. Torin gets to car and takes off. Meanwhile the farmer has his gun on David and the alien. Vincent loses control over the alien. After scoffing at Vincent's story of aliens, and just as one of the aliens attacks, Claudia is forced to kill an alien intruder using Vincent's gun, but the body vaporizes, thus putting Vincent back in control.

Torin gets to see the Colonel, but is cleverly diverted by the aliens and killed. When the aliens dump Torin's body back at the farmhouse driveway. Aliens hook up a machine to a nearby electric pole connected to a van – a modified regeneration machine. Vincent decides to head for Belding Army Base taking Claudia with him for her safety, leaving Cyrus to guard the alien leader who now needs regeneration within three hours. The racist Cyrus says, "If he dies those wild Indians out there will come in here and scalp me and the girl!" The alien is duping the farmer, the former poet, into getting his poems out there for the world to hear. The alien tells the farmer that his poems are about a world with no war, no disease. "Who would read them in a world of slaves?" the alien asks.

David tells a story: "When I was in college, I drew p plans for a city. No one was standing around waiting to read those plans, but I drew them because I had to, because I knew that someday somebody might build that city. There has to be somebody to create for."

Meanwhile Scoville has arrived at Camp Belding and senses that bogus soldiers have been at work. Scoville is worried about Torin's disappearance and David's safety, so he asks Colonel Gentry for some troops and a jeep. The aliens again cleverly capture Vincent and Claudia and bring them back to the farmhouse. Claudia gets away, but Vincent is himself electrocuted at the regeneration van when he fights with the aliens. Cyrus makes the aliens bring David back to life in return for the alien leader's safety. That was the ransom. The aliens put David in the regeneration tube, and it doesn't work the first time. They try again, and in the words of Dr. Frankenstein: "He lives!!!" In other words, the safety of the world was sacrificed, not for a white woman this time, but for David himself.

The aliens pack up and disappear before Scoville arrives. A brief concluding moral makes the point: "David Vincent, given life by his enemies, continues his search ..."

.35. "Task Force"

The same upbeat militaristic sounding sound track opens the episode (akin to the one that opened the episodes "The Summit" and "Summit 2"), and the camera focuses on huge buildings using a wide angle so it is implied that something very important is taking place on the upper levels of one of these skyscrapers.

True enough, it is the Vance Publishing Company. David exits an elevator and it met by a man, Bob Ferrera, who shakes his hand and says, "Chance. A fighting chance." They enter a meeting. "There'll be a couple of others there, can't help it. That's the way he runs his shop," Ferrera tells David before they enter. June Murray is introduced and she's Mr. Mace's executive secretary. He refers to her as "Mace's right hand, left hand" and so on. Two men in suits exit Mace's office and walk past David and Ferrera. One stares back over his shoulder and the two men leave.

Ms. Murray leads David and Ferrera into Mace's office, and introductions are made to a man who is seated on a plush couch adjacent to his huge desk, simply grunts and nods his head. But he is merely an aide of some kind. An elevator door opens and out walks Mace, an older man who introduces himself and Jeremy Mace, his nephew. The old man opens up: "We are a news-gathering organization, Mr. Vincent, the greatest news gathering organization in the history of the publishing world. And yet, despite all of our so-called expertise, we can't discover what is happening within our own organization. But you and our gifted Mr. Ferrar – you can tell us."

Mace continues: "You two have the answer, no matter how fantastic. You can say definitely why our key executives continue to leave without reason." Jeremy interrupts and adds, "The theory gets a little slippery around there, Mr. Vincent …" The old man cuts him off, "Jeremy." The young man apologizes and is seated. Mace says, "And you can tell us who these people are who are pressuring to buy control of the company. In other words, inspired by some other-world wisdom, you can tell us what the devil is going on." David, looking cocky as usual, tells the old man, "We happen to have our own levels of expertise."

Ms. Murray asks, "And just who is WE, Mr. Vincent? David tells the people in the room that "there are seven of us right now." Mace asks Ferrera if he is in the group and Ferrera nods to the affirmative. He then mentions the name Scoville and the man who was seated when they walked in says, "You can't tell me you believe this stuff – alien beings here on Earth? Come on." Ferrera says, "we believe it. I know it." Jeremy says that some black coffee would help and is ignored as David begins his usual bloviating: "Now either aliens are here, or a man whose mind you respected until now has gone off his rocker, and you're badly in need of another associate editor." Mace says, "I see. That's your hook." "That's my hook," David says. "And the fact that you're a curious man."

"Am I?" Mace asks. David stands and says, "Yes you are. There was nothing like a modern news magazine before you came along. You invented it. You put it together because you have an insatiable thirst for facts. From the moment a reliable man like Mr. Ferrera handed you my summary, you read it – you were hooked. And there's nothing you can do about it now, you know, you've GOT to know." Mace looks up at him from his chair: "Vincent, nobody's talked to me like this." "I'm sorry," David says. "But just how far do you think I'd get with you if I used the gentle approach. Do you realize what this means to us? Do you know what we'd do to get your backing?"

Mace looks over his shoulder at Ms. Murray, who is seated behind him. "Did you contact Edgar Scoville?" She says, "He's on hold." She gets up, gets the phone and puts him on and hands the phone to Mace. "Edgar, your friend Vincent is rude, hostile, boorish and arrogant – and I'm going ahead."

A man steps out of a car (that black Lincoln Continental again) and goes into a business called Resources Incorporated. He walks in, takes off his hat, and walks up to a wall that opens up. He enters a hi-tech room. As the man walks in to a meeting table, the narrator tells us, "William Mace made the most important decision of his life, and hours later members of an enemy force began to assemble in an office building in downtown New York, executives of an alien task force summoned to an urgent summit meeting – another calculated step in their planned annihilation of our civilization."

The man who walked in his giving his "report to the executive committee." The man is told to proceed. "Steps one through four of the infiltration on the executive level of the Mace Publishing Company have now been achieved. The two remaining targets are presently being exploited." One of the aliens says it may be necessary to "make an adjustment" when it comes to Mace himself. The alien making the presentation explains, "His nephew is heir, however, and it imminently suitable for our purpose, fortunately. Circumstances have changed within the last few hours. There is a group of men aware of our presence. They have convinced Mace and have gained the promise of his support, which means the entire resources of Mace Publishing. It is my recommendation that Mace be immediately destroyed and we pursue the ultimate plan." All in attendance nod their heads in agreement.

Meanwhile Mace is in his office barking out orders: "I want it set up as if we were under a number four alert from Washington," he says. "I'll see all reports personally with carbons to Edgar Scoville, here. Our staff members are to believe we are working with the Pentagon seeking confirmation that enemy forces are attempting to penetrate the defenses of this country." Scoville interrupts: "I think it's best to keep it general, Bill. If the word gets out that we think there are aliens here before we have the proof, either the people will panic or you're going to get laughed at." Mace says, "I'm not in this business to scare people, and certainly not to be laughed at. Alright – say that we're investigating another country which is using the cover of 'men from space' scare. A 'scare' – nothing more, which we are trying to suppress. I think that should assure us of secrecy as well as eliminate any tendency toward panic or sensationalism."

Mace turns to Emmett, the editor in chief, who Mace says "has carte blanche." He tells him "use whomever or whatever you need. Don't hang up on expense. The slightest suspicious circumstances, anywhere in the country, is to be minutely investigated. Clear?" With evaluations to be made by Ferrara, Mr. Scoville and Mr. Vincent here." Then he says he wants the editor-in-chief's reaction. The editor in chief says, "Well, Mr. Mace, working with you I expect to be continually astonished and I am never disappointed. I tell you this: if there is such thing as an alien in this country, we'll find him."

Mace turns to Jeremy who smugly replies, "Let's see: my assignment is very blunt – to find out who is trying to buy an interest in this magazine. Got it." Mace then says, "I think that's all." The men all leave the room but for Scoville and Vincent. Scoville approaches Mace and tells him, "You understand, don't you, that you're putting your life in danger." Mace is not afraid and assures him, "I've weathered quite a few risks in my time." "I know you have," Scoville says as he leaves with Vincent. As David leaves Jeremy says, "You may not believe me but you will get my full cooperation for the duration."

After the men are all gone only Ms. Murray and Mace are in the office. She asks him if there is anything else and he says, "No, thank you," and she leaves. Mace is sitting at his desk in deep thought when five suited men with pistols, including silencers, come through the secret elevator. One approaches Mace with the hypnotic orb.

Back at Jeremy's office he washes his face in the bathroom sink. Ms. Murry is sitting on his desk and asks him if he's had "a six martini lunch." "Does it matter? Does it really, really matter?" he asks her as he dries his face. She says that it doesn't add to his attractiveness, "and he hates a drunk." Jeremy comes over and kisses her. He says that a few weeks ago they really started something big. She says "it seems like three months, three years." "Is it that bad?" he asks. "What happened?" She tells him that they both have busy jobs and she says it's partly her ambition.

She refers to the weekend they had three weeks ago. They got the centerfold they wanted and the magazine got their $100,000. But now she tells him he's "a darling, sweet boy" and that she had to work very hard not to fall in love with him. "I am not a boy," he says. She explains, "Boys take girls to Puerto Rico for the weekend. Men do their work." She tells him that he is speaking of "the glories of sweet surrender." He hugs her and gets on the phone. He calls Murph on the phone wondering if the studio will be in use that evening. He tells him "about ten o'clock" and then hangs up. Ms. Murray acts as if she's not sure about seeing him that evening.

Then the phone rings. It's a hypnotized Mr. Mace, still surrounded in his office by the aliens. "Jeremy, will you come in for a moment? It's important. Very. Alone, please." He agrees. Then the lead alien calls the secretary and hand Mace the phone. He tells her, "My nephew will be along in a moment. We'll leave shortly. Meanwhile I don't want to be disturbed for any reason."

Two of the aliens wait behind the door and the lead alien remains standing behind Mace with another one at the elevator. Jeremy walks in and is grabbed immediately. "Hey, what is this?" he asks. The hyno-orb is then shown to him and now, like his uncle, he is under alien control.

Back at the alien stronghold, both Mace and his nephew are marched in. The alien leader tells them, "We've put you back in control of yourselves because there is something we'd like you to see." Mace, no longer hypnotized, looks at the alien leader and says, "You're responsible for this. All of it, so it's true." The alien tells him, "You believed David Vincent, didn't you? Why did you back him?" The alien says that he sometimes finds it difficult to follow human reasoning. He calls it "illogical logic."

Jeremy asks them what is going on and is begging for an answer, but his uncle is more direct: "Come on, we're leaving here," he says. The alien orders to guards to take Mr. Mace with them as Mace claims, "No matter what you do, my people won't stop." Jeremy is still left behind and after being restrained from going after his uncle who has been escorted out of the room, the lead alien tells him, "Jeremy, be quiet. Our mission is to take over the news media of your country. The first step will be to gain control of Now magazine, so you can understand why you are so important to us." After calling them "mad" several times, Jeremy begins to cough as the alien leader tells him, "Watch this wall over here."

It is a giant monitor of what the two aliens are doing to his uncle. As Jeremy watches the screen, a giant tube is lowered over Mr. Mace. Red lights begin to go off and Mr. Mace begins dying, very slowly. The screen is then lowered and the alien tells Jeremy, "He was not a weak man, Jerry. Don't bring more harm to yourself. The slightest threat to us, either from your magazine or from you, would mean the execution of the people closest to you. The next one will be June (referring to Ms. Murray).

Meanwhile, there appears to have been some kind of accident on the highway. It's Mr. Mace's body made to appear as if he's been in some type of car accident. The ambulance carries the body away. Vincent and Jeremy are on the scene and watch as Mr. Mace's body is placed into the ambulance, and after it leaves, they too drive off.

During the drive with Vincent and Ferrera in the front and Jeremy in the back seat, David explains that it couldn't have been a heart attack. Jeremy says that no matter how much of a coincidence all this seems, there is no other story. "He had a heart attack, I couldn't grab the wheel in time, now there were no other worldly creatures" who were a part of that. Jeremy was in the car with Mace and tells David and Ferrera, "The story is exactly as I told it to them." Jeremy says that he's facing a responsibility for the company that he does not want and asks David to "please get off my back."

The following day a meeting is called and Jeremy announces that they are going to turn to Mr. Lund who is going to make a sizable contribution to Mace Publications. Not only that, but Lund will be in charge of managing the company and, according to Jeremy, "will function as my executive assistant." He adds that, "In that capacity, his voice will be considered the same as my voice." Lund is introduced and he stands and says, "Gentlemen – Ms. Murray – I know it is difficult for people in a closely-knit organization to suddenly have an outsider thrust upon them. It is entirely human in such a circumstance to harbor a certain hostility toward the newcomer. Nevertheless, I should like to speak a word of caution. We are attempting to overcome a very real tragedy. We will have difficult days ahead and neither Mr. Jeremy Mace nor myself can accept such an attitude as an excuse for anything less than complete and total cooperation with the new management.”

Lund begins walking around the room and continues pontificating: “One of Mr. William Mace’s most distinct characteristics was the fact that he pretty much ran a one-man show. In the matter of policy, he tolerated no ones opinion other than his own. His view of the news, his position in regard to the news of the day were the views of the magazine. I think you should know from the outset that Mr. Jeremy Mace intends to pursue this exact policy.

Mr. Morgan, has a question. “Mr. Lund, this new management you speak of is something else again. The dictatorship of personal policy …” He is interrupted by Lund who says, “Yes, Mr. Morgan? Morgan asks Lund, “What are your qualifications for the job?” Lund says, “I rather think this is just what I was cautioning you about.” Mr. Morgan says it’s “a legitimate question,” but Lund interrupts and says, “It is hostile, it is resentful, it is divisive …” Mr. Morgan says, “Whatever it is, I think it should be answered.” “You are making a serious protest then, Mr. Morgan?” Morgan replies, “If you’d like.”

Lund then says, “I assume that you are offering your resignation, Mr. Morgan?” Morgan hesitates, Jeremy look stunned as Morgan looks around and says, “If you like.” Lund says he will accept it “with our deepest regrets.” Jeremy looks around and then repeats, “You have our deepest regrets.” Lund pompously says, “And now if you’ll excuse us Mr. Morgan while we get on with the business of the meeting.” Morgan gets up and walks out.

Later David is in an office talking with Ferrera and Scoville. “Just like that, huh? How long was he with Mace?” Scoville is there as Ferrera answers, “Thirty-one years – from the beginning,” Ferrera replies. Scoville says that he can give him a job and that he can name any salary he wants. Ferrera says, “He’s a proud guy. He still thinks that we’re the three witches from ‘Macbeth.’ “He was fired, Mace was murdered and Jeremy sold out,” David says. “The message must be getting through.” Ferrera says, “Poor Jerry. Poor scared rabbit. How do we reach him?” “They have him in a vise, obviously. The problem is we don’t know what kind,”Scoville asserts. David asks if Jeremy has a family and Ferrera tells him, “No, Mace was it.”

Scoville says, “Sorry I have to cut out on you now but if I don’t get back to Syracuse the whole business comes down around my ears. I’ll stay in touch.” Then he leans over and tells Ferrera, “You have to get to Jeremy. Somebody must have a hold on him.” This prompts Ferrera to say, “June Murray.”

Cut to Jeremy's office as Ms. Murray walks in. Jeremy is having a drink and she says, "Make one for me, light of my life." He walks over to her and hands his drink to her and begins kissing her on her neck. They dialogue back and forth about what she wants him to be and it is clear she is taking advantage of his lust for her. He tells her about how when he first came how the employees were tripping all over themselves because he was the boss' nephew but how Mr. Mace would send him out for coffee and cream. "But he wanted it black so he sent me out again and then he turned me over to a nineteen year old kid until I learned how to run copy. And then he taught me how to proof read, he taught me how to set up an advertisement. He even taught me how to cut a clean stencil so I wouldn't have a heart attack if my secretary was out to lunch. He taught me everything I know, and I had to be sharp!"

This doesn't move Murray in the least. He wants to meet with her but she summarily rejects his advances: "Sorry light of my life. I forgot the address." She walks out and he continues guzzling the alcohol.

She walks into the downtown parking garage and in her car, in the back seat, are David and Ferrera. She gets in. "Sorry, we didn't want them to see us," David tells her as she seats herself in the front seat. They ask for her help. David tells her that "Jeremy Mace is in trouble" and she says, "Jeremy Mace has been in trouble ever since he was born." Ferrera tells her that Jeremy is in love with her and she says, "I am an alp, a glacial alp. I have no time for love." She says that she is NOT in love with Jeremy.

David tells her that Jeremy is "walking a thin line. He won't make it by himself." David tells her that she doesn't have to believe them about the aliens if she doesn't want to, "but why would he let Emmet Morgan be fired? Is he simply indifferent? You know better than that." Ferrera adds, "June, Jeremy was with Mace when he was killed – when Mace was murdered, as we're sure he was. They took Jerry at the same time and worked on him. When they brought him back he must have been pretty badly bent." "He's obviously acting under their orders," David says. "We've got to break him loose."

Now she seems concerned. She walks over to the nearby phone and calls Jerry's office. She says she's scared and wants to see him tonight. He agrees to meet her, but when she hangs up we see on the other end the aliens heard the whole thing.

They're supposed to meet at the studio where she and Jeremy usually rendezvous. Vincent and Ferrea are in the car with her but when they pullup, two aliens with pistols (with silencers) are there to greet them. Ferrera shoots one who glows and dies. They continue to shoot. As they head away, they see that Ferrea has been shot and killed. They're at a pay phone outside of a garage on a side street waiting for a call and it's Morgan. With David listening in by standing very closely next to her, Morgan informs them that Jeremy has gone to Eric Lund's camp at Lake Shorewood. He says he got the information from Jeremy's housekeeper. "They'll be at the camp, some sort of a fishing lodge, for the weekend – possibly longer," Morgan tells her.

He asks her if she's in trouble and she says no. He adds, "Bob Ferrera hasn't been filling you full of that junk, has he?" She thanks him and hangs up. "They're keeping him on ice," David says. She asks David, "how many men do they have?" and then adds, "David – I'm scared." He says, "I'm not taking you up there if that's what you're thinking." She tells him that she is the only way to get through to him.

It appears to be the next day because the sun is out as David and June sneak through tall grass overlooking the camp where Jeremy is being held. Two aliens walk the grounds as guards. She's got on a skirt and heels – ain't that a bitch? A helicopter is about to land nearby and the slide under a fence – no panties revealed. And they find Jeremy. "There's a helicopter coming in," David tells Jeremy. "They killed Bob Ferrera," she adds. She's trying to de-program him but tells her she has no understanding of what they are like. He wants to help them but is afraid. "You haven't seen what these creatures are like – that hero stuff doesn't cut it!" he tells David and then immediately apologizes.

David says they have one chance to stop them. "You can't make a deal with them. They made the game and the rules," warns David. The helicopter has landed and Nivin exits with a briefcase. "Tell Lund we're in here and act like you're double-crossing us," David tells him, hoping that the ruse will give him time to get the gun from Lund. Jerry says he'll do it and leaves to go outside and set the plan into motion. David and June are looking out of the window.

Nivin and two other aliens are coming up the road. Jerry can hardly speak because of the control. "Yes Jerry?" Lund asks. Jerry looks down at the ground and they begin walking off with him. She thinks Jerry is "very much a little boy. He was always afraid that he was going to be afraid," she says. The aliens bring Jerry into Lund's office. They have information that a phone call was made from a service station and a man and a woman were spotted asking for directions to the lake. "It might indicate they are headed here," one alien says. Lund says, "I think they might be here already."

Jerry is coughing up a storm as Lund questions him about the whereabouts of David and June. Lund orders aliens to search the stables. Meanwhile, David and June are making a run for it – back up the steep grassy hill they go. An alien guard spots them and takes a shot. Lund hears the gunshot and they all head outside to see David and June in the distance running for their lives. They continue to scale the hillside but are cut off by an alien with a rifle. They attempt to backtrack but are cut off by yet another armed alien.

"Bring them here," Lund orders. As David and June are escorted back down the hillside, Jerry takes initiative, wrestles with one, takes his gun and shoots him. Now he has the gun on Lund. "He tells the aliens who are walking up with David and June, "One move and he'll die! Got that?" Still coughing, he orders Lund to walk with him over to the helicopter. As they are walking Lund says, "Jeremy, this is the greatest foolishness. I'm sorry for you." Jeremy tells him to "shut up," as Lund continues: "Do you actually think that you can bring this off? Oh my dear boy!" Jeremy orders Lund to keep moving.

Lund, still walking with Jeremy's gun in his back, asks him, "Jeremy do you remember what you were allowed to see that day? Under no circumstance will they allow me to be taken captive. Jeremy, your position is hopeless. They will order me sacrificed the moment they think you have any chance at all. By the time we reach that helicopter, undoubtedly." The aliens are communicating with one another about the location of Lund and Jeremy

There are five aliens with guns all trained on Lund and Jeremy as Lund tells him, "They have us in their sights. They are only awaiting orders." Jerry threatens to kill Lund and they continue walking. Having watched all the while David and June descend down the hill where Jerry is, near the copter. Jerry hands the gun to David and evidently he knows how to fly a chopper as he and June get in first. Back at the main headquarters the lead alien tells the one at the ranch, "They must be stopped at all costs."

The man in the ranch office says, "Execute them," and the aliens, most with silencers on their pistols, begin firing. The helicopter takes off but David is wounded. The aliens continue shooting. Lund is trying to jump out, but David is blocking the door. Lund leaps out of the helicopter, killing himself. He does – and dies. David tells Jerry to land the copter so that David, who has been hanging on for dear life, can readjust and re-board. Once that's done, the trio takes off again.

Jerry is now in charge and all is well. Heis in charge and reiterates the late Mr. Mace's statement about Mace Publishing being the greatest newsgathering organization in the world. The table in the room is filled and Jeremy announces that "our science editor, John Nivin,is no longer with us." Morgan is back, Jeremy says Nivin won't be missed and for him to send copies to Edgar Scoville.

Mace wants to be member of David's group, and is accepted with Scoville says, "we're glad to have you as a member. Jeremy is still hot behind June, but when she walks over (in a tight hot pink dress) to offer him a rather large pour of whiskey, he says, "No thanks. David and Edgar walk out together.

Moral: "Two more to be added to the handful of believers. A cool young woman and the editor of an important magazine... They will go on with David Vincent watching, waiting and fighting the Invaders..."

.36. "The Possessed"

A restricted laboratory, and a man enters through a fence. He jaunts across a small courtyard and uses a key to enter the building. Once inside, the man – whose name is Ted Willard - goes to the through a laboratory and uses a sliding door to go into a side room. Flashlight in hand, Ted approaches a file system and pulls a file labeled "James C. Garner." As he prepares to leave the room with the file, he opens the door and immediately walks into a man with a metallic disk. The two men begin fighting and the alien (the man with the disk) knocks Ted out with a nearby lead pipe and retrieves the file.

The alien is about to place the metallic disk on Ted's neck when a suited man bursts in and asks him what he's doing. The alien, who goes by the name Adam, tells the suited man that "he had the Garner file." The suited man, whose name is Martin, tells him not to kill the man because it's his brother. Adam the alien fears that he could have been taking the file to someone. Martin argues, "That's all the more reason not to kill him. We've got to find out who he's contacted, what he's told them.

Adam is then told by Martin that, "I can make sure he cooperates." Adam doesn't like it but Martin says that "he can be one of our tests." Adam argues that they've had other tests, Garner and the rest of them. "Do you think I'd take a test with my own brother if I wasn't sure this time?" Martin asks. Adam asks, "If it doesn't work?" Martin tells him, "If it doesn't work, we haven't lost anything. He dies like the others."

The next site is Willard Sanitarium, named after Martin. David arrives in a sleek blue convertible, top down, and pulls in through the front gates. David is there on Ted Willard's invitation. The narrator walks us through: "Willard Sanitarium – a place of rest and help. But for David Vincent, there will be a terrifying vision of the future waiting at the end of this peaceful road."

As he drives down the long roadway to the main building we see white people clad in white aide uniforms pushing people in wheel chairs and generally appearing to be helping those most in need. In other words, crazy muthafuckas. Inside, Ted - Martin's brother - is being tended to by a nurse. Martin comes in and snatchers her away. "You stay away from him. Tell Martin I'll take care of him!" He places a band aid on the back of Ted's neck and asks him if he feels better and

Ted says, "Except for the headaches."Martin is obviously a doctor and he runs a short checkup on his brother. He tells Ted to "come see me later at the lab."

Martin takes the nurse with him telling her that "the housekeeper will look after him." The duo leaves the plush living area and get into a station wagon and drive off just as David is pulling up from the other side. The housekeeper opens the door and David says he is there to see Dr. Willard. Ted recognizes him and tells him to come in. Ted tells him he was just on his way over to the lab for a checkup but that he has a few minutes. Ted's memory seems to be in and out. He remembers that David is an architect and that he wrote him and says, "You've been in and out of my mind," and then he remembers he was talking with Martin about him. "Of course. Architect, pavilion!" He asks David if he would be interested in designing the new pavilion research center "that Martin needs for his work."

The now deceased Mr. Garner left the money for Willard to build a research pavilion. "Isn't that what I wrote you about?" he asks. David tells him that he didn't say anything specific. Ted tells him, "It's Martin's baby, really – maybe that's why I didn't. He's the one you have to meet. I shouldn't say anything at all until you see him. He's going to take David over to the lab to meet Martin. As Martin heads to the door David has that suspicious look on his face. As they prepare to walk out he tells David that he is glad to see him.

At the lab Martin and Adam, clad in lab coats, are discussing the project. "Sure you don't need my help?" Adam asks. Martin assures him that he has things under control. As Adam prepares to leave the phone rings. Since he's got his hands full he orders Adam to "get it." Adam picks up the phone, hangs up and tells Willard that, "Janet is coming to the lab." Martin looks surprised. "Janet? I don't want her to run into Ted. How did she get in here?" Adam says, "What difference does that make? Stop her!" At this point it's difficult to tell who is giving orders to whom.

Martin stops her down the hall and tells her, "Janet, this is a restricted area." She tells him she has a right to be there because it's her father's money and she's paying for his work. "I know that dear, but I can't talk about it now, I'm sorry." She's adamant: "Neither can Ted. I've been to the house twice and each time your housekeeper sent me away. Martin, I want to see him." Martin says, "That's impossible." When she asks why Martin tells her that Ted "is not well enough. He can't have visitors and he can't leave the house." She tells Martin, "I'm his fiancée – I have a right to see him." She then adds, "Something is wrong. He called me the night of the accident. He said that he wanted to see me. I waited and he didn't come." Martin mumbles, "So you're the one" and when she asks him to repeat it he brushes her off and tells her "Just go home now. You will see him soon. He'll be alright."

Martin goes back into the lab and Adam says, "More hysterics, huh? Maybe we ought to let him see her." Martin declines, stating "not until I'm sure Ted's under control. I did find out it was Janet he contacted. Now we've got to make sure she doesn't find out and why."

On the way out, Janet runs into Ted and David. Ted introduces them and she asks, "What are you doing out like this? Martin said you were too sick to leave the house." Ted, like a henpecked bitch "explains" to her that, "He told me to come here. I've got an appointment to see him." Then he sheepishly turns and tells her, "We've got to go now. David has to meet Martin." She asks David if he's going to be working with Martin and David explains that he and Ted were roommates in college. He tells her that they have to go but promises that he will see her later.

She leaves at which time David and Ted go inside where Martin tells him, "We've seen pictures of your work and we admire it very much," but then adds that at the present time they are not ready to commission an architect. Ted reminds Martin that he sent for David "right before the accident." Martin tells David that "I hope you haven't come on a wild goose chase." He tells Ted to wait for him down at the lab and when Ted leaves the room, Adam walks in and is introduced. "Ted sent for Mr. Vincent, Adam," he says. He then informs David, "Adam is my right hand and "designed all of the mechanical equipment.

Adam says he has some papers for Martin to sign and when he places them on the desk, the mutated pinkie finger is exposed. Martin asks David to make himself comfortable and after he gives Ted his checkup he'll show him around. "We're doing some fascinating things here." Adam interjects: "Aren't you going to be busy. I'll be glad to do it." You get the feeling that Adam saw David checking out his finger and knows that David knows he's an alien.

Cut to David in a pay phone reporting in to Edgar Scoville. He tells him that Ted heads up the psychiatric division and his brother heads up the hospital division. "Are you sure this Adam is an alien?" Scoville asks. "I'm pretty sure," David answers. "And they've gotten to Ted. How it adds up, I don't know." Scoville asks him, "What about subsidiaries? Hale Electronics services the sanitarium's data processing equipment? I'll get somebody down there. I think I should take a look myself." David says, "Good idea. I'm at the Brownwood Motel and says he's alright.

Back at the lab the nurse hands Adam a file. "Yes, it is the same Vincent," he says. He turns to her and says, "I'll take care of it." After the nurse leaves, Adam goes into the back room and re-boots the computer. He dictates a communication of some kind: "Behavior pattern one. Assuming full behavior control," he says.

David goes to motel and on the way in, he's nearly run down by a car. Next day David is over to visit Ted, as an unmarked van pulls up and parks nearby watching his every move. David goes into the home and Ted is in his robe. David tells him that the previous night someone tried to run him down in front of his motel. Ted says he is going to call Martin, but David stops him. "I should have never brought you here," Ted apologetically states.

David says, "It's about time you started levelling with me. What's going on here?" he asks. "Is that why you wrote me? Not a new pavilion, you need help!" Ted says, "I called you because you're an architect, because I needed you." David says, "Hospital design is a specialty. You could have hired an expert!" After Ted again insists that he specifically wanted David, David tells him, "I know what Adam Lang is. Your brother's working with him. Why?" "My brother," Ted says in denial. "You know they're here, don't you?" David asks. Ted begins walking around hold is head. "I don't know. What are you talking about?" He tells David to get out. When David asks him what's wrong he says, "Just headaches – like Mr. Garner had."

He continues to tell him to get out despite the fact that David is pleading to let him help. Ted says he knows what to do and David finally leaves. As David walks out he sees someone messing around with the inside of his car underneath the steering column. David walks up on him and snatches him. "What do you want?" "Mr. Vincent? He asks. He then explains that he is Burt Newcomb, the guy who Scoville sent and he was just checking around. He went to the motel and waited but decided to come out. "How do you know Scoville?" David asks. "I work for him – Albuquerque plant." David looks over, sees the van and the license plate, and is convinced. They shake hands. His name is Burt.

David tells Burt he's going to have to get into their files. Their office services their machines, he tells David. "It depends on what you want." David tells him that he has to know what kind of treatment was given to two men: Dr. Ted Willard and Mr. Garner. And check further to see if anybody else has received similar treatment recently." Ed then takes off in his van.

In the next scene Martin is angry at Adam because he used his brother in the experiments. Adam is pissed because he knows Vincent knew about him and is therefore upset that Martin is being so protective. "It's not what you think of as murder," Adam says. Martin tells him that as long as he is in charge here and then he is interrupted by Adam, who says, "You're NOT in charge here and you haven't been since I came." Martin says, "When we started this thing you told me we'd be saving lives. Hell, I know how strong you people are, you could kill us all in a minute." Adam says, "No Martin – you're making that unnecessary. We won't have to kill your people – not if they don't oppose us." "I want to know what I'm doing this for: to save lives or to give you murderers," Martin screeches. "You're doing it because if we achieve control, first with machines and then without, nobody will have to be killed. That's a beautiful thought, Martin. But first we've got to get there. One man against millions that can be saved!"

David now has his nosey ass out at Ted's wife's house. Janet says that just because her money is funding that research doesn't give him the right to walk in there. He asks her if she knows about the experiments they're doing. She tells him, "There's no secret about that" and explains that it's behavior control, some kind of way to control mental illness. "Through surgery?" David asks. She says she thought he came there to tell her something about Ted. He says he will but then fires a question, "Did your father have his operation because he had an accident like Ted?" She says that her father's operation was to relieve nerve pressure on his neck.

David follows up: "Was his operation a success?" She said it was, and adds, "at least for a while." David asks, "Then what?" Janet says that "He began to complain about pain on the back of his head. I thought it was just strain from getting back to work too soon, but dad said he had so many things to clear up. He was so concerned about business, his health, making his will." "The will leaving the money for the new pavilion?" David asks and answers. "I hardly knew him. He kept saying there was something in his head – they PUT something in his head. One night he grew so irrational I called the sanitarium, and they came for him." She says that the second operation was a failure.

"Your father was operated on . So was Ted. You say your father behaved strangely – like someone you didn't know. They way Ted is behaving right now," David surmises. "Mr. Vincent, that may sound logical, but I've known Martin and Ted for three years. Martin loves Ted as much as I do, and he would never do a thing to hurt him. Would you please go?" David thanks her twice and then leaves her home.

Back at the lab Burt is looking through machinery and data under the pretense of making repairs. David and Edgar are outside in the car waiting. Adam is in the lab and walks up on Burt and asks him what he is doing. When asked who told him to do it, Burt says it's in his service contract, every ninety days. Adam says in a mean tone, "Well next time, call first." Burt is walking down, but Adam gets suspicious and tries to stop the technician from leaving, but Vincent and Scoville come to his rescue. Burt is walking across the lawn and the nurse signals an alien wo watches as another alien gets up from a wheelchair and they attack Burt and begin kicking his ass.

David beats the shit out of one and throws a second in the water. David pulls one off of Burt and they rush to Edgar's car and take off with the quickness. They get back to Burt's van in one piece and the technician confirms that there are mind control experiments using earth made equipment going on and that Janet's father's death was caused by a head implant device. Three men are dead because of devices on the backs of their necks, according to Ed's reading of the data. Scoville deduces that these men get operated on, come back two weeks later, and then they die.

"Did you have time to check any invoices?" Scoville asks Burt. "Yeah, just barely. They bought some pretty sophisticated gear, like somebody might use for ultra-high frequency transmissions. Does that do anything for ya?" "Let me tell you what some of our people are doing in Syracuse plant. You alter a brain pattern in and out electronically, you change his behavior. Send an impulse signal and you can get someone to charge a tiger if you tell him to," Scoville explains. "Behavior control," echoes David. Scoville nods.

Back at the house Martin walks in and heads upstairs but Ted is sitting in a chair in the living room and summons him. Martin walks into the room and Ted says, "David – somebody tried to kill him." "How do you know?" Martin asks. "He told me, and I saw who did it." Martin is alarmed. "You WHAT?" Ted explains that he could picture what was done with a car, out on the road." "How much of the stuff have you had?" Martin asks. Ted says, "Not much," and then adds, "Martin, tell me the truth: I couldn't have known what happened how it happened, but I did. You know why I could see it, don't you?"

Martin looks away and then back and says that he knows that Ted is still sick. "You're imagining." Ted tells him, "Martin, you're lying to me," and Martin bows his head. Ted continues: "I think I was driving the car, and I don't know why. Martin, you've always helped me before, help me now. Tell me the truth."

Martin gets up and says, "Come on, get upstairs because you need to be sleep," but Ted is adamant. "Please Martin, I'm begging you to tell me the truth!" Martin continues talking down to him and puts his hand on his shoulder: "Ted, have I ever done anything to hurt you? You've been in an accident. Your mind is playing tricks on you." Ted stares at him. "That's all you can say?" He turns away from him and says, "Leave me alone – I'll find my own help." Martin walks off and goes upstairs. Meanwhile, Ted has brief flashbacks of David fleeing and jumping out of the way of the car that he is driving.

Later in the day, David finds a car with dent on fender, a dent caused from running into a sign. It is the same car that almost hit David, the one that the hypnotized Ted was driving. David looks inside the car on the overhead visor and sees that it is registered to Ted Willard of the Willard Sanitarium, 10o17 Old Lane Road, Las Palmas, New Mexico.

David goes and confronts Ted, and he accuses Martin of being involved. He tells Ted that "I'm not saying that you knew what you were doing." Ted replies,

"But you said it was my car. So you must think I'm working for these aliens." David is blunt: "You could be – just as Janet's father could have been. One man that can tell us for sure." "Who?" Ted asks. David explains, "Ted you asked me to come here because you wanted help, you had found out about the aliens. Just how is your brother involved?" Martin is eavesdropping from the next room as the conversation continues.

"Martin isn't involved in anything, I promise you," Ted says. "Alright," says David. "There's no reason to protect him, then. You help me check it out." "But David, he's my brother," Ted says. "I can't do anything to hurt him!" David isn't moved: "Will you listen to me?" And then Martin reveals himself. "No, YOU listen Vincent! Ted is sick and you're making him worse. Now you get out or I'll throw you out." David still looks at Ted and asks, "How about it Ted. Will you help me?" Ted just shakes his head and says, "He's my brother, David." Vincent turns, walks past Martin and leaves the house. Martin walks over and puts his hands on Ted's shoulders who looks him directly in the eyes and says, "You're my brother."

David is back at Janet's house again. He tells her, "There's no doubt about it, it was Ted," and then he tells her that all the police have to do is match the dent on the car and the sign that he hit. Janet says that Martin would never do anything to hurt his brother and David is quick to tell her that Martin doesn't have anything to say about what happens to Ted. Then he goes into one of those long spiels of his: "Six weeks ago your father was killed because they had what they wanted from him, the money for the new pavilion. Now who knows what they want from Ted or how long they'll let him live. Janet, you couldn't do anything to save your father, but you can save Ted. Will you help me?"

She hesitates for a long while but then asks, "What do you want me to do?"

Janet is at the medical examiner's office and she wants her father's body exhumed and re-examined post-mortem. She says she's complied with all the rules and asks the doctor, "Will you do it?" 'As coroner, I have the right to refuse a request for a post-mortem if you don't give me a valid reason," Dr. Raymer says. An assistant, who was going through the file cabinet says, "I found it, Dr. Raymer." "The death certificate, yes," Raymer says. "Everything seems to be in order. You can see Dr. Willett's signature," Raymer tells Janet. But she's adamant: "Please don't try to make me change my mind. I'm the only surviving kin. If I just wanted to have my father's body removed, I'd have the right, and if you try to deny my request, that's exactly what I'll do. I'll have my father's body removed and have the post-mortem performed elsewhere." The doctor says, "Very well. Step into my office and we'll sign the necessary papers."

The mustached man who had gone through the files for Dr. Raymer watches as he and Janet go into the inner office. Once they leave he makes a beeline for the telephone and makes a call to Adam Lang.

Back at the lab, Martin is getting the word from Adam about Janet's move. "No, it's Vincent who's made her do this. We can stop that post-mortem," Adam says. Martin tells him that she's already signed the papers, but Adam informs him that they won't have any reason to go through with it if Janet suddenly dies. Martin turns to him and says, "No more killing." Your future and your brothers depend on stopping that post-mortem," Adam reminds him. "There's only one person who can get to her." Martin stares him down and says, "Maybe you didn't hear me. I said no more killing."

Adam ain't hearing that shit and tells him, "Your brother is programmed to give us exactly what we want." Martin says, "I'm warning you. If you go ahead with this I'll go to the police." Adam is standing at the door. "There's one way to stop this, and that is to kill me," he tells Martin. "It would be the end of this project, and you know that." Martin stands there like a knot on a log saying nothing as Adam walks up to him. There is a long silence and then Adam says, "Alright Martin. We'll find another way to do it."

Ted calls the motel where David is staying. He tells David he's given it some thought and he wants to help. David says he'll meet him at the lab and wants to know how soon, but then Ted begins having one of his seizures. He's holding the back of his head and manages to stagger upstairs.

Adam is in the lab making notes about Ted Willard. Just like that Ted comes down the stairs, still having headaches. He turns the stereo on up loud but the headaches keep coming. He gets back over to the phone and calls Janet. He doesn't say anything and she keeps asking, "Who is this?" She hangs up as the music blares in the background.

Back at the lab David walks in and looks around. He ducks behind a counter as the nurse comes in. But in the adjoining room David overhears Lang talking into microphone, giving orders to Ted. "Nothing must arouse her suspicions. You know the way, Ted. Choose a time when no one will see you enter. The rest is up to you. Now remember, if she lives, if she carries out her plan, your brother will be destroyed. You can't afford to let her (Janet) live, can you?"

David rushes out to car, which is conveniently parked right out front, as usual. Adam finishes up his orders by saying into the microphone, "It's in your hands, Ted." Meanwhile, the doorbell rings at Janet's house. It's Ted. All this rich bitch does is sit around the house all day in a short dress glancing through magazines. That is what we are led to believe. At any rate, Ted walks in with a shiteater's grin on his face. She hugs and kisses him. He tells her that he has a guilt complex for neglecting her. "Come," she says, "Talk to me about the weather, the stock markets, baseball scores – anything!"

He walks over to her and she tells him she's missed him. He turns and says he's feeling a little restless and then asks her for a cigarette. Here comes David pulling up in front. Janet tells Ted that she knows what's going on because David told her. "I should be grateful," he says. She says "you don't have anything to worry about. We'll stop them." He looks at her smiling and says, "yes." Now he's got his hands around her neck and is strangling her.

David walks in just in time because this weak bitch wasn't even trying to resist. Now he's strangling David then throws him to the floor. He charges but David judo flips him and Ted is knocked out. Back at the lab Adam is barking more orders into the microphone. "When you've finished, report immediately. Immediately!" He walks out and around the corner come Martin and the nurse. The nurse leaves and Martin asks Adam what he was doing in the other room. Adam says, "I was checking the equipment" to which Martin reminds him that it had just been checked on Tuesday. Adam says "Well some of my people are coming next week and they'll want to check our progress."

Martin doesn't believe him. Martin walks into the other room and angrily shouts, "You've been transmitting! That's Ted tape. It s on absolute control!!!" "Get away from there," Adam says walking up on Martin. Martin says "you used Ted," and Adam says, "I'm sorry Martin, it had to be done." Adam tells him he can't change anything because "it's over."

Martin goes to the telephone and Adam walks up. "Your brother did kill her? That's what you're going to tell the police?" he asks. Martin slams the phone down and then backhands Lang. "Your brother's work for us is done," he tells Martin. "And I don't think you'll try that again," he says walking right past Martin.

At the house Janet and David have Ted on the couch and have revived him. "My neck," he says. He seems to be his former self. "They must have put a device in the back of your head when you had that surgery," David explains. "Behavior control. It didn't work with Janet's father or the others but it worked with you." Isn't he calling Ted a weak-minded muthafucka?

Anyway, Ted recovers and goes back to the lab with David after David gives Janet a phone number to call which will send in reinforcements. Ted says, "I have a plan." At the lab Ted is holding David at gunpoint under the pretense that he captured him after killing Janet. "Congratulations Martin. You did a fine job on me," Ted says. But Adam knows that Ted was programmed to forget all about the operation. Adam walks over because he knows the plan. He begins to scuffle with Ted over the pistol. David gets Adam in an arm lock as Ted has the gun pointed at Martin.

Ted tells Martin off and Martin blurts out, "David – he knows how superior they are! We don't stand a chance unless we cooperate! They'll wipe us out, every one of us. But if we can get to the G-men of the world, and control them, then there won't be any resistance. We'll all survive!" David adds, "As their slaves." "Like I was?" Ted asks. Martin says, "Ted, they're going to win!" Adam makes a move and David falls to the ground. Adam pulls a metallic disk and threatens to use it on Martin.

Adam and Martin leave the room with Martin under Adam's threat and David and Ted rush out after them with Ted still holding the pistol. Ted accidentally shoots Martin, David grabs the gun and chases Adam jumps in a white car just as Burt and Janet are walking up. He takes off with David madly firing at the car. Burt joins in with some gunfire of his own. The car crashes into a tree and they run over to it. Adam falls out, glows red and dies. Burt is astonished. Inside Ted tells Martin that it's over. Martin lives long enough to claim he wanted to help Ted. Then he croaks.

Burt and David visit Janet's house before they prepare to leave town. Ted is there. Ted says he feels like being a doctor again. The police are out looking for Lang and working to solve Martin's murder. But as we know, it's all for naught. There's still a pavilion to be built and research to be done, Janet reminds everyone, once again arm-in-arm with Ted. "Say buddy, you've come a long way to help me. I want to thank you," Ted says to David. "Don't mention it. If it'll be any help I'll send you a list of people who specialize in building hospitals," David replies.

David and Burt exit

The moral: "A defeat for the aliens. A victory for the world. Four people – each with an unfinished mission. And work to do."

.37. "Counter-Attack"

David Vincent is working with a Dr. Kramer in order to advance the fight against the aliens by jamming their saucer's signals. "It's our first offensive action," Kramer tells David. As they are leaving Kramer's building at night they are attacked by two aliens. Vincent manages to overpower the aliens who are both killed in the scuffle, but Dr. Kramer is also killed after being pushed down some steel stairs. . Kramer's briefcase with important material is taken by David, as Kramer requested before dying, just as the building's security guard arrives, whereupon Vincent tells the guard to call for an ambulance. Vincent keeps one of the alien's guns as he leaves the premises.

We learn that the brief case contains a computer program that will enable Kramer's "seven friends" (he believers) to go from defense to attack." The key is in jamming the navigational signals that aliens use to get from their planet to ours.

David is picked up by Edgar Scoville who learns of his friend Kramer's death. Scoville takes Vincent to a meeting of the believers where he is introduced to Colonel Archie Harmon a friend of Scoville's, but a skeptic and not a part of the group. Scoville tells David, "I'll talk him into helping us." At the meeting Scoville hands over the briefcase material to his chief engineer and group member Jim Bryce with instructions to advance the material now that Kramer has died. Scoville's niece Joan is another member of the group – a very beautiful member who is totally committed and just happens to be Scoville's niece.

Meanwhile detectives under Lieutenant Connors have arrived on the scene of Kramer's death. They finds two .38 slugs at the scene, one near Kramer's body. David shot the aliens with their own gun, but the security guard didn't see it. He tells the cops that he saw Vincent leaning over the body of Kramer and that Victim left with Kramer's brief case. The cops suspect Vincent of killing Kramer for the brief case.

At Scovill's house Jim, the Colonel, Joan and Scoville discuss how close they are to completing the transmitter. Scoville tells them, "Complications are competed. Everything you need to start the transmitters." Harmon tells them again that he's not buying what the group is selling. David I s getting ready to head to the Lab with Jim, but Scoville is adamant in demanding that he get a good night's sleep at the hotel. Scoville believes David is overworked and in a way, blames David for his friend Kramer's death. He wonders how the aliens found out that David was going to meet with Kramer. David says that they communicated using the university's system and maybe the aliens had it bugged. Scoville doesn't believe that Kramer could be that stupid. Joan plays mediator and calms the quarrel and Scoville apologizes.

The next day David arrives at the construction work site and the cops catch up with him. They decide to hold him for questioning. As they get into the car and head to police headquarters, aliens are following. They baldly accuse Vincent of killing Kramer and taking his briefcase. They also find the alien's plasma pistol in David's car. The aliens under Lucien, however, are closely monitoring Vincent even at the police station.

Joan is arrives at the station, having rushed there after hearing of David's arrest. She assures him she will do something to help get him out. While she's back at the house Scoville has copy of the morning paper which accuses David of killing Kramer. Scoville is pissed "I can't jeopardize the group just for David!" Joan is shocked at what she hears, having heard about all the sacrifices that David has made. Joan goes and meets with David at the station and tells Vincent that Scoville is still upset over Kramer's death and that he is reluctant to help Vincent.

They finally release David after an attorney files a writ of habeas corpus. David doesn't know who did it but a man named Alex out of Chicago was summoned by Joan to act as David's attorney. After being released David heads over to the construction site, but learns he has been fired from a building project owing to the bad publicity surrounding the Kramer accusation. The foreman tells him that even though he designed the project, the board decided it was best to let him go. "You'll receive a pro-rated check in the mail," he is told.

He goes to a bar to drown his sorrows where he is befriended by blonde floozie named Louise. He's drunk and they converse, leading her to ask him, "Would you like to talk? My apartment is right down the street." David is tempted but turns down the invitation. Unbeknownst to him, Louise is an alien and who swaps out his cigarette case for one with a listening device. On the way out of the bar he gets knocked down by Kramer supporter. The scuffle is broken up and David exists. David, however, isn't as looped as he looks and realizes what she has done. Since Joan is there, he fakes a conversation knowing he is bugged. He tells her he's finished and wants her to go away with him. "I believe in you and me – nothing else matters." She's shocked and tried to talk him out of it, but he tells her. "If that's the way you want it, ciao."

After pretending to be all washed-up, Vincent lets himself be taken by Lucien, the alien. Three of them kidnap David right in front of Joan and take him to what appears to be Lucien's home. They offer David all kinds of things to come over to their side. "You're an outcast. Your only refuge is with us." Lucien promises to take care of all David's needs. David suggests that they read Faust, "a man who sells his soul to the devil." They offer David two million dollars to side with them. David convinces the aliens that he will play their game and give them transmitter details, in return for status and money.

Meanwhile Jim has the transmitter fully automated. Joan calls Sackville, who is also at the alb with Jim, and tells him she is worried. "David has allowed himself to be taken by the aliens," she says. Sackville reassures her that, "That is all part of the plan. He did his job –now we do ours."

Back at Lucien's house, they bring in Joan, who they've kidnapped, and hoe her to David. They take Joan, David and some aliens into the car and head to the Lab, whose vicinity David has shares with them. Cut to a flying saucer crash landing in the ocean because the transmitter is working! The aliens hear about the crash almost immediately and this gives them cause for concern.

Inside the Lab, Scoville, Jim and the colonel have something set up. Aliens are there and take a laser rifle out of the trunk of the car. One alien is in a field nearby holding June while David and another alien go to the door of the lab. An alien with the laser rifle begins burning through the security lock on the door. They get into the Lab, but what we finds is that Scoville, Jim and the Colonel are in a separate secret room and are watching the aliens in the Lab room on a monitor!

As two aliens and David enter the Lab, David pushes them, bolts and locks them in. At the same time he grabs the laser rifle which has been left outside, automatically knows how to use it (yeah, right) and shoots down the alien in the nearby grassy field who has been holding onto June. Scoville and Jim gas the two aliens who are trapped in the lab. They aliens then succumb to the gas fumes and lose consciousness.

Jim puts on a gas mask and goes to retrieve the two aliens, placing them on gurneys for analysis. The Colonel notices about one alien, "His brain transcripts – not close to human, are they? Ten, one of them begins to glow. "He needs regeneration!" David shouts. The alien burns up and dies. The second one threatens the group but he's dying as well. David tells him to look at the camera. The aliens have been taped! He also burns and dies.

A special study committee is being set up. Colonel Harmon is now convinced and calls Washington knowing that he has the evidence of the two aliens. They're all gathered at Scoville's house going through paperwork. Joan says her goodbyes to David and the two of them head into the other room with the other believers.

`Moral: A new war. A war in which the ability to attack is no longer the sole prerogative of the Invader."

.38. "The Pit"

A man looking rather haggard in a suit is making his way down a sidewalk as several people shout, "Good morning professor." He ignores them and continues his stagger/walk in front of the Slaton Research Center. As if in a dream state he thinks he sees guards signaling t one another. He thinks he sees a flying saucer go by and runs down some stairs. Everyone he sees appears to be out to get him. He flees to a pay phone (conveniently) and has enough sense to dial the phone. He makes a call to David and says, "They're here."

A doctor approaches and knocks on the pay phone door. "Julian! Julian! Are you alright?" He breaks for it and runs back up the stairs to a parking area where he thinks he sees another flying saucer. He gets dizzy and takes a header.

The narrator gives us the update: "Professor Julian Reed, a member of one of David Vincent's Believers has been hospitalized as insane. But is he a victim of the aliens or of his own mind?"

David pulls up outside of a house in a taxi, goes to the porch and rings the doorbell. A woman, Pat Reed (Julian's wife) is sitting there with her child and answers the door. "Hi Kathryn," he says giving her a hug. She invites him in and introduces him to their son, Frankie. "Mr. Vincent is going to be spending a few days with us," she says. He asks her how Julian is and she sends Frankie off to bed and as is the case on television where the kids are obedient, there is no problem as he tells David goodnight and promptly goes to his bedroom.

She holds his hand and walks him over to the couch. "You needn't have come, David. There's really nothing you can do," she says. "How bad is he?" David asks. She tells him, "I don't believe he's insane, I just believe he's emotionally tired, that's all." David asks her how it happened and she avoids the question, asking him to sit down. She says for him to give her a day or two, but David asks where he is. "Brookside," she says.

The next day David is at the hospital. He walks into the recreation room and there is Julian sitting at a table alone. When he walks over, Julian appears glad to see him. "Hi David, glad to see you." When David asks him how he's doing, he replies, "a lot better, thanks." He tells David, "I had a few wild hours there, hallucinating, paranoia – I'm glad it's all over now." David asks him how long he's been in the hospital and he says a couple of week and that he's "still uneasy about a couple of things."

He's looking around (as is David) and directs David to move to another part of the room with him because he suspects everyone. They go and are seated. "They told me I had a visitor and I thought it might be Pat," he says. "How is she? How's Frankie?" David tells him that they're doing fine and that he and Frankie are getting to be friends.

He leans over and is now speaking under his breath. He says, "David, it's no accident that I'm here. The psychosis that I had was induced deliberately. They used a dream machine." David says he doesn't exactly know what that is. "What is a dream machine?" David asks. Julian says, He tells him that it's a project he's currently involved in and then asks, "how much do you know about the Slaton Research Center"? David says, "Just what I've read in the newspapers and magazines." David says it's a "think factory." Julian says that General Slaton has gathered together some of the finest minds in the country to think out problems related to our space program, many of them highly secret. "I'm not sure if the aliens are merely observing or actively interfering. Some of the projects have already been cancelled," Julian says.

"So you think they're here?" David asks. "I'm sure of it. My assistant, Jeff Brower, is one of them. He knows that I found out about aliens being in Slaton, Julian says. "He tried to discredit you, drive you out of your mind," David deduces. Julian nods in the affirmative.

They stand up as if David is preparing to leave. Julian says he wishes he could be out of the hospital helping him. "We haven't got much time David. Find John Slaton." David tells him to take care of himself and he leaves.

In another office is the head man, Slaton who from behind his desk tells David, "The aliens are the result of Julian's sick mind, not the cause." David tells the man, "Why don't you have a talk with him? He's as rational as you or I." Slaton says "You should have heard him two days ago. He began using himself in his own experiments and I guess they just got away from him. Mr. Vincent: accept it as a tragic accident." David's a long way from convinced, responding, "Is it logical for a man like Julian Reed would put himself in a position where he would be driven insane – even accidentally?"

Slaton says, "Scientists are a strange breed, Mr. Vincent. In their zeal for knowledge they'll push themselves beyond normal limits." "To the extent of playing Russian Roulette with their sanity?" David asks. "Yes! Look at Pasteur. He risked a hideous, painful death by injecting with rabies, not certain that his treatment would work," Slaton explains. "That's pushing, wouldn't you say?" Slaton then gets up from behind his desk and tells David, "I've given you all the time I have to spare." David walks to the door and says, "All I'm asking is that you investigate all your employees." "My associates," Slaton says, correcting David. "Whatever," David says.

Slaton says he doesn't want to go poking around in the dark for something that isn't there, but adds, "I didn't want to instigate a witch hunt on the say-so of a deranged man." David then asks, "You don't mind if I ask a few questions?" Slaton says that he does mind, but adds that Scoville is a good friend who he does owe "a few good turns" and then he asks David, "Where do you want to start?" "The dream machine," David says without hesitation.

To the dream machine lab he goes where he meets Dr. Jeff Browser.

Browser explains to David that, "actually it's an electroencephalogram (which we know today simply as an EEG). Browser continues: " We call it the dream machine because it measures brain impulses and it indicates when someone is dreaming." "What do dreams have to do with sanity?" David asks. Browser then becomes hesitant, claiming that he is a busy man and asks, "Forgive me for sounding rude, but are all these questions necessary?" David says, "I think so." Browser continues: "The need to dream is so strong that when people are deprived of them they actually dream while awake – hallucinate. When a person is continually deprived of dreaming he becomes mentally deranged." "It's hard to believe," David says. "I assure you, I am not making it up," Browser says.

David asks him how it works. Here is the explanation which I am not going to share with you but will use in an essay I plan on writing about all this "dreaming" that grass roots activists are always babbling about. At any rate, Brower explains: "The electrodes are attached to the scalp. The electrical impulses that the brain gives off are rested here. When the dream starts, a bell will automatically ring, which wakes the subject. At this point he has total recall of the dream, which we record on tape for our records."

Hmmmmm. At any rate Browser takes off his lab coat and tells David that he's on his way to lunch. David wants an explanation as to why Julian Reed became psychotic. "Before I left for the night I turned on the machine" he says, leaving Julian alone which is the usual procedure. In that way, nobody has to stay up all night. He said that after five interruptions, this switch turns off from the sheet and allows uninterrupted dreaming for the rest of the night. He said that professor Reed was dreaming for too long, to the point of breakdown. A device that records pulse and heartbeat is attached to the machine. David picks it up and places it on Browser. "What are you doing?" he asks. David sees the heartbeat, puts down the device and says "thanks for your help." Then he leaves.

David meets with Pat and as they walk she tells him he's quite a celebrity with the staff, who want to know if he actually believes in planetary intruders or it's a magnificent put on. He says he's used to that kind of stuff and says he's checked out everything Julian told him and then Pat interrupts him: "And found nothing because there's nothing to find." David is going to see Julian and asks Pat to come with him. She says, "I can't, David."

She ignores his question about "why not" and instead introduced him to two security dogs. "These are our two friendly night watchmen, Ralph and Alfie." They continue their walk, right past the human security guard. When the dogs spot him (because he's an alien) they begin barking fiercely.

During the drive, with David behind the wheel, David tells her, "Pat, he wants to see his family." She says she doesn't want Frankie to see his father like that, not until he's better. David says, "He is better. He's calm, he's rational, he's fully aware of what happened. Anyway, you wouldn't have to take Frankie." She says she knows. "You haven't seen him since he's been there," David says. She says she doesn't feel guilty but she will go see him soon. Even though she adds, "I promise," Vincent still has to get the last word by saying, "I don't understand."

At the house she pours and serves David a cup of coffee, admitting that she probably seems "cruel." As she wrings her hands and paces she tells David, "My grandfather was a wonderful old man, and I loved him dearly. When I was seven, we were left alone – my parents had gone out and all of a sudden he just lost his mind, just went berserk, just smashed everything in the house. Only the neighbors could subdue him. It was the first time in my life I ever felt terror, I suppose. I've just never been able to forget it." David says, "It's all very unfortunate, but it's a long time ago."

She continues babbling, her back to David all the time: "First my grandfather, then Julian. I keep looking at Frankie – he seems so withdrawn ever since Julian…" David interrupts, stands up and grabs her by both arms. Their faces are less than a foot apart as he tells her that she knows that insanity is not hereditary. She's more concerned about the weakness because "Julian's always been so strong, and I need him now, I need him the way he was." "He needs you, too," David replies. David tells her to sleep on it and he will give Julian her love. She says, "No, I'll give it to him."

Back at the hospital David strolls into Julian's room. Julian is laying down, all covered up as if he has a chill. The first thing Julian does is ask about Pat and right behind David she walks in with a smile. He gets up and they embrace one another with David looking on with his arms crossed. He asks about Frankie and she says he's fine (by the way: Frankie doesn't look like either one of them). He tells her his pulse is normal, that he's "ready to get back to the wars," and that he's homesick.

He then turns to David and asks him if he's seen Brower. When David tells Julian that Brower is not an alien. "He's kind of pompous but he's not an alien – I checked his heartbeat." Julian says it's a trick and it's wrong, while David counters by claiming "there's no doubt about it." Julian says he rigged the machine and David says that Brower claims that the relay broke the machine. Julian keeps insisting and says, "You don't believe me do you – neither of you do." He says that "the only one that does (believe him) is Frankie."

Julian looks at David's hand in through a kind of dream state sees an extended pinkie finger like the aliens. He gets up: "You're one of them. I never saw it before." "Saw what?" David asks as his hands are perfectly normal. Julian and David begin tussling and an orderly comes in and grabs Julian who is screaming, "He's an alien! He's an alien!" at the top of his lungs.

David and Pat are in the car driving back to her house. "You won't let me drive you to the airport," she asks. David says he'll catch a cab. He asks if she and Frankie will be alright and she says yes, that they will work very, very hard and "kids bounce back." When they pull back in to Pat's job, the security guard is feeding the dogs. The guard feeding the dogs opens the gate to leave but the dogs charge past him and attack the other security guard, the one who is an alien. David runs over to help and though the guard was badly bitten, there is no blood.

As the other guard holds the dogs, the alien guard makes a run for it. The dog, David and the other security guard are giving chase. After turning a corner, the alien guard falls to the ground, turns bright red and dissolves.

Inside her office Pat is still saying that "it seems impossible." David tells her, "Julian wrote me before his illness and told me about the aliens. He was right. They are here … He thought they were here because of the sophisticated projects going on here. Can you tell me anything about the projects?" She says, "They cover a pretty broad area – environmental systems, space medicine, nutrition – my own project is a theoretical propulsion engine." David asks, "Electromagnetic?" She wants to know how he knew about it. He tells her that some of the people that he works with think that's the kind of engine they use to propel their spacecraft." He then follows up and asks her if she's had any unusual problems with the project or any interference?

She says no, but in regard to other projects she tells him that some get scrapped, including "some we had high hopes for." David tells her, "It could be sabotage" and again she tells him that it's impossible because they send reports to Washington and "keep records of everything." She said she doesn't send them herself she sends them to – John Slaton.

Now they're back at Pat's house again and David is immediately on the phone with Scoville informing him that the reports are going through Slaton's office. Scoville says Slaton couldn't be one of them, "I've known him for years."

David asks what if he sold out and Scoville says that Slaton was more than cordial when he told him that David was coming out. David says, "If I were an alien, I'd give priority to a propulsion system that they're working on here. It happens to be Pat Reed's project." Scoville says he'll put in a call to Washington. As he hangs up Frankie storms through the house, apparently having just gotten home from school. He walks right past David who then follows the kid into his room. "Mind if I come in?" Frankie looks up and then looks back down at his books without saying a word.

David said he called him last night when he saw his dad and Frankie told his father he had seen something. "What was it?" he asks. Frankie says, "I don't know what he meant." David says, "Something strange, something spooky." Frankie says, "I didn't see anything – honest." David tells him that it's important but the kid still denies anything. He then gets up, walks across the room and sets his books down. He turns and says, "Mr. Vincent, he made me promise not to tell anyone." David assures him, "He won't mind you telling me."

Vincent then learns from Frankie that he had been down on the pier fishing near the amusement park and he "saw a couple of creepy looking guys" go in there." David asks him why that was strange and Frankie replies, "Because it's all shut down for the winter. Anyway, I climbed the wall just to take a look. And there was a lot of funny-looking machinery. I told my dad and he started poking around there. The next thing I knew, he was ….”The kid is getting distraught and David comforts him. “Frankie, it wasn’t your fault.” Frankie’s afraid that if “they” find out, “They’ll do it to me, too.” David tells him not to worry about that.”

David glances at his watch. “Your mom will be home in a few minutes. Will you tell her I went to the amusement park?” Frankie tells him that the park is on the west side of town and off David goes, solo once again.

David scales a wall, hops a fence and then scampers across a small quad area. He spots two men conversing, and one uniformed alien ducks into the security office. A silent alarm goes off inside the office as the guard says on the phone, “there’s someone in the restricted area.” At least five aliens congregate and begin running over to the area. David is running and hiding all over the park, ducking into various outside exhibits. David ambushes one guard and knocks him out with one punch and grabs his gun. Four are now on David’s tail. David shoots and kills one who falls into the water below. Three others give chase. David jumps into the water himself and swims off – suit coat and all.

David apparently finds his way back to Pat’s home, where he just walks right in and sees Pat in the living room conversing with three men. She asks him where he’s been but she would have already known if Frankie had told her the way David asked him to. At any rate David tells her, “At the amusement park.” One man quips, “Fall off the rollercoaster?” Pat introduces the men: Arthur Whelan, Paul Myers and Jeff (Browder) I think you know.” One man standing, says, “Vincent – aren’t you the fellow who …? David interrupts and says, “I’m the one.” The man then replies, “I thought so. We were just discussing going to other planets. Sit in. Tell us about your space men.” David says, “I can do better than that. I can show you some. After all, if we can go to other planets why can’t people from other planets come here?”

The man says, “We’re not saying there’s no such animal. We’re willing to acknowledge the possibility of life on other planets. But in the absence of proof, we rather doubt that that life is here right now.” David again says, “I can show you proof.” The man seated tells him that what might be proof to David “might not be proof to us.” David keeps babbling: “There’s alien machinery at the amusement park.” Another man asks, “At the penny arcade or the tunnel of love?” David says, “You’re beginning to sound like Julian. “What kind of machines?” Browder asks. . “I don’t know,” David replies as Frankie is peeking from around the corner and listening. He tells David to describe them. David says, “I was jumped before I could see them. I only heard them.”

Browder says, "Jumped? By whom? Julian's psychosis must be contagious. Feelings of persecution, Mr. Vincent?" David stares him down and says, "Would you stop playing psychiatrist for a moment? I'm not being paranoid." Pat pulls rank and tells everyone, "The meeting is over." David is still pleading: "All I ask is that one of you come with me!" The men file out as if David doesn't even exist. David says, "I thought scientists explored every possibility." One man stops and says, "On a cool night, we also weigh the probabilities. Good night." And then he joins the others in evacuating the premises.

When the men walk out Frankie comes out of the back room. "I saw them, too. So did dad," he tells his mother. She orders him to "march out of here mister and go to bed." When he tries to tell her that he also told Mr. Vincent, she says, "Move!" and he does. When Frankie's door closes she walks up on David and says, "I won't have you involving my son in your fantasies!" She says she won't listen to him and that's she's sick of hearing about aliens: "My husband has had a nervous breakdown and now you're trying to involve my son! I like you David but, I think it would be better if you found another place to stay."

He tells her he doesn't like the idea of her and Frankie being alone. He says he's sorry and she says, "You're sorry, I'm sorry I guess the whole world is sorry. I guess too much has happened to me in too short a time." She again says she needs Julian and says, "I'm so weak without him." Then she turns and walks away leaving David dumbfounded.

Cut to the high rise offices of Edgar Scoville in Syracuse, New York. He's on the phone with Vincent: "David, I just had a long session with Washington. They're reached a decision yesterday on Pat Reed's project. They're going to cancel it." "Did they give any reason?" David asks. Scoville says something about Paul Reed and things being "pretty esoteric," and his project is no further along than it was six months ago." Both men express their regrets and Scoville tells David she'll be notified by Washington tomorrow.

David, using Pat's phone as she walks into the room without his realizing it, asks Edgar if it was possible for someone to have changed the reports before they got to Washington. Edgar says it possible and he'll check it out and get back. David tells him he'll be staying at the Rancho Motel. He turns to see Pat, stands up and tells her that the report on her project was "rather negative." She begins talking about how they've made a real breakthrough and David tells her that it is possible that somebody tampered with those reports before they got to Washington. She tells him she doesn't believe it.

David's cab is blowing outside. He tells her to call if she needs him and off he goes. David ducks to enter the cab and there is Browder. The cab driver, standing outside, knocks David over the head and ushers him into the back seat of the taxi, next to Browder.

Cut to David on a table in the lab being fitted for a dream experiment by Browder and an assistant. The plan is to drive David insane with the dream machine in the same way that he did David. The electrodes are in place on David's forehead and the machine is on. David is entering a dream state reflecting back on Julian's tantrum about David being an alien. An alarm goes off and the dream continues as David is thinking about his debate with Browder and the other men in Pat's living room. They are laughing at him as he continues to utter, "I don't know, I don't know." Browder and the assistant are watching.

Pat is talking with Slaton about the reports and she tells him that it doesn't come as a surprise because David told her last night. Slaton says he'll check it through. "Meanwhile you got out and buy yourself an expensive lunch," he tells her.

David is still being programmed and bells are going off. Browder tells someone on the phone that he will take care of his end and then hangs up. Meanwhile, Pat has called the hotel and they say that he never registered. She then asks for a "Mr. Scoville" and he hasn't come by but if either of them does, have them call Pat Reed, please. In walks Brower and she tells him she's glad he's there. She tells him about what has taken place and about David's disappearance. He tells her, "There are answers to these things. Vincent will show up." She asks him about her project and why it was cancelled like he said it would be.

Brower says, "I know it's a blow, but back off for a day. Give Slaton a chance to follow through." She says "no, it was going too well. I've got my research notes, and I'm going to get them to Washington now." He tells her, "good idea, if I can help …" She tells him no and adds, "You're very dear to offer but I'm going to take them (the notes) straight to the top." She's going over Slaton's head and tells Brower that "David has a friend, a man named Mr. Scoville."

Meanwhile, Scoville meets with Slaton in Slaton's office regarding the Magnetic Propulsion project. Slaton looks in the files and they are all gone – Pat has the reports. "He'll turn up, Edgar. Chances are he's out looking for aliens someplace," Slaton quips. "Don't put him down, John," Scoville says. Slaton pours two four-finger drinks of Scotch and as he comes back to the desk to serve them he says, "I'm not putting him down. It's just that he's created quite a stir among some of our people." Scoville interrupts and says, "Let me tell you something. These aliens you're scoffing at are possibly responsible for some of your projects being cancelled."

Slaton looks at him and says, "Edgar, a week ago if anyone would have tried to talk to me seriously about invaders from outer space I would have tossed them out on their ear." Edgar says, "What about today?" Slaton says, "Today I'll buy any explanation for what's going on, rational or otherwise." He continues: "That magnetic propulsion engine is one of our key projects. Pat Reed has one of the most extraordinary facilities for blending science and imagination. I've read all of her reports, they're excellent." "Then why did they cancel it?" Edgar asks.

Slaton says, "I don't know,' as he is seated back at his desk. "Edgar, what's it all about?" Scoville reaches in his brief case and hands Slaton a file. "Here's a copy of your report – the way it arrived in Washington. I suggest you read it." Slaton begins looking it over as the receptionist's phone rings in Slaton's outer office. It's Pat looking for Edgar Scoville. The secretary lies and says no one has come in since lunch, so Pat leaves a message for Scoville to call her at the lab. "It's very important," she concludes and then hangs up.

Back inside the office Slaton says, "Edgar these are not the reports I read." Scoville says, "They're the ones that went to the government. Who had them after you?" Slaton says, "Nobody. They were typed up fresh and sent in," he says. "Who typed them?" Scoville asks. "Why Mrs. Deely, my …." Now they know whose been sabotaging the reports. Slaton gets on the phone and calls the secretary, but no answer. He and Scoville go outside into her area and the files are all gone. Pat Reed's report is gone but Slaton says that they have her research notes. "That'll be good enough," Scoville says as Slaton gets on the phone.

He calls Brower's office and Pat is standing there. Brower says, "Sorry, she's not back from lunch yet." He hangs up and then lies to Pat, telling her that it was "somebody for your assistant. It sounded like a boyfriend." She tells Brower that she's going over to Scoville's office to wait. "Maybe I can get those reports to Washington." "Want me to come with you?" Brower asks. "I'd appreciate that very much," she says as they both leave together.

As they get to the elevator she notices the extended finger of one of the technicians. She tells him to go ahead she forgot something. Brower stays with her. Brower asks her what's wrong and she says, "That man – his hand – didn't you see it?" "David said some of the aliens have hands like that, a mutated finger." She tells Brower she's afraid to head to Slaton's office and Brower recommends that she come over to his lab: "You'll be safe there. I promise you I'll find Scoville." She agrees and off they go.

Slaton and Scoville are still trying to find Pat wondering "where in the devil can she be?" When Slaton attempts to leave a message for Pat with a security guard he is informed that "Miss Reed got back almost an hour ago." He further informs Slaton and Scoville that "she just left the building with Mr. Brower a couple of minutes ago." They summon the guard to come along with them as they now are looking for Brower.

Pat and Jeff head over to the lab and after they enter Pat doesn't see Brower locking the door behind them. She walks through the lab to go to the phone to call Scoville again and through the giant window she sees David on the table hooked up to the dream machine! She's stopped by an aide as Brower walks over and snatches her notes out of her hand. She looks at him: "Jeff, you can't be one of them. The heartbeat." Brower coldly glares at her and says, "Figure it out – you're a scientist." "A mechanical heart – a pacemaker," she deduces.

There is a knock at the door and when Brower goes to open it, Pat wrests away from the guard, runs up on Brower and snatches her notes back from his grasp. She begins screaming, but here come Scoville and Slaton. Slaton orders the guard to break the door open as inside Brower is ordering that Vincent be finished off. The security guard shoots the female assistant and she glows red and dies. David is fighting his way out of the straps on the table. Pat gets away from Brower, the guard shoots again and Brower glows and dissolves.

Pat rushes in to where David is being helped by Scoville. "David, are you alright?" she asks. "This is what they did to Julian," she deduces. David tells Scoville that he's glad that he's there.

At a table in the hospital lounge, Julian and Pat are playing chess and he's just won. David is watching and smiling. "I have a plane to catch. Take care of yourself," he says shaking Julian's hand."Mr. Slaton's going to put you back to work." Julian thanks him as Pat walks him to the door. "Have I told you how much I appreciate you?" she asks. "Not for half an hour," David jokes. "Don't worry, he'll be alright. He's responding to treatment," David tells her. "If you hadn't come I don't know how this would have turned out," she says.

They hug and say their goodbyes.

Moral: "Perhaps it has ended for the Reed family. But for David Vincent, it is still the beginning."

.39. "The Organization"

The site is a dock. A red Ford Mustang fastback pulls up and it's Vincent. David made good time because Edgar Scoville let him use his plane. David meets newsman Mike Calvin from the *Chronicle News* reports are that a meteor collided with a weather satellite in full view of a nearby ship. "This the ship that saw the collision?" David asks. "This is it," says Calvin. David said he read Calvin's article in the Chronicle, "Meteor Collides With Weather Satellite." Calvin says that was the air forces opinion and he "did it from their angle." David asks him what he thinks and he says, "I don't know" but adds that there have been reports of flying saucers in that area.

David looks up at the huge docked ship and says, "Let's have a look" and they head toward the vessel. An officer meets them and asks "Are you from the Chronicle?" Calvin says that he is and tells the man that his captain said they could look around. "Help yourself," he says. David asks the officer if he saw the collision, to which he replies that he's not even sure it was a collision. He said "all of a sudden it started raining junk." David asks "what kind of junk?" He says, Pieces of metal, tubing, wire." "That all?" David asks. "That all?" the man says obviously frustrated with David's inquisitions. He tells them he's going upstairs, turns and walks away.

A black car pulls up (must be aliens) with two men in it. They wait for the officer to walk into a nearby building and then they get out of their car and board the ship where David and Calvin are e. So far all David and Calvin see are sacks and barrels. The ship docked at ten this morning Calvin tells him. "That's over five hours ago," David says. "They could have beaten us to it."

As they keep looking they walk into the two men who are armed with pistols. As one is searching David, he pulls down a sack of material and hits the alien in the head. David says "run," and Calvin does just that as David is left to do battle with the aliens. The fight is on. David knocks one out but gets the shit knocked out of him as well.

The narrator comes in and informs us: The search for evidence of an alien spacecraft has led David Vincent into the hands of a ruthless enemy. Unaware that the freighter he searched carried not one alien cargo, but two"

The two aliens drag David's unconscious body out of the back seat and drag him into a closed down hotel. They lie him down on one of the beds and one of them gets on the phone and tells someone, "It wasn't there. We did look and it just wasn't there. That's right, number three hole. We sure did – two of 'em. No, one of 'em got away. Vincent, David Vincent. Yes sir." Then he hangs up the phone and tells the other one, "He's on his way."

They grab David off the bed and sit him upright in a chair. One of them grabs David by the tie and says,"Alright Vincent. Let's start over again. Who told you about the shipment?" The other one asks, "How'd you know where to find it?" Back to the one that is holding him: "Where's your partner?" David, still groggy says, "He got away." The other one walks over and says, "We'll find him, and you'll tell us where." Then he slaps the shit out of David.

Meanwhile, Calvin is in a pay phone booth. He has contacted Edgar Scoville who pulls up in a chauffeur-driven black Lincoln Continental. Edgar bolts out of the back seat and says, "What happened?" Calvin says that they blew it, the wreckage wasn't there." Scoville says, "But THEY were. How far did you tail 'em?" Calvin says along the docks of the river, about a mile east of here." "That's where you lost 'em?" Scoville asks." "Yeah," Calvin says. Scoville says, "Okay you start here and work your way back. I'll head west as far as Pinewood." Calvin says, "That's four miles." Scoville tells him he'll take the guards with him. The plan is for them to split up and Scoville tells him that he has a phone in his car. "If you find him, call me." Calvin runs over to his own car and says, "I will if I can."

A chauffeur-driven black Rolls Royce pulls up at the abandoned motel. Out steps a dapper man named Peter Kalter, who a mob leader. Inside he says, "Well Mr. Vincent, you've had a difficult time. I'm sorry, but you did bring it upon yourself." He orders his two guards to wait outside. "You know Mr. Vincent, I left a very spectacular cocktail party just to come here and meet you," Kalter says, standing up and holding a cigarette in a holder like some 1950s gangster bitch. "My name's Kalter – Peter Kalter."

David asks, "What are you going to do with me?" Kalter tells him, "What happens to you is entirely your decision. So now: where do we find your partner? He has something that belongs to us," Kalter says seating himself directly across from where David is seated. "All he got away with was his life," David says. "You know, your loyalty is almost poetic when you consider the consequences of it." Vincent tells him he has nothing to say. Kalter says, "This was your first job, wasn't it? If you were experienced you would never hijack something you can't possibly handle."

David looks at him and asks, "Why not?" "Because It takes an organization like ours to get that much stuff cut and distributed it," Kalter tells David. "I didn't know anything about your shipment when I went aboard that crater," David explains. "I'm not a naïve man, Mr. Vincent," Kalter replies. "I'm no hijacker," David responds. "Then what were you doing in that cargo hole, looking for something – for what?" Kalter angrily asks. "Pieces of metal, electrical cords. Look, there were several crates in that cargo hole, maybe yours was taken with the one I wanted." David tells him that "they took your drugs by mistake." Kalter looks at him: "Who, Mr. Vincent? Who are 'they'?"

"A group," David says. "A group. What kind of group? Where can I find them?" Kalter asks. "You can't, " David explains. "Do you know who I am?" Kalter asks. He tells David that his organization has a very long arm, and then he asks again "who are 'they'?" He whistles for the two men to come back into the room. "He's stalling," he tells them. One of them pulls out his gun.

David says, "Alright, I'll tell ya." Kalter says, "Your life depends on whether I believe what you tell me," taking a long drag off his cigarette.

Meanwhile, Calvin pulls up slowly, stops and pulls a pistol out of the glove compartment. Kalter's guard gets out of his car and spots him. He pulls his gun as well. He gets the drop on Calvin. Back in the room where David is being interrogated we hear Kalter shout, "Invaders from space!? A man faced with dying ought to be able to offer a more plausible story in his defense!" David has his forehead in his hands and is standing as he counters, "A man faced with dying doesn't lie." Kalter shouts, "THAT can be your epitaph!"

In walk Kalter's armed chauffeur, shoving Calvin in front of him. He apologizes to David and tells him, "I had to come back for ya." The chauffeur says, "I found him prowling around – with this," showing the pistol to Kanter. "He's the one who got away," says a second man. "You still expect me to believe your story about creatures from space?"Kanter asks David. He orders the chauffeur to "look around outside." "David who are these people?" Calvin asks. "Hoods," David says. Kanter rears back his hand to slap the shit out of him but hesitates and simply says, "I don't like that word, Mr. Vincent." He walks over to Calvin: "Now, where's our shipment?" Calvin and David look back and forth at each other and Calvin tells Kanter, "I don't know what you're talking about."

"I'm talking about life and death – yours! Now where is it?" David interjects: "He's telling the truth – he doesn't know." Kanter looks at his watch and says, "Well, it's getting late and I want to get back to my cocktail party. I don't think there's any reason to keep them alive." Each of the thugs takes out his gun and points it at each of the two men, Calvin and David.

Cut to the black Lincoln Continental cruising the town streets with two cops in the front seat and Scoville barking orders from the back. "Circle the town again. If we strike out this time we'll head back toward the river." Meanwhile, David and Calvin are being marched out to a wooded area where their murders can be carried out. Calvin is pushed to his knees. David pleads for him: "He doesn't know anything." Kanter doesn't believe it and tells him that it's his last chance: "Where's our shipments?" Kanter lights another cigarette as the gun is held to Calvin's head. Just in the nick of time Scoville pulls up and tells the guards to "be ready."

Their search begins. Kanter is merciful. He tells David, "If you were stupid enough to take our shipment, you wouldn't be stupid enough to die for it." They march back to the cabin. When they walk back into the room Scoville is there, with one guard behind the door and the other at his side, both with pistols drawn. "Let them go," he orders. Kanter recognizes him. "Scoville. Edgar Scoville. An unexpected pleasure." Scoville tells David that he was right. Kanter asks Scoville if David and Calvin are friends of his and he tells them that they are.

"I didn't know that,"Kanter says. "Does that change anything?" David asks. "Of course it does. I know Victor Scoville – although he wishes he didn't know me," Kanter replies (Note: I thought his name was "Edgar" Scoville?)

Kanter walks up to Scoville and asks, "This story of Vincent's – you believe that?" Scoville tells him, "We're working together." Kanter says, "Why don't you tell me what this is about – maybe I can give you a hand." Scoville declines the offer prompting Kanter to counter, "Scoville – who do you think you're talking to?" Scoville doesn't answer. "I would have hurt these friends of yours if I was what you think I am," Kanter says. "Just how could you help us?" David asks. "If I believed you? I don't know – in a lot of ways. I have a big organization with connections." Scoville says, "Not interested," then summons David and Calvin to join him in leaving.

Kalter's assistant walks up to him when they leave and asks, "You're not thinking of tying up with guys like that, Mr. Kalter?" "Of course not," he answers. "They're crazy," the aide says. "They'd have to be," answers Kalter as he takes a drag off his cigarette.

In the car headed back to town David and Edgar are in the back seat talking. "What did they want with you?" David asks. "They were bringing in narcotics, thought we took their shipment," David explains. "I'm amazed he didn't kill you," Scoville says. "Peter Kanter is the worst kind of gangster there is." David says, "For a while I thought he was going to kill me." Then he asks, "What do you imagine he could do for us if he were on our side?" Scoville says, "Kill a lot of people. Some of the aliens, some of us if he felt like it. But he's not on our side. We've got all we can do fighting one war at a time."

David asks Scoville if he's basing what he's saying on newspaper events. Scoville shares a story of a powerful man who wanted to testify against Kanter. "They're still dragging the Hudson River for Harold Beal," he says.

Then Kanter offers some background on his relationship with Kanter: "I met him myself last year. A member put him up at the Uptown Athletic Club. I blackballed him." Then he got shown around so that people could see what a prince Kanter was. "Everybody else was for taking him in. I blackballed him again. One's all it takes, and then I resigned from the Uptown Athletic Club. Peter Kalter doesn't like me, I don't like Peter Kalter. And I don't like what you're thinking, David. Come around to my office tomorrow morning. I want to show you a letter that Howard's wife sent me when he couldn't deliver some parts on time. Then somebody broke both his arms." David sits quietly.

Next scene is a stately manor with a Rolls Royce parked in front. You know it's Kanter's place. As he plays pool an advisor tells him that they have obligations to the suppliers, the wholesalers, the distributors and to the users. It isn't right to promise and not deliver." "No, I know it isn't Mr. Weller," Kanter replies. "So, can you recover the shipment?" Weller asks. "I don't know. To be honest with you I've reached a sort of dead end," Kanter tells him as he chalks up his cue. As Weller takes his shot he says, "We're talking about ten or twelve million dollars. I think you should make another try." "Yes sir, of course," Kanter acknowledges.

"David Vincent and his associates. Could they help you," Weller asks as another man enters the room. "I don't think they're any closer to it than we are," Kanter says. "They do have some story about who has it," Weller reminds him. "Mr. Weller, Mr. Vincent's in with some tough people: a reporter, a man named Scoville who's a millionaire. They're hard to push around,"Kanter says circling the table. "Are they? Really?" Weller asks. Kanter tells him, "I have a bad feeling. I don't like Vincent or Scoville. I'm not sure we can trust them," he says. "Maybe other solutions will present themselves. I think you can handle them," Weller assures him. "I'll try," he says. "Good," says Kanter as he puts down his cue and says "Thank you, Pete" as he leaves the room.

The man who came in when Kanter and Weller were talking walks up after Weller leaves and hands him a glass of Scotch, as he has one as well. "Call David Vincent for me," he tells the man. "ASK if I can see him."

Cut to Scoville's high-rise office with David going over some papers. "Sounds like a fine woman," David says. "She is. Her husband was a fine man." David says, "Well, I agree with you Edgar. Kalter deserves everything you said about him but…" Scoville interrupts: "But what?" "He has an organization, hundreds of connections all over town who can help us find what we're looking for. Now what's your first responsibility: to fight people like Kalter or aliens?" David asks. "Aliens!", Scoville expeditiously replies, "But that doesn't mean we have to use Kalter.

David, still pacing, turns to his older counterpart: "We know the aliens have his narcotics. And he has the manpower to get them back and maybe the crates containing the saucer fragments. Maybe we should give it a try." "No," says Scoville. "We can always get the crates back and maybe uncover some good evidence," David continues to insist. "No!" Edgar adamantly responds. But David is persistent: "Look Edgar, if it doesn't work out you can forget it ever happened." Scoville says, "But it WILL happen. You'll get his narcotics back and you know too much. He'll never let you out. No. We all know the morality of it, when is it alright to fight fire with fire? But what really worries me is you get into this thing and you'll see something you shouldn't. And you could end up like Harold Beal, at the bottom of the Hudson River.

David says, "I know that. But I still think that we should give him a chance." Just then Kalter walks in. "You didn't return my call," he says. The secretary closes the door as Kalter walks in. "How did you get in here?" Scoville asks. Kalter says that he's been calling since last night – your apartment, here." David glances at Scoville. Scoville says, "No calls came here." Kalter says he heard him say that they might work together." David asks, "If we do, what do we go after – aliens or narcotics?" Kalter says, "One hand washes the other, Mr. Vincent."

David says, "No deal. We're going after aliens. If we find narcotics, they go in the River." Kalter quickly agrees and says, "Let's go." Scoville watches intently as David and Kalter walk out of the room.

Meanwhile, Calvin is on the phone talking to Scoville and promising him that he'll listen to what is being said. He walks into the next room where David and Kalter are seated (they're in Kalter's house). Calvin says, "Alright,what do you want?" "A story in your paper," David says. "Saying what?" Calvin asks. "A crate containing wreckage from that collision between the weather satellite and the meteorite is being moved from Pier 56 to Compton Air Base tomorrow." "A trap story," says Calvin. He continues: "Edgar was right. You lie down with dogs, you get up with fleas. It's starting already. You want me to put a phony story in the paper."

Kalter interrupts him and tells him, "Yeah and then we'll ask you to trip a blind old lady walking across the street." The point is, according to Kalter is that he (Calvin) wants them as much as he does. He adds, "Scruples are marvelous, but for once do yourself a favor: forget 'em." David pleads, "Mike, how about it? Just one favor. Calvin agrees, but with one condition: he then drops the money that Kalter had stuffed in his hand and walks out. When he leaves Kalter laughs and picks up the bill.

Cut to David driving a white pickup truck with Kalter in the passenger seat. "Where are your aliens, Mr. Vincent?" he asks. The story has been in the paper already and David says maybe they didn't see the story in the paper or maybe they saw it and didn't believe it. "Or maybe I just talked myself into it because I wanted to believe it," quips Kalter.

As they cruise down the highway a motorcycle cop pulls out and begins trailing them. They've got two large crates in the back and are nearly at the air base. David tells him, "We're being followed." The trap is working perfectly. Kalter is getting fidgety and wants to turnaround. When David tells him they're being followed, he continues to tell him, "Pull over, I don't want any trouble." David asks him what the speed limit around there is and Kalter tells him sixty-five; David tells him he's only doing fifty.

David says there is no siren or red lights but the motorcycle cop is edging up on them. "I don't think he's a cop," David says. The cop tosses a grenade into the back bed of the pickup truck then speeds off. The explosion rocks the truck, with the bed starting on fire and the truck billowing smoke and flames. The truck crashes and turns on its side. David gets out of the driver's side and goes back to rescue Kalter. He manages to pull Kalter out of the passenger side window although it's nearly pinned to the ground. "Let's get outta here, this truck is gonna blow!" David shouts as he rescues the thug.

As they make it across the street the truck does indeed blow up. "Why'd ya do it, Vincent," Kalter asks. "I wanted you alive," David says. "Because we're such good friends?" David says, "So you can tell your people what you know." Kalter says "You saved my life. Now we're quits."

Back at Kalter's Web Weller is quizzing Kalter and asking him if saw any of those "things" that Vincent was talking about. "They hit the truck – that ought to prove something," Kalter declares. Weller asks him what the motorcycle cop looked like and Kanter says, "He looked like a cop!" They both put down their pool cues as Weller tells him, "This Vincent is running you in circles. Maybe he's trying to make a deal for our stuff with somebody outside the country." Another man in a suit has been listening and walks over to the door and tells the suited guard, "Bring him in." In walks David.

Weller says, "Mr. Vincent, we don't want any harm to come to you or anyone else for that matter. We'll forget that you know something about our operation. Now what is this all about? Tell us the truth." David says, "I've told you everything I can." The other suited man scoffs and talks about those people with no heart or pulse? The phone is ringing but Weller decides that David is wasting their time. "Good day Mr. Vincent," he says. "If I walk out of here, how far do I get, Kalter?" David asks. Weller says, "Kalter is out of it now." The phone has been ringing all this time and Kalter finally picks it up. "Oh hello, Mr. Scoville. No, I'm sorry, he's not here," he says into the phone.

Kalter tells Scoville that Tom called several times yesterday and Scoville told him that David wasn't there, either. There is a long pause and Kalter hangs up the phone. Kalter looks into the next room where a man is sitting. He summons him: "Don." The man walks over. "Yes Mr. Kalter?" "How many times did you call Mr. Scoville yesterday," Kalter asks. Don says six or seven times. Kalter calls him a liar. "You didn't call at all." Weller interrupts and asks, "What is this foolishness, Peter? How do you know he didn't call?" He tells him that Scoville told him. "You take his word over one of your own?" Weller asks.

Kanter closes the door behind Don and David walks over: "Maybe he has a reason for not having called. Maybe he wanted to keep us apart." Don says, "What reason?" Kalter says, "You're a liar – why?" David tells him to feel his pulse and see if he has one. Don tries to walk across the room but David stops him. Kalter calls him and Don asks, "Mr. Kalter, you're not going to listen to this guy?" Kalter says, "You've had your pulse taken before. Hold out your hand."

Don makes a run for it, but Kalter shoots him in the back. He glows red and disintegrates in front of everybody. "Like I said, no blood, no pulse or heartbeat. When they die they incinerate," David says. "Are there many of them?" Weller asks. "No," David replies. "Now will you work with us? We'll have to dig them out." "And find our shipment," Weller adds. The other guy says, "Pete – give Mr. Vincent whatever he needs." David and Kalter lock eyes.

Later we find David pulling up in a red Mustang fastback as a man peers out of the window inside and tells another, "He's here." David is introduced by the man who opens the door to another man who is seated and drinking a mug of coffee. "There's your man, Vincent. His name is Amos Foster." Foster walks up and informs them that he has an office down at City Hall and therefore wants to know why he was "dragged" all the way out to where they are meeting. It seems that Foster is an officer with the Building Permits Bureau, which he corrects by adding, "Industrial."

David's concern is that Foster has a list of factories and warehouses that have been given permission to use high voltage lines, the maximum that the city allows. "Recently?" he asks. "The last three or four months," David informs him. "There aren't too many of those. I could have it for you by tomorrow." David tells him, "I need it today." He scoffs and the other man tells him, "By noon," at which time Foster walks out. "Can you depend on him?" David asks and is informed that Foster is on their payroll and they pay him as much as the city pays him. David says, "When he brings the list I want every place checked. Do you have enough men?"

He says he has enough men and David continues with the orders: "Look for places that are abandoned or seem to be out of business. If you see any activity, call me." David then leaves.

Back at the home of Weller, he tells Kalter and his aide that "Vincent's war is not ours. We have to be careful not to get involved." The man who set up the meeting with David and Foster walks in with a list and tells Weller and the others that Foster came through with a list of three places: two warehouses and a private museum. Vincent wants to get on it right away," he says. Weller says, "Alright – you know what to look for." The other man says, "If you find the shipment, bring it to me and uh… THANK Mr. Vincent for us."

As the man prepares to leave Kalter stands up and says, "Wait a minute! I could care less about Vincent, but these aren't hoodlums we're fighting. You saw what happened with Dom. Vincent's right – we're gonna need him." The man on the couch, Weller's colleague reiterates, "It's not our fight. Let's look out for number one, eh, Peter?" Kalter is concerned.

Meanwhile, in an abandoned railroad car, we find inside the aliens using it as a regeneration chamber headquarters. Inside an alien is self-regenerating and outside, David and two men are watching the freight car. The guy who set up the meet with Foster says that someone at the railyard heard a humming sound coming from inside the railroad car. There are no power lines leading to it. David is surprised: "No power lines? Let's check it out," and the three men approach the freight car. Another alien, inside the car watching over the one being regenerated, spots the three men through an open door. He signals for the other one to come out of the regeneration tube and check out what is going on.

They continue to watch as David opens a sliding door and finds nothing. "Maybe the next one," he says as they approach where the aliens are. They walk right past and David notices a thick wire running into the car. "If there's anybody inside, take 'em alive," he says. The aliens push the self-destruct button, the rail car glows red and then disappears.

Back at the house Kalter is still arguing: "But you can't meet with them," he says. He tells Weller that "we know what they are because Vincent's told you!" Weller tells him, "I don't care what they are" and once again emphasizes that all he wants is the shipment. Kalter says that Vincent was thinking of the well-being of the gang and has warned them. Weller says, "Relax Peter: if they take over the world, they'll have to take it over from us."

A two-door gold Lincoln Continental pulls up outside. In walk two men, one identifies himself as "Dorcas." After turning down the offer of a drink he gets right to the point: "We would like for you to leave our installations alone." Weller tells him, "No." Dorcas says, "We know why you're applying this pressure." Weller's colleague says, "Then you know how you can stop it." Dorcas admits that they have the shipment and the aide suggests that if he gives the shipment over to them, "we'll work this out." Dorcas says, "That's one condition. We also want David Vincent." Kalter immediately says, "No deal." Dorcas says, "There is no deal without Vincent. We'll destroy the shipment."

Kalter walks up to him, cue stick in hand and threatens that, "we'll destroy every other installation of yours that we can lay our hands on!" Dorcas is convincing Weller that the offer is a good one, especially when he adds that he will return the trucks and other materials. "You know what they'll do to Vincent," Kalter says. Dorcas tells him not to worry, that they will take Vincent dead or alive. "If you like it you can kill him," Dorcas tells Kalter. "But of course we will need proof." Weller walks across the room and tells the man, "Dorcas, you have yourself a deal." He turns to Pete and says, "Pete, take care of him, will you?" Weller leaves the room as Kalter and Dorcas glare at one another.

Meanwhile. David meets with Mike Calvin and Scoville. There's a contract out on David, so Scoville suggests that David go into hiding. Will meet Weller at the Red Lion's Club. David packs his gun and goes into the club owned by mobster Kalter.

He pulls a gun on David and they depart from the club. They head to the Fergus Museum. David, Peter and two gangster thugs enter and meet the alien Dorcas. Peter tells Dorcas, "Here's my part of the deal … Do your own killing." They take David but Weller says, "Hold it – open the crates." David gets the drop on them and shoots an alien. Peter has the drugs but feels guilty for selling David out. David tells him, "Go – you don't owe me anything!"

Peter shots an alien and then uses Dorcas as a shield. David warns Peter of an alien who is about to shoot him. Peter shoots the alien who falls on top of a crate of drugs, incinerating him. Peter walks off and we learn later that he is killed at a booth in his own club.

Moral: "Two hours after making the decision to save David's life, Peter Kalter left the organization for good. He had joined the fight against another organization, a fight which David Vincent will continue …"

.40. The Peacemaker"

David is ushered into an underground parking lot, escorted by military personnel. They are locking up a man who is handcuffed. The officer gets out of the front seat and tells the driver, "Go on Corporal – and keep your mouth shut."

David, the officer and several military personnel enter a building. They shove the handcuffed "man" into a cell and have an officer stand guard. The officer tells the guard, "I expect to find him that way when I get back." He leaves while David waits behind in the hallway, lighting up yet another cigarette.

The officer goes into General Concannon's office and tells him, "We've got one." The general says, "Fine." He wants to see for himself. Meanwhile in the hallway a man in a uniform stops and asks the guard "what you got in there?" he guard doesn't answer so he slides open the window on the cell and sees the handcuffed man inside. Unbeknownst to the guard, he drops a small white pill into the cell and the handcuffed man bends over to get it. He goes to his knees and swallows the pill off the floor. The uniformed "officer" then sides the window shut and quickly walks away.

The guard opens the window in time to see the man glowing red and disintegrating. "He's on fire," the soldier shouts pulling his gun. David looks in and sees the man – an alien – disappear. The guard tells the officer, "Halt or I'll shoot." He shoots and in front of General Concannon, David and others, the being glows red and distintegrates, just like the guy in the cell.

The men walk over to where the officer disappeared. "The one in the cell is gone, too," David says. The general scrapes up some ashes, hands it to a soldier and tells him, "I want this stuff analyzed by nine o'clock tomorrow morning."

The site is now Washington, DC. The narrator informs us that, "For two years, David Vincent has been waging war on two fronts. One against the alien invaders, the other an attempt to enlist allies in high places – while there is still time. Now finally, with the help of some friends in the military, David Vincent is opening the second front.

Colonel Harmon gets out of the car to enter a building from an underground parking lot but is stopped at gunpoint by suited men. They order him to accompany them. The man next to Harmon in the back seat tells Harmon, "Yesterday, you kidnapped one of our people and brought him in here. We want him back." Harmon says, "Sorry," but the man says, "We'll exchange you for him." Harmon tells the man, "He's dead." He man says, "No – we would have heard." Harmon tells the man that the dead man's name was Vance and "you won't be hearing form him again." The man then orders the driver to take them to Colonel Harmon's apartment. "I'm afraid you've lost your bargaining position, colonel," the man with the gun tells him.

Meanwhile Scoville and David are in a Harmon's apartment waiting for him and discussing the situation. "All that hassle. I hope you haven't blown it," Scoville says. "At least we have the government," David says. "Maybe," Scoville replies. David tells Scoville that Concannon saw one of the aliens die which "puts him on our side." "That could be an advantage," Scoville replies. "I don't know." David tells Scoville that he heard that "you and Concannon don't get along very well." Scoville tells him, "That's a personal thing – nothing to do with this." He adds, "So the government's in on this. That means we might get some action."

Harmon is walking up the hallway with the two aliens. They knock over a plant and make enough noise for David and Scoville to hear the commotion. David and Scoville take cover as the aliens tell Harmon to open the door. David is behind the door and when one alien walks in, gun drawn, David pushes the door on him causing the second alien to be trapped in the hallway with Harmon, where a fight ensues. The alien in the apartment kicks Scoville over a couch but David jumps him. The alien is kicking David's ass but while on the floor David grabs a pistol and shoots him. He glows, turns red and dies. In the hallway Harmon is receiving a similar ass kicking. But the alien he was battling managers to break free and run away.

David walks past Harmon's knocked out body and then runs back into the apartment and looks out the window in time to get the license plate off the car that the escaping alien is in. David goes back out into the hallway and helps Harmon to his feet. Harmon tells David that Concannon wants to see him and when Scoville asks what he wants, Harmon says, "All I know is that he said he was speaking for the President."

Later, both Harmon and David are in Concannon's office. Concannon acknowledges only David and they shake hands. "You're in this with Edgar Scoville, am I right?" Concannon asks. "Yes," David says. He asks how Edgar is doing and when David tells him, "Fine," he replies, "That's good. I've always liked Edgar." He adds, "We had a spat a few years back, and I don't see much of him anymore. It was probably my fault. Tell him I asked, would you?" After David says that he will do so, Concannon then sits down at his desk and prepares to share information.

He tells David that what he is about to say "I want you to read between the lines and draw whatever conclusions you think are warranted." He leans over the desk and tells David, "We know they're here. We know who they are and what they are and we mean to do something about it. I'm saying this on the highest possible official level … Now before I tell you what our approach MIGHT be, how strong are they militarily?" David says that Colonel Harmon has had a look at the files and would be more qualified to answer that question. Harmon says, "Strong and getting stronger. We'd guess they won't attack until they get more gear and people down here. When they do, it won't be much fun."

Concannon gets up and begins pacing the room saying that they don't want war and that there's no reason why "we can't get along and live peacefully with these people." He asks Harmon, "Will they talk to us?" Harmon tells him he doesn't know. David adds, "They seem to think that they can get what they want by taking it." Concannon asks, "What do they want?" "Everything," David hastily replies. "We can give them everything – within reason," Concannon says. He adds that, "Once we know how much land they need, facilities, technology. Will they talk about that if they think they have nothing to lose?" "They'll be afraid we'll try to expose them, unite the whole world against them," Harmon says.

"Expose them? Oh good Lord no! All we want to do is talk with them, privately. A few of our people, a few of theirs. See if we can't settle this thing responsibly, that's all." David says, "I'm inclined to agree with Colonel Harmon. If they know you know they might try to speed things up and we'll find ourselves in an all-out war." Concannon, still pacing, says, "Mr. Vincent, do you know what a

Doomsday Device is?" When David admits that he doesn't, Harmon explains, "In theory it's an automatic self-detonating bomb designed to go off under certain rigidly defined circumstances, destroying the whole world. The ultimate weapon."

"If we can't get together with these people we can tell them that we're going to build one of these things," Concannon says. "I don't know whether we can or can't. But if they think we can, if they think that we'll blow up the world before we'll hand it over to them, they might have to sit down and bargain. What do you think about that?" David says that he thinks they'll listen. "Good," Concannon says. "So do I."

"Now," Concannon says, "About finding another one of these aliens." David says, "What about the one that got away? I saw the car and the license plate number, I'm sure it can be traced." "Fine," Concannon says. "You let me know if there's anything I can do. You've been carrying a heavy load. Let me know if there is anything I can do to help you out." David gets up to leave and Concannon tells him to let him know if he finds "one of these people" that we can talk to. They shake hands and David leaves Concannon and Harmon in the office. Concannon turns to Harmon and says, "That's a fine boy, Archie. He'll do it."

Meanwhile a man exits a cabin and gets into a car with Maryland license plates. David is waiting in the back seat and puts a gun to his head. "Better shoot now. You'll never get me to your people," he says. "I don't wanna shoot, I wanna talk," David replies. "Let's go inside." They get of the car and re-enter the motel room. Two other suited men are watching them as they do so. Then they get out of their car.

Cut to the Concannon's house as he enters with Harmon. He greets his wife Sarah with a kiss and immediately goes over to the bar and pours drinks for himself and Harmon. He asks Sarah about the woodchucks and she says it's no big deal but he tells her that after dinner maybe he and Billy will go outside and shoot some. Sarah tells him that the gardener said that they could spray the grounds and that would be the best way. "And have you breathe that noxious stuff and have you get sick again? Oh no," Concannon says. "Archie, do you want to shoot some woodchucks with us after dinner?" Concannon asks, taking a seat. "If they want war, I'll give them war," he says.

Sarah passes out hors d'oeuvres and asks Harmon how their day went. "Maybe you ought to ask the boss," he says. Harmon and Concannon click their glasses together and Concannon says, "We've solved the problem." Sarah tells him he talked in his sleep but he didn't remember. He asks her to repeat it and that it's alright to talk in front of Archie. Sarah says he was talking about Armageddon, doomsday, like the end of the world. You know I never ask about your work." "No you don't, Sarah,' Concannon says.

"He's working too hard, isn't he Archie? I mean, it's not as if we're twenty years old," Sarah says. She turns to Harmon: "Why don't you get him to slow down?" Harmon says, "Nope." She turns to her husband and says that "When you don't sleep at night I worry," she says to Concannon, rubbing his head. In walks Billy who greets his father and Archie. He asks Billy if he wanted to shoot some woodchucks. The boy hesitates but looks at his mother and then agrees. Concannon tells Archie and Billy to go on to dinner so that he can talk to Sarah for a moment.

When they leave he grabs Sarah by the neck with both hands and his look turns to anger. He stares at her and says, "Don't you ever, ever, ever say that I'm too old to do my work in front of Archie or anybody else!"

Meanwhile, David and the other guy come out of the cabin with the man saying that all he can do is "take you to the man I report to." David, unaware, is then attacked from behind and knocked unconscious by the other two men. They load him into the car and drive off.

The next morning Edgar Scoville walks into Concannon's office. Concannon, who was sitting behind his desk, seems ecstatic to see Scoville, gets up and walk around to shake his hand. Scoville, on the other hand appears less than enthusiastic. "Well, well, well Edgar! How good to see you again!" He invites Edgar to sit down and Edgar turns down a cup of coffee. He asks him if he's heard from David and Concannon says that he's given him a big task. "Rome wasn't built in a day," he says. Scoville fires back, "Caesar was killed in a minute." As Harmon looks on, Concannon asks Edgar. "What do you think about this Doomsday Device?"

Edgar, who has taken a seat, says, "Very effective. If anything can make them talk, that's it." Concannon agrees and then ask Edgar if he could build one. Scoville asks, "why" and Concannon asks him if one could be built: "Could YOU build one?" Scoville is flustered: "No, I wouldn't build one. And I wouldn't if I could." Concannon is insistent. "Can anyone? I mean, hypothetically." Scoville fires back, "I hope not. It would be insane. To put us at the mercy of a machine that couldn't be shut down? There's an accident factor that would be impossible to calculate." Concannon is hesitant but says, "I suspect that you're exactly right, Edgar. However if the time ever came, I'm sure there would be other opinions." Scoville is staring at Concannon as if he (Concannon) has lost his damn mind.

In another scene a gold Lincoln Continental pulls up in front of a house. It's the alien leader, Ryder. Inside David is sitting nearly alone in a large room with a long table. The alien leader walks in: "Nice to see you again, Mr. Vincent. Have my people been treating you well?" he asks. "Oh yes, very. In fact they gave me aspirin for the headache I acquired when I was clubbed," David quips. "Forgive them. They were under the impression, as usual, you meant us no good. But this time, you do have our best interests at heart. You want to give us a helping hand, land, peace – things like that?"

David tells him, "I'm not in a position to offer you anything. I'm here to ask you if you'll talk to the man who can." The alien, Ryder, says, "Who says he speaks for your president?" "Yes," David acknowledges. "What do you want in exchange for these things that you'll give us," the man asks. David says he wants a cease fire. A suited man at the door says that if the leader trusts them and sits down with them they'll use it as a chance to expose you and use it as a chance to unite." David interrupts: "Create any safeguard you like, we want only to talk." The man at the door says, "He's lying. He's been trying to tell the world for too long."

David says, "It's all in the open now! One of your men burned in the general's office building yesterday. They know you're here. Either you talk with them or they'll begin building the Doomsday Device." The head alien says, "Mr. Vincent, you and the general come here tonight at eight o'clock. Drive in slowly, in one car. Don't tell anyone you're coming or bring anyone with you. Then, if I feel like it, we might talk.." David gets up and walks past them both out the door. When he leaves the leader tells the guard, "Go after him. Watch him."

Scoville pulls up and David gets into the car. The alien guard follows them in his car. David tells Scoville "We're talking tonight." Scoville remains silent so David asks, "Edgar, do you know something I don't know?" David says that this is big news. "You want me to honk my horn," Scoville sarcastically asks prompting David to counter and ask him "what is going on between you and Concannon?" David says Archie said he served with him for 28 years and would walk through Hell with him. Scoville says that he knew Concannon for five minutes and went through hell with Concannon. Scoville explains that he was sub-contracting with Concannon on some early moon shots. "Remember when the rocket blew up on the pad?" he asks David.

"It's happened a couple of times," David says. "Well this time it killed two people," Scoville says. "Two men, two boys. Concannon ordered a board of inquiry." He said that the finding was "human error" and that somebody pushed the launch button before the fuel chamber was secured. "Concannon blamed you," David says. Scoville said that his exact words were that "Scoville murdered those boys just as sure as if he'd shot them in the head." Scoville said that the one reason that Concannon had for holding him responsible was "he told Archie Harmon that the public needed a scapegoat and he was going to give them one – me."

After noticing that a car is following them David nevertheless tells Scoville that he thinks he should go along with the meeting. "He is speaking for the President," David says. "That's what he says," Scoville opines. "We're being followed," David says. "You trust them, we have nothing to worry about," Scoville replies. "If you trust Concannon." David looks over at him.

At the Concannon house, Sarah tells her husband that she has good news, that the lobsters came early this year. And old friend of Concannon's sent them, as he does every year. Concannon then walks over and shares a tale about his love for lobsters with Harmon who, for some reason, is still seated in the living room. She walks over and asks him if he'd like to have one tonight and he says he'd love to have one. As she goes to prepare it, Concannon sits down on the couch next to Harmon and says, "Yes, we've crossed a lot of bridges together since the Philippines, haven't we Archie?" "I'd say so," Archie agrees. Concannon says, "And this is the toughest one yet." "You'll get us across there, you always have," Archie says.

"Sometimes I don't know why you put up with me, Archie. I'm a mean old croc, aren't I?" Concannon asks (saying to this man what he ought to be saying to his wife). "Sometimes," Archie says. "You know I don't mean anything by it. You're family to me," Concannon says and Archie agrees. Archie recommends pouring Concannon a drink and the latter says, "If you'll join me."

Scoville drops David off at Concannon's house but doesn't come in. When he takes off he passes by a man in a car who has been watching the house. Concannon rushes Sarah to "just bring me one lobster, no salad or anything" he says. He tells her that she and Billy can eat after he's gone. (What?) He offers David something but he turns it down and is seated. He takes the papers that David handed him and is looking it over. "This is fine, fine work, Mr. Vincent. It'll only take me a minute to eat." He shouts, "Sarah! Sarah! As quickly as you can!" as he continues looking through the notes.

"What conditions did they make?" Concannon asks. "Two people – the general and myself. And they'll be watching the meeting place," David explains. Incidentally, they sent someone to follow me here." Concannon asks, "You really think they'll talk?" David says, "I think they'll talk about talking." Sarah brings the lobster in with a napkin. "Are you sure you won't join me?" he asks Harmon and David. They turn it down and he digs in.

He cracks open the lobster as David tells them, "They took me to a farmhouse in Virginia." Harmon asks, "Who did you meet with?" David says he's met with him before, that he's one of their leaders. "Does he trust us?" Concannon asks as he stuffs lobster in his mouth. "Not really," David replies and says that they'll take the first step. Harmon quotes a Chinese proverb that a journey of a thousand miles begins with the first step.

As Harmon says, "We're on our way, buddy," Concannon begins choking and repeats, "I've been poisoned! I've been poisoned!" An ambulance arrives and in the next scene the three men are standing around as a doctor examines Concannon, who is laid out on a bed in his bedroom. "Is it food poisoning?" Sarah asks. The doctor says, "Poison poisoning" and then asks that the lobster be wrapped up in some wax paper. The doctor asks who did it and Concannon can only say "whoever it is, I'll get him." He then sends the doctor home.

"Nice people we're dealing with, Mr. Vincent," Concannon says. "They don't trust us." "Soon as you tell them we're here, this happens," Harmon says. "They wanted to talk – they could have killed ME," David reminds them. "They don't want you, they want him," Harmon says, pointing at Concannon. "There are easier ways," David reminds him. Concannon said that the meeting is off. "I wanted to talk to them, I tried to talk to them, you know that," he reminds David.

David wants to go talk to them again and Concannon says no, that if he did he'd be committing suicide. David walks out of the room. In the next scene he's meeting with the lead alien named Ryder. "Mr. Vincent, until the General had this trouble, you were going to live up to your part of it," the alien says. "Every part of it," says David. "The General too, I suppose." "Yes," David affirms. The alien tells David that by himself, he's "useless to us, you have no authority." But David is quick to remind him that, "I do have the authority to arrange another meeting. Mr. Ryder you'd better be interested – they're about to build the Doomsday Device, remember?" "Is that a threat Mr. Vincent?" Ryder asks. "Yes," says David.

Ryder tells David that if his group still wants to talk that would be his (Vincent's) decision. David says that he's not sure that the General would come. "Let's see if we can't arrive at satisfactory terms," Ryder suggests.

Back at the house, still lying in bed in his pajamas, Concannon is in deep thought. In walks Sarah who asks him how he's feeling. He sits up in bed and says, "Come sit by me, Sarah." She walks over and sits on the bed and tells him, "Dr. Jacob says you'll be fine." He asks her how long they've been married and she quickly responds, "Twenty-three years." "Good years?" he asks. She says if he makes it sound that way there will be more. Suddenly a mood change and he grabs her and charges her with trying to kill him, of trying to poison him. He tells her those lobsters weren't sent but indeed, that she purchased them from the market. He continues squeezing her arms, all the while asking, "Why? Why?"

She confesses: "To stop you! To keep you from what you're going to do!" You talked about it in your sleep!" He's not shocked but is surprised that she would go so far as to try to kill him. She says she didn't want him to go to the meeting that night but she wasn't trying to kill him. The phone is ringing as she cries out her confession. He grabs her and hugs her just as the teenaged son walks in the door. Concannon picks up the phone and it's David who tells him, "They still want the meeting, General." "After THEY tried to poison me?" he asks with

Sarah right there staring at him. David tells him, "They said they didn't have anything to do with that." Concannon says, "I believe them. What conditions?" David tells him, "Tomorrow, twelve noon at the farmhouse." David further tells him that the aliens will have their top people there from all over the world if you will, too. Concannon asks "how many," and David says, "No more than six." Concannon agrees and hangs up.

David turns to Ryder and says, "He'll be there." At the house Concannon softly tells Sarah to get out his uniform, "would you dearest?" The son is still standing there looking, saying nothing. Concannon gets on the phone as the boy walks over and sits next to his father. Concannon, talking on the phone, says, "Archie, set up a meeting in my office in one hour," and then names all the people he wants in attendance. "Have Scoville there, too. See you there."

After he hangs up the son asks why his mother was screaming and Concannon explains that "she was just worried, but she's fine now. Thanks for asking." Then Concannon gets up and walks off.

The meeting is filled with top brass and an anxious Scoville is already there. Concannon arrives and convenes the meeting. "Gentlemen, you all know me. I'm not a dramatic man, I'll just say what I have to say and leave it at that. We're into something pretty big. Unless we act together, correctly, immediately, our country and our world may not survive." He gives each of them envelopes and tells them to take them to a farmhouse, two hundred yards from a school, four-point-two miles from due east from the intersections of the routes nine and one-oh-six in Virginia. Arrive at it before noon. Do not open the envelopes until noon. Your instructions are inside." One officer attempts to make a comment but Concannon interrupts: "There will be no discussion. I have been given these instructions. That's all gentlemen. Good luck to you."

The men adjourn but Scoville remains seated. One officer takes a long hard look at Concannon but doesn't make a comment. He leaves. As Scoville prepares to leave Concannon stops him and says, "Edgar, I know how you feel about the Doomsday Device, but you must, without argument, be present at that meeting to convince the other side that it can be built – not WILL be, can be." When Scoville attempts to make a comment, Concannon again interrupts and tells him that he has been given these instructions. "Yes sir," Scoville says, and then leaves.

Harmon was standing in a corner and when everyone is gone and Concannon goes back to his desk, Harmon slowly walks over, carefully looking over Concannon as he (Concannon) loads his gun. He takes out a note from his desk that says, "To be read in the case of my death" and then gets on the phone. He calls another general and tells him that he and Harmon want to fly a practice bomb run, claiming that Harmon needs to get his hours in and that tomorrow would be fine. The time? Eleven o'clock. He fires off some numbers and requests that the plane be "gassed and ready at Andrews Field." He thanks the general and hangs up the phone.

Col. Harmon has always been extremely loyal to General Concannon but now has doubts as to the general's sanity. He asks Harmon to sit down and has to repeat the order because Harmon is flabbergasted about what he just heard. After he takes a seat, he listens as Concannon talks into a dicta-phone:

> "This is General Samuel Arlington Concannon, Minister of Defense for the United States of America. For thirty-six years I've served my country as soldier, statesman and patriot. No one can question my love for America. In recent days I have learned that our country faces the gravest danger ever in her history. We have been invaded by beings from another planet, beings who bear us great malice, and who will not be content while any of us remain alive. I am as a consequence determined to take immediate and forceful action against them, although this action will certainly cost some American lives, including some of my most devoted friends and possibly my home and that of my devoted aide of twenty-eight years, Colonel Harmon. What we have done is this: we have invited the top leadership of these beings to a meeting where they will be destroyed. Without leaders, soldiers have no army. It is our hope that they will go home, retreat from the battle and leave us with our beloved America. Militarily the plan is sound. With God's help, it will succeed."

Switch Concannon's place with that of Sitting Bull or Geronimo and you would have a good idea of how the First Nation people felt about these white people, these Caucasian "aliens" coming in and "invading THEIR beloved land!

At any rate, Concannon then looks over at an amazed Harmon and asks, "Did I leave anything out?" Harmon, who says nothing, should have said, "Yeah muthafucka. You left out tellin' ME that you were about to pull this bullshit!" But Harmon remains quiet as Concannon and speaks into the dicta-phone and says, "God bless America." He then takes the tape and places it in an envelope where his suicide letter was. He gets up and is on his way out of the room. Harmon stands up and grabs his gun from the desk and is about to shoot him when Concannon turns and says, "Oh, I would have forgotten that," calmly takes the gun and says, "What would I do without you, Archie?"

Vincent learns the true meaning of events from Sarah Concannon and rushes to the farm realizing that the bomber is on its way. After an attempt to dissuade the general by radio, Vincent agrees with the aliens to have the bomber eliminated by an alien saucer. The saucer destroys the plane with a laser shot. The meeting group splits up and everyone goes their separate ways.

Moral: "David Vincent returns to his war against the Invaders. He returns to his search for another day and another place when the powers from both sides can meet again, and an armistice can become a reality."

Armistice? With the white man? Did Quinn Martin not read his own history? White people don't even know what an armistice is in terms of what such a relationship represents. According to Dictionary.com, an armistice is, " … is a formal agreement of warring parties to stop fighting. It is not necessarily the end of a war, since it may constitute only a cessation of hostilities while an attempt is made to negotiate a lasting peace." In other words, it is on-going, not permanent. And that means more time for both sides to plot and plan the elimination of the other. And that is why the narrator used the word "armistice" because the entire premise of the show is based on both sides seeking the genocidal elimination of the other. No mercy.

.41. "The Miracle"

Two young people are rolling around in the grass making out near a religious shrine. A car pulls up and a man in a suit exits. He has a black bag in his hand. He is glancing at his watch and is evidently waiting for someone. He then hears the girl giggling. She gets up to go get a drink of water from the nearby faucet near the shrine. The man with the bag is not paying attention and is bitten by a rattlesnake. The girl gets up after hearing a commotion as the man struggles to gain possession of the bag he dropped. He gets to his feet, staggers over to the girl and as he drops he hands her the bag and utters, "She will come for this."

The girl takes the bag and then watches as the man glows red and disintegrates before her very eyes. The boy walks up to her and asks her what happened several times. All she can do is look up at the shrine, cross her heart and say, "It's a miracle!" She clutches the bag to her chest and stares intently at the monument.

The narrator tells us, "News of a miracle finds David Vincent and draws him to a small New Mexico town. Here, according to legend, the virgin appeared to two Indian children and wept. Her tears forming a stream known as Las lagunas de la hem, which according to my translation means "lagoons of the hem." The narrator says it means, "The stream where he is later." A young girl was presented a gift by a vanishing creature. A gift that is in fact the heart of an awesome new weapon aimed at mankind."

David is walking around the shrine and the area where the girl was supposed to have been. He gets into his snazzy white convertible and heads off. In a stereotypically lazy Mexican village where even the dog is napping, the girl gets into a pickup truck. A young blonde boy asks her where she is going and adds, "Where's your halo?" She drives off just as David is pulling up. The little boy runs up to David's car and asks him if he wants a car wash for fifty cents. He answers, "Nope," and the boy says, "how about a shoe shine? Two bits?" David again says no as he walks into the place of business with the boy in tow.

The boy, whose name is Johnny, continues bugging the shit out of him as he walks up to the bar. Harry, the bartender walks up and says, "Johnny, leave that man alone. Scram!" David orders a beer (draft) and Harry tells David not to mind the kid: "He's just an orphan. I let him hang around – sometimes he gets a little too pushy." David asks him, "You're Harry Ferguson, aren't you?" The man says, "Yeah – do I know you?" David says, "I read about your daughter." Harry laughs as he downs a peanut, "You ask me, she was high on something," he says.

David continues digging: "The paper said that the man who disappeared gave her a crystal." Harry tells him that the claim was true and in fact, "it (the crystal) is right over there." Harry has it encased in a glass box that he calls "the shrine." It is sitting right in the middle of a pool table. Harry tells David that people come in and "stare at that thing for hours." David asks he can have a look and Harry approves. The cowboys looking seem hypnotized. Harry and David walk over and David asks, "Ever think of selling it?" Harry says, "Oh, I thought about it, alright. I borrowed the case from a jeweler friend in Santa Fe. He says if it was red it would be a ruby, then it would be worth plenty." David says he'd offer him fifty bucks for it.

Harry asks why and David says, "Curiosity. I collect stones." "Well it seems possible that we might come to some sort of an agreement," Harry says. Harry says, "Okay boys, show's over for the day," and the cowboys get up and leave. He adds, "I'm afraid I have business to discuss." They all leave, but one man remains in the bar leaning on a table. Meanwhile Harry says to David, "Man, it's hot. Why don't we go over there and sit by the fan. You can finish your beer and we can finish our business."

"Now the point is," Harry begins, "It's not really mine. My friend offered me seventy-five. Maybe you could see your way clear to offer a little more." The man who was eavesdropping walks out of the bar and runs around the corner. In the meantime, Beth is lighting a candle at the site of the shrine. Ricky, the kid who likes her, pulls up on his motorcycle. He tells that he hasn't seen her in a while and declares that he was at the site with her and he didn't see any such thing as what she described. She brushes him off and tells him she has things to do.

He tells her she can't change just like that, after all the things they had going. She says she can and she did. He tries to kiss her and she rebuffs him twice.

"Leave me alone," she declares. The eavesdropper is trying to find a side door or window into the bar. He gets into a side door and sneaks out into the main room where David and Harry are. He wants to steal the box and the crystal. David agrees to the price of one hundred dollars. But the would-be thief is clumsy, grabs the crystal but knocks something to the floor. David and Harry hear it and rush to cut him off. David tackles him and the crystal falls to the floor. Harry picks it up as David and the thief engage in combat.

David gets his ass kicked and the thief runs out the front door. Harry is watching and goes to help David. David runs to the front door and looks out but doesn't see the thief. Meanwhile Harry puts the crystal back into the box and takes it. The man is an alien and is communicating on his device. He tries to take a suicide pill after the man on the phone tells him he will have to be replaced. Vincent se sim and they fight again. This old man is kicking David's ass. He falls back on a bed, glows red and dies. He must have taken the pill.

Beth pulls up in the pickup truck and goes into the bar. The kid, Johnny, is teasing her and says, "You know why you get headaches? Your halo is screwed on too tight." Harry tells him to get out as Beth notices that the crystal is not on the pool table. "Where is it?" she asks Harry. Harry tells her that he put it in the safe because somebody tried to steal it. "I think I better lock it up." She asks who tried to steal it and Harry says, "some bum."

He tells her he wants to talk to her. He tells her this guy came in and he wants to buy the crystal. He tells her he could get a hundred and she tells him "it's not for sale." She tells him, "It's not to sell. It's a gift." Harry says that with a hundred bucks he could buy a couple of new bar stools, fix up some fancy booths, "Make this place a little more attractive, things would pick up." He tells her he tried to get a loan from the bank and "they wouldn't even talk to me." She tells him he doesn't understand: "It's a gift from God. It's not about bar stools, and it's not for you to fix up your saloon."

He tells her: "Now you listen – I don't know about miracles but I know about money. I know what it costs to feed you, and I know what it costs to put clothes on your back, and I know what it costs to send you to Saint Teresa's. I know. I got no wife to help, I been both mother and father for ten years. And I'm goin' under baby – I'm goin' under." She says, "Sorry, Pop." He tells her "It's not that much of a sin to sell it!" she says she knows what it costs him, how much it would cost to pay a waitress or come in and clean up the way Billy does. She says, "We don't owe you Pop – you owe us."

"A guy tries to be a father, tries to make a decent living, tries to keep a lousy saloon from going under." Just then David walks back in and Harry asks him, "Did you catch that guy?" "No," David says. "Well," Harry says and slides David a beer "on the house." David hands over some money anyway and Harry tells him "My daughter owns that thing, and I can't sell it to ya." David says, "Wait a minute – we have a deal. David has the money in his hand and is extending it, but Harry tells him that he loves his daughter very much and would rather put a bullet in his head than to hurt her. "The crystal's not for sale. I'm sorry." David puts his money away and walks out.

Beth overheard everything her father said. They stare at each other.

Later, Beth is walking down the street and David gets out of his white Lincoln Continental and stops her. He offers her a ride and she is impressed with the car. "Is it yours?" she asks. She likes it and says she's wanted one for years, ever since her mother died. But then she says, "No thanks – I'll walk." David walks beside her. "Did you come to offer me more money for the stone?" she asks. "Would you accept more?" he asks. "No," she tells him. "Beth, there are other people after that stone and because of that, you're in danger. So is your father," David says. "And you're the only one that can help. For a man who collects rocks you've got quite an imagination," she says.

"I know these people – they're dangerous," he says. "Who are they?" Beth asks. He tells her that it's a long story and he doesn't know if she'd believe him. "Does anyone?" she asks. "A few. I've tried to convince other people. You know what it's like, having seen something and no one will believe you." She asks if the man in the bar was one of them and David tells her "yes." She turns to walk off and he grabs her by the arm and tells her she has to believe him. She jerks away and says, "Don't touch me. I don't like being touched. I'm sorry, but you can't add my rock to your collection." Then she walks off.

Meanwhile, Beth is back at the saloon surrounded by people who want to see the crystal which she is holding in her hands. Ricky is there as well. A Catholic priest walks in, accompanied by David, and Beth recognizes him immediately. "Father!" she says. Accompanied by another man he says, "Miguel, Pancho, Sancho, I'm sure we have work to do," he tells the Mexicans, who are obviously laborers or farmhands. "Beth, put that thing away – and get the confession," he orders. "After all these years of fighting ignorance and superstition, then you come along with little magic rocks," the priest says. Harry walks out of the kitchen and is listening.

"It was a miracle," she says. The priest yells, "Don't tell me what's miraculous! That's not for you to say. The church performs miracles!" "Yes father she says sheepishly as she hands the crystal to him. The priest gives the crystal to Harry and then apologizes: "I'm sorry. I have a harsh and brutal temper. I'm sorry," he tells Beth. "It's alright father," she says turning away. He walks up beside her and says, "Beth, miracles are rare and special. Often our eyes tell us things that are not so. So no more magic shows, alright?" "Yes father," she obediently replies with David in the background watching.

The priest tells David he'll walk back to the church and then leaves. Beth walks up to David and asks, "Is there anything, any one you won't use?" He tells her no and adds, "If you don't want the money I'll give it to the church" and offers five hundred dollars. "You can't buy God, Mr. Vincent!" she says and then storms out. When she leaves Harry tells David, "Her mother was just like her, full of fire. She ran off about ten years ago. I been father and mother to that girl ever since." David turns to walk away and Harry summons him back: "Mr. Vincent – I'll sell you the stone." David tells him, "It's not yours," but Harry says, "Oh, I'll take care of Beth, alright. Only the price has gone up."

David tells him, "Listen to me: There are others who are willing to kill you for that stone. You'd better sell and sell now." "A thousand," Harry responds with the quickness. David says he'll go to the bank in Santa Fe and will be back. Harry offers him a beer but he turns it down and leaves.

Back at the shrine, Beth is kneeling as Johnny runs up. She tells him to go away but he starts babbling anyway: "In town they're saying they offered five hundred. Five hundred, and that's what we need. Bus fare, food – and money for your uncle!" "My uncle? Oh that was a long time ago. He might not even remember me," she says. "It's just silly talk to me." But Johnny says, "It wasn't, it wasn't. He's your uncle. He said he liked you." "It was after my mother died, he felt sorry for me," she says. Billy says the man lives alone has his own house and she agrees that they could move there and she could cook and sew. "He has a dog and he likes kids," Johnny further claims.

She is dreaming about it: no more glasses to wash, no more men grabbing and touching me." Johnny says he can get a ride there and she says no, "it's a dream, it's like a movie. After it's over you go home, you wake up." Johnny tells her, "It doesn't have to be." She says she doesn't know what's real or what isn't any more, but Johnny says, "The five hundred's real, and the bus tickets." She looks at him and says, "Maybe Johnny. Let me sit here and think about it for a while" she says as she remains kneeling and peering up at the shrine.

After Johnny leaves (or pretends to), a nun walks up to the kneeling Beth and says, "My child: I've come for the gift." As Johnny looks on, Beth breaks into a smile, gets up and walks away with the nun.

Back at the saloon, Harry is drinking alone and going through some magazines when Beth rushes in. "Where is the crystal, I must take it now! A nun, the most beautiful person, daddy!" He stops her and tells her he's got great news, and that it is that David Vincent has offered them a thousand dollars for the stone. She tries to snatch away to get to the safe but he grabs her back; "Wait a minute! A thousand! A thousand dollars for it Beth. I can fix up the place and we can start makin' a profit. We can rent a little house – I don't want my little girl living over a saloon!" he says as he kisses her hand. She tells him that she won't do it: "You can't do it papa, I won't let you!" she says.

Then he tells her, "Your mama wouldn't have run off if I would have had money! You would have had your mama, Beth. The only reason she run off she couldn't stand the bar and livin' upstairs and taking care of you up there!" Beth says, "She ran off because she was no good!" Harry hits his hand on the bar: "It was the bar and no money!" She snatches away and says "I'm going to take that stone!" Harry grabs her and says, "Over my dead body! You ain't givin' that stone to no nun," he says. "She wants it, let her pay for it. They got plenty! Like everybody pay for everything. But I ain't openin' that safe for nobody unless they pay as much as David Vincent!" Beth snatches away and leaves out the door. When she does, Harry takes his seat and continues flipping through the pages of magazines, looking for things to buy for the bar.

It's late night and Beth is up in her room pacing the floor. David drives up to the bar and enters. Two aliens are nearby. Beth stops him at the front door and says, "You offered my father a thousand dollars. Please don't do it." David tells her he has to, that he just got back from Santa Fe. She tells him that her father is obsessed with that thousand dollars and has an idea that the money will help bring her mother back. Vincent says, "I thought your mother was dead." Beth says, "My mother ran away ten years ago with a whiskey salesman," and adds that, "She was no good. She's my mom, I'm her daughter – I'm no good, either."

She says she's no good and tells David, "What do you think I was doing by that stream?" David pulls her off to the side and they are seated at a table. "My life was ashes. Dirt. Then he came along and gave me that stone. Now I'm clean again. Don't you see?" David says, "Beth I know what you think that stone is, but you're wrong." She asks, "Then what is it?" "A part of a weapon," he says causing her to ask, "Then why would the church come for it?" "Who came for it?" he asks. "A sister – she came for it at the stream." David says, "I doubt if she was from the church."

Just then Johnny bursts in and shouts, "Beth come quick – your father's been robbed! They took the crystal!" David and Beth break through a small crowd outside and enter to find Harry on the floor. Beth helps her father revive and when he does she asks who was it? Harry says, "Two men." The sheriff comes in and Harry declares that he was robbed. Harry turns down the sheriff's suggestion that he see a doctor and when asked what they looked like he simply says, "They came up from behind. Two men – big." When asked what they got Harry says that he had a hundred dollars in a safe. The sheriff escorts him out to the car to come to the station to make a statement.

Beth walks up to David and says, "Now that you've got what you want, when are you leaving?" David says, "I don't have it." She says, "You did it – or had it done. Now get out of here and leave us alone!" David asks her, "Who else wanted it?" She walks away, goes outside and gets into the back of the police car with her father. The car drives off with Harry and Beth on board.

David goes to his hotel, and is asleep but for some reason he leave the door unlocked. An alien comes in with chloroform, knocks him out. The man is searching drawer after drawer looking for something – more than likely the crystal. Meanwhile, back at the bar and grill, Ricky pulls up on his motorcycle. Beth is mopping the floor as Ricky, who also works there, walks past, grabs a soda and tries to converse wither. She keeps informing him that "we're not open." Little Johnny says, "She said we're not open." Billy looks over at him and says, "You keep quiet, hot shot. It isn't any of your affair." Beth tells him to leave the boy alone so he turns and follows her as she arranges chairs.

He says that since the place is closed maybe they could go on a date. "It's been such a long time," he says. After she once again tells him to go away, he grabs her arm and asks about Harry. She tells him that the hospital released him and that he is currently at the police station looking over some pictures (mug shots most likely). He's holding her hands and suggest that they "get out of this firetrap." She again declines but nevertheless they madly kiss. After it's over he says, "This afternoon," and off he goes.

Beth then heads back upstairs and Billy goes out the front door. When he opens it he sees two men in a car across the street with the nun. "He either has it hidden where I couldn't find it or he didn't take it," one man says to the nun after she requests a progress report. The nun claims that Vincent stole the rock and then doubled back. "Stay with him – you know where I'll be." She gets out the car and walks back up the street to the convent/hideout.

Ricky gets on phone and calls David. David is still knocked out from the effects of the chloroform but by the time he wakes up Johnny hangs up. Johnny, the little boy, follows the nun. There's an abandoned building being constructed on a country road near the town.

Meanwhile Beth comes to David's room and appears to adorned in her special slut clothing, looking much different than usual. "What did you do with the crystal?" she asks. David tells her he doesn't have it. "You've got it – and I want it," she says. "I'll do anything to get it, implying that the pussy is there if he wants it. David again denies having it. "You have it – you're a man. You take what you want" she says, going over to the bed and sitting on it. "Men do take what they want, don't they David?" she asks lying on the bed. David tells her she doesn't have to do that and goes on to explain that he works with a group of about six people. "We're after that crystal, we don't have it yet, but we want it to take it to Washington to prove to the government that I'm not lying."

"About what?" she asks. "The other people who want the crystal aren't human," David says. "They're from another world, another planet. They make themselves appear to be human. And when they die, they begin to glow and disappear." Beth says, "Are you asking me to believe that the man at the stream …" David interrupts: "…and the nun. They're here to destroy us." She counters by saying, "You're an evil man Mr. Vincent – plus insane. I hope God can forgive you." She storms out of the room. She goes downstairs and there's little nosey-ass Johnny. "Did you get what you can for it?" he greedily asks. "What do you think I came for?" she asks. The boy says, "A piece of junk – your miracle."

She slaps the living shit out of him but immediately kneels and says, "I'm sorry Johnny. "He didn't give you back your piece of junk did he, no matter what you did?" the child asks. She says no, and Johnny says, "He couldn't. He doesn't have it." She asks him who does for him to tell her. David is in his room looking out of the window and sees Beth and Johnny scurrying down the street.

The phone rings – Harry, the father, calls David with yet another proposition. Meanwhile Johnny and Beth venture to the area where the nun went. They see the aliens and machinery emanating a bright red glow. In fact, the nun is in one of the regeneration chambers. They run back to town but are spotted by an alien as they scurry back to town up the dirt road.

David heads out and while walking up the street runs into Beth and Johnny. Beth excitedly tells him that she saw everything including "the nun in a glass tube." David says, "We'll take my car" and off they go now that Beth knows he was right and they head back. The place has been cleaned out, and the machines are now gone. Beth asks who they are and what do they want. David tells her, "The world." He tells her that the crystal is a part of a very powerful weapon. She says, "I should have let my father sell it to you. I'm sorry, David." He just looks at her and then they head back to the car.

That night back in town David straps on his gun, complete with holster. Where has it been all this time and why hasn't he worn it in many of the previous episodes? At any rate, Beth leaves in her pickup to Santa Fe for some medicine her father needs. David's car is still parked out front, and when he opens the door he notices two men parked in a car across the street. So he goes out back door. The two men exit the car and head into the saloon but David has gone down a back hallway to Harry's room. Harry lets him in and the first thing he asks is, "Did you bring the money?" David says, "Where's the crystal?" Harry tells him, "It's in here" and they walk toward the safe.

The two men have come down the hallway and are outside of Harry's room. They have a key and open the door. They lurk and hide in the outer room while David and Harry are in the back making the exchange. It seems that Harry had the crystal all along, and faked the break-in to get it away from Beth. "Why the phony robber?" David asks. "I had to keep it away from Beth, didn't I? A man needs to keep his daughter's respect" Harry replies as he counts the money. Harry and David walk to the outer room and Harry puts the money in the safe. "Now only you and me know that money's in there. Let's keep it that way, okay?"

David hears something and pulls his pistol. He kicks open a side door and it bumps an alien who knocks loose a live wire. Harry pushes some wooden crates down on another one. The second one fires but David is quicker and shoots him. He then shoots the second one, both glow and turn red and start a fire. They run for it, but Harry stops: "The money!" David tells him, "This place is going to blow any minute!" Harry pulls away and again shouts, "The money!" and runs back into the bar. There is fire engulfing the entire bar. The room blows up and Harry dies in the blast.

Inside the bar old white men play chess as Beth and Johnny sit back. David comes downstairs, already having packed and she immediately asks him if he's saved the crystal. She says there was no medicine at the drug store so she knew what was going on. He said he's taking the crystal to Washington and asks her if she was able to save anything. "A fifty dollar bill," she says. David says, "That money was for you," but she says "No thanks – no more lies. He didn't want it for me – he just wanted it." "Where will you be staying?" he asks. Johnny says "I don't know and looks up at Beth as if to say that he's going wherever she goes. She tells David that she has an uncle in Denver and she looks at Johnny: "We can stay there." "For real?" he excitedly asks. "For real," she smiles and replies.

David tells her that he got some extra cash in case her father decided to raise the price again, which is a lie. "I'd like you to have it, please," he says. She gratefully accepts it and they say their goodbyes and walk David out to the car.

Moral: "So David leaves Lacunes, New Mexico with a crystal from an alien planet. He leaves behind two orphans who have met in the desert, who have lost everything, but gained a new life."

.42. "The Life Seekers"

People in maroon sedan speeding on the highway, heading north. A policeman, Joe Nash, sees them, gives chase with sirens blaring, and pulls them over on Highway 34. The cop forces them onto the shoulder of the road, walks back to their car and asks, "Are you trying to kill yourself?" The driver says that the man in the back seat is his uncle, and he's had a heart attack. The officer says "follow me" and is about to help them but the man in the back seat begins to glow with a reddish color. The officer asks, "What's that?" giving the driver just enough time to pull out a pistol and bust a cap in his ass.

The driver backs up and for some reason gets out of the car. The cop shoots twice and hits him, he falls to the ground glowing red. The woman gets out of the back seat and takes the driver's seat. As the man in the back continues to glow, she peels out, leaving the officer lying on the ground.

The narrator tells us: "A critically wounded officer, a garbled account of glowing vanishing assailants, a phone call from a physician who has come to believe in invaders from space. And David Vincent moves into the center of the widening dragnet."

There are stop points and David comes to one and the cop asks for his keys and his license. David complies as one checks the trunk. He asks him where he's headed. David tells him "Redstone," and the cop says, "Fine – let him through." The next scene is the emergency room at the hospital where the cop who got shot is lying in a bed connected to an IV. A doctor walks in, accompanied by David. The doctor tells the nurse to "just give us a few minutes" as they walk over to the bed.

The cop's name is Joe Nash and he is introduced by the doctor to David. The cop says, "I asked you not to bring him here." The doctor says, "He can help find who shot you.' David tells him that the police don't know who they're looking for and Nash says, "Two people who don't want to be brought in," referring to the woman and the glowing man who was in the back seat.

David reminds Joe what he was talking about but Joe claims he was delirious. David tells him that the old man and the glow he was talking about. "That means there's a facility nearby for what they call regeneration. Now we can find that facility …" Joe cuts him off: "I've got nothing to say, Mr. Vincent, now butt out." A man walks in, a police Captain Battersea. When the doctor attempts to introduce David, Battersea gruffly says, "I know who he is. Why do you think I put a 24-hour guard on this room?" David says, "I'd like to help if I can."

Battersea isn't in the mood and says, "Listen Vincent, I'm running a manhunt not a three-ring circus. You're not going to jam my switchboard with crank phone calls and send my officers and send my officers out after buck rousers (?)." He turns to the doctor and says, "I'd like to speak to Joe – alone. And don't give me any medical reasons why I can't have it. I'm not some crank you dragged in here," he says, glaring back at David. "I'm like his next of kin."

The doctor says, "Two minutes. The doctor and David leave. But before David closes the door he says, "Joe, if you change your mind, I'll be at the hotel." He leaves. Walking down the hallway David asks the doctor, "What did the Captain mean by 'next of kin'?" The doctor explains that, "He brought Joe up after his father was killed." Back in the room Battersea asks Joe, "What did you tell Vincent, Joe?" Joe says, "I told him to leave me alone." Battersea says, "You said some things when you were brought in." Joe says, "I was out of my mind." "You sure?" Joe asks, "Why would I lie about it?"Battersea suspects a couple of crazies like the Tanner kids. "Just find the people that shot me," Joe says.

Joe comforts him by telling him that whoever they were, they'll find them because they have the plate number, make of the car and "the biggest dragnet you ever seen." Roadblocks on every road out, we got dogs coming and I've asked the state police for a chopper. I promise you, we're gonna search every square yard in this county." Joe nods and says, "You give 'em the devil." Battersea tells him to get well, turns and leaves. The news blares, "Although Vincent would not comment to the press, it is clear that he plans to stay in Redstone until the manhunt is concluded." The man who was previously glowing and the woman – Claire - are in a room watching the news account on television.

"Try him at the hotel," the man says twice. She says it's a mistake: "If it were anyone but Vincent …" He ignores her so she goes over to the phone and dials the hotel (as if she knows the number by heart). "Mr. Vincent, please..." She is connected. "My father and I we heard about you on the radio. We were hiking and we came across this terrible thing. It seemed to be half-human and half – something awful." He asks her, "Have you called the police?" She says she thought the cops would think she was insane. "Mr. Vincent, this monster – is it one of those aliens you talk about?"

"I don't know," David says. "Who are you and where are you?" Evidently they agree to meet, so David hangs up the phone and prepares to head out. He walks over to his suit case, pulls out his holster rig and checks his gun. Meanwhile Clara puts on her jacket and walks out of the cabin. She strolls across the farmyard on foot.

Two men, Lieutenant Rawlings and Captain Jim Trent, walk into the police station and up to the desk of Captain Battersea. They introduce themselves and tell him they are from the state police. "We came down to see if we could help out," Trent says. "Appreciate it," replies Battersea. Battersea walks them over to the map and Trent tells him that his request for helicopters came through. They ask him if he needs dogs and Battersea says, "Whatever. I'm not too proud to ask. About ten cars and twenty men could have nailed him but … whatever you can do." Trent says, "We don't think very much of people who shoot cops, no matter where in the state it happens. This boy, Joe Nash – is he gonna be alright," Trent asks. Battersea quickly answers, "If praying helps," then turns back to the map.

We got there ten minutes after it happened so we have to believe they're still somewhere in the grid," Battersea explains using the map as a visual aid. The men listen intently.

Meanwhile Claire is waiting outside of a small country store. Vincent pulls up, she walks up to the car and identifies herself. "Get in," he says. "Now where's this thing?" he asks. She says it's on a dirt road just up the way. "I'll show you." They take off and take a turn at Old Mill Road, a sign that also says "Private Property – No Trespassing." Naturally, David ignores it and they pull onto the road. As they ride she asks, "What are you going to do with this creature, Mr. Vincent?" David says he hopes to keep it alive, which is why he brought oxygen along. "Oxygen?" she says in a panic. She utters something about oxygen can kill and grabs the steering wheel causing the car to veer off the road onto a grassy hillside area.

David stops the car and Claire runs off And David gives chase. This bitch has speed! She runs back to the farmhouse where she was, and David is in hot pursuit. Gun drawn he heads up the stairs and busts into the cabin. He then heads down some basement stairs into a dark room and a voice says, "I'm not armed Mr. Vincent. And neither is she – otherwise you'd probably be dead by now." Here are computers in the dark room. "Keith, he won't listen to you," says Claire but ___ tells Vincent, "We need you." "For what?" he asks. "To help us in our search for peace," he says. "You mean surrender, don't you?" David asks, his gun still drawn.

"We are hardly in a position to dictate terms, are we?" Keith asks. He stands up and tells David "Clara and I are fugitives from our own alien compatriots as well as from your police. We're marked for death because we favor the abandonment of Earth as an objective." "Keith, don't trust him!" Clara demands. "We have to," he says. David says, "I don't have to trust YOU." Keith tells him, "Mr. Vincent, we don't have any time. This is a primitive regeneration system, one of the last left on Earth. It saved my life. My compatriots knew I needed regeneration and they'll be coming here soon. Now will you listen to me?"

David gives him no answer and is still pointing the gun. Keith says, "Then SHOOT!" David says, "I'll listen to you first."

Cut to two suited aliens getting directions from a gas station. The man driving gets back into the car and says, "Three miles." Back at the cabin, Keith tells David, "Yes, we used gases before we brought the rejuvenation tubes down. They are quite harmless to you. He says he effects are "similar to what you would find in your own deep sea decompression chambers." He explains: "I was one of six leaders chosen who came here to clarify your assault. I had been on Earth a lot before I realized that we had been deceived by the expeditionary forces. The human brain is a subtle, complex, highly efficient organ. It would be a crime against creation to destroy it. The ten billion planets to choose from, it would be ruinous to continue our fight against this world. As soon as I saw that, I planned to return home to fight against the coming slaughter. That was the night they decided to kill me."

"What would stop them from killing you at home?" David asks. "I have many friends there, powerful friends, leaders. And I have this…" He opens up a laptop: "This is a memory bank. It contains a million facts about about man, his philosophy, his science, his civilization, his world. It could change a great many minds," Keith tells David. Claire sits in the corner silently staring at the two men.

The two men from earlier find the turnoff and head toward the cabin. Inside Keith tells David that they have already made contact with the space craft that will carry them home. We were to meet at nine o'clock tomorrow morning. Then …" David interrupts: "You're not asking me to help you through the dragnet after all the nice things you said about the human mind?" David asks. Claire interrupts; "I told you. He's obsessed. He doesn't want peace." "If you want peace you'll let me arrange your arrest with the authorities," David says. Keith asks David to think about the catastrophe that he is trying to avoid. He said that his forces would be compelled to attack and "your planet would be destroyed."

An electric security eye shows that the aliens have arrived. Keith says that he (David) will be witnessing an execution, and asks for help one more time.

The aliens pull up (of course in a black car) and get out and walk to the porch to meet Keith. One alien runs past him into the house and the other, standing outside, tells them "We've been authorized to spare your lives. You will give us the time and place of your rendezvous tomorrow and the names of your collaborators." Keith is standing on a lower rung of the stairs that Claire, looks up at her and tells the man, "We are ready to die." The alien looks at Claire and says, "There's no reason for you to die too." "Get it over with," she says.

The alien points the laser then two shots ring out, he falls, glows red and disintegrates. Keith takes Claire by the hand and they scamper down the stairs. David runs out of the barn where he was hiring and fired the shots, ducks behind the house with Claire and Keith and when the other alien comes out, he shoots and kills him as well. "Thank you, Mr. Vincent. I'm afraid it's only a reprieve. They won't stop trying," Keith says. "Let's get inside," he says as he walks up the stairs, picks up the brief case that the dead alien dropped. Claire and David follow.

"You are absolutely sure you have a way to get out of here, Mr. Vincent. I would like you to have the attaché case," Keith says. "He'll take it to the authorities," Claire warns. Keith says that "That in itself will convince them of nothing. There are others who think as I do. If they come at you, give it to them. Say that it came from a leader. I am sure it would be to your benefit," Keith explains. "How much of a chance are you willing to take?" David asks. "To do what?" Keith asks. "To get through the road block and meet the saucer tomorrow," David answers. Claire again warns that David is leading him into a trap, but David says, "The whole scene outside could have been staged for my benefit. But there are several billion lives at stake so I'll go along with you."

Keith contemplates and David says, "If you don't want to try, that's alright, too." David then begins reloading his pistol. Later he's on the phone with Scoville who says, "Of course I see the implications, David. We could win with one big play. But you'll never make it." David says, "There's no other way. The farm house is right in the middle of the search area, we can't go four miles in any direction without running into a road block." Scoville asks, "Is there any way you could get the police on your side?" David tells him, "The Chief of Police down here won't even listen. I told you about Officer Nash. There's something going on here and I don't understand it. But I have to make a move."

Scoville tells him, "I have to catch a plane. I'll be in Redstone before midnight." They terminate their call. David, cigarette in hand, picks up an envelope of some kind and leaves his room.

At the police station, Battersea is again at the map issuing instructions. "As soon as they finish at the river bank, I want the main force to spread out in this direction: up toward the Old Mill Road. Okay? Anybody wants me I'll be in the Photo lab." As he heads off he runs into David. "Vincent, get out of my way," he says. David says he has something that Battersea might be interested in. In the envelope was a license plate. "Aren't you interested in that license number?" he asks. "Where'd you get this?" David says, "You wouldn't believe me. But I'll take you there – alone."

"Don't give me that alone baloney," Battersea snaps. "I'll have you behind bars for obstructing justice." David says, "That won't solve your case, will it?" David interrupts one of Battersea's rants and says, "Either you come with me alone or you don't come at all." Battersea hesitates and then goes over and picks up his jacket and his police hat and off they go.

Battersea and David are in a station wagon and pull up to the road block. A cop says, "Alright, let 'em through." David tells Battersea to take the Old Mill Road, which he does. "There's a farm house down this way," Battersea says.

"That's not where we're heading, is it?" Battesea asks. "Is there something wrong, Captain?" David asks, looking at him suspiciously. Battersea gives no reply.

Inside the cabin in the back with the technology, Keith and Claire are waiting but not speaking to each other. David and Battersea pull up in the station wagon. They get out of the car and walk toward the farm house. Battersea is hesitant but follows at a distance. They enter the outer room and then David leads him to the next room where the basement stairs are located. As they descend, Battersea sees nothing at first. Then David pulls his gun and pins Battersea to the wall. Claire then walks up to him with the hypnotic orb and says, "Captain Battersea: you will remember nothing about what is about to happen. You will remember nothing."

Back at the hospital Trent and Rawlings come into the room where Nash is still recuperating. He re-introduces himself and Rawlings, his aide. "Joe, the Captain left his office with David Vincent. Can you think of any reason why?" Trent asks. Joe looks confused. "He isn't buying what Vincent is spouting is he?" Trent again asks. Nash says, "You know better than that." "I understand that you met with Vincent earlier today," Rawlings says. Nash says that he did. When asked what he said Nash just tells them that he said that he (Vincent) was bad news. "Whether we like it or not, he's gotten himself involved," Trent says. "Joe, if you think of anything, would you give us a call?" Trent asks. "Yeah sure," Joe replies.

Nash asks if Battersea is in trouble and Trent says, "I hope not."

Back on the road the station wagon comes back to another road block. A cop tells Vincent and Battersea that a Captain Trent is down at state police. headquarters. Battersea says, "I know him. He's a good man." The cop senses that something is wrong with Battersea. "Is everything alright, Captain?" he asks. The cop looks into the back of the station wagon, sees nothing and gives them the go-ahead to take off. The chief pulls up behind David's car and asks "Why are we stopping here?" David hops out and under some quilts and covers are Claire and Keith. David helps them out. They load into David's car. Battersea is attempting to pull his gun, but David wrestles with him. Claire walks up with the orb but Battersea knocks it out of her hand

They all pile into David's car with Claire behind the wheel as Battersea threatens that "when they catch you they'll throw away the key." "Get in!" David orders as he and Battersea pile into the back seat of the car.

Later, some men in suits, along with some police officers have located the station wagon and are searching the area around it. T rent comes across the broken orb that Battersea knocked out of Claire's hand. These guys appear to be aliens, too!

On the road, a helicopter appears to be flying overhead and David orders Claire to "get off the highway. Stay out of sight until we get to a phone." They turn into a little town called Travistock. Back at the police station men are still looking over the map. "I've alerted every peace officer in the northern half of the state," Rawlings tells Trent. Trent orders forty units be transferred up there. Trent and Rawlings are hard at work. As Rawlings walks off, in walks Scovillle who introduced himself:"captain Trent, Edgar Scoville. Chief Dusek and I are pretty good friends." They shake hands.

"Oh yes, Mr. Scoville. I've heard him mention your name. What can I do for you?" "Captain, I think you are setting the stage for a tragic mistake in regard to David Vincent." Before Trent can remark on David's gooniness, Scoville continues his rant: "What I think of his theories is beside the point. He is neither a criminal nor dangerous to your men." "Then just what are you afraid of, sir?" Trent asks. "Now in this atmosphere, you're building to shoot first and ask questions later." Trent says, "I can assure you, that will never happen on this police force." "Good," Scoville says. "Thank you for your time, Captain." He leaves.

When Scoville leaves, Trent gets up and walks over to Rawlings. "Watch him," he says. Trent is showing concern.

Meanwhile it's nightfall. David walks out and tells Claire and Keith, "We have adjoining cabins, and hands them their key. He opens the car door and says, "Come on Captain, come on!" Battersea's hands are tied and as he gets out he says, "I don't know what you think you're doing. I just hope you know what the ante is." David escorts him into the cabin they will share. Outside Claire tells Keith, "I guess I was wrong about Vincent. Now they'll kill him." Keith says, "We can't concern ourselves with that." She says, "Can't we? Isn't he as good an argument for humanity as the case you're carrying?" Keith is silent.

Inside David ties Battersea to a chair. "You think we're kidnappers, don't you?" David asks him. Then there is a knock on the door. David grabs his pistol, but it's Claire. He lets her in. "David I came to see if I could help," she says staring at Battersea. Battersea says, "If you two want to be alone …" Claire interrupts: "Captain! You've been chief of police in Redstone for a long time, haven't you?" she asks. He doesn't answer. "Remember the Tanners, Captain?" she asks. "You remember the Tanner children, twins, 16 years old, a boy and a girl? One day they came to you with a story. Outside their farmhouse they saw a man burn up and disappear. The man who shot at them was imaginary … that's what you told them. Because you investigated and found nothing. We're very good at covering our tracks, Captain." "That farmhouse hasn't been used in years," Battersea says. Claire continues: "The real trouble didn't start until the children read about David Vincent and decided what they'd seen were aliens. You laughed at them but they insisted. And then one night the Tanner house burned down – no one escaped. Aliens set that fire, Captain, to keep them quiet." "That's garbage!" Battersea shouts.

She says that that is what Battersea had been telling himself for years because, "If we exist, and you didn't care enough to find out, then you're responsible for their deaths. Well we do exist!" She holds out her arm to him: "There's no pulse in that arm, there's no heart in here. And no blood" she says as she cuts herself. "No blood!" "Vincent – get her out of here! Get her out of here!" Battersea screams. David walks Claire to the door, opens it and she leaves. "How could you help them?" Battersea nervously asks. "All they want to do is get to their own planet and stop their people from making war with us," David explains. "You've got to kill them, you understand? You've got to kill them," Battersea declares.

Back at the hospital, Captain Trent and the doctor come back in. Nash is more coherent now and thanks the Captain for coming in. He tells him he thinks they'd better be alone and the doctor, along with the nurse, excuse themselves. After asking Trent if there's been any word and getting a negative response, Nash says, "I think there's something I'd better tell you. I wasn't delirious. That first story I told – that's the way it really happened. About the …" Trent interrupts: "…glowing man who disappeared."

Nash says he remembers something about the Captain and something that happened about a year ago. "If he knew there really were aliens …" Nash is beginning to put it together. Trent says, "I see…" and then goes into deep thought. He casually walks over to the door and locks it. In his other hand is a metallic disk. Nash asks, "What is that?" as Trent walks toward him. Trent places it on Nash's neck and as we know, he's a dead man.

The phone in Scoville's hotel room rings. It's David. David tells him that "They almost found us twice. We'll need another car." He tells Scoville that they are in a motel on the other side of Travistock. Scoville tells him he'll get started right away. David walks out of the pay phone and Claire is outside. She asks him if he has a minute for them just to sit and talk. He agrees. They are seated and then she asks him, "What's going to happen to you if we get away?" "Nothing good," he says. "Police Captains don't like to be kidnapped." He tells her that it's worth it to "get your people to stop making war with us. That's all that matters." She looks at him: "And you spend the rest of your life in jail?"

She asks him why and he tells her, "You know what your people are like, what'll happen if we don't fight back." "Sooner or later you'll be killed," she says. "Or wind up in Captain Battersea's jail," he says. She's staring into space as David rhetorically asks, "What else can I do?" She says, "You've been told we have no feelings, haven't you?" But David says that on the contrary, he's seen it. She tells him he's seen the murderers, the executioners. "David, some of us are able to feel with our minds as deeply as you feel with your heart."

"You're a woman here, Claire but are you …." She cuts him off: "A woman? She gives him some bullshit explanation and then he leans over and kisses her. Meanwhile, Scoville is on the way but is being followed by Rawlings. Rawlings is ordered on the phone to pull the car over and detain the passengers for six hours. Meanwhile, on the radio in the hotel room they are in it is reported that Officer Joe Nash has died from wounds received in a gun battle some thirty hours ago. Battersea is flabbergasted. He is working to get loose from his bonds.

He manages to get his mouth free and turns over the table and gets to the phone. His hands still tied he manages to get a message out to the operator and inform her who he is and where is located. Meanwhile, outside David tells Claire, "They can't stop us now. My friend is on the way here with a car. From there on in, it's all downhill." "For us, not for you," she says. David is rather nonchalant about it: "I don't know. Battersea will see the saucer tomorrow and if that doesn't convince him, maybe I'll hitch a ride with you." He smiles. She says, "Goodnight, dear." "Good night" he says as she walks back to her room.

"That's right, Riverview Motel, outside of Travistock," Battersea is saying into the phone. David walks in and immediately hangs up the phone.

David, Claire, Battersea and Keith are back in the car again. Scoville was held up on the highway by Rawlings in an intentional attempt to stall him. It worked. Without the car that Scoville was to provide, the group now has to use the same one that they escaped in. A police helicopter is flying above them and they have to make it until nine o'clock, which is when the saucer will arrive. Back at the roadblock, Rawlings tells Trent, who is now on the scene, that "The copter has spotted them." Rawlings tells him that there is no way out, and Trent circles the spot on the map which is lying across the hood of a police cruiser.

Rawlings calls Unit 22 and informs the officers that "subject car is headed North on Route 10." He orders that a road block be set up at the intersection. Two cops get the message, turn around and are on their way. Keith informs them that they have another half hour and as they come to a bend in the road, they spot a roadblock. Claire does a perfect one hundred and eighty degree turn and peels out in the opposite direction. The two cops from earlier are firing their guns at the escaping car. She pulls over as David says, "Mr. Battersea, millions of lived depend on whether these people get to that spacecraft or not. Get us through this roadblock!"

"After what they did to Joe – and the Tanners!" Battersea shouts. The cops run up on the stalled car with their guns drawn, but David has his gun pointed at

Battersea's head. He orders them to back off and drop the guns. They comply. He then forces Battersea out of the back seat as Claire and Keith exit the car as well. "We'll take their car," David says. They walk back up the street just as Rawlings pulls up. Rawlings fires a laser gun which destroys the police car that the group was headed for. They make a run for it. Before they give chase, Rawlings turns and shoots the two police officers with his laser gun as well. Battersea saw it all from where he and David are hiding and David tells him, "That's what this is all about." He unlocks Battersea's handcuffs.

He hands Battersea a revolver: "Here take it, come on!" They run to catch up with Keith and Claire. Rawlings, Trent and a cop all give chase and are searching what appears to be a park of some sort. Battersea comes out of hiding to shoot Trent in the back and watches him glow red and then disappear. In the meantime, David guns down both Rawlings and the other cop, also an alien. They also disintegrate. The four of them gather together.

Battersea says, "There's eight minutes. Let's see if we can get to that spaceship!" Having snatched another police car, the foursome arrives at the pickup site. They look to the skies and David glances at his watch and then you hear the piercing sound of a saucer. Keith shakes hands with David and says, "David – we're going to try." Claire walks over to him and he asks her if she'll come back. She tells him, "No David, I won't be back." She rubs his face and kisses him on the cheek. Off she goes. Battersea is staring in amazement. The duo climbs on board and the saucer takes off.

Moral: "For David Vincent and his new ally, sadness for what they have lost, and hope for what they may have gained. Already tens of thousands of miles away an alien saucer speeds through the void on a mission, not of death, but of life."

.43. "The Pursued"

Suzanne Pleshette returns for this episode as an entirely different character after having been featured in an earlier episode ("The Mutation," episode 3). Somebody is speeding up a long driveway to some kind of bed and breakfast type building in a car that looks a lot like one of the cars that David Vincent was driving a few episodes back.

The driver, a female, backs into a parking space and speedily walks into the Sycamore Guesthouse. She goes to the counter and asks if David Vincent has checked in yet and that she doesn't have much time. The woman says she doesn't see the name and tells her she'll double-check and leaves the desk for a moment.

The old woman sits down at the telephone system and phones a man who is presumably her husband. "Henry, a young lady is here asking if David Vincent has checked in." Henry grumbles back, "How would I know? If he hasn't registered he isn't here" and hangs up.

A car can be heard screeching to a halt outside. Two men leave a car and look into the auto she was driving. She asks for the back door and ducks into a side room to hide. The men come in and walk to the counter. An older man says he's looking for his fiancée: "She's a pretty girl, about so tall, long brown hair, wearing a beige coat," explains to the receptionist. The woman lies and says the girl was here and asked for breakfasts but that she sent her to the café on the corner. The two men leave, but one stops to get cigarettes from a machine. Then he exits.

The receptionist, Hattie Willis, says she's going to call the cops. The young woman, Anne, pushes the old woman and turns violent. She picks up a pair of darning needles and stabs the old woman several times in the back. She then makes a run for it, gets into her car and takes off.

The narrator offers the following: "The Sycamore Guesthouse, Arbor City, Massachusetts. Scene of a vicious, senseless killing. David Vincent had been summoned here by a woman he never met. Her name: Anne Gibbs. Her reason for calling him, she had been marked for death by creatures from an alien planet.

Inside the hotel/guesthouse, Henry is seated in the lobby pining away: "Who could have killed her? Who could have killed my Hattie?" he keeps asking himself. The sheriff, Tom Halladay, tells him, "That's what I'm trying to find out, Hank." Then adds, "Hank I want you to tell me everything that happened in here this morning." Hanks explains he was in the back office and that Hattie called and said there was a young lady asking about a reservation for a David Vincent." He tells Halladay that Vincent hasn't checked in yet. The cop tells another one to "make a note of that name." Henry concludes, "She is the one most likely. She is the one who most likely killed Hattie," he tells the officer.

Hank is an ex-cop and reminds Tom that he helped him get his badge two years ago. "I can still out-sheriff you any day," he adds. Tom asks if anyone got a look at the young lady and Hank says no. A man from the back of the crowd that has gathered in the lobby says, "I did." Tom tells them to let that man through. His name is John Corwin and he says he came into the lobby about an hour ago to use the cigarette machine. "That young lady that was talking to Hattie – what did she look like," Henry asks. Corwin claims she was about 45, a big woman with blonde frizzy hair, nowhere near what Anne looked like. Tom asks Corwin to come down to the department with him because "I'm going to want all the details." He leads him out.

As he leaves Tom shouts, "Hank, if that David Vincent fella shows up you let me know about it right away." A crowd has gathered on the outside of the guesthouse as well and Tom tells them "the show is over" as he proceeds out with Corwin. Vincent walks up to the counter. Henry is on the phone with Anne who is asking for Vincent. He hears his name and tells Henry who tells him he can "take that phone over in the lobby." He and Anne are talking. She tells him she can't meet him at the hotel and that she'd better not go near the town.

She tells him she is at an antique shop in Shelter Point, "it's on the main highway about three miles north of Arbor City." He tells her to stay there and that he's on his way. Henry was listening in the whole time. David heads out and a suited fellow watches and then gets into his car and trails David.

Anne is waiting as David pulls up. She introduces herself and wants to talk inside. "Are you sure you weren't followed?" she asks. David claims that he's sure but she tells him, "They know more than you realize." He tells her, with that cock hounds look on his face, "You seem to be very familiar with them." She tells him, "I should be – I'm one of them." As they talk, two customers enter the area and they move to another section. Outside the alien who was trailing David pulls up. He talks into a communications device and says, "Shelter Point Antiques – meet me here."

Inside she's telling David, "I'm not like the others. That's why they want to destroy me. I'm a threat to them." She further explains, "They've been experimenting with human emotions. I'm one of their failures. When I get angry I lose control, I get violent, wild." David tells her that he doesn't believe her. Anne tells him, "A woman was murdered this morning at the hotel." "Are you telling me you did it?" he asks. Anne tells him, "She wasn't the first. That's why they want to destroy me. I'm a danger to them. If your police should ever catch me, they'll find out that I'm from another world. David please – help me," she pleads.

"Why should I?" David asks. "Because I can help you," Anne says. "I can tell you what you want to know about the invasion, I can go with you to your government and tell them why we're here." David says, "In other words you're selling out. I don't buy it." She explains, "I'm not turning against them – they turned against me. I'm not one of them anymore. My life has become valuable to me. It could be to you."

David tells her to wait where she's at while he goes to make a phone call. As the alien outside continues to wait for reinforcements, David is making a long distance call to New York, person-to-person to Edgar Scoville at Scoville Electronics. The alien outside grows impatient and decides to enter the antique shop on his own through the side door. The two people in the shop, one of whom is the proprietor, enter the area and delay the alien from approaching Anne. David is on the phone telling Scoville that, "I'm sure she's telling the truth and she's willing to go to Washington with us. We have to move fast."

Scoville says he'll send a helicopter to pick him up, "But we can't possibly get there before three o'clock." David tells him, "That's a long time to stay out of sight. The aliens are after her and so are the police. Now you know this area so how about it?" Scoville picks up a map, puts on his glasses and tells David Sean McCabe a summer camp not too far from Arbor City in Cape View. He tells David to "start looking for us at about three o'clock. There's a baseball field there."

David hangs up as the two people in the shop walk back outside. David asks the man how far it is to the cape and is told that it's about 75 miles. He is asked if he sees anything interesting in the shop and tells the man he's still looking. Meanwhile the alien has grabbed Anne and David walks in and sees it. The alien pulls a gun and David leaps across a huge amount of furniture to tackle him – the most athletic move he's made since the series started (read: stunt man). They begin to fight. The alien grabs a mallet but not before David launches a well-placed judo kick to the gut, forcing the alien to spin and fall back, impaling himself on a nearby spear of some kind. He turns red, glows and disappears as they all do.

Anne watches it and appears in shock. David grabs her arm and they prepare to leave. Henry pulls up in his station wagon and sees Anne getting into the car with David. David speeds off headed down the road to Cape View. How would Henry know what Anne looked like? He didn't see her, remember?

At any rate they get away but Henry is serious. In the back seat of his station wagon is his hold police holster and gun. Meanwhile, old man Hank Willis, the husband of recently killed Hattie Willis, is on a mission. He's looking for the men who killed his wife. Three aliens in a Black (figures) station wagon pull up and look around. One says, "Funny – he told us to meet him here." One walks up to Henry's station wagon and with all the windows rolled down, it is easy for him to reach in and take out the holster rig that Henry had on the back seat.

Henry is in the shop and the proprietor recognizes him. "Hello Mr. Willis." Henry asks about "that young couple that just left here – do you know them?" The man asks, "Should I? Are they some kind of fugitives?" "Why would you say a thing like that – do you know somethin'?" Henry asks. The man tries to walk off but Henry stops him, reminding them that he's been sheriff there for over twenty years and anything he has to tell the current sheriff he can tell HIM. He reminds him, as he lights up a cigarette, that "Sheriff Holloway is one of my best customers."

The guy wants a bribe. Henry asks him how much a trinket is that he picks up. It's ninety-eight cents but Henry pulls out a ten and says he has no change. "I thought so," says Henry and stuffs it in the proprietor's shirt pocket. The man tells

Henry that they went to Cape View. He asks, "Are you sure?" The man says that he is the one who gave them directions. The sheriff walks in as Henry is leaving and asks, "Find some antiques, Mr. Willis?" Henry says, "Never mind" and keeps walking but is cut off. Corwin, the alien who took his gun rig then says as he shows Henry his gun rig, "I found this in your station wagon. The grief-stricken husband seeking revenge." Henry snatches it out of his hands and the man says, "Why you must know something the sheriff doesn't know. " Henry says, "I know you told a lie about that woman – fat, forty, blonde, frizzy hair." Henry walks out as the alien Corwin asks, "Have you seen her?" Henry says "May be," as he walks out the door.

Corwin follows him outside and stops him. "Mr. Willis: I lied to the sheriff for good reason," he claims. "I wasn't busy elsewhere, this case is bigger than anyone realizes." He shows Henry his identification. "Justice Department?" "Special investigator," he says. Henry looks at him. "Do you know Warren Jacobi. He's with the Justice Department, used to be my deputy five years ago." Corwin asks, "Where's the girl, Mr. Willis? It's not cops and robbers any more. This is national security." Henry tells him, "She's gone to Cape View with David Vincent." The man says, "You've done your job, Mr. Willis – now stay out of it. We will not tolerate interference from anyone. You understand that." Corwin then walks off.

David and Anne are speeding toward Cape View. "Is the camp open this time of year?" Anne asks. "No," David replies, "Professor McCabe and his son lived there. He's a retired geologist." "Do they know about uh …" "Aliens," David interrupts. "Oh yes. They know about aliens." As she stares at him, obviously enamored, he tells her, "Charlie and his wife were on a field trip once. They ran across an alien outpost. Your friends began chasing him for miles. Charlie was driving like a madman, car went out of control and he had a head-on collision with another car. His wife and the other driver were killed. He was convicted of manslaughter, he just finished eighteen months in prison."

"Why, was it his fault?" Anne asks. "What could he tell them? Creatures from another planet were chasing him?" David replies. "Does Professor McCabe know I'm an alien?" she asks. "I'm sure Scoville told him." "David, I don't want to go to that camp," she says. "They're expecting us. The helicopter is meeting us there to take us to Washington." She gets loud: "David, my people turned his life into a nightmare. How can you expect him to help me?" David tells her, "By helping you we hope to end this nightmare. That's what this is all about." "I'm not going to that camp!" she insists.

David tells her that she's in no position to be dictating terms. She turns to him and says, "What do you mean?" He tells her, "Figure it out for yourself. You killed my people, your people don't want you." She tells him to stop the car and he tells her, "No chance." She grabs the wheel and David brings the car to a halt. "I'm getting out!" she's shouting. I'm not your prisoner, I'm nobody's prisoner!" she screams. She gets out and begins running down an incline. David gives chase. She turns and swings but he ducks. She takes off again and this time hurls a rather large rock which misses. David grabs her and forcibly brings her back up the small hill and places her back into the car.

"Now you know what I'm like," she says catching her breath. David stares at her, starts the car and off they go.

Outside of his cabin chopping wood, McCabe is keeping busy. He lives in the cabin with his son. He picks up an armful of wood and carries it into the house where Eddie is seated. His father reminds him that he asked him to start a fire and Eddie asks, "Sorry dad. Won't things get warm enough without it?" The elder McCabe explains that "Mr. Scoville is landing his helicopter on the playing field. I hope there aren't too many gopher holes." Eddie says, "I think we'll need them to hide in if the police show up." "They won't," the professor says. "Are you sure? She's running from the cops. If they find her here they'll …." Eddie replies. The professor cuts him off: "It's a calculated risk."

Eddie isn't backing down and tells him, "You're the one with the record. You're the one who might go back to prison. Nobody seems to care about that. I don't want her here, dad." McCabe replies, "Eddie, I know how you feel. Maybe I feel that way, too. It'll be okay. Okay"? he asks putting his hand on his son's shoulder. Eddie hesitantly complies.

David and Anne pull up in front of the McCabe cabin and are let in. "Well David, it's good to see you again. Come in," McCabe says. Anne Gibbs is introduced to both Charles McCabe and his son Eddie. Eddie does not respond but the elder invites David and Anne to sit down. He offers Anne a drink and she turns it down. David asks if there is somewhere he can hide his car and McCabe asks Eddie to show David a place. Eddie, still putting logs on the fire, replies, "I ain't showing him nothin'. He's got no right putting your life on the line like this." When the father insists, Eddie begrudgingly walks to the door with David to go find a place to hide the car.

When they leave the professor says, "My apologies Ms. Gibbs. My son is a bit over-protective." "He's just more honest than the rest of us," she says. "One of the privileges of youth," he says. "You have those same privileges," she replies. He turns to her: "I think you already know my opinion of you. I'm a little surprised you came here." She tells him that it wasn't her idea and "believe it or not, I don't think I have the right to expect you to help me." McCabe says, "I don't believe you."

She tells him "I think I'd better leave," gets up and heads for the door. He tells her she's not going anywhere, "not until we tell you to" and blocks the door. "You have no right to keep me here," she says. "Haven' I? I paid for the right, Miss Gibbs, with my wife, my leg, my career. Now you sit down," he tells her. "Get away from that door!" she shouts and charges him. She strikes him with an iron poker and he falls to the floor and she strikes him again and again.

Eddie and David are running back up to the house, unaware that Anne has just beaten the living shit out of McCabe. "Dad!" Eddie shouts as they walk in the door as Anne kneels beside the body with the poker still in her hand. "David help me," she says through tears. "Now do you see?" Eddie says, "She killed him" and then runs out the door. David can't catch him but goes back over to McCabe's body. "He's still alive. Get some water," he orders Anne.

In the meantime, a station wagon screeches to a stop in a residential neighborhood. The leader gets out and orders the other two to search every cabin. The car just so happens to stop in front of a house that Eddie pulls up to in the van. He jumps out, with the alien leader watching, and enters the house. David puts a cold press on McCabe's forehead and he begins to come to. David tells her they have to go because there will be plenty of company and Anne says, "I'm not leaving him – he's our ride." David informs her that Scoville's helicopter is due in forty minutes and "we have to avoid the police and your people during that time."

"You know, sometimes I think you're less human than I am," she says to David. "You're perfectly willing to just leave him here?" David tells her, "I didn't hit him, I didn't kill anyone, so don't give me lectures on humanity, alright?" They head out the door but before they do she tells David that she's sorry about everything. David gives her no response and they leave.

Eddie runs out of the house and goes back to the van, which has "Cape View Summer Camp" plastered all over the side of it. Corlin walks up to him and Eddie just spills his guts: "There's been a murder up at the Cape View camp. My father." "Oh I'm sorry. Is the sheriff on it?" Corlin asks. "He's up at Pine Ridge, they just radioed him. He's on his way in," Eddie says. "Any idea who did it?" Corlin asks and Eddie tells him, "A woman." "Know her name?" he asks. "Ann Gibbs." Corlin shows some kind of identification but Eddie isn't paying attention. When Corlin asks where he can find her Eddie says that some kind of helicopter is coming to pick her up at the playing field to take her to Washington. Corlin tells him not to worry, "we'll take over."

The helicopter with Scoville in it, will arrive in twenty minutes.

Meanwhile, the sheriff walks into the Sycamore Guest House and asks Hank for a signed statement regarding what happened at the hotel earlier that day. "There's a murderer running around and you're worried about statements," Hank says. The sheriff tells Hank that her name is Anne Gibbs and she's wanted for attempted murder down at Cape View. He tells him he heard it over the radio. "She and that David Vincent fella." Hank says, "While you're standing here letting grass grow under your feet."

The sheriff says, "Hank, you know that's not in my jurisdiction" and Hank tells him, "That girl could kill a dozen people before you get started." "Hank – we're workin' on it!" the sheriff says. He adds, "There's a report of a helicopter going to pick them up and take them to Washington." Hank is staring ahead and the sheriff gets fidgety and begins walking off. As he leaves Hank tells him that if he needs any help in Washington, DC, he has some connections. My old deputy Warren Jacoby is a big muckety muck with the justice department." The sheriff tells him, "Hank, I can handle this. Now you just file that statement, alright?" Then he leaves.

When he leaves Hank makes a long distance call to Washington DC.

Meanwhile, David and Anne has arrived at the hill above the baseball field. He comes to a rapid stop, they get out and run down the hill to the meeting point. He wait at the edge of the field as the helicopter appears overhead. A station wagon with Corlin and two other aliens is speeding down the highway and they, too, spot the helicopter. David and Anne watch as the copter slowly lands. Up drive the aliens, three of them including the leader. They begin shooting as David and Anne get into the copter.

Up goes the copter leaving the men shooting on the ground. Scoville says, "Anne, sorry it's been so tough on you. We'll see that you get treated better once we get to Washington. Some very important people waiting to meet you." "Some of ours, some of hers," David says. "My wife's cousin has a place just outside of Washington. We'll stay away from the airports, land in an open field someplace," Scoville explains. "The Justice Department has lined up a number of top meetings with half a dozen people," Scoville further explicates. "You can pick any of twenty different groups in Washington. There's no way they can stop us now. Sit back. Enjoy the scenery."

Corlin, the lead alien is communicating telling someone about the Washington Tracking Station and the copter is coming in from Virginia and he wants to know exactly where it lands.

It's late night and a taxi pulls up in front of a residence. David, Scoville and Anne get out of the cab and head to the house. A car with Corwin and another alien is speeding down the highway and he's in contact with people at a communications tower. Scoville puts them up at the home of one of his relatives. The aliens have tracked them and know where David and Anne are. Corwin has been told that "every man in the area has been made available to you."

Inside the house Scoville is on the phone and is telling someone that he has a job for them. "It's confidential, it's urgent and it must be done by six a.m. I want you to go to the motorpool at our Washington plant," and he continues as we cut to Fairfax Taxi Company. Someone walks in side and turns off the radio on a sleeping man's desk. It's Corwin. He tells the man, "At three fifty-five this morning a helicopter landed in Fairfax Park. One of your taxis went into that park empty and came out with three persons." Corwin flashes identification and says, "I want to know where your cab took those persons. I don't have much time."

The next morning the aliens are parked down the street (in a black Lincoln Continental) from where Scoville, David and Anne are staying. Scoville tells them, "The car should be here at six sharp, just a few more minutes." Anne asks, "Will we go straight to Washington?" Scoville tells her they're going to an official meeting and takes her cup to get her more coffee. He adds, "Think of it: you're about to become the most important woman on two worlds."

She turns to David and asks if he will be with her at the meeting. "I'll miss you," he says. "It frightens me. The most important woman in two worlds and I don't fit into either," Anne says. A white van from Camp View pulls up and the man blows the horn. Scoville looks out the window and tells them that the van has arrived. "Let's go – out the back door," he says. A second car comes slowly up the street, passes by the waiting aliens and turns the corner.

The van is a decoy – the real transportation was the old car that pulled out back and they are now loading into it. A kid on a bike (an alien) sees the car pass by and gets on his communicator and calls it in. "They're riding north to Hudson Boulevard," he says.

Cut to the nation's capital. The old car pulls up in a nearby parking lot outside of a huge building. Hey get out but the black Continental comes barreling down the parking lot and a shootout takes place. David sends Scoville for help and tells Anne to follow him to cover. They scamper and continue to get shot at. David re-loads his pistol (of course he has extra ammo). David shoots one who has scampered up an outside stairway and he glows and burns. Anne runs out and says "I'm giving myself up." It's Corwin. ""Alright now let's all go quietly," Corwin says. Anne hits his arm and then grabs his gun while he beats the shit out of David. Security guards rush out and shot Corwin, who glows and dies. "Corwin says "We'll cover you in case any more of them show up."

David and Anne are inside. David asks her how she feels. She says "Nervous, or even worse, scared." "They're waiting," David says. "Alright, let's go." Down the hall they stroll, but out of a side door extends a pistol and Anne is shot in the back. It's Henry!

Just as they were preparing to enter the high level meeting Hank Willis guns down Anne explaining, "She killed my wife." Hank surrenders his gun. Anne poignantly says David's name one final time as she begins to glow red, falls to the floor and dies. Anne disintegrated in front of a hall full of witnesses including Hank, a general and four high ranking men in suits. They now know that aliens exist. The men in the meeting join the others in the hallway in time for Hank to be turned over to authorities.

Hank comes out of a meeting with more than twenty other people and asks Sackville, "Do you think I convinced them?" Sackville points out that half a dozen people testified to how she died and they can't believe that they're all cranks. Hank boasts, "I was a sheriff for twenty years – they can't think I'm a crank." David is sad. "A rotten shame," Scoville says. "She could have ended this nightmare once and for all. She could have helped every one of us – the whole human race." David replies in regard to Hank, "If he hadn't been so damn human."

Moral: "Eyewitness testimony to the presence of the Invaders – another piece in the mosaic. And soon the picture that David Vincent sees there will be seen by all. Today, the road ahead seems not quite so steep."

.44. "Inquisition"

The final episode.
It's been two years and it all comes down to this.
The site is the nation's capital and David and Scoville are in the office of an official, Senator Breeding. "Now let's get this straight, Mr. Vincent. You say that a member of the top echelon of government is involved with these people?" "Yes sir," David replies. The man they are talking about is a technical advisor to the National Security Council.

They charge a close friend of his, Arthur Koy, of being an alien and always being in the vicinity of known saucer activity. The problem is that Koy is a close friend of Breeding's. He explains, "Arthur Koy has eaten spare ribs at my house, he's played leap frog with my granddaughters and he scammed me out of twenty four dollars last week in five-card stud." "We happen to have facts," David says to which Breeding scoffs, "Nonsense."

"In the last few weeks our tracking stations have been picking up evidence of increased saucer landings. In every instance, Arthur Koy happened to be in the exact area where all these landings took place," Scoville tells Breeding, showing him paperwork. Breeding tells Scoville that he appreciates all the work he's done for the government but then adds, "Do you know what you sound like?" David gets out of his chair and says, "Of course we know what we sound like! Do you think this is fun for us?

Breeding turns to David and tells him, "Mr. Vincent, I have a lifetime of experience with people who know that the enemies of the republic are hiding under every bed and behind every curtain!" David tells him that he has nothing to lose and he could give them the benefit of the doubt if you listen to us. If you don't listen to us, if you don't do anything about this you'll have to live with your conscience." Now Breeding is really pissed: "Mr. Vincent, don't you lecture me on my responsibilities. You sashay in here with this outrageous charge against Mr. Koy and expect me to swallow it whole? Me. Koy is a loyal American and I will not subject him to any witch hunt!"

He then turns his ire on Scoville telling him that he doesn't think that he is the kind of person that the government should be giving their defense contracts to. David and Scoville take their paperwork and leave as a female stenographer is seated on the couch and Breeding walks out. There is a brief case that was left behind and the stenographer walks out to catch David and Scoville. "Mr. Vincent, did you forget your brief case inside the office?" David tells her he didn't have one and just then there is a huge explosion. They rush back in and Senator Breeding lay dead.

The narrator tells us: "Minutes after the violent death of one of Washington's most beloved Senators, David Vincent and Edgar Scoville are hustled to the office of Special Assistant to the Attorney General, Andrew Hatcher." Hatcher allows friend journalist Joan Seeley to sit in on the interview. "You're going to question suspects in a murder case and you want me here?" she asks. "Oh Andrew, what are you up to?" "Just trying to throw you a bone," he says as he walks over to the door. A male aide invites them in and Hatcher asks them to have a seat.

Hatcher is direct to the point: "Who planted that bomb? Do you have any idea?" "No sir, we do not," Scoville replies. "I've been going through the notes made by Senator Breeding's secretary at your conference. You claim that an advisor to the National Security Council is a traitor, or worse. Have you made these charges with any other government agencies," Hatcher asks. "No sir, we haven't," says Scoville. "Well I suggest that you don't for their sakes," Hatcher says. "What are you driving at, Mr. Hatcher?" David asks. Hatcher answers, "You make reference to our tracking stations. You say 'we are trying to stop them.' What is this collective entity you keep referring to?"

David tells him that he is referring to "a few people like ourselves – believers. A group, a small group of ordinary people." Hatcher tells him, "Ordinary people don't have tracking stations, Mr. Vincent." Scoville explains, "I put my facilities at the disposal of the group, Mr. Hatcher." Hatcher stares at both men and then asks, "Who are these people? What are their names? Where can we find them?" Scoville says, "I'm sorry – I can't tell you that." "How many of you are there?" Hatcher asks. "I can't tell you that, either," Scoville informs him. "You don't know …" Hatcher assumes as Scoville again informs him that "we can't tell you."

"What does your company do, Mr. Scoville?" "Research and development and advance electronics, laser design and guidance systems." Now they've got Hatcher's attention. "Armaments and ammunitions?" he asks. "Yes sir, that too," answers Scoville. "I presume that's what the senator meant when he said that 'I seriously doubt whether you are the kind of man that our government should give its defense contracts to'," Hatcher says reading from the notes taken by the secretary. Scoville stands up and walks over to Hatcher, informing him, "Before you get carried away, Mr. Hatcher …" but Hatcher interrupts. "I'm just trying to be logical, Mr. Scoville. I'm sure you couldn't be unhappy over the death of a powerful enemy."

Scoville informs him, "I didn't consider him an enemy. He was an honest and dedicated man who saw the truth differently from me." Hatcher, in a gruff tone, says, "He was a man who could have ruined your business, exposed and destroyed you, and in your terms, opened the way for an invasion of the Earth." Hatcher adds accusingly, "Now wasn't it your duty to eliminate him?" David looks up: "Making an accusation?" "What do you think, Mr. Vincent?" Hatcher asks walking across the room. David tells him that he's looking for a scapegoat. "Not a scapegoat, Mr. Vincent – a murderer," Hatcher says, tossing the file on his desk.

David gets out of his chair and says, "I hope you find him." Hatcher says, "Thank you for coming gentlemen." "You'll be available if we need you," he says looking at Scoville. "Of course," Scoville says as he and David exit the room. Once they leave the room Joan gets up and says, "Alright Andy, I have a documentary record of the attorney general at work – or was it at play? Do you want me to print this?" He tells Joan that it's up to her because he thought he was doing her a favor. She tells him, "I'm never sure whether I can afford your favors." She continues by asserting, "The way I see it, you're building yourself a case, a case without much evidence but with a great deal of outrage over the death of a beloved senator, and you want me to help you make that case, don't you?"

He looks at her and asks her if she's being a little suspicious. She turns her back to him and says, "Yes, and I have good reason to be." He fires up a cigarette and says, "One little incident," to which she replies, "I'm sentimental that way. That one little incident nearly wrecked two careers. It was mine." She says goodbye and leaves the office. After she does Hatcher is on the phone. "Get ahold of John Connolly, NSA. Have him send over the security file on Edgar Scoville. Make it a rush." He hangs up and there is a knock on the door.

"Come in," he says taking his seat behind his desk. It's the male aide from earlier. "I just spoke with the lab. They'll have the report on the bomb fragments … How did it go with Laurel and Hardy?" he asks. "About what I expected," Hatcher says. "They had the motive and the opportunity. They've hooked up some kind of underground organization." He plans on getting information and taking it before a grand jury.

Meanwhile, Joan pulls up in front of a residence but is intercepted by a man at gunpoint. He rushes her into the house and orders her to sit down. David comes out of a back room. David starts in on the questioning asking her what her line of work was since he saw her taking notes. She introduces herself as Joan Seeley and she's a reporter. She says that Hatcher asked her to stick around. She thought it would make a good story. David asks, "You expect us to believe that the press was called in while he was questioning us?" The man with the gun says "Ask her how she knew about this place." She claims she had the phone number traced but that they need not worry about her letting Hatcher know. "Why not?" Scoville asks.

"He wants to hang you. I just want a story," she says. "You want us to share our secrets with you," David surmises. "You don't trust me," she begins, "But you're going to have to." When David asks why she stands up and tells them that they come into Senator Breeding's office ranting about invaders from outer space and accuse the Koy of the NSC of being one of them and that you even have an organization set up to combat these aliens. She says "Hatcher could hang you from a sour apple tree!"

David says that they'll worry about Hatcher when the time comes. She tells them, "You'd better worry about him now. While you're out shadow boxing with ghosts, you're about to be a very talent for this kind of thing, and an ego to match." The man with the gun says, "I still think Hatcher sent her." David says, "Let's give her a story to take back." David and Scoville say "Come with us" and everyone goes into the next room.

Hey head into a basement and into a room where men are operating a control room. It is an area where they can trace the alien landings and, according to David, can break their codes. Joan looks around and says "impressive," and then adds, "Do you know what Andrew Hatcher could do with this? He would have front page headlines all over the country: 'Secret group led by mad industrialist in a plot to overthrow the government."

David asks one of the men to show he film to Joan. David turns off the lights and the film is on. "This is a film we got back from the lab an hour ago," David tells her. It shows a man with a brief case exiting a cab and walking into a building.

The man is Dr. Koy. "He just had a two hour session with the National Security Council," Scoville, who is seated behind her, says. The man in the film meets with another man who David identifies as an alien. Koy opens his brief case and shares a report on the latest developments in communications interruption devices. "Why that?' Joan asks. "We don't know yet," says Scoville. "We're working on it now. They've had four meetings in the last two weeks. This is the first time they've given him something," Scoville narrates. "Money?" Joan asks. "My guess is it's an operational plan, something that Koy would be in a position to program for them." The film concludes.

Scoville turns the lights back on and says, "Well, what would the journalists have to say about that?" Joan says that a government advisor and a childhood friend exchanged letters. David questions it and she asks him to prove it. The phone rings and Scoville answers. "Koy just made a ten p.m. plane reservation to Paris," Scoville reports. "That means we have to move now," he tells David. "Take me with you" Joan requests. David tells her that she's seen enough and for her to "go back to Hatcher now." She tells them, "Andy Hatch and I grew up in this town together. Three years ago he leaked a story to me about an impending federal indictment of a United States congressman, one George Neal. The day after I turned in my story all the other papers picked it up." "Yes I remember that. I was in Washington at the time," Scoville says.

"Well then you also know that the story wasn't true." She says that the indictment was never sought and that Hatcher's real target was a group of lobbyists who were close to the Congressman and he leaked the story to her just to scare them off. Now gentlemen, you are his stepping stone." Scoville looks over at Vincent and David decides, "Alright, stay with us. We'll leave at seven."

Back at Hatcher's office the aide comes in and tells Hatcher, "The lab report just came in. The bomb was made from a new type of explosive charge called Keldonite. There's only plant that produces Keldonite – Scoville's." "He'll say it was stolen from him or purchased," Hatcher replies. "We need more than that." The aide says, "We have something more –a witness." He goes to the door and in walks Dr. Frederickson. The aide introduces them. Frederickson tells Hatcher that, "up until today I was a member of the Believers. I want to tell you about them."

That night Koy walks into his house and the lights won't come on. Joan is hiding behind a curtain as Koy picks up a flashlight and begins looking around. He enters the next room and gets a file. Out of a closet comes David, revolver drawn: "Don't move," he says. Koy tosses an envelope to David that lands on the floor and when David bends over to pick it up, he runs to a drawer and grabs a gun and they begin shooting. Joan shouts "David!" and David shoots Koy who hits the ground, glows red and dies. He was an alien.

The next morning Joan is in her office as Hatcher walks in. "Your receptionist is out to lunch so I took over," she says. He walks over to her desk and looks at a file: "More material for your monthly axe job on the ruthless and ambitious Andrew Hatcher?" She seductively gets up and walks around the desk. "Ooh Andy. We used to be friends once, remember?" He tells her that he remembers very well. She flashes a smile, turns away and he walks up behind her, turns her around and they kiss. "Why did you really come down here?" he asks.

She tells him she came down there because she likes him. "Because I want to stop you from doing something that's going to end up hurting you," she adds. He laughs and says, "Such as?" "Prosecuting Edgar Scoville," she says. He changes his mood and says, "Oh that. It isn't just Edgar Scoville. I'm going to nail all of them." He walks over to pour himself a drink. "Even if they're telling the truth?" she asks. "It's a lie Joan, on the face of it, it's a lie," he tells her. "I've got evidence." She asks him "what evidence?"

"Does your evidence include Arthur Koy? Because on Tuesday Scoville and Vincent charged Koy with conspiring with the aliens and on Wednesday he booked himself on a flight to Paris." Joan says. "Which he never took," Hatcher says. Hatcher, cigarette in hand tells her, "Joan, you are facing the wrong fox." "Won't you at least listen to them, won't you let them come here and show you their evidence?" Joan asks. "That would only prejudice their case," Hatcher tells her. "The Grand Jury meets one hour from now. If they return an indictment, they'll have ample opportunity to defend themselves, " Hatcher explains.

She looks at him and says, "And you're going to have ample opportunity to put on your usual vaudeville show." "So what else is new?" he asks standing up and staring at her. She tells him she's sorry and that she really came there to be friends. She asks, "Can we?" He asks, "You mean, can we recapture the past?" "Well uh, re-discover it maybe" she seductively replies. He asks her about later on tonight and she tells him she will be at the Tiki Club at six o'clock. "And if you think that we can stop studying each other for an hour or two, I'll buy you a drink." He says, "Alright." Off she goes.

Elsewhere the phone rings. It's Joan. She tells David that Hatcher is going to the grand jury at nine o'clock and that she "set up the other thing." David asks her if she said anything about Koy and she says, "No, that's up to you."

The hearing has started and the questioning has begun: "You were at this meeting with Edgar Scoville, David Vincent, James Bowlin, Ann Lampier, Alexander Goldman, Venita Morrow, John Merritt." "Yes sir," answers Frederickson, who is on the stand. "There was some decision reached at this meeting, some decision regarding Senator Robert Breeding." "Yes sir, Frederickson says. "It was decided that Vincent and Scoville would go to Senator

Breeding and demand that he take action against Koy." "I see. And if he failed, was there a contingency plan, some plan to be carried out in case Scoville and Vincent failed?" "Yes sir," Frederickson says. "What was it?" Hatcher asks. Frederickson hesitates for a while and then says, "Kill him." Joan gets up and storms out of the hearing room.

David and Joan meet and she tells him that Frederickson testified that you planned Koy's death a month ago. "He named you, Scoville and five others," she said, showing David her notes. David is reading the notes and walking around the room. He says it was a set up in an attempt to get rid of the Believers for good. One of the Believers, Boland, runs upstairs from the basement sees Joan and asks David if he should talk in front of her. David says she's alright. Boland tells David there is a problem, that the papers that they got from Koy's safe are in a multiple series. "They're in a top secret code," Boland explains. "We broke through the first layer, the easiest one." Boland again looks over at Joan and David tells him, "I want her to hear this." So Boland continues: "They're planning a general assault.'

"Does it say that specifically?" David asks. "No, that and the time and the place and the method are buried in the other layers. We've got to find a way to crack them," Boland explains. "How did you draw your conclusion?" David asks. Boland explains that they had learned some months ago that they had they had tipped a general assault by drawing a key man from the field. They'd begun to do that. The stuff we broke consists of orders for a general pullback. "They've ended their reconnaissance, David. They're going to make an all-out attack." Boland says. "How soon?" David asks. "We don't know yet, and we don't know how they're going to do it," Boland replies. "That's why they killed Breeding, to frame us now," David deduces. "We've got to stay free to break the rest of this code" David says.

Then he looks over at Joan and asks, "Is there anyone who can stop this indictment?" Cut to Hatcher walking into a night club for his "date" with Joan. They are seated and make small talk. The waiter brings their drinks. "Whos' turn is it?" Hatcher asks. "Last time it was about ten years ago." He says he's reminded of that old song, "What happened to us"? She says she lost him to the American public and he became a great man, guardian of the public wheel, to whom in his honorable cause or misdeeds …" "You?" She said she became thirty years old and and decided it was time to find a permanent mate. "But you didn't," Hatcher says. "It's true. After you it's going to be difficult," she tells him.

"I couldn't have been all bad," he says. "You were – but you spoiled me anyway," she quickly replies. He then asks her if she wants to come back to his place. "House boat, tape recorders and ghosts of medical victims. I have a new place. You might be comfortable there," she seductively offers. He kisses her hand.

Later they enter her apartment. She turns on the light and there stand Scoville and David. "Oh dear – unexpected guests," she says. "Forgive me, Andy," she says. "It's all part of the game," he says. "Well I can't help you gentlemen. I suggest you get an attorney," Hatcher tells Scoville. "There's no time for that," Scoville informs him. Hatcher walks around the chair and says, "Mr. Scoville, you may have your ideas positively reinforced by what Ms. Seeley told you, but I have some dictatorial authority in this case, well I don't. I don't like having to prosecute a man of your stature and reputation. But I'm charged by law to do so." "You're charged by law to find the truth," David says.

"Not in our system. Judges and juries find the truth. My job is to make a case and its your lawyer's job to make a better one," Hatcher explains. Scoville approaches Hatcher and asks him, "If we convince you of the danger, will you kill the indictment?"

Boland has partially cracked the code for the aliens' plan, which is to attack by using a sophisticated computer decryption program.

David and company foolishly trust the power-oriented Hatcher. Joan lures Hatcher to visit and listen to Vincent and they show Hatcher the plans they got from Koy. Hatcher pretends to be agreeable and says he will back off, but the next day he has all the believers indicted. Jill reports to David about the Hatcher betrayal.

Warrants are sworn for the believers' arrests, and Joan goes to warn them. But she also has a confrontation with Hatcher.

Meanwhile, the police arrive, just as they leave the house and Scoville is wounded, but Boland and Vincent get away. Meanwhile, reports come in that Boland and Vincent have been seen in the vicinity of Scoville's research facility. Hatcher orders the police to capture them.

Storming into his office, and blurts out, "Someday, people are going to find out the most important fact about you!" He asks, "What's that?" and she tells him, "You can't be trusted about anything. You are a liar and a cheat!" He is at his desk and brushes her off saying, "That should make good reading in the Times." She walks closer. "It will," she says to which he replies, "And it won't hurt your career any, will it?" "Is that what you think this is all about? We stand here and trade insults while the world is coming to an end?"

Hatcher stands up: "Why? Because your little squad of Believers says so? You've been brainwashed!" She tells him, "I saw them!" Then comes the conventional "gaslighting" response of an impotent male: "You THINK you've seen them." She tells him, "Andy, I saw Koy shot, and burn up, and turn into ashes in about one second flat!" He replies, "I don't believe you" as he walks toward the wall of the office (this is known as an "avoidance technique"). But she walks over to where he is.

She asks him what if he's wrong. She tells him that the grand jury hearing was a frame-up. He gets on the phone and then tells her that they are going to go "meet a Believer." He's talking about Frederickson. Hatcher takes Joan to meet Frederickson at a safe place, but when they arrive, nothing is left of Frederickson except some ashes in the bathroom. "Time is running out, Andy – call of the hunt," Joan says. Hatcher says that the ashes were a trick. "Andy – in the name of Heaven!" Hatcher gives an aide permission to send state police into the area where Vincent and the others were spotted.

The believers need a better computer than they have in their basement, so Scoville supplies a backup at a research facility. Boland is giving the instructions and David is following them. They found the transmitter: it's in the Wyndham Hotel, "right here in town," and the attack will commence tonight, "five hours from now!"

Meanwhile, Vincent and Boland crack the remainder of the aliens' invasion plan and locate a transmitter in the basement of a hotel. Joan arrives at the Scoville research facility just before the police. This white woman saves the day. She takes David's car so the cops will follow her, giving David and Boland a chance to get away. One police car with two cops in it? Give me a break.

At any rate, they take out after the car with Joan driving it. She gets cut off by another police car up the road, turns around and of course, wrecks the car. As she creates a diversion, she is injured in a car crash, allowing Vincent and Boland to escape and head for the hotel. While Vincent and Boland pose as telephone repairmen, Hatcher visits Joan in the hospital. She's bandaged up and the first words out of her mouth are an apology! He decides now, of all times, to talk about them starting all over. She claims he was the only man who ever met anything to her. It makes sense that she would die holding his hand.

Vincent and Boland scuffle with aliens after David lies and tells one of them that they are from the phone company and are there to check a wire box. They get inside and find a key control box on the wall. Hey go downstairs and are approached. "This is the generator plant," he says. They kick the suspicious aliens' ass and continue looking around the room. They find a high voltage area but no meters. They descend even further by stairway and locate a side room. Aliens come in and they hide. A shootout begins. An alien is hit, glows and dies. David shoots another one but Boland is killed. His last words are, "Tell hatcher I'll wait for him in Hell." He dies.

Vincent destroys the vital transmitter. Thereafter, Vincent meets Hatcher at the hospital, but Joan has died. Hatcher is finally convinced and promises help for

Vincent. When Hatcher asks what he can do David tells him that he can help them because the aliens are going to try to rebuild the transmitter. He says he'll do what he can.

The narrator's moral ending: "And now Andrew M. Matcher joins David Vincent in his struggle against the Invaders. Edward Scovill will recover from his wounds, and these three will be in the vanguard leading the fight against the aliens from space. Invaders who must be stopped."

And that's how the series ended: a convoluted and confusing ending promoting white unity with ne'er a mention of including the majority of the world's people – *people with skin color*. It is, as Dr. Frances Cress Welsing wrote over forty years ago and as stated earlier in this book (the point should be reinforced):

> The Color-Confrontation theory further postulates that whites are vulnerable to their sense of numerical inadequacy. This inadequacy is apparent in their drive to divide the vast majority of non-whites into fractional, as well as frictional, **minorities.** This is viewed as a fundamental behavioral response of whites to their own minority status. The white "race" has structured and manipulated their own thought processes and conceptual patterns, as well as those of the entire non-white world majority, so that the real numerical minority (whites) illusionally feels and represents itself as the world's majority, while the true numerical majority (non-whites) illusionally feels and views itself as the minority (Welsing, 1974 – emphasis original).

Again, a superior species *from another galaxy*, with all of that technology, nevertheless opts to land in the most violent, barbaric and racist nation on the face of the earth. Not only that, but chooses to adopt the human form of the worldwide racial minority and literally exclude any concerns about the history and human potential of African or Asians. But Quinn Martin is a white man and they can only write about what they know and believe. And folks: this is it!

Season 2, Episode 22: Fade to Black?

Speaking of white creative limitations and how people write about what they know and believe, check this section out.

"This particular episode of "The Invaders" has been intentionally singled out by me, this episode - Titled "The Vise" (who knows why) -- was the first episode that attempted to deal with Black issues – or should I say "negro" issues in a white system? It was also not even addressed until the second season of the show. And as I will show, it was poorly addressed, totally "whitenized" even though there were sporadic attempts to deal with issues of race (but only as it relates to merit, promotions and working in the white man's system).

Why do I call it "fade to blacks." This is a play on the term "fade to black," which in television and movie parlance means, "To end a film or a scene of a film by causing the image to disappear and become black." According to one website source, the origin of the term comes from the movie industry, where it was customary to end a scene or session of filming by closing off light to the camera, sometimes for dramatic effect, but often as a practical measure." This brings me to the reason for the analogy and juxtaposition.

The late idea to deal with race is so typical, even though during this time the country was a cauldron of racial turmoil and tumult. The series started in 1967, and a major "black breakthrough" permeated the media during that same time: The Black Power Conference in Newark, New Jersey. According to the African-American Registry website,

> On this date we mark the assembly in Newark of the first Black Power Conference. In the tradition of the antebellum African American convention movement and the early Pan-African congresses, the National Conference on Black Power was a gathering of more than 1,000 delegates representing 286 organizations and institutions from 126 cities in 26 states, Bermuda, and Nigeria. They met in Newark, NJ., from July 20 to July 23, 1967, to discuss the most pressing African American issues of the day …

Take note of the dates, and you can only imagine the impact that this had on this white nation. And that includes Hollywood and Quinn Martin Productions. Even as they were considering scripts, filming and scouting locations for each episode, they had to open up newspapers and see the concept of Black Power in full effect, from the Black Panther Party and the US organization on the west coast to groups like the Revolutionary Action Movement, the Weathermen, the Brown Beret and others, the groups that met in those rooms discussing upcoming episodes had to know that Black people all over the nation were pissed off. But in those days, unlike the "march and prayer vigil" oriented Negroes of today (except for those in Ferguson, Missouri), Black people were ready to fight. This made the role of the white media all that more important: to put shows on television that promoted whiteness and as a result, pacified the white viewer and made him/her feel "safe" from the nightly news and those "angry negroes."

In addition,

> The conference held workshops, presented papers for specific programs, and developed more than 80 resolutions calling for

emphasis of Black power in political, economic, and cultural affairs. Only one resolution, a Black Power Manifesto, won official approval, but others were adopted in "in spirit." The Manifesto condemned "neo-colonialist control" of Black populations worldwide and called for the circulation of a "philosophy of Blackness" that would unite and direct the oppressed in common cause ...

White people had to be in shock. Throughout 1967 there was but a smattering of the back presence on all the major networks. The only shows that included even a token black presence were "I Spy," "Mission: Impossible" and "Ironside" and in 1968 it didn't get much better, adding "The Mod Squad" and "Land of the Giants." White folks just didn't want the world to be anything else other than white. And "The Invaders," as I have shown, contributed to this lily-white universe that we know as "television programming." And that's not all.

And in 1968, an anthem of Black Power was powerful enough for Quinn Martin Productions to have at least offered up more on the television screen than they did. That anthem was James Brown's "Say It Loud, I'm Black and I'm Proud." As one website documents,

> "Say It Loud – I'm Black and I'm Proud" is a funk song performed by James Brown and written with his bandleader Alfred "Pee Wee" Ellis in 1968. It was released as a two-part single which held the number-one spot on the R&B singles chart for six weeks, and peaked at number ten on the *Billboard* Hot 100 … Both parts of the single were later included on James Brown's 1968 album *A Soulful Christmas* and on his 1969 album sharing the title of the song. *The song became an unofficial anthem of the Black Power movement.* (emphasis added).

All this pervasive, new found black pride and images on television of black people making threats and, unlike today, backing them up. The TV programs had to deliver a powerful whites-only message. And in 1967-68, the shows that did that were, in 1967: "The Andy Griffith Show", "Gunsmoke," "Gomer Pyle USMC," "Family Affair," "Bonanza," "Beverly Hillbillies," "Bewitched" and "The Jackie Gleason Show" , to name a few from the top 20.

In 1968, it was even more white. While a number of the previously mentioned shows repeated, add to the list "Green Acres," "the FBI," "Lassie," "My Three Sons," "Rowan and Martin Laugh-In," and "The Lucy Show." See? Even amidst all the social upheaval and gains that black people were forcing to be made, their television – the entity that is in the living room of white households – remained almost lily-white, serving not as a social engineer but more like a therapeutic catharsis.

Now we have context: we see the design and intent of American television during one of the most racially torn periods in the history of this country. White folks didn't want to see blacks on television, and that was what fed into ratings, advertising revenue and of course, profits.

Not only were there hardly any black people in the entire 1967 first season (a black butler in one episode, an occasional "negro" police officer or ambulance driver), but in this episode it appeared as if something were hastily put together and the black actors may as well have been white. The conflict between "tokenism" and "qualifications" and the battle for acceptance by the white man is at the crux of the theme of this episode. While many black people may have loved the idea of seeing two black men and a black woman in lead roles, we have the benefit of retrospect and can therefore see how insidiously insulting the entire script for this episode truly was.

Oh, and one more reason for my naming this section "Fade to Blacks," with the emphasis on "fade." The series went off the air in March of 1968, meaning that this episode, which took more than a year to materialize, was one of the last ones that ABC aired. So as interest and ratings 'faded,' so did any interest or intent on dealing with any social issues. You would think that a show addressing an attempted takeover of the world would have included more members from the worldwide majority – people of color – than it did.

Remember, the year was 1968, and this episode was aired on February 20, 1968. Just a half a year earlier as "The Invaders" was originally airing, there was the Newark riots on July 12th and then on July 23rd, came the Detroit riots, On February 8 of 1968, the same month this episode aired, there was the Orangeburg Massacre, when cops killed three college students at S. Carolina State College.

Let the analyses begin.

First, let's look at how TV.com describes the episode in its synopsis: "Racist issues arise between David Vincent and the Baxters, a black couple, when David produces evidence that another African American in line for an important position with the space program is actually an alien." Racist issues arise? This implies that black people can be racist. Racism, for one thing, implies power. If there was a racist it was Vincent; he was white, he had the government behind him, and he had the power to do almost whatever he wanted to do. In simple terms, racism can be defined as, "an ideology, a violent imposition, and an institutional arrangement."

Secondly, check out this all-star cast: Arnold Warren is played by Roscoe Lee Browne ("The Liberation of L.B. Jones," 1972; "Uptown Saturday Night," 1976; "The Connection," 1962. James Baxter is portrayed by Raymond St. Jacques ("Cotton Comes to Harlem," 1970; " "Come Back Charleston Blue," 1972; "The Sophisticated Gents," 1988). His wife on the episode, Celia Baker, was played by the beautiful Janet MacLachlan ("Sounder," 1972; "The Man," 1971; "Uptight," 1968). These three great actors dominated this episode with their acting, but their sterile and stereotyped roles left a great deal to be desired. When you have a fucked up script written by white people, what else can you expect?

Now, for the episode, "The Vise."

Gas station attendant sweeping up. Scoville and David sit and watch as an alien brings a briefcase and passes it off to the attendant. They've been watching an alien suspecting the station is a alien meeting point. Car pulls up for gas – it's the alien. He hands the attendant a brief case. He takes it. David follows him into the station. David has a gun and he and the alien fight. 'Scoville blocks the other alien's car as David kills the other one, who disintegrates. The other alien manages to get away as Scovill runs inside, and puts out a fire that was started when the previous alien burned up. David has the briefcase and gets information. A black man's photo is inside. It's a photo of Arnold Warren.

David is able to determine that the aliens have infiltrated high government circles in Washington and that one important alien Arnold Warren, who happens to be black, is about to be promoted to oversee an important space tracking project, thus facilitating alien landings. The question is why? Why would aliens who have come so close to infiltrating American institutions, labs, facilities and compounds over the years decide that they are going to transform a black war veteran into someone who can infiltrate a white racist hierarchy and do their bidding? This script has tokenism written all over it.

At any rate, standing in Warren's way is ex-policemen and now senate investigator James Baxter, also a black man. One black man pitted against another as there is an obvious attempt to play "good cop, bad cop" with white viewers lest their racism get elevated with only an "alien black" being the key.

Warren is being considered for a post in the space program, and David has reason to believe he's an alien. David has 24 hours to prove it. The Committee investigator, Baxter, meets with David for five minutes at his (Baxter's) home. David tells him about aliens and that he has info on Warren, including his background. Baxter's wife Celia and son enter the room. My wife, "Mrs. Baxter," is how he introduces her. David knows that Warren was with a military unit that "wasn't integrated until six or seven years later."

Celia, who cares about race issues, is all for Warren's promotion, as she would like to see more Black people get promoted, but she doesn't know Warren is an alien. At the same time, she recalls when the army was integrated – but her husband didn't know. Warren lied about his role in the army, and Baxter confronts Warren. Warren says he was a cook in the army, having worked in a field kitchen. Baxter has his doubts, and just in time his wife pulls up in the car and blows horn for him. "I hope that clears everything up," Warren says as he leaves in his car. Baxter gets in his car after Celia scoots over so that he can drive. He's still not satisfied. "I didn't mention Vincent – they did," he tells her. Even when he's not there, David is the topic of discussion.

In the meantime, David is calling Scoville. Aliens in car see him in phone booth. David walks to flag down a cab, and the aliens attempt to run him over. He dives out of the way, and the car gets away. Celia has a lot of questions about the report being ready. "Heading up that tracking station is a pretty important job for a negro isn't it?" she asks. Her husband says, "Just because he's negro, I'm not going to white wash it." Whitewash it?

Their son, Michael, comes in and Celia, trying to make a racial point, asks him who the best baseball player is. Michael says, "Willie Mays." She then asks him who the best football player is. The child says "Gale Sayers." Then she sends him off to bed and turns to her husband: "He needs heroes – black ones" she says. But of course, just because someone can hit or catch a baseball or football doesn't make them a hero in one's eyes except for white people and sick negroes. Speaking of sick negroes, her husband then shouts to the kid, "Hey Michael, who throws the football better than anyone else.? The kid says, "Johnny Unitas." He proved is point I suppose. His wife is conscious and he's a tom. He has to ask her, "Now what was your point, Celia?"

This is the kind of shit that only a team of white writers (with token black input) could create and concoct and then put it on the television screen as a sign of being "progressive." We have to remember that when white boys set all these records the various sports leagues were just getting out of racial segregation so there were very few black people. And when the records were actually set, there were NONE. This is especially true for football and basketball. There should be an asterisk by the names of these charlatans, white athletes who benefitted because there were no black men to compete against.

Back to the episode.

The doorbell rings. It's David. David is grilling Baxter and feeding him intel (information) at the same time. There is a plant at River Road, and he wants Baxter to meet him in the south parking lot at 10:00 tonight. David and Baxter meet in high rise office, but find out that Scoville isn't coming. But they do have him on closed circuit television monitor. He's in Syracuse, and when he asks Baxter why he came back Baxter replies, "The trusting part of me tells me to keep an open mind; the cynical part says I should give you enough rope to hang yourselves." What? Baxter continues: "Call it a cop's intuition, call it what you want. There's always been something about Warren that didn't quite jibe." Scoville interrupts; "...something that wasn't human…"

It gets worse. After explaining that aliens don't bleed, we find that two years earlier, Warren was on a job in South America. There was an explosion, and 18 men were cut up. Warren didn't bleed. The natives called him, "the man who couldn't bleed." Scoville flashes a picture of Warren and Baxter catches it. "Look at his hand and look at mine," he tells David and Scoville. "The palms of his hands are much darker. I never saw a black man like that before," Baxter says. What the fuck?! This is 1967 and these people are still walking about the shade or color of black people's palms?

Baxter's stupidity apparently knows no bounds. We find that there is a regeneration station near a place where Warren is scheduled to go fishing. David and Scoville want to postpone the hearing, but Baxter is doubtful. He's tired of all the doubting. He says, "If, if, if. If I had a hundred legs I'd be the Rockettes." What?? This white script has a black man using, as an analogy, the legs of white women who dance. There are three types of assimilation: structural (joining institutions), marital (marrying into the white race), and cultural (accepting and buying into white norms and values). It is clear that Baxter, as reflected in the lines that white screenwriters handed him, is guilty of all three.

Here comes more racism. We find that Celia's brother was killed. David asks, "Vietnam War?" Baxter, her husband, says, "no, the one in this country – Detroit." The riots in Detroit had taken place in real life just the year before, and was one of the bloodiest in American history. The riot, referred to as the 12th Street Riot, started after some cops harassed some black people outside of a bar called The Blind Pig. Brothers started lighting cops up and cops ran and came back with the National Guard. The result was 43 dead, 1,189 injured, over 7,200 arrests, and more than 2,000 buildings destroyed. By comparison and in retrospect, the scale of the riot was surpassed in the United States only by the 1863 New York City draft riots during the U.S. Civil War, and the 1992 Los Angeles riots.

The point here is that the writers had the wherewithal to mention the Detroit riots, but didn't have the cultural compunction to feature any black people in "The Invaders" series in 1967 and only one time in 1968.

At any rate, Baxter calls some senator and informs him of the delay in the Warren hearings. He says, "I know what I said senator – I hate to throw a monkey wrench into it." Celia is eavesdropping and is pissed and goes to the bedroom and locks the door. David goes to visit Warren's father, pretending to be a reporter doing a story on his son. "So you ask me any old thing you have a mind to," the old man tells David. David gets the background information he needs and leaves the old man sitting on the porch.

Aliens are listening in. Elsewhere Warren comes to Baxter's office to find out what's wrong. Warren asks if there is anything he can do because he's going fishing over the weekend (in reality, he's going off to get a re-charge in one of those alien regeneration chambers). Baxter says no and Warren replies that it seems to him that "you're not being very loyal to your race." Baxter snaps back, "What race is that – negro or HUMAN?" There's a pause and Warren exits.

What? Why would an obvious Uncle Tom like Warren bring up race loyalty? At no time is he shown living anywhere near or saying anything about the plight of black people. In fact, the mentioning of the Detroit riots is the only reference to a black event in the whole one-hour episode. Then, for Baxter to counter what "race" Warren was referring to is more evidence that this script must have been written by some suburban white boys who believe they know something about "the negro condition."

Racial inferences continue as two cops walk up to David's car and as one would have in this "salt and pepper" episode, one of them is black and the other one is white. The fact is, they are both aliens. Again, why? Why would these technologically superior extraterrestrials give a shit about integration? Why would they take time to add color to the synthetic skin of one of their people so that they can "blend in" when the society they are trying to take control of or destroy shows no concern about improving race relations?

As can be expected, the black cop is shot and burns up. The other one – the white one – reports by his communications device, "Vincent got away." That evening Baxter comes home and Celia has more questions and wants to know what's going on . When he tries to explain about the record, he repeats his idiotic observation regarding the color of Warren's palms and she goes off. "The color of his skin? If this were a white man you wouldn't' be saying such a thing!" She continues: "You're playing whitey, trying to find any little thing just so you can prove you're better than he is." But you can't convince and Uncle Tom when he's in the wrong. Her husband replies, "Well I am better." As evidence of his trials and racial tribulations he explains that he mows the lawn twice a week so their house can look better. "You want black heroes. Fine. I want them too, But I want real heroes with no flaws." What???

Let me explain something right here. What was just described is a classic case of the "negro" mentality. In his speech on "The Black Revolution," Malcolm X taught long ago that, "This modern house Negro loves his master. He wants to live near him. He'll pay three times as much as the house is worth just to live near his master, and then brag about "I'm the only Negro out here." "I'm the only one on my job." "I'm the only one in this school." Bragging about mowing a lawn when you're paying as much (or more) for your house as your white 'neighbor' pays for his is the epitome of self-hatred and anglophilia as far as I'm concerned.

Celia, getting increasingly pissed, fires back, "So we've got to run faster just to stay in the same place, is that it?" And her bootlicking husband looks his wife in the eyes and says, "Yes, that's it." And do you wonder why black women, over the years, have assumed increasingly stronger roles in the family and have gradually shown a disrespect and disdain for black men? These are the kinds of "niggers" that most blacks deem "successful" and yet look at how they think and more importantly, look at what they (don't) do.

Cut to David is running down an alley. What kind of episode that features blacks would it be without an "alley" or two? The cops see him, so he hides behind some boxes. After eluding them for the time being, he enters the back door of a place called Ollie's. It's a black club, of course – the first one we've seen in a year and a half of David sitting, drinking and conversing in bars all over the nation. As can be expected, there is only a small clientele sitting around looking stupid and getting fucked up – par for the course.

David asks to use the phone and calls Baxter's house. Celia answers the phone and immediately hangs up on him after saying 'wrong number' obviously trying to keep David away from her husband.

After that she takes the phone off the hook. So here is a black man trying to save the world against aliens and the one person who is working with him calls the house. This black bitch, pissed because her husband is an Uncle Tom, decides to sabotage the safety of the world so she can make a point. The fact is, David needed help and was calling to tell Baxter that he was pinned down by cops.

Ollie (Lou Gossett) is the bartender and owner of the bar that David is now "trapped" in. Cops all over the place outside the bar, as is the case when you have an episode about black people and a bar is a part of the setting. David looks outside. Ollie gives him change and orders a beer. While at the cash register, Ollie slips gun in his belt. In the meantime the aliens are bringing the regeneration machine for Warren. At Baxter's house Celia is at the sewing machine, and Baxter is nervously waiting to hear from David. "Do you have to run that thing?" he asks. Now check out her answer: "Yes, if you want Michael to have some clothes to wear." What???

Some clothes to wear? This bitch lives in the suburbs, her husband makes good money and she's still making clothes for her kid? This is that "mammy" perception that white writers have of black women. I'm surprised they didn't have her on the back porch with a scrub board singing, "Jesus Lifted Me"!

Baxter knows David was supposed to call. As he paces through the house he finds phone off the hook and confronts Celia about it. He assumes it was Michael, and Celia, manipulative as can be, tells him, "If it was important he'll call back." Now comes the statement that establishes the depth of Baxter's Uncle Tomfoolery.

He tells Celia, "I don't think you know what you married. I'm a cop. I'm a guy who's trying to keep the lid on. And that's all I'm doing now."

Keep the lid on? Why don't you start by talking to some of those racist colleagues of yours who keep gunning down black people? They were doing in 1968 during the airing of this episode and today, in 2015 they're still doing it: kids killed by cops include 16-year old Kimani Gray (New York), 16 year old Tavares McGill (Florida), 25 year old Aaron Campbell (Portland), 18 ear old Erven Jefferson (Atlanta), 22 year old Oscar Grant (Oakland) and how about Timothy Russell and Melissa Williams, who were killed in Cleveland after cops pumped 137 rounds into their car? Baxter couldn't keep the lid on then, and the cops are out of control (lid thrown away) to this very day.

While Celia's in the kitchen fixing him a sandwich, Baxter gets his revolver out of the desk drawer and leaves the house. She's talking her ass off in the other room trying to make a date and adds, "It seems like a million years since we've had some time together, you know?" She realizes he's gone and notices that he's left the drawer open and now she knows he has his gun.

We learn that Ollie doesn't want his place busted. He tells David "I've got a sign out there that says I've got the right to refuse anybody. You look like anybody to me. Now split!" This is the first time a black man has stood up to Vincent, but never fear – the bootlicking is on the way (as it is in any white-written script). David lies and tells Ollie that he killed a cop and asks Ollie to call the police station and send some cops there. He claims that there is a reward.

Ollie locks David in the store room in the back, and gets on the pay phone (why? Doesn't he have a business phone?). Alien cops come in and look around. Ollie finds out that those badge numbers don't fit. The aliens locate David and they walk him to the hallway and search him.

One young brother comes forward from the bar and tells the cops that they have to advise David of his rights. Ollie comes out with a gun and orders them to "leave that man alone." "You ain't no cops. You're even wearing phony badges," Ollie says. Two black men save Vincent's life. Ollie tells David he can leave. "Everything's copacetic," he informs Vincent. David runs out back door as Ollie is forced to shoot an alien cop. David flees out the back door and runs right into Celia who is coming down the alley in the car. (What timing). He jumps into the driver's side as she slides over. Alien cop dies in front of her. David and Celia take off.

Let's look at this. First of all, she's audaciously disregarding her husband's job and role to fight aliens. Secondly, she's in her car, but when Vincent runs into the alley and spots her, she immediately scoots over for him – the same way she did for her husband in an earlier scene. Remember, readers: this shit is *scripted,* and what is being done is the way that white people believe it should be.

The alien Warren is about to give his speech as David pulls up outside a building and leaves Celia in the car. Warren is weakening. He prepares to get on the set, give a quick speech, and then to the regeneration chamber. David and Baxter are together as Baxter orders wife back into car and he and David join her. Now they are a team of three but at this point, it seems as if Celia is calling the shots. But don't worry: any sign of black audacity is immediately squashed by the scriptwriters.

Here comes the van with the regeneration equipment on board. Warren aide goes out to meet it and orders them to be ready in fifteen minutes. "The regeneration station came to him," David tells Baxter and Celia.

Next, check out the following dialogue:

> Baxter: It won't be easy with just the two of us.
> Celia: Three of us! Jim, please I fought you so long on this, let me help you now.
> Baxter: No, you're out of it and that's final.
> Celia: But the two of you can't do it alone.
> Baxter: Then it won't get done.
> Celia: David, you talk to him. Tell him nothing will happen to me.
> David: I'm not going to lie to you.
> Baxter: We can handle it ourselves, can't we?
> David: I'm not going to lie to you, either.
> Celia: Well, now that you've talked me into it, there's just one thing: somebody's going to have to tell me what to do.

Ain't that a bitch? She talked all that shit, told those lies, and acts as if she's so pro-black and what does she do when the chips are down? She says, "Well, now that you've talked me into it, there's just one thing: somebody's going to have to tell me what to do." Up to this point nobody told her what to do; she made her own decisions to confront her husband, to hang up the phone on David, to take that phone off the hook and allow her kid to be blamed, to get in the car and inadvertently bail David's ass off the hook. But now she's a "defenseless little female" who has to be told what to do? This is bullshit!

The aliens are hooking the van up to power grid outside and are charging the regeneration chamber in preparation for Warren. Celia exits car and goes inside the station. Her jobs is to engage Warren in conversation when she gets the chance. When Warren is off the air, she approaches him and claims to be a columnist and wants to talk to interview him. Outside of the studio, Baxter is stereotypically pretending to be a drunk nigga. He asks one of the aliens, "You seen my car? A red convertible." Yeah, white boys: a red convertible like most niggas prefer.

After his stalling tactic, Baxter knocks out an alien, and David gets the other one. Celia sits with Warren and continues to stall him. But alas, Warren recognizes her. She runs but gets caught. David fights an alien while Baxter and Celia run for the car. Baxter has Warren and an aide at gunpoint. Baxter gets caught off guard (as can be expected), and Warren is getting gradually weak. Baxter shoots him in the back and also shoots the alien that was kicking David's ass. The last remaining alien abandons Warren and escapes with the regeneration van.

Washington DC. hearings in progress. Testimony is over. Technicians and Baxter both testify. Celia, still engaging in wishful thinking, says that she hopes that whomever they appoint to take Baxter's place "will be a negro."

So why is the name of the episode, "The Vise." I believe it was because of the squeeze that Vincent and Baxter combined to put on Warren. A black man and a white man teaming up to oust and then eventually kill another black man. And we are led to believe that aliens would send a black man to infiltrate a lily-white hierarchy. Again, this is what happens when white scripts get into black hands. In May 2005. Dave Chapelle walked out when white boys wanted him to wear a dress in one of his skits. Their job (white screen and scriptwriters) is to humiliate, degrade and stereotype us every chance they get. This episode of "The Invaders" was simply one more example.

DAVID VINCENT: THE PERSONIFICATION OF 'WHITE PRIVILEGE'

To far too many white folks, the world IS white, in spite of the fact that, as a racial grouping, they are a shriveling minority of the people on this planet. But you would never be able to tell this when you turn on the television dial: they are all over the place, from reporting the news and broadcasting sporting events, to starring in daytime soap operas and later-night talk shows.

For those of you who can't figure it out, "white privilege" is defined as, "White privilege (or white skin privilege) is a term for societal privileges that benefit white people in Western countries beyond what is commonly experienced by non-white people under the same social, political, or economic circumstances." According to McIntosh, whites in a society considered culturally a part of the Western World enjoy advantages that non-whites do not experience. She goes on to describe the "daily effects of white privilege" that "as far as I can tell, my African American co-workers, friends and acquaintances...cannot count on most of these conditions."Here are a few of the more than 100 examples provided by

Macintosh. My views of each and application of how they apply to David Vincent in his battle to expose "The Invaders" will filter in and out:

> 1. I can if I wish arrange to be in the company of people of my race most of the time.

In the white man's world (or at least his version of it), the Caucasian racial group exists even in the far reaches of outer space, even while occupying but a small minority here on planet Earth. With a mindset like this, how can you not help but understand and venture to capitalize on the concept of "white privilege." David Vincent did throughout the series and the aliens, while occupying Caucasian-looking bodies, did the very same thing. In both cases, entering and exiting, coming and going as they please, were everyday realities that both the aliens and David Vincent took full advantage of.

> 2. I can avoid spending time with people whom I was trained to mistrust and who have learned to mistrust my kind or me.

This is true of most people, but David Vincent took it one step further; throughout the series you will find him interacting, cutting deals and even befriending the aliens. And since this book makes it clear that there were no people of color in any of the episodes other than two, it is clear that white skin becomes a literal "cultural universal."

Before this allegation is lambasted as being stereotypical, merely look at how the American white man deals with his enemies if they are also white, and then look at how, today in 2017, the overwhelming majority of American's enemies are either brown or black. Even Russia, who they claim to hate, is being treated with kid gloves even after having sabotaged an American presidential election. Being "trained to mistrust" those who mistrust the white race was a recurring theme on "The Invaders." Though white, they were able to become a part of American life through the skillful manipulation of white privilege and Vincent apparently resented it.

Moving on:

> 3. If I should need to move, I can be pretty sure of renting or purchasing housing in an area which I can afford and in which I would want to live.

This is another recurring theme on a number of levels throughout "The Invaders" series. As already mentioned, David Vincent traveled anywhere he wanted to and if you notice, in most cases it was some lily white rural, suburban or urban area where he very rarely ran into any people of color. In fact, the aliens must have known this about the American way of life and therefore set up shop in areas where there would be no "colored" interference.

The concept of "freedom" has to have something to do with being able to go anywhere you want to go as long as you're not impeding on anyone else. And it is for this very reason why black people have always been "controlled" in a number of ways. Whether you are talking about redlining, steering and restrictive covenants when it comes to where they could live, rent or buy housing, or the "racial profiling" that continues to be practiced and imposed during travel, it is clear that David Vincent never had to undergo any of these obstacles. And neither did the Caucasian-appearing aliens. As a result "social activity" or movement were allowable and, in fact, anticipated.

> 4. I can be pretty sure that my neighbors in such a location will be neutral or pleasant to me.

David Vincent moved around too much to have any "neighbors", per se. But that white skin sure enabled him to make "friends" and "pals" with some powerful people, even those from his "pre-invader" past. He was tight with generals, political figures, corporate leaders and so forth. Some of them end up being alien impersonating humans, but how would David know: they were all white! He told Dr. Lindstrom in the second episode that he knew the aliens better than the astrophysicist did, and yet in every episode he (Vincent) gets duped or fooled because of the white skin issue, a built-in key to "social acceptance."

Continuing:

> 5. I can go shopping alone most of the time, pretty well assured that I will not be followed or harassed.

Vincent was continually harassed and followed, but it wasn't because of his skin color – it was because he was sticking his nose in the aliens' business and they were trying to kill his ass! White privilege means shopping alone even when you walk into a gun shop and order thirty or forty rifles the way that white boy, 64-year-old Stephen Paddock did before he shot up those people in Las Vegas on Sunday, October 1st.

Now you tell me any incident of a black man not being "followed" when he's shopping for a gun? Purchasing bullets? Hell, a black man is being followed around Wal-Mart, Best-Buy and Costco while shopping for a pair of draws! I think you get the point. And this point is why the aliens were able to infiltrate corporations, businesses and political systems all over the place – they were white and they acted that way. This gave them a veritable "license to kill" just like another black man, James Bond, is able to secure by working for a group of British white folks.

> 6. I can turn on the television or open to the front page of the paper and see people of my race widely represented.

Although the aliens kept a low profile and because Vincent could never secure any physical evidence of their existence, there is no doubt that they learned about this planet and about the history of white people through their scouting and research abilities. They knew who to look like, who to imitate and where to infiltrate. Their version of "reading the papers" may have been far more advanced, but it is clear that anyone black who picks up a newspaper or turns on the television is going to see white people in every section (except for sports). And when you DO see a black person, the role he occupies or the part he's playing is not worthy of emulation.

The key is that "wide representation" by these white humans is a defense mechanism to cover up what Dr. Frances Cress Welsing refers to "deep-seated feelings of genetic inferiority and numerical inadequacy." Simmel (1907), for one, wrote in his book *The Philosophy of Money*, that money is the ultimate confounding of things. Among the things it can do is make the small look large and the weak appear strong. America is a capitalist society and white folks control the capital which also controls the media. This means that what constitutes "news" and "information" is totally under their control.

The benefits of "white privilege" and how they apply to David Vincent and the masquerading aliens continues:

> 7. When I am told about our national heritage or about "civilization," I am shown that people of my color made it what it is.

It doesn't matter if the white child or adult is "told" about being the key to the creation of civilization or not, the institutions of America are going to make sure that the information is ingrained and imparted into every single child's mind in the educational system, which makes the concept of "compulsory education" synonymous with "mandatory brainwashing."

When black people fought to get into those schools they were fighting to be there because they felt that the education they were receiving was "inferior." Perhaps that was the case; but the one that was waiting in the so-called "public school system" was even more devastating and harmful to the black psyche. How else to explain all these sellouts, Uncle Toms and potential corporate quislings walking around college and university campuses and all these confused millennials in high school and middle school, confused into thinking that they are "Americans" and that indeed, despite the white man's on-going messages to the contrary, that "black lives matter" and "black votes matter." How confused can one racial grouping be?

But this is how the myth of white superiority has been globalized and institutionally circulated. And that is what the aliens played upon, why they were able to say the right things, look the right way and infiltrate the right institutions in their quest to come to this planet and take it over from the white humans that had already attempted to do so!

A related fact regarding "white privilege" follows:

8. I can be sure that my children will be given curricular
    materials that testify to the existence of their race.

When you are the recipient and beneficiary of white privilege, this privilege is automatically extended to your children, hence the institutional circulation of the myth of white superiority articulated earlier. These white people know what they're doing because what they did in order to mass produce and distribute this myth was again used in the reverse to simultaneously circulate the myth that any person of color was inferior to any white person, be that person black, brown, red or yellow.

Interestingly enough, this was one of the major flaws in the thinking of the aliens. They went after and imitated white adults and in none of the episodes were children affected. In real life the white race went after the children and the women, the latter being the carrier of the seed of life. Then they tortured and killed off the men so that black women would have scarce resources to choose from. Today if you look around, increasing numbers of sistahs are dating outside of the race and it is for good reason: black men are either on the down-low, outright gay, locked up in prison or being gunned down by cops or each other.

The curricular materials are a reflection of the attitude and ideology of the system that requires that such one-sided bullshit be circulated. It is then endorsed by people who are deemed educated and credentialed, but who nevertheless subscribe to the tenets. Can you imagine how many people and committees sat together and mutually agreed that "Little Black Sambo" was required reading for all kindergartners? How long did it take to circulate curricular lies such as Columbus discovered America, George Washington never told a lie, and

Pocahontas was not a victim of statutory rape by a white boy but indeed, fell madly in love with this strange white man? And the list goes on and on.

And the curricula is global in its impact. The myth of "Sinter Klaus and Black Pete" is circulated all over Holland and Norway and has landed in the public schools of America as well. In case you don't know, Sinter Klaus is known as Santa Clause in the Americas, but Black Pete is his sidekick in most cultures. If the children are good Sinter Klaus brings them presents and goodies; but if they've been bad, Black Pete beats the shit out of them with a birch rod. And black Pete is this little dark re d devil-looking creature who rides a black mule while Sinter Klaus is on a white horse.

In comparison, "The Invaders" was a televised version of a similar form of "education." The show draws on white supremacy and mythology and then creates a belief that white people have long held: that they are the victims of jealous intergalactic aliens who are coming to Earth to do to them what they did to us. This is one of their major recurring themes in movies like, "Independence Day," "War of the Worlds", "The Day the Earth Stood Still," "They Live," "Invasion of the Body Snatchers," "Men in Black," "Pacific Rim," "Signs," "The Blob" and so many, many others. Just as the myth of the white female's universal desirability and beauty is circulated and accepted, the belief that Earth is a mecca for aliens in galaxies far away is also a show stopper. Whoever pitched the idea for "The Invaders" knew what they were doing.

> 9. I can do well in a challenging situation without being called
>   a credit to my race.

This may be a unique one. But in certain respects, this was one of the more subtle themes of the show. David Vincent, as are most "heroes" who are white, is portrayed as being fearless, courageous and intelligent. His only vices appear to be women and cigarette smoking, more of the latter than the former. This portrayal of this "lone wolf" white man is an integral part of white literature when, in reality, the white male is more likely to attack in mobs, crazed crowds or as some organized cadre of racists. White history, whether you are talking about the Roman empire, the U.S. cavalry, today's military or some mob marching for "white rights," the reality is the antithesis of the lone wolf image.

On the show David Vincent is admired for her persistence but nevertheless considered a "nut" by many humans that he comes into contact with. But by the end of each episode he was managed to "win over" one or two people who indeed, consider him a credit to his race – the HUMAN race.

> 10. I am never asked to speak for all the people of my racial
>   group.

And yet each and every week Vincent is a self-appointed "ambassador" for the entire human race. That translates to mean for "all white people" since in their culture and literature THEY represent the entire human race. All other people are deemed inferior, subhuman or as they continue to name us, "minorities."

Nobody authorized Vincent to do the things he did. He was on his "quest" because he believed in what he was doing. He never had to report to a job because he was an architect. Where did he get the money from to finance his escapade? Who knows? But one thing is for sure: he was convinced that he represented the views of the entire human race and as the television show progressed, increasing numbers of aliens read about him and feared him even though it was clear he was alone.

In a related matter,

> 11. I can criticize our government and talk about how much I
>   fear its policies and behavior without being seen as a
>   cultural outsider.

Throughout the series, David Vincent criticized the government for its laxity and narrow vision. And yet he fought tooth and nail to meet with government officials, both on the mainland and at an international conference in his quest to spread the word. He was able to win over a number of government officials and in fact, it appeared as if he was the one giving the orders in many cases. But this is how white supremacy works: rank and titles are just a façade; the most important thing is skin color (or lack thereof) and cultural background (Anglo).

Vincent was no cultural outsider because he had light colored hair and blue eyes. He was white in the truest sense of the word, which is why he was able to win over those who originally doubted his sanity. But again, because of his colorlessness, he was able to get the benefit of the doubt and as the final few episodes make clear, attained the necessary contacts and networks to get to a major body and present his case.

> 12. I can be pretty sure that if I ask to talk to the "person in
>   charge", I will be facing a person of my race.

This is one component of "white privilege" that was apparent in every episode of "The Invaders" including the only one that featured black people. As in American life when you scale up the ladder far enough, there will be a peckerwood in waiting. It's known as a racial hierarchy and it is a concept that most black people don't understand. Black people believe that if they see a black with a title like "mayor," "undersecretary," "councilman" or even "president", that this means that this person has the final decision making power. That is not correct.

These kinds of people are merely window dressing, token appointments or some kind of patronage anointing mainly used to appease larger groups of people of color. The white race knows that no person of color is ever going to have ultimate decision making power, even if elected president. President Barack Obama wasn't a passive person, but he was "controlled" and he knew it. But to black people, dark skin is better than "the other." But most don't understand that "white doesn't represent a color, it represents a mentality that is anti-black" (Karenga, 1967). And that is why so many dark-hued people can be as anti- black and harmful to the race as any white man.

> 13. If a traffic cop pulls me over or if the IRS audits my tax return, I can be sure I haven't been singled out because of my race.

David Vincent was the victim of a number of traffic stops by police officers who were really aliens. This was an example of a white man being "profiled," and the "race" was "human." Vincent never had to worry about being "singled out" because the aliens began to learn who he was and where he was headed in almost every episode.

Being "singled out" is far easier when you are one of the few who dares to stand for something. That is why it was so easy to execute Malcolm X, Martin Luther King Jr., and any others. It was because black people have a "messiah complex" and the white man knew it. Even J. Edgar Hoover, as freaky as he was, issued an edict to his agents that their main concern during the 1960s was to "prevent the rise of a messiah." This singularity of leadership tendency was one of the major flaws of the movement. White folks in power knew that if you cut off the head (or control it), the tail will follow. That's why so many of our leaders ended up selling out, being imprisoned or getting killed off.

> 14. I can easily buy posters, post-cards, picture books, greeting cards, dolls, toys and children's magazines featuring people of my race.

It is clear that the aliens had done their "recon" on Earth activities and values before deciding to land in America. They knew how egocentric these white people were and as a result the aliens that were sent were always physically put together with nary an ailment. By the white Earthlings' standards they were prototypes. And this is related to the previous statement on "white privilege" on an important respect.

The television show itself had to be one that centered on white physicality. Although there are no real scenes where David Vincent is shown working out, he is nevertheless in tip top shape with endless energy and an ability to fight that appears based more on wit and the mastery or any martial art. Because this image is important, the posters and picture books are secondary. What is of PRIMARY importance is the message: an average white man with no prior investigative or combat experience can nevertheless overpower stronger aliens with superior weaponry and t technology. With such a white supremacist message, the pictures, dolls and toys are nothing more than support mechanisms, the aesthetic support needed to buttress the ideology itself.

> 15. My culture gives me little fear about ignoring the
>   perspectives and powers of people of other races.

This is another dimension of "The Invaders" that white viewers need not have worried about: no episode addressed the issue of race relations on Earth. Nothing about black people rioting, civil rights or white earth racism. Other than a single episode, which was laughable at best, there were no blacks of any importance anywhere in Vincent's life or his plans. In simpler terms, "The Invaders" was about as lily-white as a TV program, even in America, can get.

In light of this fact, as far as the aliens and their focus was concerned, and as far as David Vincent's lack of cultural competency was concerned, there were no "other races" to give consideration to. In a couple of episodes, as I've discussed, there was an international conference and in the lobby area a few black people dressed in African garb were shown congregating but played no major role in the episodes. In the same way that the early movies used white men and women and made them up to appear Asian, Native American and Mexican, it is clear that the so-called Africans in these two episodes were just black people from America clad in dashikis and kufas.

Moving right along:

> 16. I can chose blemish cover or bandages in "flesh" color and
>   have them more or less match my skin.

This was the glaring concern regarding skin color and one that continues to skim right over the heads of people all over America as these aliens both directly and indirectly make it clear that the only race that is of worth is the one with the pink skin. The "flesh" colored crayon was in the boxes that I was exposed to as a kindergartner in Hastings, Nebraska and we referred to it as such. Of course you had to have access to the large 64-crayon box to see it, but the kids whose parents could afford it saw it loud and clear.

The same way with band-aids that are known as "flesh colored." But this is a potential teaching moment that I cannot let get away from me. Follow me for a moment back to the morning of December 14, 2016, when two women appeared on "CBS This Morning" to talk about a new business they had started, a business geared toward re-defining the term "flesh" and what it meant as a color designation. This is a concern that I have stressed for over two decades so the question is, what took them so long?

At any rate,

> Finding the right shade of clothing or makeup that matches the skin tone can be a challenge for women. But two recent Harvard Business School graduates, working from their kitchen table, are hoping to change how the retail industry sees and sells to women of all skin colors. (Oliver, 2016).

I'm not one to knock creativity as I'm an innovator myself. But the concept of "the right shade of clothing" and "skin color" doesn't seem to jibe with me unless the woman wants to appear to be "naked." Why would that be the case? Aren't they the ones who have historically complained that men see them as "objects" and "sex toys"? Are you telling me that they want to be seen as butt naked and enticing – and then when the man responds to it they can shout rape or charge him with sexual assault. Today in 2016, that appears to be the game.

According to the story about these two incredible women, "The problem, according to entrepreneurs Nancy Madrid and Atima Lui, has been fashion's limited range in the color nude, reports Meg Oliver of CBS News' digital network, CBSN." (Oliver, 2016). The women have the right general idea but it is clear that they are avoiding the fundamental reasoning for the existence of this issue: white racism.

Their concerns should have been evident as they walked the campus of Harvard University, a Latina and a dark-skinned woman from Sudan. As they sat in on their classes in the Harvard Business School, they had to notice lily-whiteness of it all; hell, it's in a system known as the "Ivy" league. But by limiting their scope to fashion, they can avoid some of the racist realities that they would inevitably tackle – and lose at attempting to conquer. But along the way they make some errors when it comes to attribution:

"We are the first to tackle this problem for fashion," Madrid said. "When you were growing up, what did the color nude mean to you?" Oliver asked. "It definitely meant beige. I have a lot of stories of wearing beige, nude hosiery and just having ashy legs," Lui said. (Oliver, 2016).

These two women are not "the first to tackle the problem" for fashion. They are the first ones to emphasize the issue of skin color, but black people have always fought against the white aesthetic and along the way, created a kind of "cultural aesthetic" of our own. So the foundation and the concern for recognition were always there; the belief in the need to define ourselves was laid out in early African-American history. So they are wrong on the "first" aspect of their endeavor. They are the beneficiaries of proud people who came before them, black and Latino, and they should pay homage to that fact.

But more specifically, the issue of the color "nude." When asked what it meant to her when she was growing up, the African sister says that, "it definitely meant beige." To tell the truth, the concept of "beige" is actually flattering to white people: they ASPIRE for that color because it is a synonym for "tan," another color in the coloring box. The sun tan industry is a billion dollar a year enterprise, and what white folks want is to darken that pale, pasty white skin and get it to the point where it appears "beige." But what they get is a shade of orange, what we artists would refer to as a "Portland Orange" or perhaps "Cadmium." Look at Donald Trump's skin color and you'll see what I mean. It's a long way from being beige.

While promoting these "color types" of "flesh" and "nude," the white man and woman nevertheless have combined to make the skin tanning industry a multi-billion dollar enterprise. They risk skin cancer and come out a shade of orange that is akin to the tone of President Donald Trump. How can you seek and admire skin color for yourself and then take vacations to islands that are filled with black and brown people (Virgin Islands, Puerto Rico, Tahiti, other parts of the Caribbean) but drive home to a suburban home in a lily-white community and call black people in this country "niggers" and Mexicans "spics"?

The final example of "white privilege" offered herein, follows:

> 17. I have no difficulty finding neighborhoods where people approve of our household.

In simpler terms, white folks are white in a society that re=wards whiteness. If you don't believe it ask yourself this simple question; how many time have you come across someone in a decision making position who was so stupid, you just knew they got the job because they were white?

A key part of this is believing anything positive you hear about white folks and only doubting when it is extremely negative. This brings us to The Invaders" and the premise that this white man, who is basically talented but jobless, can nevertheless afford to travel all over the nation and seen internationally, to chase down aliens and, in the process, stay in the best hotels and motels and, when he needs to, find a job and money is never an object. Again, to quote from a narration from the episode, "The Peacemaker," "For two years, David Vincent has been waging war on two fronts. One against the aliens, the second an attempt to enlist allies in high places – while there is still time."

And while engaging in this 60-minute televised fantasy about "fighting alien invasions" take place in living rooms all over America, keep in mind that right outside of their windows, on the front pages of the newspapers and on the evening news, Black people, in real life, were rising up against *real* invaders and were burning the country down and demanding equal rights.

A key point to remember, as it relates to white privilege in general and David Vincent, in particular, is, "Power from unearned privilege can look like strength when it is in fact permission to escape or to dominate (McIntosh, 2010: p. 175). And that is what most white people, directly or indirectly tend to do. The ones who claim not to are still guilty because they do nothing about the ones who do exploit their whiteness overtly. So they opt for the covert method and pretend as if they've "earned" what they have.

So now we come to David Vincent and the Invaders.

To begin with, these aliens had to know something about white privilege and how it works. Whose racial characteristics did they adopt? Who do they imitate and which nation do they come to in order to take over the world? They come to Americas, a place where white privilege pays and where white people can run around with relative ease, limited restrictions, purchase properties and infiltrate the highest ranks of office, and never get found out. And why is that? Because they're white, that's why!

And here's something that the "eracism" and "I'm colorblind" people need to pay close attention to:

> Disapproving of the systems won't be enough to change them. I was taught to think that racism would end if white individuals changed their attitudes. [But] a "white" skin in the United States opens many doors for whites whether or not we approve of the way dominance has been conferred on us. Individual acts can paliate, but cannot end, these problems (McIntosh, 2010: p. 176).

The point goes deeper than just the fact that white skin opens up doors for white people; hell, as far as I can see they own the doors and the house anyway. My point is that they lie about the fact that the door is open to people regardless of race, creed or color, and then turn around and hire pit bulls and beast-like cops to not only make sure the door stays closed to people of color, but to make sure that those people don't have enough resources to build a house of their own! Racism is more than just disdain for people because of their race – it's also a violent imposition and an institutional arrangement.

McIntosh, though on the right track, makes another erroneous assumption about the power and pervasiveness of white privilege in the following paragraph:

> It seems to me that obliviousness about white advantage, like obliviousness about male advantage, is kept strongly inculturated in the United States so as to maintain the myth of meritocracy, the myth that democratic choice is equally available to all. Keeping most people unaware that freedom of confident action is there for just a small number of people props up those in power, and serves to keep power in the hands of these same groups that have most of it already (McIntosh, 2010: p. 176).

Again, it's not just about the myth of meritocracy. It's about a more blatant and sinister reality: if you're white, there's a place for you. When she writes that, "Keeping most people unaware that freedom of confident action is there for just a small number of people props up those in power, and serves to keep power in the hands of these same groups that have most of it already," she is missing an essential point. Group identification is not just for the "white few;" it is something that the "white majority" can feed off of culturally, socially, politically, economically, ideologically, legally, and even morally (their God is even white with blue eyes). In other words, the myth is real and it is shared with white folks in all areas, and is magnified and intensified when those areas have something to do with the racial hierarchy (that they created).

David Vincent is the personification of white privilege. The only real "problems" that he has are the ones he voluntarily imposes on himself in his quest to expose and eliminate the alien Invaders. He has an education, a brother who is a doctor, and evidently one hell of an American Express card! This guy seems to have no qualms or quibbles about expenses at all! He can carry a gun whenever he needs to and when cops pull him over, they are usually aliens and they never question is identification or ask for an insurance card. He can go into a black bar as he did in the episode called "The Vise" or he can enter rural pubs or Mexican tavern and have no problems.

Following are a few ways that David Vincent and his white alien pals benefit from the "white privilege" that permeates American culture and society.

Money is no object

David Vincent is an architect and, as we know, it is a job that generates a nice income. But since he rarely worked (he was commissioned for a few projects, but please!) his access to money and privilege is totally unbelievable. For the purpose of time and space, let's look at how he was able to: rent cars; (2) book hotel rooms; (3) wear tailor-made suits and shirts and (4) travel via airplane, as extensively as he did for the sole purpose of "investigating" (read: chasing) alien life.

The Car Rentals

Time and time again David would begin a new trek with a rental car. And these weren't those old hoopties from Rent-a-Wreck or Ugly Duckling Rentals. These were new cars and as we recall, back in the 1960s, these were rather large automobiles. I'm talking about the Mustang fastback, the Ford Fairlane, the Ford Falcon and the Pontiac Tempest. They never actually showed him going through the changes of renting the car, which was much easier in 1967 and 1968 than it is today, but he never lost a step once he got off the plane or that bus: he had wheels and never had a problem getting to where he was going, whether it was a luxury hotel downtown or some farmhouse out in the sticks.

His credit cards must be charged to the hilt because he's flying all over the country, he's dining and drinking like there's no tomorrow, staying in four-star hotels and quality motels and wearing the nicest of tailor-made sharkskin suits. But the car rentals are the key because they show on-going control of credit cards despite the fact that we only saw him actually at work less than five times in two years.

Hotel Rooms

Speaking of hotel rooms, David never scrimped when it came to hotel accommodations. Many times they were paid for by the people who needed his help or were interviewing him for a job. But most of the time he had reservations and never had any problem flashing that credit card once he arrived at his destination. This is white privilege at its finest: even at a time long before identity theft, white folks were able to write and pass bad checks and never even be questioned. Today, in 2015 just go to the store and stand in line. The white woman pulls out her checkbook and easily gets her merchandise. And yet these are the people who are kiting checks – that is, a form of check fraud. Online websites describe it as, "taking advantage of the float to make use of non-existent funds in a checking or other bank account. In this way, instead of being used as a negotiable instrument, checks are misused as a form of unauthorized credit." This is how white collar crime thrives: white folks trusting other white folks and get taken to the cleaners as a result.

I mention this because this is a flaw in the thinking of the aliens. If they really wanted to take America under, they would use their white skin and white appearance to write bad check after bad check, then disintegrate themselves, then repeat that action time and time again. This would have bankrupted the system and made it all the more easy to conquer. But I get ahead of myself. David Vincent was white privilege personified and over 44 episodes, was never asked for a form of identification to cover a check he wrote or a credit card he flashed.

Clothing (suits, shoes, shirts) –

In "Dark Outpost" (episode 25), Dawn Wells (Mary Ann from "Gilligan's Island") noticed that Vincent, who came across them in a mountainous desert, was wearing "$30 shoes." But it was more than just the shoes, you can be sure.

David Vincent wore tailor made suits of the sharkskin variety. For those of you not familiar with a sharkskin suit, they are expensive and have a sheen to them. No matter who he fought, where he dove, what hills he climbed, how he fell and so on, he kept those suits together. He had metallic blue, silver gray, navy – whatever you want to name. When season @ came he began to dress more casually, but that still included suits, even when he was doing investigating where he knew he'd be either getting his ass kicked, getting shot at or scuffling with aliens. The fact is he knew they could be replaced which means he had the financial wherewithal to do it: money and white privilege combined.

Air Travel –

Look at some of the big cities and hick towns that David travelled to, after reading a newspaper article, upon being summoned, because he heard a radio broadcast or saw something on the news – he was up and running all over the nation and during a European Summit, even traveled to the Baltics.

Some of the places he traveled included Maricopa County, Arizona; Harper County, Vermont; Carterville, Wyoming; San Franciso, California (twice), Washington, DC., Kentucky, Jackson City (twice); West Virginia; the Florida keys; Kansas, Utah, Philadelphia, and Houston. These, to name but a few.

The Lincoln Continental: Re-habbed or Contractual?

I paid close attention to each episode of "The Invaders" and one of the many things I noticed was the types of cars that Vincent and others who were main characters would use from episode to episode. Although he would exchange cars because he would rent them or somehow just appear in one, there seemed to be a recurring use of the Lincoln Continental, the one with the suicide doors (as they called them back in the day) that would appear throughout the series. Sure, it was 1967-68, but the car was considered high end for the most part.

The Lincoln Continental would appear in different colors from time to time but either it was altered and re-habbed between episodes or perhaps Quinn-Martin had a contractual arrangement with Ford, who made the car. But then again you would also see an occasional Ford Thunderbird. But as for those doors on the Lincoln Continental, one source informs us:

> After World War II, the use of suicide doors was mostly limited to rear doors of four-door sedans. The best-known use of suicide doors on post-World War II American automobiles was the Lincoln Continental 4 door convertibles and sedans (1961–1969) and Ford Thunderbird 1967–1971 four-door sedan .. The British Rover P4 cars also used rear suicide doors until their demise in 1964. German Goggomobil saloons and coupes had two door bodies with suicide doors, until these were changed to front-hinged in 1964 (Wikipedia, 2017).

Following are some of my observations during my viewing of more than forty episodes of "The Invaders" as they relate to the role, relevance and appearance of various models of the Lincoln Continental by Ford in various episodes of "The Invaders."

The Lincoln Continental appeared in the following episodes: "The Leeches," "Doomsday Minus One" (silver version), "The Innocent" (again, silver), "Counter-Attack," "The Watchers," "Summit Meeting (Pt. 1), "Task Force" and "The Organization." The car was usually a chauffeur driven limo type, either owned by

Edgar Scoville or by one of the aliens who was in charge of some big company. In a word, the car was a status symbol.

Purchase of buildings, warehouses, real estate, etc.

This pertains more to the aliens and their on-going investments than to the circumambulating David Vincent. The thing they have in common is that both David Vincent and the overwhelming majority of the aliens had white skin, similar physical attributes (and of course the psychological obsession with being in control). These alien beings were smart, and knew the importance of real estate and land ownership. Either they purchased it outright or took it over by killing, bribing or taking over the minds of the people who *did* own it. Sometimes, as in the case of abandoned mines or small radio stations, the aliens just moved right in. In other words, these beings from another galaxy not only had the finances to get the land and the property, but to also construct and transport their computers, regeneration chambers and other complicated equipment just about anywhere they wanted to.

Some of their capital accumulations and assets include, but are hardly limited to: abandoned mining camps, closed down radio stations and power stations, Newport Sea Lab, Vikor Enterprises, Now magazine, Midlands Academy, Carver oil fields, several power stations, Mace Publishing, Willard Sanitarium and several closed-down hotels.

Immediate contacts and access

Here is a man who is an architect by trade and yet because he tells people that there are aliens on Earth, he is able to gradually establish a network of contacts rivaled only by the director of the FBI himself.

Among those contacts: the Federal Bureau of Investigation (FBI), the United States Air Force (USAF), NASA (National Aeronautical and Space Agency), Col. Stanhope of UFO Investigations, the U.S. Army Proving Grounds, Mace Publishing, Col. Harmon, The Slaton Center, Members of the MAFIA (mob leader Peter Kalter), a room full of high ranking military officials and Edward Scoville, co-founder of The Believers. And these are just a few.

What is the importance of this lone man establishing, at almost a moment's notice, all these contacts and support systems, both individual and institutional? It's called "social capital", and I've written enough term papers to have a good idea what it is and the value it represents. In a nutshell, social capital is Social capital is the value that comes from social networks, or groupings of people, which allow individuals to achieve things they couldn't on their own.

Bourdieu (1983) explains that, "Social capital is the aggregate of the actual or potential resources which are linked to possession of a durable network of more or less institutionalized relationships of mutual acquaintance and recognition" (p. 249). Let's break each of these components down and show how they fit when it comes to David Vincent in his quest to expose and then vanquish, the Invaders.

Aggregate of actual or potential resources. Vincent slowly but surely put together a network of supporters that held powerful positions. The one who weren't killed off (largely due to David's interference) stayed around and helped him put together potential resources, from papers and photos (those that weren't destroyed) to finally, by the last episode, have some material facts to go along with the reams of newspaper clippings about "sightings," "rumors," "alien pranks" and so on that David had amassed over the years.

Secondly, these have to be linked to possession of a durable network of institutional relationships. As stated, David's evidence moved from his gaining the support of individuals to groups and finally to important institutions.

Third and finally, with all this being done, there has to be mutual acquaintances and recognition. See the second point.

But make no mistake about it: that social capital was a lily-white as can be and it was geared toward equating "saving the human race" with the only humans who count: white ones.

ANALYSIS: SPACE INVADERS VS. ANGLO INVADERS

As stated earlier, "The Invaders" lasted two seasons, from 1968 through 1968. These were tumultuous times for and in America, and therefore I believe that this program was the kind of pacification device that was needed to re—define issues of "race." This society was being confronted by black people for its racism and Martin Luther King, The Black Panther Party, and a number of other pro-lack organizations were on the news each and every night. Try as it might, society worked hard to give the nonviolent civil rights leadership the lion's share of the publicity, but chants of "black power" and the police confrontations with the Back Panthers, the Black Power Conference in Newark, the advent of the US organization and a host of other "militant" activities, scared the living shit out of white people who were wondering what to do with the negroes.

Along comes "The Invaders," the perfect therapeutic catharsis. Take skin color out of the equation and make it a "human versus alien" scenario. Even in that, this show featured hardly any blacks, and only one episode where blacks were featured. In other words, even in fighting for humanity against aliens, white people behind the cameras, the script writers and producers nevertheless saw the world as "the white world" and in numerous episodes "the world" is white America, white aliens are considered "men" or "women," and this came at a time when white people were still referring to black people as "negroes."

Let's deal with the concept of an Invader as one that relies heavily upon an intrusion of sorts. And let's frame it within the context of law and use everyday examples to show how the alien invaders from the television show have a great deal in common with the Anglo invaders right here on earth. Let's deal with the four elements of an intrusion claim and gain a better understanding of what is at stake when it comes to an invasion of any kind.

To begin with, the concept of an "intrusion claim" is akin to that of an outright invasion. According to Digital Media Law, "An intrusion on seclusion claim is a special form of invasion of privacy. It applies when someone intentionally intrudes, physically or otherwise, upon the solitude or seclusion of another. In most states, to make out an intrusion on seclusion claim." It should be clear that the invasions by both of the parties in this analysis – aliens from another galaxy and white folks from earth – are both clear-cut examples of an intentional intrusion upon people who were minding their own business. In the case of the Anglo invasions, they used three major means: the missionary, the mercenary and the military (Karenga, 1967). But an invasion is an invasion in terms of the final result.

According to the law, you have to establish four elements in order to show that there has been an intrusion.

First, the defendant, "without authorization, must have intentionally invaded the private affairs of the plaintiff." Nobody authorized white people to sail their pale asses to Africa and kidnap over 100 million black people so that they could enslave them and built a mega-economy in the South. Throughout the two years of "The Invaders," David Vincent and his pals continued to whine and lash out against their fears of an "invasion" and of being "enslaved" by the aliens. For instance, in the very second installment of the series titled, "The Experiment," it concludes with the moral claim that, "The human race can never be enslaved."

In episode 6 titled, "Vikor," the alien named Nexus guarantees Vikor: "A slave population of billions. But you won't be a slave, you'll be a master." It is therefore clear that no one wants to be a slave, but few can turn down the chance to be a master. In episode 34 titled, "The Ransom," a retired poet, now a farmer, is asked by an alien who is attempting to win him over, "Who would read them in a world of slaves?"

In episode 35 titled, "The Possessed," Martin tells his brother: "Ted – David knows – he knows how superior they are! They're going to take over the Earth Ted, we don't stand a chance unless we cooperate. They'll wipe us out – every one of us. But- if we can get to the key men of the world and control them, then there won't be any resistance. We'll all survive …" and then David Vincent adds, "As their slaves!" Again, they know about slavery and are willing to fight against it while their own history shows on-going enslavement of other people. No one wants to have their privacy and rights invaded and their lives controlled. That is why David Vincent spent so much of his own money making sure that this didn't happen to his fellow whites.

Second, the invasion must be **offensive to a reasonable person**. Of course all invasions are. But we have to define what's reasonable and who the person is. White folks, who endorsed not only slavery but the segregation that followed it (and which still exists) used their Bible and ideology to justify enslavement of Africans and the invasion of the Motherland. In like manner, the alien invaders offended the senses of David Vincent to the point where he spent his own money to follow them wherever they were and do all that he could to stop them. He killed ("destroyed") scores of them, duped them and battled them in the name of "reason." No one likes an invader, even when you do claim that it is a moral imperative, Manifest Destiny, or some form of "divine right."

Third, the matter that the defendant intruded upon must involve a **private matter**. How much more private can 'race' be? You can't determine what color your skin is or, in the case of "The Invaders," where your planet is located. In the latter, case, the home planet of the aliens was dying, so they sought out another planet to take over. America was moribund and needed a race to exploit because Native Americans weren't working out. So Catholic priest Bartolome Las Casas suggested going to Africa for human capital. A private matter? Survival of your race? Increased profits? Enslaving or conquering those you feel are inferior? It starts with the private attitude and is then elevated to a public military and ideological set of actions, policies, rules and regulations.

The fourth and final component of an intrusion – or as in this case, an "invasion" is, "the intrusion must have caused mental anguish or suffering to the plaintiff." The 300-plus years of enslavement of black people in this country was nothing short of a race war, regardless of the lies in the history books and the myths that whites use to justify its existence.

As a part of the "dehumanization process." Black people were exposed to mass brainwashing. And despite the alleviation of slavery, there was never a "de-briefing" afterwards. So the same slave mentality continues to exist in the majority of black people to this very day, and it can be seen in the self-destructive actions many of us engage in. If these are not examples of "mental anguish or suffering," then tell me: *what is?*

"The Invaders" – The Issue of Gender Bias

The old saying teaches us that, "The hand that rocks the cradle rules the throne." This has never been more true than in the case of the white race, especially since their forced migration (read: banishment) from England to what became "America" and the system that they have developed since those embryonic beginnings.

There has been and always will be gender bias in television as long as the white man and his lopsided views of male-female relationships is in charge. The ABC television series, "The Invaders," was no exception. Although some of the women played major roles, they were always beholden to David Vincent in some capacity. The following examples prove that this is an accurate assessment.

The women were always of the Hollywood beauty queen type, and even though it was 1967 and the skirts were just below or above the knee, most of the women wore dresses that were tight fitting and many were attired in business suits or tight fitting ensembles. Even the occasional "floozie" or farmer type would be nattily attired, thereby ensuring that the image of the white women would be upheld as being concerned about her appearance while white men – other than David Vincent and his believer pals – could just about wear whatever they wanted to, whatever was needed to fit the job description (beach comber wino, security guard, blue collar factor worker) could wear whatever they pleased.

Something this subtle might be considered irrelevant to most people. But the fact is we are talking about images, and about millions of dollars being invested in these television shows, which are designed to last for numerous decades, perhaps centuries. To this day, "The Invaders" still holds up in terms of the style of Vincent's suits, his hair and although the cars are older models (and rather large), they are not hoopties; they are a reflection and reinforcement of the well-to-do and even if only middle class, the scenario and the characters within still show clear-cut benefits of "white privilege" and an inherent anti-female bias.

Many of the women who were white and appeared to be Earthlings were really race traitors against their own people. Why they sold out was usually based on some sense of conscience, fear that a plan might go bad or just an inability to control their emotions. But whatever the reason, they would join up with and in some cases fall for, David Vincent, who was supposed to be their sworn enemy.

And here is another important point. The white woman has been the focus of a number of decisions that were made by Vincent where he literally "gave in" or sacrificed the safety of the planet to save one of these females. In addition, several titles of these episodes and names of the female characters carried Biblical references. When you combine these two facts you come to one conclusion: there is gender bias that is based on the stereotypes (myths) of "sacred white womanhood" and "white man's burden:" refer to those bullshit marital vows about, "till death do us part." But I doubt it meant sacrificing the entire planet for a piece of pussy. And yet as you will see, David Vincent did just that on several occasions.

Finally, in some of the episodes, the woman is viewed as a hot piece of ass that is so horny that her actions end up in jeopardizing one of Vincent's "missions" and in doing so, jeopardizing the world. This role of "scapegoat" is usually overlooked because David "the white knight" Vincent is usually there to bail her out. Even though this may be the case, the implication is still a biased one because it implies that women are weak-minded and mistake-prone.

In episode 3, titled, "Mutation," the leading female is a white woman who is an alien. Her name is Vikki, and she is played by Susanne Pleshette. She actually would appear in another episode much later (episode 43, "The Pursued") once again playing an alien. This is essential to the point that I am driving home in this essay.

Here we have aliens who want to create beings that will blend in once they come to earth. If that is the case, you would think that they would create some ordinary looking white bitches, you know, the kind that black men seem to find attractive! All kidding aside, this woman is a superstar and as such, she would not simply blend in. There would be hounds galore after her and if this were the case, this would run totally counter to what the aliens were seeking, which was anonymity.

At any rate, they take their time putting together this nice looking white girl and then, for some reason, they can't even control her! As I write elsewhere, Vikki is not like the rest of the aliens: she's a "mutation" and as such, she can experience love. Quite naturally then, she helps David and falls for him. Now here is a woman who is a stripper, who probably gets more than her fair share of dick, falling for a guy who is out to destroy her race. Sounds like a lot of black women I know. At any rate, the scenario takes place in Mexico of all places. By the way, the Mexican wife of the farmer who helps them is dressed like she's been plowing a potato field all day long; this, in contrast to the tight jeans clad Vikki.

At the conclusion of the episode, David shots down three of the ambushing aliens, but they shoot and kill Vikki. She dies because of her commitment to the white man, David Vincent. This is that old 'Gunga Din' theme where when you give your life for one of them they bend over your dead body (as they did Gunga's) and whimper, "He was black, but he had a white heart." To white folks, this is the highest of compliments. In this case, Vikki betrays her own race and the closing narration explains, "Two people, star-crossed, from alien worlds." Strangely, interracial marriage wasn't legalized until 1970, and yet here is an earth man falling for a woman from another galaxy. If this ain't "interracial," then I don't know what is!

In many of the stories the woman is a slut or some backstabbing unsatisfied wife who falls for Vincent for some reason. This is what took place in episode 4, "The Leeches."

A woman named Eve Donegan is screwing Tom, the bodyguard who is supposed to be her husband's protector and best friend. In the end both Eve and Tom are killed. But her husband lives and becomes one of David's first allies. Biased? You be the judge.

In episode 5, we have yet another Biblical reference. We've had one with a woman named "Eve" as the central character, and now we have an episode called "Genesis." In this one, a woman named Selee Lowell is the director of the Newport Sea Lab, which has received a grant to build another wing. But the wing is really for "secret experiments taking place at the lab." The fact is, the aliens are creating life, and experimenting with what they call "primordial conditions."

This weak minded woman is approached because it was her station wagon that aliens were found in at the beginning of the episode. When questioned she tells Vincent that "everybody has the keys to the station wagon." What major laboratory do you know that would have such a lax policy? Of course, that policy exists because a woman is calling the shots and as such, discipline is supposed to be lax and lacking.

In "Vikkor," episode 6, we once again find the "unfaithful wife" type, married to a man who came back from the war "changed." Vikor's wife turns on him and sides with David because the changed "Vikkor" is a man who has won a lot of military awards, but craves power. And he's been promised as much by the aliens if they do his bidding. In other words, Vikkor has chosen power over his wife (who he's been neglecting anyway).

So answer me this: what bitch do you know in her right mind that would turn down ultimate power (because as you know, if Vikkor is given the power to control millions of people as the aliens promised him), she's going to be right there by his side, just like she's by the white man's side helping maintain the white supremacy system today. She supposedly has morals, but in reality, since she wasn't getting dicked properly, she was vulnerable to the seductive Vincent's crusade.

Episode 7 is titled, "Nightmare," and revolves around a schoolteacher named Ellen who stumbles across an alien machine (regeneration tubes) in a barn. Vincent starts probing and asking questions as if he's some kind of official, and this pisses off Ellen's fiancé.

Once again, the white woman is kidnapped and it's David to the rescue. The barn, which she owned, had a broadcast station in it but she was apparently too stupid to know that. So here comes Vincent from across the country to not only discover what those hicks in Kansas couldn't figure out, and he has to rescue the damsel in distress – something her own fiancée couldn't even do. The myth of the defenseless white woman is thereby perpetuated and once again, David Vincent is literally the knight in shining (white) armor.

In episode 10, "The Innocent," we find that David is placed in a dream state where everything he's always wanted is right there: a major architectural firm, a beautiful city and his ex-woman, Helen. The head alien, Magnus, tells him that, ""Injury, disability – these are human concepts, Mr. Vincent" and it's "A world where what we want most can be obtained."

Where does the white woman fit in? In addition to Vincent's imaginary ex-flame Helen, there is the wife of a drunk who says that he saw a saucer. But the aliens have the drunk, and they say they'll kill his wife and boy if he and Vincent don't both tell the media they were lying, out to get publicity. David and Greeley meet with the captain, and they are discredited. Again, sacrificing for the white woman at the sake of the very planet he (Vincent) purports to be out to "save."

In "The Ivy Curtain" (episode 11), we find an old ass white man named Barney Cahill who is a pilot who is basically smuggling aliens in exchange for money. He is married to this young blonde chick and she's a gold-digger who wants to make some money – so she sells him out. In the end Barney chooses to crash the plane into the academy and destroy it all rather than have the aliens win. But this raises a question: what about his wife's job? She was a dispatcher at the Academy that the aliens were in charge of. Oddly enough, she got away with her treachery while Barney paid the ultimate price. Talk about art imitating life …

In episode 12, "The Betrayed," David has only been at work at Carver Oil in Houston, Texas for three months and he's already fucking the boss's daughter, Susan. He's working to "design a plan," but what he's doing is using her to find out about some aliens. Another important female is Evelyn, who is Carver's secretary and, for some reason, lives with them on the upper level.

Without going into a lot of the plot, which is done on the segment dealing specifically with this episode, let it suffice to say that Evelyn is threatening to blackmail Carver if he doesn't do the bidding of the aliens (she's one), and toward the end of the episode, the aliens use the hypno orb on Susan and she spills her guts. After that, they kill Evelyn and the aliens call and order the space ship to turn back, because they have been found out by David and Taft.

The white woman is seen as having given it all for good ol' mother Earth. The closing narration claims, "A girl's life. For David Vincent, a very personal reason why the fight must go on … Why the Invaders must be destroyed." But let's look at the underlying message.

Susan was screwing David Vincent and apparently there were no strings attached. Her father was filthy rich and he appeared to like David. A man who is hated is retained by Vincent (Taft), but at no point does he bother to act as if he is serious about this woman. It's been three months. If he was looking for juice, why not marry this ho, inherit the father's money, and use those millions to kick the aliens off the land and purchase new weapons? Why the on-going solo act? Why do women, no matter how rich or beautiful or sluttish, continue to get short shrift from David Vincent?

"Storm" is the title of episode 13, and it features Lisa, the daughter of a priest who is leader on an island that is being plagued by a spate of storms and is headquarters for, you guessed it: the Invaders.

One scene in particular stands out. David is interrogating the hell out of Lisa (as he has a tendency to do with women, including grabbing on them to get their attention when they give him that, "here's that crazy muthafucka with the martian stories" look), so to counter-act his man-handling her, she yells and in comes the island menfolk just in term for her to tell them that David assaulted her. Joe, the so-called Christian, sees her torn blouse and, believing that David tried to bogart the pussy, knocks the shit out of David. Afterwards, he says that he felt guilty about the way that he treated Vincent, but Vincent gets locked up nonetheless.

What the episode shows is gender bias in reverse. Every time the white woman bats an eye and claims she got assaulted, the damn military busts in, beats the shit out of the man, and that's how it's handled. In my manuscript, "Never Hit a Woman?", I make it clear that the ass whipping has to be two-way. If she hits you, knock the shit out of her – *but not until or if she hits you first*. If you don't then that is what constitutes sexism: treating her like some frail little kid which gives her the green light to take your fuckin' head off. And that's what many of them do.

Even in 1967, these women knew it was wrong to unjustly accuse someone of assault or to imply sexual abuse. They were doing it in the 18th and 19th century whenever they'd get caught with their legs gapped. In this case, it is glossed over because it was white on white. But imagine what would have happened if Vincent had been a brutha!

"Panic" is the title of episode 14, and once again, the woman (in this case a very young one) is weak minded and falls for the first guy she sees, therefore jeopardizing the entire planet. Some guy named nick who has an alien disease freezes whomever he touches. He gets tied up to a post in a café owned by Gus Flagg, but his slut daughter falls for the guy. She ends up drugging Vincent and running away with Nick to escape. In the end Nick gets killed by an alien blast from a saucer because he's a liability, and Madeline gets put on the bus by David, leaving town now that her father is dead. And, of course, it was largely her fault.

Episode 15 is called, "Moonshot," and the wife, Angela, is the dupe who is nevertheless suspicious of her husband Hardy's actions. Oh, by the way: she's also fucking Lewis behind her husband's back. And then she had the nerve to tell Hardy that she was fucking him and Hardy, brainwashed by aliens to not give a fuck about anything but the mission ahead, didn't even give a shit.

If you study, then you know. And what I know is that the July 12, 2004 issue of *Newsweek* is one that generated controversy because of the manner in which the authors dealt with their topic, "The Secret Lives of Wives." According to their bold faced thesis, "Why They Stray," the statement posits that, *"With the workplace and the Internet, overscheduled lives and inattentive husbands – it's no wonder more American women are looking for comfort in the arms of another man"* (Ali & Miller, 2004). This "breakthrough" is nothing that men of color haven't known for some time about white women – who are, after all, the numerical majority in this country.

My point here is that this episode of "The Invaders" was presenting something that the writers believed would be accepted by the viewing public. For those of you who didn't think that women were screwing around behind their husband's backs until just recently, what I have just presented to you should give you an idea of how far back such activity goes. Hell it goes all the way back to "The Scarlet Letter."

"Wall of Crystal" is the name of episode 16. It's about a rock that shrinks when it's exposed to air, but the thrust of it deals with a woman named "Grace", who is the sister-in-law of David Vincent. She's pregnant with his brother's first child and the aliens kidnap her. So guess what: he sacrifices himself for his brother so that he can be with his pregnant wife.

I don't care what anyone says, this shit is about genetics. White people working and doing whatever it takes to protect their future generations. They are already a shriveling minority on this planet and with all their studies, reports, data-gathering exercises and maps, they know what the hell is going on demographically. So they are going to do what it takes to preserve even one white life. And that is what is going on here: to them, the father is as important as the mother because he is the one who teaches the child how to say "nigger." So David's sacrifice is about the gene pool and the future of it as much as anything else.

Episode number 19 is called, "Condition Red." It's about a white woman, Laurie Keller, who is an alien. She falls off a horse and dies at the beginning of the episode but then comes back to life and somehow it makes the papers. David sees the article and hurries to the area, since the woman is NORAD Major Dan Keller's wife. Keller (the Major) is a computer programmer). She's fucking him around by placing an orb on the back of his unsuspecting neck and in turn, he keeps getting headaches. The reason is that he's being programmed by her and the aliens.

It seems that every morning she gets up at 6am and rides her horsey to pick up tapes from the aliens and then gives them to her spaced out husband to take to NORAD and use those tapes to replace the originals. He ends up killing her after seeing her packing one morning. She has already written a "Dear John" letter, and he loses it and shoots her. Since she's an alien, she distintegrates right in front of his eyes.

Here's my question: how in the fuck is your wife going to get up every morning at six o'clock, claim to be going horseback riding, and then come back into the house and not tell you shit? Is this typical for the white man and woman, or what? Had he been more attentive, he would have found out about her on-going rendezvous with alien creates bent on destroying the world. As a NORAD officer, shouldn't that agency have had a monitor on him and his wife? Again, white privilege raises its ugly head.

Two embezzlers on the lam, a white man and his woman (Bob and Ann), are the focus of episode 20, titled, "The Saucer." They are supposedly eloping and they have $250,000 worth of stolen blueprints with them that they hope to sell once they get to where they are going. But guess what? The white woman, as usual, is taken captive by the aliens, so David has to give up a chance to expose the aliens in order to save the life of ONE white female – one who has already proven to be a criminal. And that's just what he does.

Episode 21 is called, "The Watchers." In this one the aliens take over a hotel, but the focus is Paul Cook, an electronics genius who has a blind niece named Maggie. David walks up on her as she's standing next to a pool, and apparently not worried about scaring the shit out her, she turns and asks who he is and what he does. David bluntly replies, "I go around the country chasing flying saucers." David and Maggie head back to the lodge. He drops her off and heads to the power station (which is the headquarters for the aliens). This woman is blinds, and he doesn't even bother to walk her to her room.

Of all the female characters over the two year period, other than Joan (Scoville's niece) this woman Maggie was the bravest and most aware of them all. She did things on her own and she wasn't afraid to do what she had to do to expose the aliens who were running the hotel. Later in the show Maggie tells Cook that Ramsey and Sims are dead. She adds, "The people that are running this lodge – they're not people." She may have been right, but the fact is that these aliens had white skin and in many cases blue eyes. That means that they get the benefit of the doubt no matter what happens and they also happen to benefit from "white privilege."

The closing statement: "David Vincent will seek out the invaders again ... Facing a world that cannot believe him. Not so alone now. A girl of courage and spirit – a girl of vision." Why can't she be a *"woman"* of vision? This is the bravest character yet, and she is physically impaired (blind), and she is still stripped of her adult status by these white male writers. Vincent, through the years of the show, has never been referred to as a "boy," has he?

Episode 22 is the one titled, "The Vise," and the one that I analyze in some detail elsewhere in this book. But for now let's just look at a few situations that address issues of gender, but since this episode primarily focused on black leading characters, also on issues of race.

As I've written elsewhere, the role of Celia Baker was played by the beautiful Janet MacLachlan, and as I asked before, "When you have a fucked up script written by white people, what else can you expect?" By this I simply mean that the role of this black woman is one that is contradictory: one minute she's a black history buff and wannabe black militant and the next minute she sounds like a female version of Captain America! Let me explain what I mean and why her role is one of both gender and racial bias.

To begin with Celia, who cares about race issues, is all for Arnold Warren's promotion, as she would like to see more Black people get promoted, but she doesn't know Warren is an alien. At the same time, she recalls when the army was integrated – but her husband didn't know. Now this is a woman who wants to see more black people get promoted in a system that is lily-white. It is a system that she knows discriminates against her people. She is not ignorant of racism in the system and yet she and her husband are diametrically opposed when it comes to _____'s selection and potential promotion.

Since she can't make the decision on her own, she does it surreptitiously. For instance, when David phones the Baxter's house, Celia answers the phone and immediately hangs up on him after saying 'wrong number.' She is manipulating the situation by obviously trying to keep David away from her husband. Now this is a woman who willingly adapts to all the stereotypical roles: she sews clothes for her child, she cooks and cleans the house – she is basically a housewife. These roles are stereotypical, but while this sister is shown playing "Hazel," white women throughout the series are acting boldly, working in laboratories, making military decisions and the like. But my question is this: where does Celia get off getting mixed into her husband's business? Why should she get a vote?

Following the fact that she hung up on David regarding a very important (life-threatening) issue, she takes the phone off the hook. So here is a black man trying to save the world against aliens and the one person who is working with him calls the house. This black bitch, pissed because her husband is an Uncle Tom, decides to sabotage the safety of the world so she can make a point. The fact is, David needed help and was calling to tell Baxter that he was pinned down by cops. The world is in her hands and because she's got a hair up her ass, the fate of the entire world is jeopardized.

Gender and racial bias are combined throughout the episode. For instance, as David is fleeing the black bar courtesy of help from Ollie (Lou Gossett), he just so happens to run into the alley that Celia is driving down. She stops when she sees him and check this out: she immediately scoots over for him – the same way she did for her husband in an earlier scene. Remember, readers: this shit is *scripted*, and what is being done is the way that white people believe it should be.

Finally, toward the show's end, the hearings in Washington, DC are underway, and the testimony is over. Warren is dead and so are a number of aliens. Baxter and some technicians all testify. Celia, still engaging in wishful thinking, says that she hopes that whomever they appoint to take Baxter's place "will be a negro." Say what??? During one conversation she had with David and her husband, after doing all that talking, she ends up asking, "Well, now that you've talked me into it, there's just one thing: somebody's going to have to tell me what to do."

An insult to women and an insult to black people. After all those decisions she made that hampered the "mission," when invited to get involved in it, she's clueless.

Episode 24 is called, "The enemy." Gail, a woman who owns a ranch, sees a saucer crash. So she gets into a jeep and locates it, and it is f-u-u-u-c-ked up! She sees an alien pulls a box from the ship, then pulls out a ray gun and destroys the saucer. The fireball is not only seen by Gail, but by ex-nurse Gale Frazer who drives up to the crash site just as the one surviving alien Blake vaporizes the saucer in a red glow. For some reason, this white woman walks up on this strange "man" who she doesn't even know and, for some reason, befriends him.

David shows up and explains that these "men" are aliens. He ties up the one named Blake and tells her, "He's reverting to his old form." Still defending this "man" she just met, she tells Vincent, "We're the killers, Mr. Vincent …How do you know they're not here on a mission of peace? … Anything that's strange or unlike us doesn't have a chance."

Two points to be made here: (1) the white alien gets the benefit of the doubt because at this point all she knows about him is that he is white and he is a male. This white women is portrayed as being so stupid and so gullible, that she takes up for this man, and (2) this woman is willing to admit to the crimes of the white race.

At the end of the episode Blake is killed. At that time David tells her, "He wasn't a man." And check out how Gail responds: "To me, he was." You see? This is the same race and gender as women who regularly railroad black men with charges of rape, who regularly blame black men when something goes wrong (Susan Smith) and other acts. This particular episode made this white woman appear to be the perfect shill for a rapist: instead of "stranger danger," this bitch fell hook line and sinker – just what any sexual assaulter or stalker would want!

Episode 25, "The Trial," is one more example of a white woman marrying a "man" without hardly knowing him and then finding out later on that he is an alien. How could this be? Are aliens skilled in sex? Do they give alien head?

In this episode yet another dumb white women marries a man that she knew for only a few weeks. This woman was dating one guy named Gilman, leaves town and then marries this alien (Fred) while she's pregnant with the Gilman's child. She gets on the stand talk tells the onlookers that her husband didn't act quite human and that the baby she had was not his, but was Gilman's. That turned the trial and Gilman was exonerated.

Part 1 of one of my favorite episodes (episode 28) is titled, "Summit Meeting." This is an international setting and a key female in all of this rancor and rigmarole is Ellie Markham, who is Blaine's secretary, but is also an alien. Another race traitor (sort of), her view is that she has doubts about the Summit. But she - like a number of other aliens she claims, don't like the purpose of the Summit or the invaders, which will lead to mass killings.

Why not like mass killings? Because she believes that if the aliens try it and it doesn't work, Earth will strike back and kick their ass. She believes that, in her words, Earth will react "into one unified faction that will destroy us." So she doesn't give a shit about Earth casualties, only about her own people. But as they say, the enemy of my enemy is my friend. In this case it is about race and not only the human race, but almost everyone at this Summit, except for a few black men wearing African garb, is a white person.

Not only that, but an alien sees her at dinner with Vincent (in her hotel room), and alerts his commanders. Vincent's aim is to now get to the Summit, but Ellie makes it clear that she will intervene and destroy Vincent if necessary, even though she may not agree with the alien's plans. Typical woman – playing both sides of the fence. But she's white and attractive so these guys allow her to help them even though Vincent claims that he doesn't trust her.

"The Summit" (part 2, episode 29) continues the story. This white woman Ellie Markham shows how much juice she has as she's had herself reassigned to the Executive Secretarial staff so she could attend the Summit.

This woman is a suspect by the aliens, so the lead alien, Almquist, tells her that the schedule that she's requested will be in the top drawer. She then accompanies David and Scoville to the office but when David looks in the top drawer, there is no schedule. David gets the schedule but now Almquist knows he has it and the subtle chase is on inside of the huge complex.

Through it all they get to the missile in time as Halverson sacrifices himself and blows it up. Ellie reassures Vincent that the radiation will no longer be a threat as The Invaders can't live in a highly radioactive environment either. "We've been allies for a time, but not friends. I suggest that you don't count on me next time," Ellie tells David. "I didn't count on you *this* time. If you'd made a wrong move anywhere along the way, I would have killed you," David replies.

He talks that shit now. But this woman had his nose open from the very beginning. Although he kept his distance, there was definite chemistry between this white woman who was really an alien. I believe that Ellie was the third strongest female character, behind blind Maggie and Scoville's niece Joan in the entire two-year series.

Episode 30 is called, "The Prophet." David infiltrates a cult run by "Brother Avery," but the weak link (as usual) is a white woman named Sister Clara. Just like that, David becomes an "apprentice" and Brother John puts a necklace on him. He learns that Sister Clara is not an alien, but simply someone who believes in Avery's preachings. He goes into her office and fins that she has not decided what as he is going to do. It seems that her father deserted her and along came Brother Avery to help her.

This is pimp thinking: find some lonely young thang that has been abused by her father, maybe at a Greyhound station, take her in and then make her your willing thrall. Sister Clara is a true believer, but she finds out that Brother Avery is fill of shit. She meets with him and has some questions; she didn't have these questions before she met and talked with David Vincent. And Avery finds it strange that this loyal follower would suddenly be so inquisitive.

As he is on the phone, Clara goes through his desk drawers. David is outside watching out and she signals him to come inside the van. He takes pictures, but she gets caught. What do you expect? These white bitches always get caught because the white male writers want to do whatever they can to make even the most well-meaning woman appear to be an imbecile unless there is a man around to give her confidence and cunning.

Again, Vincent has photographs but because Sister Clara gets her ass in a sling (gets captured) David has to trade the film for her safety. Although Vincent is able to get free and destroy the electrical power lines, everything burns up destroying the evidence that Vincent had. And guess what? Brother Avery commits suicide right in front of David and Sister Clara. Now she is a believer – but at what cost.

This is that "but not for the woman" bullshit that a lot of these male-driven shows use as a recurring theme. How many times has Vincent had to sacrifice evidence so that he could bail a white woman out? This is a clear-cut message: the life of one white woman is worth more than billions of lives on a global level. And there can be but one reason: long-term genetic survival for the white race. She is the reproductive key to the survival of the white race.

"Labyrinth" is the title of episode 31 of the series. The X-ray technician is the doctor's wife and she finds out that the man in the office has no bone structure! The alien wakes up and kills the doctor and then walks out. David meets the doctor's daughter, Laura, and is immediately suspicious of her when he notices a suspicious-looking scar over her right fifth metacarpal. His suspicions are strengthened when he discovers that Dr. Crowell has only been reunited recently with his daughter.

Another "weak minded woman" motif is in the making. Not only is Laura not an alien, but her mother is so damn dumb she is an alien and while they were in Europe, got brainwashed. Mrs. Thorne, the alien, is bought in to testify about the x-ray results. She gets there and changes her story, denying ever having seen any aliens and discredits David.

Laura, like the others, has seen an alien disintegrate and is now a believer and says she will testify, and the University vows to continue unmasking the aliens.

Episode 32 is called "The Captive." Another female medical professional is at the center of this one. It seems that Dr. Katherina Serret cannot find a pulse and pronounces the intruder dead, whereupon he soon recovers. After further medical examination Dr. Katherina declares that he is not human, much to the shock of the delegation leader Deputy Ambassador Borke. However, Dr. Katherina, knowing something of David Vincent, and sends for Vincent "who may have experience with these creatures."

Now, this bitch is a doctor. How in the FUCK is Vincent going to have more experience with these creatures than she would have if she took the time to dissect his ass? Everything Vincent knows about these "creatures" is based on appearance and their need to rejuvenate. She would have actual internal and biological information that could be used to figure out a way to destroy these assholes. What a gap in logic.

The place where she works becomes a prison for both her and Vincent. She works there as a medical professional and therefore knows her way around the building. After she and David meet in a confidential meeting, she helps him to escape but he is immediately captured by aliens. One alien tells David, "The animosity you people have toward us is almost beyond belief." One of the aliens is being held and he only has nine days left before he incinerates (dies). David then does a deal with the invaders by saying that he can get Sanders out, but the aliens only allow Vincent two hours to do it. If Sanders isn't freed in two hours, a helicopter will be sent to "obliterate" the compound.

After involving a state department official, who is killed by the aliens, Vincent re-enters the compound after knocking out an alien and taking a gun. He scales a fence and gets to the second floor to Dr. Serret's lab and persuades Dr. Katherine to cause a diversion with Borke while he gets Sanders out before the invaders destroy the building.

So if it wasn't for Dr. Katherine, Vincent might not have succeeded. But who gets the props? Vincent because he is able to kill without conscience when it comes to the aliens. Meanwhile this woman, like those in almost every episode, are nothing more than pawns to be used and manipulated by Vincent, and then off he goes, to another alien-chasing adventure.

Episode 33 is titled, "The Believers." David is in a Tulsa Hospital, formerly run by U.S. Military Intelligence. Now the aliens appear to be in control of it. David is then put into general circulation in the alien prison where he is befriended by Elise Reynolds, a psychologist. She is full of information and anti-alien energy, and explains to him, "They needed me. Been here for three months." She informs David that the aliens plan to turn every major city into a panic-stricken mob. Vincent believes that she is also a 'captured' human and she explains that she is doing forced research for the aliens on crowd control. She says she knows a way out, so together they plot an escape and when Elyse distracts a guard, they get out of the building through an air vent. With aliens in pursuit they eventually get to the Burbank Airport and eventually to a hotel suite at the Hotel Stanton in Hollywood. He tells her that they should split up. "I have a job to do – stopping them. It's all that I live for. I can't afford to worry about what happens to you." She tells him she's independent and has no family. She informs him that the aliens have compiled a list of 300 key officials to replace on the day of the attack. "They plan to kill as any as they can," she says. She says they will immobilize communications and power systems, and "the hour after the blackout is the most critical."

She further explains that people will begin to panic. Aliens will broadcast message across all channels saying that a major earthquake has developed along the major fault line and that people should evacuate any way they can. The attack is slated for Los Angeles in five days.

Vincent listens carefully and then decides to bring her into the secret group, the believers, where she is introduced to Professor Hellman. When Vincent and Elyse return to the hotel later, Vincent sends Elyse to meet Jansen at a disused warehouse, but instead of Elyse, two aliens turn up looking for Jansen but somehow end up dead. Elyse turns up sometime later and David accuses her of working with the aliens. She admits it and says her brother is being held captive. Vincent then convinces her that her 16-year-old brother has been killed by the aliens already. Later on the phone rings and it is implied that David fucked her. After the phone call David tells Alyce, "If I have to, I'll sacrifice you, too. They knew that from the start!" Three more aliens arrive and Vincent manages to eliminate two of them when Elyse helps Vincent by creating a diversion.

"Task Force" is episode 35. At the behest of Bob Ferrara, who is one of the group of seven believers, David is meeting publishing magnate William Mace and his secretary June Murray. In a nutshell, June Murray is Mason's secretary. Two men exit the office and stare at David. Moral: "Two more to be added to the handful of believers. A cool young woman and the editor of an important magazine... They will go on with David Vincent watching, waiting and fighting the Invaders…"

See how the narrations have matured? From a "girl" reference earlier to now a "young woman." It seems that they can change everything except their views on race, views which enable them to ignore anything racial that isn't an alien vs. earthling motif. As reliable as June was, she was a lowly secretary in the white man's corporate world. Good enough to help them chase down extraterrestrials, but not good enough to get a middle management job.

"The Possessed" is the title of episode 36. This one takes place in a sanitarium, and it's really a brainwashing operation for the aliens. It's named after Ted Willard's family, and David arrives on Ted Willard's invitation. Ted tells David that he can't remember a lot of things but does remember that he wrote to David. The late Mr. Garner left the money for Willard to build a research pavilion. Ted has a brother, Martin, who is an alien, and who introduces David to his fiancée, Janet, who is the daughter of the late Mr. Garner. Martin sends her on her way, promising her she will see him later. On the way out, she runs into Ted and

David. Ted introduces them and shares with her that he and David were roommates in college. David goes to visit Janet and she immediately begins to spill her guts.

This is more evidence of what I have termed "the sluttification of the women" who are starring in these episodes. What is this woman doing running her big mouth to David just because he used to be her husband's roommate in college? She tells David that the experiments are behavior control, and the new pavilion will house other related facilities as Garner laid out in his will. But if the aliens get their way, those facilities will be used for something totally different.

David walks right in (of course), hears someone coming and hides. It's the nurse, who enters, sees nothing. David overhears Lang talking into microphone, giving orders to Ted. "You can't afford to let her (Janet) live." David rushes out to car. Meanwhile, the doorbell rings at Janet's house. It's Ted. At about the same time, at the lab, Martin walks in on Lang and angrily shouts, "You've been transmitting. That's Ted tape. It s on absolute control!!!"

Martin backhands Lang. Meanwhile, David gets to Janet's house just as Ted arrives and knocks Ted out before he can kill Janet and in the fight, dislodges the implanted device. Ted recovers and goes back to the lab with David. After a scuffle with Adam during which Martin is accidentally shot by Ted, Vincent subsequently shoots Adam, who vaporizes. Ted takes over the running of the sanitarium with Janet, and the aliens are given their pink slips.

Ed and David visit Janet's house before they prepare to leave town. Ted is there. Ted says he feels like being a doctor again.

The moral: "A defeat for the aliens. A victory for the world. Four people – each with an unfinished mission. And work to do."

"Counter-attack" is the title of episode 37, and this is where we meet Joan, one of the strongest women to appear on any episode of "The Invaders." And it is one that David evidently had a caring relationship with. And as is the case, the white woman sacrifices for her belief in her white male.

Kramer, one of the believers, was caught meeting with David and was killed following that meeting. David was able to kill the two aliens and get the briefcase off of Kramer's dying body (Kramer requested he do so), but is a suspect in Kramer's death after a security guard sees David leaving the scene.

Scoville finds out and is pissed and demands that David get a good night's sleep at the hotel. Scoville believes David is overworked and in a way, blames David for his friend Kramer's death. He wonders how the aliens found out that David was going to meet with Kramer. David says that they communicated using the university's system and maybe the aliens had it bugged. Scoville doesn't believe that Kramer could be that stupid. It is the ever-faithful-to-the-movement Joan who plays mediator and calms the quarrel and Scoville apologizes.

Joan is arrives at the police station, having rushed there after hearing of David's arrest. She assures him she will do something to help get him out. While she's back at the house Scoville has a copy of the morning paper which accuses David of killing Kramer. Scoville is pissed "I can't jeopardize the group just for David!" Joan, defending David once again, is shocked at what she hears, having heard about all the sacrifices that David has made. Joan goes and meets with David at the station and tells Vincent that Scoville is still upset over Kramer's death and that he is reluctant to help Vincent.

The episode concludes with a special study committee is being set up. Colonel Harmon is now convinced and calls Washington knowing that he has the evidence of the two aliens. They're all gathered at Scoville's house going through paperwork. Joan says her goodbyes to David and the two of them head into the other room with the other believers.

Episode 38 it titled, "The Pit." The setting is a space program and it is highly secret. Again, a man who suspects the alien presence has contacted David and then mysteriously falls from a balcony and he's then committed to a psychiatric facility. While he's in there, Vincent meets with his wife, Dr. Pat Reed, who also works at the center. Now check this out: she invites Vincent to stay, but she is reluctant to discuss anything saying that she is just concerned for their small son Frankie. Vincent and Pat then go to visit Julian at the hospital, and when David tells Julian that Brower is not an alien, Julian has a relapse and accuses Vincent of being an alien. Vincent decides to leave town and to drop Pat back at the center. On arrival, however, they see a guard being attacked by a dog. The guard runs after being badly mauled but he subsequently dies and vaporizes. Pat is still reluctant to accept that her husband Julian has been right about aliens.

Back at the lab, Brower straps David to a table and places in the dream machine in order to drive Vincent insane, just as he did with Julian. Pat, continuing to stay involved in David's business, knows that David never registered at the hotel, and tells Jeff her project was cancelled, but she still has her research notes. She says she'll get them to Washington DC and she'll give them directly to Scoville.

Later, Pat and Jeff head over to the lab and while there, she sees David strapped to a table. The aliens detain her and she learns that Jeff is an alien. Brower tries to also capture Pat at his sleep lab, but Scoville and Slaton come onto the scene with a guard and in the scuffle Brower is killed by the guard. David is released from the machine. Normality returns to Julian, Pat, and the Slaton Center.

Moral: "Perhaps it has ended for the Reed family. But for David Vincent, it is still the beginning." What in the fuck do they think is going to happen to Pat and her family? Don't they think the aliens know who fucked their plans up? David isn't the only one on this crusade; every life he comes into contact with gets entered onto the "hit list" of these aliens! And women, as quiet as it's kept, are not immune from getting their asses shot with ray guns, either!

"The Miracle," yet another heavenly reference, is the name of episode 41. Two young people are rolling around in the grass making out near a religious shrine. A car pulls up and a man exits. He has a black object in his hand, and he hears the girl giggling. She gets up to go get a drink of water from the stream and sees a rattlesnake. The snake bites the man and since the man is an alien, he glows red and then disintegrates. The man handed her the bag before he died. The boy walks over and she concludes, "It is' a miracle!" She says this having seen what she saw and is now staring up at a statue of a saint.

Now all of a sudden this bitch acts as if she has the Holy Ghost. She was just bustin' a nut in her pants a few minutes earlier, but now that she's seen this man disintegrate, she figures that the shrine that is nearby, with the help of Jesus, must have made it possible. This is how these bullshit myths get started in the first place.

David hears about this "miracle" and comes to the area. He meets with and then offers Beth a thousand dollars for the crystal, after initially offering only fifty bucks. She refuses to sell it. Beth tells David that her mother ran off because she was no good. The crystal is placed in the safe by her father, Harry who "ain't gonna open it for nobody unless his name is David Vincent." Meanwhile, back at the bar and grill, Ricky the kid with the boner who was rolling in the grass with Beth earlier, pulls up on his motorcycle. Beth is mopping the floor as Ricky walks in asking if they could see each other again. They kiss in front of little boy, and Beth says she'll meet Ricky this afternoon. Billy leaves.

Next we find a nun in a car talking with aliens. Johnny gets on phone and calls David. He wakes up but not before boy hangs up. Johnny, the little boy, follows the nun to an abandoned building being constructed on a country road. The nun enters, and she wants to know what the lead alien did with the crystal. She makes it clear that she wants it back. The boy sees and overhears all this and runs back to the bar.

Meanwhile Beth comes to David and begs him not to buy the crystal. David tells Beth about the aliens, and now she also knows that the nun is in on it. She doesn't believe him, but tries to give him some pussy. This is a young girl but she's been led to believe that she can get whatever she wants if she offers a male, any male. Some pussy. But David has turned down women a lot finer than she is, and they are interrupted by Johnny at the door.

David goes with them and sees the alien. Beth now knows David was right and they head back. By the time they get help and return, the alien machines are gone. David learns that Harry had the crystal all along, and faked the break-in in order to get it away from Beth. The bar burns and Harry is killed greedily trying to get back in and grab some cash.

David is leaving town, but before he does, he gives Beth some extra cash.

Moral: "So David leaves … with a crystal from another planet. He leaves behind two orphans who met in the desert, who have lost everything, but gained a new life." If they gained a new life, then they haven't "lost everything," asshole!

Episode 42 is titled, "The Life Seekers." People in car speeding somewhere. Policeman Joe Nash sees them and pulls them over on Highway 34 after a long chase. An alien called Keith is dying and needs regeneration and is being taken by a woman named Claire, who is in the speeding car, to a regeneration point. As the car breaks the speed limit, it is pursued by a patrolman Joe Nash who stops the speeding car along the highway. Man says his uncle's had a heart attack. The man begins glowing red and driver shoots cop. Cop shoots driver who incinerates. The woman in the car, Claire, takes off. The driver panics and shoots and critically wounds the patrolman, but the patrolman shoots and kills the driver who vaporizes. Claire drives the car away with the ailing Keith leaving patrolman Joe injured on the ground.

David makes the local news and the aliens are listening. They devise an escape plan involving David and they lure him to the farmhouse. They claim that they are dissident aliens against the invasion, pursued by other aliens, and that they need his help. Vincent is suspicious and is armed, so when two other aliens arrive to eliminate Keith and Claire, Vincent intervenes in order to save them. Claire meets David at a gas station "A dirt road, just off the highway, she says. She and David are in a car but she grabs the wheel and they go off the road. Vincent chases her into an old farmhouse and ventures into the basement. There he finds alien machinery.

Trent tries to corner Vincent, Keith and Claire with hostage Battersea, but when a road block incident goes wrong, aide Rawlings arrives and kills two real patrolmen. Battersea now realizes the enormity of the situation. Vincent and Battersea shoot and kill both Trent and Rawlings and another alien, and Battersea helps Keith and Claire to escape to an awaiting saucer. Before the saucer leaves, David shakes hands with Keith and kisses Claire.

So he talks all that shit, but when it comes to alien pussy, we have regularly seen how weak David Vincent is. Why? Because the alien pussy comes in a package that looks just like white women from Earth, that's why!

Moral: "For David Vincent and his new ally, sadness for what they have lost, and hope for what they may have gained. Already tens of thousands of miles away an alien saucer escapes on a mission …"

"The Pursued," episode 43, is the title of the next episode. At the root of this episode is an early case of woman-on-woman homicide. And again, this white woman is a traitor to her own people, but she's got some anger management issues, prone to violent rages and is pursued by alien John Corwin to the Sycamore Guesthouse owned by ex-police sheriff Hank Willis. Anne, a dissident alien that might attract police attention, has arranged to meet David Vincent saying she will defect and provide vital information.

She enters the hotel and the receptionist, and old woman named Hattie Willis, tells her that David has not arrived yet. A black car (figures) pulls up and men hurry inside. Anne ducks into a room as the men look around and retired police chief Hank's wife, Hattie Willis, hides her from her pursuers. The receptionist covers for her and she tells the receptionist that she needs a place to hide until David arrives. *When the elderly receptionist turns her back, Anne, in a rage, stabs her with her own darning needles.* Ain't that a bitch?

David pulls up at the hotel in Harbor City and cops and an ambulance are outside. David was summoned there by a woman he never met. The woman, Anne, called because she had been marked for death by "creatures from an alien planet." David is at the counter checking in and gets a call from Anne. She's at an antique shop three miles away. As he leaves to meet with her, an alien is following him.

David arrives at the antique shop and he and Anne talk. She admits he's one of them. Another race traitor. The alien who is tailing them finds David's car and calls for backup. Meanwhile, she tells David that "They've been experimenting it human emotion …" She tends to get violent and she's a danger to them. She volunteers to help. This is a great way to subtly promote the myth that women cannot handle their emotions. After all, if all she can muster up is anger, then that denotes some kind of mood disorder, does it not?

Meanwhile, old man Hank Willis, the husband of recently killed Hattie Willis, is on a mission. He's looking for the person or persons responsible for killing his wife. David and Anne arrive at Cape View, but she's running scared and wants to turn back. She runs off, but David catches her. They get back into the car. Scoville is headed to the cabin where Charlie and his son Eddie are living. The plan is for David and Anne to wait there until the helicopter arrives, and they will pick the two up at a nearby baseball field.

The copter arrives and both David and Anne get on board. Aliens arrive three deep and shoot at the copter, but it's too late. Scoville says, "There's no way they can stop us know." Coleman, one of the aliens, is having the copter tracked to its Washington DC destination. When they arrive in Washington (nearby Fairfax, VA.) Scoville puts them up at the home of one of his relatives. The aliens have tracked them and know where David and Anne are. They are watching the house.

Inside the house Scoville tells Ann, "You're about to become the most important woman on two worlds."

The most important woman on two worlds. Why? Because Edgar Scoville says so? Is she being treated like the most important woman on two worlds? Of course not. She's being hunted by one species (her own) and she's being over-protected by people from Earth so that she can snitch on her own race. It sounds to me like she's some intergalactic confidential informant to me!

A shoot out take place and Anne wants to give herself up. David and an alien fight and Anne shoots an alien.

They are almost home free. They enter the building headed for a very high level meeting, but of all people, Hank Willis has been hiding in a corridor and shoots Anne in the back, killing her. "She killed my wife," Hank says as he surrenders his gun and is carted away. Anne poignantly says David's name one final time as she dies, and Vincent is clearly deeply affected. Luckily, the room full of high ranking men saw Anne disintegrate and now know that aliens exist.

So the last thing that this snitch says before dying, is the name of the enemy of her race. If she were black she would be labeled a "super tom."

The final episode, which is number 44, is titled, "Inquisition." David and Scoville are called before District Attorney Andrew Hatcher a man with ambitions. Hatcher allows friend journalist Joan Seeley to sit in on the interview. They have no idea who placed the bomb. Hatcher wants to know who the believers are and where he can find them. Seeley, however, owing to past incidents, is mistrustful of him as Hatcher often manipulates journalists to his own ends. In this case, when they leave his office, he orders a security file on Scoville.

Joan meets Hatcher at a bar. They used to be a hot item but stopped dating as he became a powerful man. She says she turned 30 and needed a husband. She invites him back to her place.

Look how desperate this woman is made to sound. And if you saw the two of them together, you would see that she was definitely out of Hatcher's class in terms of appearance. But he had power and that was what was important to him.

Still as yet, David and company foolishly trust the power-oriented Hatcher. Seeley lures Hatcher to visit and listen to Vincent and they show Hatcher the plans they got from Koy. Hatcher pretends to be agreeable and says he will back off, but the next day he has all the believers indicted. Joan reports to David about the Hatcher betrayal. So the woman is the snitch and is playing both ends against the middle. Remember who the writers of these scripts are because this is yet another example of the low regard that these men have for women, in general.

Warrants are sworn for the believers' arrests, and Seeley goes to warn them. Meanwhile, Vincent and Boland crack the remainder of the aliens' invasion plan and locate a transmitter in the basement of a hotel. Seeley arrives at the Scoville research facility just before the police, but as she creates a diversion, she is injured in a car crash, allowing Vincent and Boland to escape and head for the hotel. While Vincent and Boland pose as telephone repairmen, Hatcher visits Seeley in hospital. Vincent and Boland scuffle with aliens and Boland is killed.

Vincent destroys the vital transmitter. Thereafter, Vincent meets Hatcher at the hospital, but Seeley has died. She died giving her life to the cause. Hatcher is finally convinced and promises help for Vincent. In addition, Hatcher also wants Joan to come back to him.

And this brings me to my final point on the issue of "gender bias."

I have recently completed a book called, "The Transformers: Sex and Gender Roles in America." In that book I offer up a theory that goes as follows: the white male is the new "meta-human," akin to his heroes like Thor, Hercules, Superman and others. The white woman is the new white man, and if you look at what has taken place in the past three decades, she has taken her audacity to new heights, learning how to fight, running his corporations, assisting him in his decision making at top levels. Bearing in mind that "the hand that rocks the cradle rules the throne," the white woman is now the dominant force in both numerical superiority over her mate and sexuality. And like the former "white male", she is just as racist albeit better hidden than that of her predecessor.

`The black man is the new gay. More effeminate than ever, the black has devolved socially, culturally and in far too many cases, sexually, into an impotent wimp to takes orders from the woman he calls "mama," which may refer to his actual mother or his significant other who he also allows to call him "baby." He walks around looking more bitch-like than she does, he gets his hair done in the same beauty parlors, he wears nail polish and skinny jeans. He is more concerned about his wardrobe than about the race and has a female-like infatuation with silk socks and draws.

Yes, the black man is the new gay. Just turn on television. If not donning a dress in some TV show or movie, he's switching his ass and screaming at the most trivial "scary" situation (e.g, Damon Wayans, Kevin Hart, Greg Robinson). In the real world the black woman has grown tired of waiting and turning on television and seeing men more eligible than the one she's married to locked up or hugging on some white bitch.

What of the black woman? She's the new black male. She is the one with the power, the perseverance and the commitment to tradition of history that the black man used to possess. The black woman is the breadwinner and in many instances literally "wears the pants." After all, she was liberated (not by choice) long before the white woman. He Black woman is the new black man in that she has the job , she earns the money, and she is now using the club scene to "prowl" for an occasional dick or two – the way we used to do in our ceaseless pursuit of pussy. Now it's her turn. In many cases she's become what I refer to as "the sister-dyke."

I'm not sure if the large numbers of black men in prison has introduced many of them to becoming acquainted with taking it up the ass or sucking dick, but it's a theory that some social scientist should explore. After all, the studies show that when these bruthas are released, most of them return to the neighborhoods that they are familiar with. And with the recidivism rate being so high, does that mean that they will be "repeat offenders" who seek money and other forms of gratification by any means necessary. Yeah, and if you don't believe it look at the next generation, the Millennials. They are the most bitch-like collection of males in the history of African-American life.

What about the gay? If the black man is the new homosexual then what becomes of the queer? He's the new black man! He's the one tanning his skin, dressing sharp and fighting for civil rights against insurmountable odds, is he not? The homosexual is not afraid to come out of the closet and is stealing the moves of former black civil rights activists. His favorite saying is, "calling me a faggot is like calling you a nigger." After he picks his teeth up off the floor, he becomes aware that this is not an accurate statement. You can steal or appropriate black culture and tendencies, but that doesn't make you black.

But that is not to say that he is not treated like a "nigger" by his own fellow white folks who shun and make jokes about him. And as the case of Matthew Shephard, the gay kid who was tied to a fence, pistol-whipped and tortured in October of 1998. This is akin to the centuries of treatment of Black people back during the days of enslavement.

CONCLUSION

For the most part, "The Invaders" had an incredible run. The locations were top notch, the cinematography was out of this world (no pun intended) for 1967-68, and Roy Thinnes, for the most part, was one hell of an athlete. The part that I found most believable was that 99.9% of the aliens were white, they could be exposed by a mutated extended pinkie finger (as many of them do to this day, especially when drinking tea), and they were as shrewd as hell.

What race of people can be more aptly described as "invaders" than members of the white race? And do they not continue to "invade other cultures in search for oil and natural resources and human capital (read: wage slaves) to this very day? Let's take a look at an incredible 1973 poem by the Last Poets titled,

"Before the White Man Came" and although the talented men who wrote it were Black, it is clearly an attempt to present the view of the First Nation people here in America:

Happy the days when once we roamed
The land completely free
Good were the times when Village Heads
Dictated policy
Great was the hunting in those days
Abundant was the game
Peaceful relations we all had
Before the white man came

Tall was the stalks of corn we grew
Large, the tobacco leaf
Healthy our bodies and our minds
Strong were our backs and teeth
Many a moonlit night was spent
Dancing around the flame
Never a hungry moment met
Before the white man came

Clear were the streams that cross this place
Fishing was at its best
Silver and Gold the trinkets we wore
In the finest of clothes we were dressed
Large were the herds of long horn steer
And buffalo on the plains
Full was the peace-pipe that we smoked
Before the white man came

And then the day of the curse arrived
And they landed on these shores
What manner of being is this? we said
We've never seen them before
But even so we extended them our hand
As we would unto a friend
How could we have known that syphilis
And daps and plague had come with them

And now it's been 400 years
Since that eventful day
But if we had known what they had in mind
They would all have died in the bay
So now we are paying for our mistake

With only ourselves to blame
With memories of the good old years
Before the white man came

And since this same race of people pulled similar tricks against African and Chinese people, can we not see a trend in the concept of the white race being viewed as "invaders" by the overwhelming majority of the world's people?

This book was intended to show one more example of how American popular culture serves as a fundamental bulwark in the white supremacist system. Though appearing to be innocent, television shows, like their big screen counterparts, are not just a therapeutic catharses: they are also brainwashing mechanisms. In the case of the "Invaders," Quinn Martin created a story about HIS world, his view of that world and his perception of race relations. This explains why there was only one episode that featured Black people while the ones that included Latinos did so in such a way that the Latinos were submissive, ultra – religious and therefore susceptible to the stories of David Vincent.

For the most part the treatment of David Vincent by his own fellow Earthling white folks can be juxtaposed with the way white people treated black people and continue to treat us. Just as we were dubbed "niggers," "negroes" and "coloreds," David was consistently referred to in person and by the media as a "kook," a "psychotic" and even as "insane." He had to wear that badge whenever his named was announced, even as the skin color of black folks is a visible tool of oppression by the same white people that castigated, doubted and mocked David Vincent.

REFERENCES

African-American Registry (2015). Black Power Conference of Newark Held. http://www.aaregistry.org/historic_events/view/black-power-conference-newark-held.

Ali, L. and Miller, L. (2004, July 12). The secret lives of wives. **Newsweek.**

Bourdieu, P. (1983). 'Forms of capital' in J. C. Richards (ed.). **Handbook of Theory and Research for the Sociology of Education.** New York: Greenwood Press.

Digital Media Law (2008, March 10). Elements of an intrusion claim. Retrieved from http://www.dmlp.org/legal-guide/elements-intrusion-claim

Karenga, M. (1967) **The quotable Karenga**. Los Angeles, California: Kawaida Publications.

McIntosh, P. (2010). White privilege: Unpacking the invisible knapsack. In Paula S. Rothenberg (Ed.). **Race, Class, and Gender in the United States.** New York, New York: Worth Publishers.

Oliver, Meg (2016, December 14). Entrepreneurs redefining "nude" fashion for women. CBS This Morning. Retrieved from http://www.cbsnews.com/videos/women-work-to-expand-flesh-toned-color-palette/

Sleeter, C. E. (2018). Learning to teach through controversy. **Kappa Delta Pi Record**. 54.

Sleeter, Christine E. (2017). Neoliberalism, democracy, and the question of whose knowledge to teach. **Teacher Education & Practice** *30*(2).

Sleeter, C. Commentary: Wrestling with problematics of whiteness in teacher education. **International Journal of Qualitative Studies in Education** *29*(8).

Stelly, Matthew C. (1985). "Television and the Sociology of 'White-Mail." Iowa City, Iowa. An unpublished manuscript.

Stelly, Matthew C. (2017). The Sociology of 'Color-Coded' Image Manipulation in Euro-American Culture: **A 25-Year Longitudinal Study of Color-Coded Language in American Media, Politics – and Beyond, 1988-2013.** Charleston, South Carolina: Create Space.

Stelly, Matthew C. (1978, July 29). 'Their Color is Why Whites Feel Inferior'. **The Omaha World Herald.**

Welsing, Frances Cress. (1974). The Cress theory of color confrontation . **The Black Scholar.**

www.ingramcontent.com/pod-product-compliance
Lightning Source LLC
Chambersburg PA
CBHW080021260726
48658CB00007B/2409